Prison Masculinities

Prison
Masculinities

EDITED BY

Don Sabo, Terry A. Kupers, and Willie London

TEMPLE UNIVERSITY PRESS

PHILADELPHIA

Temple University Press, Philadelphia 19122
Copyright © 2001 by Temple University
All rights reserved
Published 2001
Printed in the United States of America

Library of Congress Cataloging-in-Publication Data

Prison masculinities / edited by Don Sabo, Terry A. Kupers, and Willie London.
    p.   cm.
    Includes bibliographical references (p.) and index.
    ISBN 1-56639-815-0 (cloth : alk. paper). — ISBN 1-56639-816-9 (pbk. :
alk. paper)
        1. Prisoners—United States—Attitudes.   2. Prison psychology—United States.
    3. Masculinity.   I. Sabo, Donald F.   II. Kupers, Terry Allen.   III. London,
    Willie James, 1948– .

    HV6089 .P74   2001
    365'.6'0973–dc21   00-037808

"The Phone" by Michael Keck (pp. 143–44 herein)
© 1966 Michael Keck
Originally appeared in "VOICES IN THE RAIN:
The Struggle for Survival and Hope" by Michael Keck.
For performance rights, contact: PO Box 1287,
Grand Central Station, New York, NY 10163-1287

The following poems and essays originally appeared in *Men's Studies Review*
9 (1[*Men in Prison*]) and are reprinted herein by permission of Michael Kimmel:

    "The Elements of Crime" by Anthony Thomas (pp. 54–55 herein)
    "A World Without Softness" and "My Mother Death" by Willie London
        (p. 56 and p. 105 herein)
    "Slave Ship" by Steve Fraley (pp. 57–58 herein)
    "Caged and Celibate" by Mumia Abu-Jamal (pp. 139–42 herein)
    "Reflections" by Carlos Hornsby (pp. 148–49 herein)
    "Once More I Dream" by Stephen Wayne Anderson (p. 153 herein)
    "Night Crier" by Rudy Chato Paul (pp. 198–99 herein)
    "Scars" by Jarvis Masters (pp. 203–6 herein)

ISBN 13: 978-1-56639-816-9 (pbk. : alk. paper)

121808-5

Don Sabo dedicates this book to his beloved life partner,
Linda Weisbeck Sabo, and to prison educator Robert E. Hausrath,
a visionary and idealist who never lost his guts and resolve
in the face of the politics of neglect.

Terry A. Kupers dedicates this book to all the unsung heroes,
inside and out, of the struggle to progress beyond the
Prison Industrial Complex.

Willie London dedicates this book to prisoners in the struggle
and their families and teachers, especially Robert E. Hausrath,
Kathleen Boone, Roman Shchurowsky, Don Sabo,
Charles Sabatino, Obi N. I. Ebbe, and Terry Kupers,
and to all the educators with the Consortium of the
Niagara Frontier prison education program who gave life
to dead bone, water to the thirsty, and compassion
to the weary.

Contents

Acknowledgments

We are grateful for the dogged support of our editor, Michael Ames, who encouraged and challenged us during the years of work on this book. We also appreciate the expertise of Tamika L. Hughes in the Temple University Press rights and permissions area and the superb copyediting of Joan Vidal.

Don thanks his friends and colleagues John Abbarno, Kathy Boone, Harry Dammer, Steve Mokone, Martin Needleman, Ed Powell, Hugh Pratt, and Charlie Sabatino for sharing passion and ideas about the prison system. Don's dad, Don Sr., deserves special love for always being there.

Terry thanks the dedicated and wise contributors to this book; the visionary activists of Critical Resistance, California Prison Focus, and the National Organization for Men Against Sexism; and, especially, Arlene, Eric, Kimi, Hyim, and Jesse for tending the home fire while he organizes and writes.

Willie reminds us that self-pity is forgetting that everything else exists. Plain human thought would never conceive of the depths of evil as it is manifested today by silence. Willie is grateful for the support and energy of Don and Terry, without whom the words and spirit in this book would still be ringed by silence.

Prison Masculinities

Part I

Introduction

Don Sabo, Terry A. Kupers,
and Willie London

Gender and the Politics
of Punishment

Prison is an ultramasculine world where nobody talks about masculinity.

People who work with men in prison—religious leaders, educators, counselors, therapists, corrections officers, and parole officers—give far too little consideration to the ways that manhood and the patterns of men's relationships with one another influence how men ended up in prison in the first place, how they function "inside," and what happens to them if and when they are released and return to their communities. Similarly, although criminologists have long been aware of men's overrepresentation among criminals and prisoners, they reduce the treatment of gender to a demographic category. As James W. Messerschmidt's critical review of criminological theory shows, "gender blind criminology" has failed to understand how boys' and men's pursuit of masculinity is implicated in their involvement with crime (1993:2).

Prison writers and activists have decried racism and class inequality as sources of oppression within the criminal justice system, but few have dealt with issues of sexism, homophobia, and men's violence against women and children. The prison activists who founded a "nontraditional approach" to criminology during the 1980s laid out an economic analysis of imprisonment that involved class and racial inequities in the context of eroding urban communities. And more recently, writings on prison have explored the growth of the U.S. prison industry against the backdrop of privatization and exploitation of prisoner labor. These analyses have resulted in a profound critique of the Prison Industrial Complex, the intersecting web of interest groups that gain profits and power from the rapid expansion of imprisonment. What is missing in these approaches, however, is any commentary on the collusion of prisoners, police, corrections officers, corporations, and legislators in supporting certain patterns of masculinity.

Finally, feminists and even scholars in the field of men's studies have been curiously silent about men in prison. Even feminist scholars in criminology, who have made great progress in the study of women's involvement in crime, the victimization of women, and sex discrimination in the criminal justice system, have mostly limited their focus on gender to women and girls (Martin and Jurik, 1996; Naffine, 1987; Naffine, 1995; Daly, 1994). The study of men in prison can help expand feminist theory to include a critical analysis of men and masculinity. Men in prison, at first glance, present profound contradictions for much feminist theory. Within the sphere of sexual politics, for example, a certain number of men are in prison because they have enacted the worst kinds of exploitation of women—rape, child abuse, armed robbery, battery, and homicide. Of course, the majority of prisoners have not been convicted of a violent offense, but a significant number have. It is difficult to develop a feminist or profeminist theory that not only allows for understanding and reforming these men but also holds them responsible for their complicity with the oppression of women. In addition, many feminist theories during the 1980s and 1990s were organized around "we/they," "men/women," "victimizer/victim," and "male dominator/female subordinate" schema that in some ways made it very difficult to discuss or even perceive social arrangements in which women participate in oppressive practices or politics that exploit or hurt other women, girls, boys, or men.

The editors of this volume want to make gender relevant to understanding the lives of men in prison. Our standpoint does not come out of criminology, though we hope that criminologists will appreciate what we have to say. Sociologist Don Sabo taught as an adjunct professor in prisons for fourteen years. He has studied men, masculinity, sports, men's health, and gender politics since 1972 and has also contributed to the development of the field of men's studies. Terry A. Kupers, a community psychiatrist, has served as a psychiatric expert in over a dozen class action lawsuits involving the conditions of confinement and the quality of mental health care in jails and prisons. He has also served as a consultant to the Civil Rights Division of the U.S. Department of Justice, Human Rights Watch, and Amnesty International. Willie London is a poet, essayist, and prisoner in Eastern Corrections, Napanoch, New York. He has edited prison publications and pushed for prison reform, and he knows from experience how men in prison struggle to survive. He has served nine years at Attica Correctional Facility and seven years at Eastern and has also been confined at Clinton, Green Haven, and Wallkill.

This book contains writings by professional scholars, including anthropologists, criminologists, educators, historians, philosophers, prisoner advocates, psychologists, sociologists, and therapists. We also solicited writings from current and former prisoners by tapping our network of prison contacts and sending out a "Call for Prison Writings" to prisons across the United States. We invited submissions of poetry, short stories, and essays that dealt with men's lives, sexuality, family, relationships, and gender issues. After sifting through more than two hundred responses for their relevance and quality, we selected the pieces published here. Prisoners sometimes refer to themselves as the scum of the earth. This is not merely self-deprecation; it is a fairly accurate observation of where they fit into society's status hierarchy and the value that people outside the walls attach to their existence. The merging of prisoner and nonprisoner writings in this book is an effort to break down this pattern of marginalization.

The editors share the conviction that the existing prison system serves to reproduce destructive forms of masculinity. Rather than reduce crime, imprisonment in the United States today perpetuates men's violent proclivities. The abandonment of rehabilitation and the embracement of punishment by contemporary corrections exacerbates class, race, and gender antagonisms, thereby creating more toxic confrontations between elite males and lesser-status males and females. We regard much of the "war on crime" and the "war on drugs" as patriarchal policies that in fact lead to more crime and violence. Finally, although men constitute 92 percent of the current prison population, we recognize that women are the fastest-growing population of prisoners and that women prisoners, too, are brutalized.

Prisons and the Gender Order

The prison system, though it isolates prisoners from mainstream society, is not an isolated institutional element within that society. It is melded to the social landscape and to the social relations of men and women. This gender order consists of two main structures: a hierarchical system in which men dominate women in crude and debased, slick and subtle ways (feminist scholars have done a great job of exposing and analyzing this dimension of sex inequality) and a hierarchical process of intermale dominance in which groups of elite males subjugate and dominate groups of lesser-status males. These two hierarchical processes reflect and feed one another. Intermale violence in one arena (training for aggression in the homosocial worlds of football or urban gangs) fuels violence in another sector (assaults by men against women in the form of date rape and domestic abuse).

Prison facilitates and accentuates enactments of hegemonic masculinity (Newton, 1994; Carrabine and Longhurst, 1998). Hegemonic masculinity refers to the prevailing, most lauded, idealized, and valorized form of masculinity in a historical setting. Emphasized femininity reflects the cultural ideal celebrated for women. In the United States, hegemonic masculinity accentuates male dominance, heterosexism, whiteness, violence, and ruthless competition. Emphasized femininity is constructed in reciprocal and subordinated relation to hegemonic masculinity in ways that reinforce masculine power and male-dominated hierarchies. Emphasized femininity supports whiteness, heterosexism, sociability, fragility, passivity, compliance with male desire, and sexual receptivity (Connell, 1987).

These representations of masculinity and femininity are historically emergent constructs through which human beings give shape to their daily lives (Messner, 1998). Of course, conflicts and complementarities occur. For instance, some masculinities may be subordinate to hegemonic masculinity (for example, gay, bisexual, or transgendered men), whereas others may oppose or challenge it (for example, profeminist or pacifist masculinities). As Robert Connell (1987:183) puts it, hegemonic masculinity is always constructed in relation to various subordinated masculinities as well as in relation to women. The interplay between different forms of masculinity is an important part of how a patriarchal social order works. The prison tough is an exacerbated version of hegemonic masculinity that coexists with various subordinated masculinities, such as jailhouse lawyers, punks, intellectuals, and religious leaders.

Men's prisons constitute a key institutional site for the expression and reproduction of hegemonic masculinity. It is not the only site. Hegemonic masculinity is apt to take shape in any homosocial setting typified by a high degree of sex segregation, male cultural lore, and hierarchical relations among men. The Marine Corps, for example, is another institution touted for "building men" who take orders from superiors, develop a capacity for aggression, suppress emotional sensitivity, and identify chiefly with the male corps and against women (and, by extension, against femininity and homosexuality).

Messerschmidt (1993;see also the chapter "Maculinities, Crime, and Prison" in this volume) shows how men actively use crime in a variety of situations in order to make statements about their status and identity as men. He explains that "we 'do gender' (West and Zimmerman, 1987) in response to the socially structured circumstances in which we live and within different social milieu diverse forms of masculinity arise, depending upon prevalent structural potentials and constraints" (Messerschmidt, 1993:83). Class plays a big part in the types of crimes committed. Adolescents of all classes commit crimes; however, affluent boys with a future frequently stop short of committing crimes that will result in incarceration, whereas lower-class boys who have relatively fewer opportunities for higher education and satisfying work are disproportionately represented among the convicted. Thus, according to Messerschmidt, "Crime by men is not simply an extension of the 'male sex role.' Rather, crime by men is a form of social practice invoked as a resource, when other resources are unavailable, for accomplishing masculinity" (1993:85). Masculinity is basically the way men behave in response to a particular situation (Crosset, 2000).

For example, in a personal communication with the authors on July 9, 1998, a female registered nurse working in a South Dakota prison made this observation: "An agitated Native American was brought down to the holding cell, which is made of glass walls facing the booking desk on the ground floor. He was really having a stare-down with the officers at the desk there. They were ignoring him. I walked through and saw him, smiled and waved at him. He changed body tenseness, waved, shifted his hips, and smiled back. I kept walking, thinking 'What is going on here?'"

Gender expectations are essentially ideological constructions that serve the material interests of dominant groups. Hegemonic masculinity reflects and actively cultivates gender inequalities, but it also allows elite males to extend their influence and control over lesser-status males within intermale dominance hierarchies (Sabo, 1986; Sabo and Panepinto, 1990). Relations within intermale dominance hierarchies may be configured along lines of race, ethnicity, class, or sexual orientation.

The prison system encourages the enactment of hegemonic masculinity in many ways. Politicians enhance their power with tough rhetoric on crime. As Angela Y. Davis shows (see the chapter "Race, Gender, and Prison History" in this volume), corporation officers and stockholders are making substantial profits from a prison economy that employs prisoners for twenty-three cents an hour in unskilled positions or five dollars an hour in the rare jobs that actually make use of some of the prisoners' skills. Often prisoners are forced to work, but prison rules preclude their organizing for better conditions or higher pay. In many cases they are used to replace outside workers who are laid off, or they serve as scabs when strikes occur in industries outside the prison walls. Prisoners are willing to participate in this kind of slave labor because, if they refuse, they will lose their "good time" and be unable to pay for toilet paper and other amenities and for the fees they are charged for medical appointments. In some states, prisoners are even charged "rent." But the labor they do in prison rarely prepares them to enter the workforce once they are released.

Just as sports and the military are taken for granted as domains of masculinity, the prison is equated with manhood in our culture. The aura of masculine meanings attached to prison goes beyond mere symbolism; it shapes perceptions and actions. This cultural dynamic is apparent in Geoffrey Canada's critical autobiography, in which he recalls the following conversation he and some street buddies had with two older men. The older men (Ronald and Sam) were former members of a Bronx gang who had spent time in jail. Now back on the street, they enjoyed "instant respect" from the younger boys on the block.

> "Listen, when you go to jail, don't take shit from nobody," Ronald began. I was immediately stunned. Ronald didn't say if you go to jail, he said when. It was clear to me that he expected all of us to go to jail one day. I wondered why we all had to go.
> "That right," Sam chimed in. "Don't take no cigarettes, no candy bars, no nothing. If you ain't got no money, fuck it. Do without. Be a man."
> "And when they try to make a move on you," Ronald continued, "fuck them up. I mean fuck them up good. Not with your hands. Pick up something, a tray, a stool, anything you can get your hands on. Don't say nothing. Just bust them upside their fucking head. Try to tear their fucking head off. Yell and scream and shit like you a madman. Let everybody know you ain't afraid to kill a motherfucker." (1998:136–37)

Snarling and yelling, Ronald and Sam go on to tell the boys about the threat and reality of prison rape.

This scenario reveals a strange irony about men's perceptions of prison life and, to an extent, actual prison conditions themselves. At the same time, men on the outside have a clear sense of the kinds of manly contests that permeate prison life, because the same dominance hierarchies shape the fears and behaviors of men inside and outside of prison.

The Prison as a Patriarchal Institution

Many criminologists have pointed toward the irony that the creation of harsher prison conditions and the "war on crime" may actually be creating more criminals. Perhaps there are parallels between the cult of toughness that pervades the prison yard and the calls for tougher sentences that emanate from the halls of Congress. These cycles of punishment-pain-violence reflect the workings of "patriarchy," the socially structured domination of men over women and children.

Indeed, prisons exhibit four earmarks of patriarchal institutions:

1. *Homosociality:* Contact between men is the norm. Patriarchal cultures always include an exclusive space for men to gather and work out their relationships and relative power. The prisoner population is all male, and the vast majority of corrections officers and administrative staff are also men. Female guards are few in number, and they dress and act like male guards. Prison culture breathes masculine toughness and insensitivity, and it impugns softness, caring, and femininity. Men do "hard time" in prisons, not "soft time."

2. *Sex segregation:* Sex segregation is so thoroughly taken for granted in our culture that the notion of coed prison populations appears ludicrous. Patriarchal cultures

often isolate men from family and women in order to extol the virtues of masculinity as they denigrate or ignore women and femininity. Male prisoners are permitted to interact with women in highly controlled circumstances: Visits from female family members or friends are periodic and closely monitored; conjugal visits must be applied for and are infrequently approved; interactions with female guards or medical staff usually occur with male guards or staff present.

It is as if prison staff fear that sex integration would make it impossible to control the prisoners. And because the prison system has constructed a self-fulfilling prophecy, this may well be the case: The system of repression, alienation, and oppression is partly rationalized by and reinforced through, and therefore simply would not work without, sex segregation.

3. *Hierarchy:* Relations among men in patriarchal institutions are hierarchical. Male hierarchies abound, and their day-to-day operation makes prison life work. There are the administrative hierarchies and the chain of command among prison guards. The legitimacy and operation of prison hierarchies stretch well beyond prison walls to include city officials, county executives, state governors, and the federal government. The prison system is extremely male dominated, and male overrepresentation increases with each step up the status ladder. Women and prisoners hold the lowest positions in the pecking order, with women guards and professionals a notch above prisoners themselves. Status differences are also carefully regulated among prisoners, with violence-prone men at the top and feminized males at the bottom.

4. *Violence:* Relations among men in patriarchal societies are secured by violence (Loy, 1995). Violence is omnipresent in prison, even though 75 percent of new admissions to prison are for nonviolent crimes. Prisoners use the threat and practice of physical or sexual assault to maintain the pecking order. Guards rule through the threat or application of violence, keeping their batons in hand and more lethal weapons at the ready. Racism in the hearts and minds of some guards and prisoners stokes hate and aggression. Many guards who grew up watching Charles Bronson and Sylvester Stallone movies tend to "view prisoners as scum for whom incarceration itself is not sufficient punishment" (Gilbert, 1991:78). For a significant minority of prisoners, violent crimes lead to imprisonment. Others become violent, or at least act as though they are capable of violence, only after being jailed. For those who have been victimized by family and community violence as children, the specter of violence in prison is just another variation on a lifelong theme. In the end, prison violence reflects and feeds wider patterns of male violence within the entire gender order.

All men in prison help maintain the hierarchies. Administrators tend to very broad realms of influence, corrections officers monitor status relations in their ranks, and prisoners enforce their own status differences. Just as gang leaders and drug dealers act in complicity with the exploitation and devastation of their communities, prisoners participate in the violence and hierarchical competition that constitutes prison life. Roberto Rivera, a prisoner and college student, depicted the intermale dominance hierarchy of Attica Correctional Facility this way (see Figure 1): The higher the prisoner is in the hierarchy, the better is his standard of living. The lower the prisoner is, the more susceptible he becomes to abuses at the hands of other prisoners.

DOMINANT PRISONERS

Tough Guys with the Capacity and Willingness
to Use Violence to Get What They Want

PRISONERS WITH RESOURCES

Stand-up Guys,* Gangs, and Inmates Who Can Move within the Prison,
Operate in the Prison Economy Because of Their Access to Drugs and Contraband,
and Carry Out Contracts, Assaults, and Extortion Schemes

MARGINALIZED PRISONERS

Religious Groups, College Students, Individuals Involved in Prison Programs,
and Prisoners without Social Ties Who Quietly Do Their Bids
(or complete their sentences)

WEAKER, STIGMATIZED PRISONERS

Snitches, Homosexuals, Sex Offenders, Child Abusers, Bitches, and Punks**

* "Stand-up guys" know when to keep quiet, and they have the capacity for violence but are not as ruthless as the more dominant prisoners.

** "Snitches" are inmates who provide information to prison authorities. A "bitch" refers to an individual who is labeled weak, a snitch, homosexual, or feminine and who cannot defend himself or otherwise hold his own in the prison world of men. A "punk" is someone who has become the sexual slave for an inmate by force.

FIGURE I.   The Intermale Dominance Hierarchy Among Prisoners at Attica Corrections Facility, New York

Even the linguistic labels used by prisoners connote a hierarchical awareness suffused by gender, class, and race. Willie London offers these definitions:

Prisoner: a positive thinker, always thinking freedom, held against his will, respected, honorable, a leader among prisoners, not a snitch, trustworthy among prisoners, viewed as a "smart ass" and potential problem by prison officials and guards, political

Convict: convicted of a crime, has a con mentality of trying to get over on anyone in any way possible, guilty but considers himself to be a "victim of the system"

Inmate: will do anything, has no individual will or resistance, acts as a snitch or a house mouse (informer); the term "inmate" is used to deceive the public and prisoners about the abuses and injustice in the prison system

Correctional officer: a decent person, just and fair, a human being in a uniform, helps prisoners to better themselves, does not try to break a prisoner's spirit, encourages prisoners to participate in programs that can help them become healthier and stronger
Prison guard: oppressor, opprobrious

Doing Masculinities in Prison

The prison code is very familiar to men in the United States because it is similar to the male code that reigns outside of prison. For example, homophobia is a major obstacle to deep male/male friendship and to men's wholehearted participation in emotionally profound heterosexual intimacies. The guiding principle outside prison is "Don't do anything that might lead other guys to think you might be gay." So men do not hug or express much affection toward each other, except in those rare instances where such displays are condoned—for instance a slap on the buttocks of a running back who just scored a touchdown. Men entering prison merely intensify their awareness about such principles. The new prisoner, if he is to survive, has to become especially vigilant, because the punishments for violating the code are much more drastic on the inside than on the outside.

On the outside, most men are able to move on from the school yard fight scenario—in which the winner and the onlookers mock the loser as a weakling—to a less violent life. As Messerschmidt (1993) explains, most middle-class men go on to college and a career. And the majority of working-class youths, even those who commit a certain number of criminal or violent acts as adolescents, eventually turn their energies toward establishing and providing for a family. Even most inner-city youths who steal and engage in violence for a year or two in their midteens settle down and cease their criminal activities by the time they are eighteen (Sullivan, 1989). Most prisoners committed the crimes for which they were first convicted in their late teens or early twenties. But they are not permitted to settle down. They are thrown into an environment that makes school yard fights seem tame by comparison, and they are forced to continue fighting in order to survive—for the length of their term if not for the rest of their lives.

The Prison Code

The prison code prior to the mid-1980s was simple: no fags, no snitching, and no gambling. Today, because of changing values, drugs, the greater age span among prisoners, youth rage, the large proportion of prisoners confined in punitive segregation, and the progressive fragmentation of bonds between prisoners and their families, there are modifications to the code—especially in maximum-security prisons. Still, the following core commandments remain: Even if you do not feel tough enough to cope, act as if you are. Suffer in silence. Never admit you are afraid. Whatever you see "going down," whether it is the brewing of pruno (prison-brewed drinking alcohol), rape, or murder, do not get involved and do not say anything. Do not snitch—the penalty can be death. Unless you want to be branded a punk, do not do anything that will make other prisoners think you are gay, effeminate, or a sissy. Act hard and avoid any semblance of softness. Do not help the authorities in any way. Do not trust anyone. Always be ready to fight, especially when your manhood is challenged, and act as if you do not mind hurting or even killing someone (this is sometimes the only way to avoid being put in a position of having to hurt or kill).

The commandment to remain silent extends far beyond the prohibition against snitching. It is dangerous for a prisoner to talk personally. Betrayal is always possible. Men outside prison fear betrayal too, and this keeps them distant from one another. But the reprisals that men on the outside fear are relatively minor compared to solitary confinement or sudden death. Consider the options available to the two occupants of a cell in which the security staff conducting an unannounced cell search has just discovered a weapon. In this situation, most prisoners will choose solitary confinement. The consequences of the alternative—snitching—are dire. Still, some prisoners will choose to "snitch," and friendships are very difficult to maintain in a milieu where snitching is always possible. The newcomer, or "fish," learns very quickly after entering prison not to trust anyone or reveal very much about his personal life.

The commandment that a prisoner who is a man must be prepared to fight when his manhood is disrespected is ironic. It is likely that the prisoner hails from a relatively low socioeconomic class—more than half of prisoners are people of color—and has therefore suffered a lifetime of insults to his manhood at the hands of the authorities. For instance, as a young African American or Latino male, he was probably stopped repeatedly and harassed by the police. In that situation, he had to restrain himself—if he retaliated in order to prove his manhood, he would be arrested and imprisoned. In prison, unrestrained retaliation is the rule, and the men are quick to anger and to insult another prisoner's manhood. One way to avoid a fight is to look as though you are willing to fight. As a result, prisoners lift weights compulsively, adopt the meanest stare they can muster, and keep their fears and their pain carefully hidden beneath a well-rehearsed tough-guy posture.

A key locus through which domination and subordination are constructed is sexuality. The code limits men's sexual options. The act of prison rape is clearly tied to the constitution of intermale dominance hierarchies. Rapes between male prisoners are often described as if they occurred between men and women and in terms of master and slave.

Rape is by no means the whole story of male sexuality in prison, however. The code is not ironclad. For example, it does not actually preclude close friendship. In spite of the danger, there can be a certain amount of warmth and friendship among prisoners. Solidarity against the guards was the basis of the code in the first place. It is not rare for a prisoner to report that he once thought he would die in prison until another prisoner, someone who supported him or watched his back, offered him the help he needed to get through the terrifying and seemingly hopeless times of his prison tenure. The code is more complex and subtle than it seems at first glance.

Guards Subscribe to the Code Too

Staff members subscribe to the same code that governs prisoner culture. There is intense solidarity among correctional officers, and any officer who breaks ranks and informs about the abuses committed by fellow officers is likely to be shunned or harmed. Some members of the security staff try to help the prisoners when they can, but others are brutal and sadistic. An October 28, 1996, article in the *San Francisco Chronicle* alleged that guards at one of the highest-security prisons in California, Corcoran State Prison, had set up fights between rival gang members by releasing them into the yard at the same time in order to bet on the outcome. As soon as the winner became apparent, the guards would order the prisoners to cease and desist and would open fire if they did not do so. It has been reported that, since the opening of the prison in 1988, more than fifty prisoners have been shot in this manner, and seven have died. These guards take advantage of the fact that certain prisoners who have scores to settle must fight if they are given the opportunity. They must follow the code that they learned on the streets and that is played out again in prison: To display weakness is unmanly. In May 2000, eight guards were prosecuted in federal court in Fresno for setting up fights and murdering prisoners. All were acquitted (*San Fancisco Chronicle,* June 10, 2000:A-1).

It is ironic that a code established in the interest of prisoner solidarity and resistance to unfair authority can so easily be manipulated by staff to divide prisoners. Corrections officers and prison administrators have also been known to threaten to expose prisoners to a greater threat of rape in order to evoke good behavior, to punish, or to squeeze out information. And in many cases, prisoners report that they have been thrown into cells with known "booty bandits," or rapists, and left there as retaliation for having disrespected or hit an officer.

Psychiatrist James Gilligan (1996) concurs that members of the prison staff use the code to manipulate prisoners and enforce order. For instance, guards tolerate some sexual domination among prisoners because it serves to divide them into perpetrators and victims, thus diminishing the likelihood of united resistance. Hierarchy is pervasive, steeped with intimidation. Guards intimidate prisoners, and the stronger prisoners intimidate the weaker ones.

Within the prison hierarchy, guards adopt various strategies for maintaining their authority and inducing day-to-day compliance from prisoners. Criminologist James Marquart (1983) pioneered research on how gender and race enter into the reciprocal relationships between guards and prisoners (Hemmens and Marquart, 1999). The prison code confronts and guides both female and male guards as they wrestle daily with gender and sexual expectations and develop professional and interpersonal relationships with fellow corrections officers and prisoners (Crouch, 1985; Jenne and Kersting, 1998; Szockyj, 1989; Zupan, 1992).

The Will to Hurt

Not surprisingly, prison violence reflects the kind of everyday violence that men have become accustomed to in larger society. In fact, for men on the outside, prison—with its exaggerated forms of violence and insensitivity—provides a spectacle that serves to normalize the seemingly less-perverse forms of violence that are part of daily life on the outside.

Joseph A. Kuypers labels the hallmark characteristic of masculinity as "man's will to hurt," or "the male capacity and willingness to inflict pain" on others (1992:4). He writes, "Men teach each other about hurting and they structure their lives in ways that allow them to express this behaviour. They build the will to hurt into their definition of maleness and exert pressure on others to conform. And they achieve benefits from this teaching—in control, profit, social approval, status and pleasure" (p. 18).

The will to hurt plays an obvious part in men's violent crimes against women and against one another. Feminists and gender theorists have focused on the former at the expense of the latter. We view the two as integrally interconnected. We see the will to hurt as both an expression of and driving force within the construction of hegemonic masculinity. We also recognize that the will to hurt takes on both illegitimate and legitimate forms within the larger gender order.

Although the criminal justice system actively polices men's violent crimes when they occur on the streets, especially when affluent, white people are the victims, there is much less policing of corporate crime. So-called white-collar crimes nonetheless wreak pain and havoc on millions of victims. And the predominantly male perpetrators, like street criminals, share a developed capacity for depersonalizing those they exploit. Furthermore, other symptoms of men's will to hurt are taken for granted within patriarchal culture and are not even recognized under criminal law. For example, politicians are never prosecuted for inflaming public fear of crime and criminals in order to get themselves elected, even while young, black males suffer from the resulting police harassment in their communities. Corporate executives are never prosecuted when their cruel profit-maximizing strategies include the firing of U.S. workers and the devastation of local economies. Pharmaceutical companies are never punished for marketing products that lack proper safety guarantees. And even when government agencies are sued as a result of policies that foster environmental destruction, rarely are they found guilty.

Of course, tobacco company lawyers and marketers who systematically covered up evidence of the harmful effects of smoking are now being prosecuted for their advertising efforts to hook adolescents, but this is one long overdue exception that only proves the rule. In short, prison is not the only place where hurtful forms of masculinity can be found. Men's will to hurt is legitimized by the cultural codes surrounding hegemonic masculinity, but only in select circumstances.

Prisoners as Scapegoats for Dark-Side Masculinity

Some readers may be disturbed by the recognition that men's behavior in prison is not a unique aberration but an exaggeration of many culturally accepted forms of masculinity. One man is incarcerated for murdering his wife, another beats his spouse for years without public detection, and yet another dishes out daily verbal abuse and ridicule unbeknown to friends or kin. A street kid is busted and jailed for stealing a car stereo, while a store manager gets away with falsely reporting a "stolen" television to his insurance company. A prison rapist "enslaves" a new prisoner, a prison guard bashes the crotch of an inmate with his fist during a pat search, and a husband pressures his wife to have kinky sex in order to demonstrate his control. A pedophile is locked up for child molestation, while a schoolteacher masturbates in front of downloaded computer video clips of "young, hot, barely legal girls." Each man resides on a cultural continuum that reverberates the patriarchal forces of the larger gender order. Scores of "law-abiding" men fear indictment for white collar crimes or prosecution for unreported crimes of passion.

To the extent that we men on the outside of prison fear falling to the bottom of the heap, we look for psychological maneuvers to enhance our tenuous subjective sense of power and security. One such maneuver is scapegoating. And those we perceive as actually having fallen to the bottom—homeless people, single welfare mothers, the disabled, and immigrants—serve this dark purpose very well. But the criminal is the best target of all—easily stigmatized and easily disappeared. The current gender order is fueled and legitimized by men's will to hurt others in order to succeed and feel empowered. In this context, little human concern need be directed toward the have-nots, especially criminals, since their low station is believed to result from personal flaws and misdeeds. They no longer need to be counted among the potentially productive and law-abiding citizenry. In fact, the more they suffer, the more reason there is for each top dog and person of middle status to feel superior, as if relieved that "at least I'm not one of them."

The dark and hurtful sides of masculinity can be projected onto prisoners. They are the ones who have failed in life, and they deserve the horrors that await them in overcrowded and brutal correctional facilities. The darkest and most secret fear that straight, heterosexist men harbor—being "butt-fucked" and un-manned by a more dominant male—is deemed an appropriate fate for those at the bottom of the heap who have been disappeared and forgotten.

The scapegoating and lack of human concern visited upon prisoners is a continuation of the school yard training that prepares men to fight their way up in hierarchies. According to Kupers (1996), the common thread running through the prison code and the school yard fight scenario involves complicity. When bullies lash out, most boys remain silent out of fear, confusion, or a hidden sense of compassion. Similarly, because a prisoner who attempts to halt the brutalization of a punk can quickly be made the target of even greater brutality, prisoners learn not to interfere. In the school yard, all the guys were pressured to join in the fight, at least in jeering the one who was getting his ass kicked or shunning the chicken who refused to fight. The onlookers who did not join in enthusiastically enough risked becoming the next object of derision. By the same token, according to the law-and-order buffs who are calling for even harsher sentences and more executions, the only way that decent middle-class Americans can protect their precarious station is to join in the process of further disenfranchising those less fortunate than themselves. In each case, men's complicity in abusing those at the bottom is compelled and compelling. And the image of the prisoner at the very bottom of the social ladder motivates many men to buy into the whole deal.

What Is the Real Political Agenda?

With the advent of downsizing, globalization, plant closures, and structural unemployment, the American Dream had to be revised. The anyone-can-do-it, rags-to-riches narrative had to be ideologically revamped in part because too many people were giving up on that illusion. As the gap widens between the rich and poor, the rich and powerful are offering the middle class a different deal: Join us, at least in terms of identifying with our needs, and you will not fall beneath the level of creature comforts to which you have grown accustomed. But you must distance yourself from the poor—as we do—ignore their needs, refuse to pay higher taxes for social services, embrace unbridled competition and give up the idea of a social safety net, and demand that the bad apples among them be locked up for long stretches and treated harshly.

For this deal to seem credible, the poor and their advocates have to be "disappeared." For instance, more laws and ordinances that target the homeless are needed, so that they will disappear from the streets and subways. Remember when homelessness was not itself a crime and was considered problematic only when the homeless became too visible during political conventions or when they panhandled at automatic teller machines? They were locked up only when they made affluent people too uncomfortable. More recently, however, cities have been racing to outdo each other, passing ordinances to outlaw sitting or sleeping on public streets, camping in city parks, and panhandling alongside freeway exits. The criminalization of homelessness—one of the ways this society disappears the poor—removes the daily reminders of the social injustice in the richest country in the world. Is it mere coincidence that the current prison-building binge commenced just prior to massive cuts in welfare, legal aid programs, and public housing subsidies?

When social policy is aimed at disappearing a large proportion of the have-nots, it is not very difficult to see that the stated purposes of imprisonment—to correct or reform offenders—are far from the real functions of incarceration. Throwing young, male offenders who have never been convicted of a violent crime into overcrowded prisons results in their being attacked relentlessly by other prisoners as well as by guards. In order to survive, they learn to toughen themselves and become numb to the pain of others. Some become more prone to drug abuse, crime, and violence after they are released—and almost all young prisoners are released in two to five years. Similarly, a growing proportion of prisoners are being locked away for years at a time in punitive solitary confinement in supermaximum-security units. There they remain idle and isolated in their cells for nearly twenty-four hours a day, and they are ineligible for counseling and transitional programs. As a result, many go directly from solitary confinement to the streets, filled with rage and confusion and grossly out of touch with basic social amenities. And many almost immediately find themselves in serious trouble.

It is becoming apparent that the prison system is designed to fail. But this is precisely the point. In order to understand the gendered politics of punishment today, we need to ask who benefits from the failures of imprisonment. Once we see through the media hype about "superpredators" and rising violence in our midst, it becomes evident who benefits from the "war on crime"—politicians who base their prospects for election on "tough-on-criminals" rhetoric, contractors who build the new prisons, vendors who supply the prisons, and corporations that run prisons for profit or utilize prisoner labor to undercut competition.

Selective attention to the manly gladiatorial battles on the prison yard only serves to divert attention from the real domination hierarchies: the widening gap between rich and poor and the consolidation of political power among very small elites. Analysis of the growing gap between rich and poor is not new. Unfortunately, gender is rarely identified as a critical factor in the mix of political, economic, and cultural processes. The original piece of the puzzle that this collection on men in prison provides is the part that gender dynamics play in the overall power relationships.

Revisioning Punishment

Around the country, attempts have been made to establish model rehabilitation programs in prisons. Many enlightened criminologists and prison administrators agree that overcrowding and idleness in prison lead to more violence and higher recidivism rates, whereas focused, well-run rehabilitation and education programs help prisoners gain the vocational skills and social competencies to succeed at going straight after they are released. The problem is that the model programs receive minimal funding and reach only a small proportion of prisoners. The large majority of prisoners are left to their own devices, or, as Christian Parenti explains (see the chapter "Rehabilitating Prison Labor" in this volume), they are exploited in low-paying prison jobs where they learn skills that are of little use to them once they are released.

Many immediate steps need to be taken to improve our criminal justice system. Some are matters of social policy. For example, in order to halt the growth of our prison population, we must divert a large proportion of nonviolent offenders to noncorrectional settings. We must view drug addiction as a treatment issue rather than a rationale for harsh and inhuman punishment. We must end racial disparities at every level of the criminal justice system and promote equity in the way that laws are used to imprison people. We must develop aggressive, well-funded programs for counseling and educating juveniles instead of sending so many to prison. And we must reverse the trend toward harsher punishment for every variety of crime. Inside the prisons, on a practical level, we must utilize what we have learned about drug counseling, vocational preparedness, domestic violence, ending rape and other sexual crimes, and helping men relate in nonantagonistic ways. We must provide extensive opportunities for rehabilitation and education. We must provide extensive counseling services and visitation opportunities to prisoners. We must establish many varieties of group experience so that prisoners can sort through their lives and their goals as men. We must make participation in violence-prevention programs and diversity training mandatory for both prisoners and prison staff. We must reverse the current trend toward confining ever more prisoners in punitive solitary confinement units. And we must expand preventive health education programs and interventions, including self-assessment programs, HIV and AIDS education, and stress-reduction workshops.

This is, of course, only a partial list of the steps that need to be taken. We must also apply the lessons of feminism and the men's movement to reforming men who have gone astray and landed in prison. As we pursue this discussion in correctional, legislative, and public policy circles, we must introduce and expand the use of gender studies and men's studies in criminology departments, law schools, and law enforcement programs, and we must foster research and scholarship that explores the gendered dimensions of men's involvement in crime.

Our work with men in prison must forge conceptual frameworks and practice agendas that at once hold men accountable for their oppressive actions and facilitate personal and political change. But we must recognize that the male dominance hierarchy intrudes in the process. Simply challenging the existing system of harsh punishment runs the risk of having the effort labeled as "soft on criminals" and as backed by "limp-wristed liberals." Nevertheless, the contributors to this volume have set ourselves the larger task of advocating not only helping prisoners "correct" what sent them to prison in the first place but also helping correct the gender order that surrounds and supports the prison system. According to Don Sabo and Ross Runfola, "Perhaps the most essential problem of men's liberation is getting men to understand themselves individually as victims of sexual inequality without losing sight of why they are the collective oppressors of women" (1980:337). We believe it is necessary to rethink and reshape our understandings of the prison itself as an element within the larger gender order. We are all, in a sense, prisoners of hegemonic masculinity and its institutional and cultural moorings. By sorting through the gendered aspects of punishment today, we will be in a better position to change ourselves and the institutions that hem us in.

References

Canada, Geoffrey. 1998. *Reaching Up for Manhood: Transforming the Lives of Boys in America.* Boston: Beacon Press.

Carrabine, E., and B. Longhurst. 1998. "Gender and Prison Organisation: Some Comments on Masculinities and Prison Management. *Howard Journal* 37 (2): 161–76.

Connell, R. W. 1987. *Gender and Power.* Stanford, Calif.: Stanford University Press.

Crosset, T. 2000. "Athletic Affiliation and Violence against Women." In *Masculinities, Gender Relations and Sport*, ed. J. McKay, M. Messner, and Don Sabo. Thousand Oaks, Calif.: Sage, pp. 147–61.

Crouch, B. M. 1985. "Pandora's Box: Women Guards in Men's Prisons." *Journal of Criminal Justice* 113 (2): 535–48.

Daly, Kathleen. 1994. *Gender, Crime and Punishment.* New Haven, Conn.: Yale University Press.

Gilbert, D. 1991. "These Criminals Have No Respect for Human Life." *Social Justice* 18 (3): 71–83.

Gilligan, James. 1996. *Violence: Our Deadly Epidemic and Its Causes.* New York: Putnam.

Hemmens, C., and James. W. Marquart. 1999. "The Impact of Inmate Characteristics on Perceptions of Race Relations in Prison." *International Journal of Offender Therapy and Comparative Criminology* 43 (2): 230–47.

Jenne, D. L., and Kersting, R. C. 1998. "Gender, Power, and Reciprocity in the Prison Setting." *The Prison Journal* 78 (2): 166–85.

Kupers, Terry A. 1996. "Men, Prison, and the American Dream." *Tikkun* 12 (January–February): 60–79.

Kuypers, Joseph A. 1992. *Man's Will to Hurt: Investigating the Causes, Supports and Varieties of His Violence.* Halifax, Canada: Fernwood.

Loy, J. 1995. "The Dark Side of Agon: Fratriarchies, Performative Masculinities, Sport Involvement and the Phenomenon of Gang Rape." In *International Sociology of Sport: Contemporary Issues. Festschriff in Honor of Gunther Luschen*, ed. K. H. Beffe and A. Ruffen. Stuttgart, Germany: Verlag Stephanie Naglschmid.

Marquart, James W. 1983. "Cooptation of the Kept: Maintaining Control in a Southern Penitentiary." Ph.D. diss. Abstract in *Dissertation Abstracts International* 45 (A): 307 (University Microfilms AAC 8408457).

Martin, S. E., and N. C. Jurik. 1996. *Doing Justice, Doing Gender: Women in Law and Criminal Justice Occupations.* Thousand Oaks, Calif.: Sage.

Messerschmidt, James W. 1993. *Masculinities and Crime: Critique and Reconceptualization of Theory.* Lanham, Md.: Rowman and Littlefield.

Messner, M. A. 1998. "The Limits of "'the Male Sex Role'": An Analysis of the Men's Liberation and Men's Rights Movements Discourse." *Gender and Society* 12 (3): 255–76.

Naffine, N. 1987. *Female Crime: The Construction of Women in Criminology.* Boston: Allyn and Unwin.

———. 1995. *Gender, Crime and Feminism.* Brookfield, Vt.: Ashgate.

Newton, C. 1994. "Gender Theory and Prison Sociology: Using Theories of Masculinities to Interpret the Sociology of Prisons for Men. *Howard Journal* 33 (3): 193–202.

Sabo, Don. 1986. "Pigskin, Patriarchy and Pain." *Changing Men: Issues in Gender, Sex and Politics* 16 (Summer): 24–25.

Sabo, Don, and J. Panepinto. 1990. "Football Ritual and the Social Reproduction of Masculinity." In *Sport, Men and the Gender Order: Critical Feminist Perspectives,* ed. M. A. Messner and Don Sabo. Champaign, Ill.: Human Kinetics.

Sabo, Don, and R. Runfola. 1980. *Jock: Sports and Male Identity.* Englewood Cliffs, N.J.: Prentice-Hall.

Sullivan, M. 1989. *Getting Paid: Youth Crime and Work in the Inner City.* Ithaca, N.Y.: Cornell University Press.

Szockyj, E. 1989. "Working in a Man's World: Women Correctional Officers in an Institution for Men." *Canadian Journal of Criminology* 31 (3): 319–28.

West, Candace, and Don H. Zimmerman. 1987. "Doing Gender." *Gender and Society* 1 (1): 125–51.

Zimmer, L. E. 1986. *Women Guarding Men.* Chicago: University of Chicago Press.

Zupan, L. L. 1992. "The Progress of Women Corrections Officers in All-male Prisons." In *The Changing Roles of Women in the Criminal Justice System,* ed. L. Moyer, 323–43.

Part II

Historical Roots and Contemporary Trends

Forms of punishment change over time. Michel Foucault (1977) documents a major shift in the late eighteenth century, from public floggings, brandings, stocks, and other forms of corporal punishment to the beginnings of the modern prison bureaucracy, where punishments look more rational, almost clinical. Barbaric forms of bodily retribution gave way to the purportedly more "humane" modern prison system, with its whistle-clean solitary confinement units and video monitoring. But Foucault insists that the whole idea of progress is illusory. Although he does not throw gender relations into the mix, his explanation of the interconnections between punishments, culture, and politics has obvious ramifications for gender theory.

The history of imprisonment in the United States contains many major shifts, yet there are striking continuities throughout centuries. One example of a shift is the alternating cycle of harsh punishment and kinder rehabilitative efforts. For example, from the late thirties to the late seventies a large number of politicians and prison administrators favored the rehabilitative model of incarceration. By now, however, most have switched to harsh punishment, claiming that rehabilitation and all efforts to correct are useless because prisoners are incorrigible. Efforts to rehabilitate prisoners have been curtailed or at least downsized considerably. Today, the conservative law-and-order lobby urges us to deny prisoners educational opportunities and even to remove the exercise weights from the prison yards.

Along with the shifts there are continuities. Consider the theme of manhood that runs throughout the history of punishment in the United States. In colonial times, a man entering prison lost his manhood in the eyes of the citizenry (see Mark E. Kann's "Penitence for the Privileged" in this volume). After the Civil War, when a large number of former slaves were imprisoned only to be leased out to work for their former plantation owners, the prisoners' manhood was literally and symbolically at issue (see Davis's "Race, Gender, and Prison History" in this volume). White racists, obsessed by the idea of sex between a black man and white woman, carried out castrations and lynchings. Today, a prisoner's real or imagined manliness plays a very big part in shaping his prison experience.

Race is another critical factor. People of color are much more likely than whites to be stopped by police, searched, arrested, defended by a public defender with a huge caseload, convicted, and imprisoned. Over 50 percent of new admissions to U.S. prisons today are black, another 15 to 20 percent are Latino, and Native Americans are also vastly overrepresented in the prisons. The number of people of color imprisoned increases with each security level, until, in a supermaximum-security unit, where prisoners remain in their cells nearly twenty-four hours per day, people of color constitute an overwhelming majority. More than 90 percent of the "supermax" population in some state systems is black. And 40 percent of the occupants of death row nationwide are African Americans. When prisoners of one race are outnumbered by those of another, the disproportion can lead to extreme violence. Race is a critical dividing line in prison. Like that other line between the strong and the weak, racial lines are a constant consideration. After all, it would be deadly to make the mistake, for example, of being among men of a different race when a race fight breaks out.

Gender and race are inextricably linked in the daily lives of men in prison. As the harshness and brutality of prison life intensify, the lines that separate men inside become ever more rigid, and many of the worst aspects of ultramasculine behavior come to the fore.

Reference

Foucault, Michel. 1977. *Discipline and Punish: The Birth of the Prison.* Trans. Alan Sheridan. New York: Pantheon Books.

Mark E. Kann

Penitence for the Privileged: Manhood, Race, and Penitentiaries in Early America

The American founders coupled the concept of manhood to the language of liberty. Benjamin Franklin proclaimed that his grandfather's essay on liberty was written with "manly freedom," and Thomas Paine explained that *Common Sense* was meant to prepare the way for "manly principles of independence." John Adams praised his ancestors for their "manly assertion of . . . rights" against tyranny, while Thomas Jefferson applauded his American brethren for demonstrating "manly spirit" by declaring independence.[1] The founders' use of gendered language to urge men into battle was a typical offspring of the ancient marriage of manhood to militarism. However, their use of manhood to promote self-discipline in the exercise of liberty, to deter and punish criminal activity, and to rehabilitate some convicts and restore their liberty was innovative.

The founders led a revolution in the name of liberty only to encounter what they considered men's tendency toward licentious behavior. They believed that ordinary male vices, such as swearing, gambling, drinking, promiscuity, and greed, fostered conflict and criminality that subverted the new republic. Accordingly, they urged men to consult religious doctrine, examine enlightened self-interest, commit to republican virtue, and follow their moral sensibilities to promote self-restraint in the exercise of liberty, social harmony, and law-abiding behavior. They also invoked the dominant norms of manhood to prompt men to moderate their conduct.

In general, the founders defined "manhood" as a combination of individual independence and family responsibility. They saw this mix as a positive source of social order and stable citizenship. They also relied on it to deter white men from engaging in criminal conduct and to punish and rehabilitate white convicts. Prison reformers in the early republic threatened to deprive lawbreakers of their manly freedom and dignity by incarcerating them and isolating them from their families in newly conceived penitentiaries. Men who were actually convicted of crimes and imprisoned were encouraged to use their isolation as an opportunity to repent and reform in order to regain their manhood and liberty.

The founders' Enlightenment optimism about deterring crime and rehabilitating criminals had racial limits. Many white leaders considered black males as inherently unmanly because they lacked individual independence and control of their families. This putative absence of manhood precluded public officials from deterring and punishing black men's crimes by threatening to confiscate their manhood. It also eliminated any incentive for rehabilitation, because black convicts had no manly freedom to redeem. Black convicts were often considered incorrigibles. For them, the new penitentiaries were not innovative houses of penitence but old-style prisons for punishment.

Male Licentiousness

The American founders were obsessed with maintaining order in the ranks of men. From the first protests against British authority in the 1760s, through the Revolution, and into the turbulent politics of the 1790s, patriot leaders wondered whether most American men would ever consent to be governed and comply with legitimate political authority. Once the rhetoric of liberty and equality was unleashed, many men used it to justify rebellions against parents, masters, teachers, ministers, and magistrates. Bernard Bailyn writes, "Defiance to constituted authority leaped like a spark from one flammable area to another, growing in heat as it went." Men's defiant attitudes and licentious conduct were symbolized by the figure of the libertine. He represented all males who were enslaved by passion and who acted in ways that had a destructive impact on lovers, families, and neighbors, as well as on republican society.[2]

The founders were especially concerned about men's lustful tendencies, because they believed that men's failure to discipline sexual desire represented a more general failure to restrain passion, impulse, and avarice. For example, during the Great Awakening—a general revival of evangelical religion in the American colonies—congregational ministers attacked New Light evangelicalism not simply by interrogating its theology but also by associating its spiritual individualism with devastating images of "sexual anarchy," "sexual libertinism," "sexual promiscuity," and "a generally sexualized climate" that destroyed individual faith and reason, family integrity, and social stability. Men's sexual transgressions were seen as indicators of their potential for moral, social, economic, and political subversion.[3]

Consider the young men in post-revolutionary New York City who constituted "crowds of 'bloods' . . . who lounged on city sidewalks and, affecting the contemptuous stance of the aristocratic libertine, tossed provocative remarks at any single woman who passed." These young rakes were known for their aggressive sexuality and their tendency to make contempt for women an "emblem of high style." Some of them went beyond provocative words to violent deeds only to be charged with "attempted rape" or "rape." "Attempted rape" referred to coercive sexual acts up to and including forcible penetration; "rape," the more serious charge, involved penetration and ejaculation. Legislators had two concerns: First, they wanted to reduce the number of single mothers and bastard children who made claims on the public treasury. Second, they believed that the crime of rape was rooted in "the sudden abuse of a natural passion" and "perpetrated in a frenzy of desire." Rape indicated that liberty without self-restraint resulted in abusive, frenzied actions that were inconsistent with liberal reason and republican order.[4]

The founders consistently condemned rape as "a horrid crime" that excited "universal abhorrence." Certainly, some American men, however, blamed the victim. In one notorious case, a defense attorney claimed that the accused rapist had actually been seduced by a carnal thirteen-year-old. But most civic leaders blamed rapists for impassioned violence against innocent females. Josiah Quincy and others expressed outrage at the "brutal ravisher." William Bradford declared rape an unmanly crime that demanded manly vengeance: "Female innocence has strong claims upon our protection, and a desire to avenge its wrongs is natural to a generous and manly mind." Like most founders who prided themselves on gentility and civility, Bradford saw nothing manly in sexual promiscuity or sexual violence.[5]

American leaders also associated same-sex relationships with subversion. Same-sex relationships represented a "potential in the lustful nature of all men" and "a potential for disorder in the cosmos." During the eighteenth century, public perception transformed sodomy from a mortal sin against God into a passion "against the order of nature" and therefore an abuse of natural laws that regulated "the peace, government, and dignity of the state." Why did private sexual acts among consenting adults have public meaning? John Winthrop's explanation was the enduring one. He argued that same-sex relations "tended to the frustrating of the ordinance of marriage and the hindering [of] the generation of mankind." Like the libertine, the sodomist separated sexual pleasure from marital restraint, unleashed passion and licentiousness, and thereby undermined men's commitment and conformity to stable family life.[6]

Following the Revolution, men's licentiousness appeared to be expanding. Many founders saw libertinism, along with itinerancy, pauperism, frontier bloodshed, slave unrest, military disorder, and criminality, as the crest of a wave of male degeneracy swelled by men's dealings in blasphemy, alcoholism, gambling, prostitution, adultery, fighting, dueling, thievery, and murder. So many men seemed to be "intemperate zealots"; so many took part in "the most shameful depredations"; so many joined mobs that committed "indecent outrages"; so many followed "factious demagogues."[7] In part, the founders responded by invoking the dominant norms of manhood to urge males to discipline desire and channel passion into family responsibilities and sober citizenship.

The Dominant Norms of Manhood

Eighteenth-century Americans debated the meaning of manhood. Images of traditional patriarchy vied with aristocratic ideals of the gentleman, republican images of benign fathers, and nascent notions of self-made manhood.[8] However, two facets of manhood were common to all contenders.

First, manhood required individual independence. A mature male was an autonomous thinker and actor. He disciplined passion and impulse, consulted reason, and relied on virtue to guide his actions. A mature male was also self-supporting, determined the nature and pace of his labor, and kept free of other men's patronage and government relief. He could afford to resist adverse pressures and exercise his own will to defend his liberty, property, and community. He was an independent agent of his personal and public destiny. His independence stood in opposition to slavery in particular and subordination in general. Judith Shklar writes that a white male's sense of dignity, reputation, and public standing was a function of distinguishing himself "from slaves and occasionally from women." He measured his worth by his distance from dependency. The main marker of that distance was suffrage, which functioned as "a certificate of full membership in society." A man without the vote saw himself and was seen by others as slavish, effeminate, or childish.[9]

Second, mature manhood entailed family governance. The founders saw "a bachelor of age" as a slave to desire and greed. They presumed that a family patriarch assumed sober responsibility for provisioning and protecting his loved ones, continuing his family line, and caring for his posterity. His deep and abiding commitment to his family provided him an enduring stake in social stability and the public good. Although popular culture warned that a married man might be degraded by a domineering wife, Benjamin Franklin explained that "Every man that is really a man is master of his own family." He governed firmly but lovingly. Ideally, he ruled his household by joining traditional patriarchal authority to republican benevolence.[10]

Many founders saw patriarchal family status as a basis for citizenship. Thomas Jefferson wrote, "I cannot doubt any attachment to his country in any man who has his family and peculium in it. . . . I [am] for extending the right of suffrage (or in other words the rights of a citizen) to all who [have] a permanent intention of living in the country. Take what circumstances you please as evidence of this, either the having resided a certain time, or having a family, or having property, any or all of them." At the Constitutional Convention, George Mason proposed enfranchising family patriarchs, arguing that "the parent of a number of children whose fortunes are to be pursued in his own country" merited "the common rights of their fellow citizens."[11] In early America, independent manhood, family patriarchy, and social stability were nearly synonymous.

Ideally, males who exercised the self-discipline associated with independence, assumed the responsibilities of family life, and exhibited the long-term caring conducive to citizenship would voluntarily limit licentiousness and obey legitimate laws. After all, if a husband could restrict sexual passion to the marriage bed, then he could also make the small sacrifices necessary for republican order. Of course, some husbands were adulterers who indulged lust despite their marriage vows. Jacob Rush asserted that their adultery constituted a "cruel breech of trust" that fostered a "universal depravity of morals" that "must utterly destroy society."[12] The founders hoped that most men would exhibit manly self-restraint and marital fidelity, but they knew that many men failed to discipline desire only to run afoul of the law. They continued to rely on state coercion to deter criminal activity and punish criminals, but they infused traditional state coercion with an Enlightenment ethic of benevolent reform.

Traditional State Coercion

The American founders believed that criminal behavior on a prosperous continent could not be justified. Crime in class-divided Europe was understandable. There, William

Bradford explained, an impoverished "wretch" had little or no opportunity to transform his labor into individual independence or a family estate. Lacking alternatives, he engaged in crime to support his family or better his children's prospects. However, poverty was different in America, where "every man is or may be a proprietor" and his "labor is bountifully rewarded." Here, even the poorest man could invest individual effort in economic opportunity to build a stake, start a family, and accumulate patrimony for the next generation.[13] Because America was a land of economic opportunity, a man who turned to crime as a way to wealth had no legitimate excuses. The state had a duty to use its coercive apparatus to deter crime and punish criminals.

In colonial America, state coercion focused on capital punishment, corporal punishment, and public humiliation. Many crimes were capital crimes. Magistrates and ministers designed public executions to display the supremacy of civil and religious authority over the forces of chaos and evil. The scaffold was a sort of communal pulpit for warning spectators about the lethal consequences of criminality. Civic leaders used lesser penalties, such as public whippings and the pillory, to punish and humiliate lesser offenders and to deter onlookers from future crimes. After the Revolution, criminologists added public labor to their roster of punishments and humiliations.[14]

Humiliation was an effective punishment in some circumstances. The first Continental Congress drew up a strict code of moral conduct that banned vices related to "unbridled sensuality": cockfighting, horse racing, and the theater. Communities enforced the code by way of social pressure, stigma, and ostracism. Local committees pressured offenders to recant. They stigmatized men who tried to conceal their vices, by accusing them of "unmanly equivocation," subjected them to ridicule, and urged them to confess and conform. Finally, they forced perpetrators beyond persuasion to endure rituals of shame that included being tarred and feathered or drummed out of town.[15]

Prisons played a minor part in colonial criminal justice systems. Few cities or towns had prisons. Where they did exist, Kermit L. Hall observes, "Incarceration was a temporary rather than a punitive measure." A man might be detained or warehoused in a local jail until his trial. If he was found guilty, he was more likely to be sentenced to be hung, whipped, branded, or subjected to the stocks or public labor than to be remanded to the lengthy custodial care of the state. For the most part, "The colonists placed a premium on schemes of punishment that emphasized retribution, humiliation, and shame." Jails were for short-term detention, not long-term punishment.[16]

In the late 1780s, significant opposition to traditional state coercion surfaced in Pennsylvania. Critics suggested that republican ideals militated against cruel executions, draconian physical punishments, and barbaric humiliation. They also pointed out that extreme public punishments failed to deter crime. For example, some critics contended that capital punishment actually invited more crime by providing degenerate males with an unearned opportunity to redeem their lost manhood. In 1788 "A Citizen of the World" complained that audiences at hangings were more concerned with the conduct of the condemned than with the justice of the sentence: "The populace depart, either applauding the criminal's hardness, or as they term it, his spirit, in 'dying like a cock'—or else condemning his weakness—'He died like a d****d chicken hearted dog.'" To die like a cock was to be remembered as a man. It was as if a manly performance on the scaffold could erase a lifetime of immorality and crime.[17]

The most notable case in which a criminal was executed only to redeem his manhood involved British Major John André, who was hung for spying during the Revolution. On his capture, André sent to General George Washington a letter marked "with a frankness becoming a gentleman and man of honor and principle." He asked to "die as a soldier and man of honor [by being shot], not as a criminal [by being hung]." Washington denied the request but praised André for exhibiting "that fortitude which was to be expected from an accomplished man and gallant officer." When a teary-eyed servant brought André a dress uniform for the scaffold, he ordered, "Leave me until you show yourself more manly." When André was hung, observers reported, "the tear of compassion was drawn from every pitying eye that beheld this accomplished youth a victim to the usages of war." Alexander Hamilton was one of many Americans who memorialized André for having been "a man of honor" whose final request was "to "die like a brave man."[18]

More than a decade later, Benjamin Rush was still rankled by André's celebrity. He wrote, "The spy was lost in the hero; and indignation everywhere gave way to admiration and praise." Men who believed that a shortcut to manly dignity was to exhibit courage before the gallows had an incentive to commit capital crimes. Moreover, the "admiration which fortitude under suffering excites has in some instances excited envy [and] induced deluded people to feign or confess crimes which they had never committed on purpose to secure to themselves a conspicuous death." According to Rush, a proper punishment for terrible crimes should deter would-be criminals and dissuade innocents from confessing; it should not invite them to seek manhood through criminal notoriety.[19]

Critics also charged that most public punishments were counterproductive. On one hand, criminals' presence in public places was dangerous. The penal scene became "a vortex of viciousness, ominously seducing and contaminating the larger society." Philadelphia official Caleb Lownes opposed punishments such as street cleaning and road repairs because they afforded criminals an opportunity to engage "crowds of idle boys" in "indecent and improper conversation." Criminality was infectious and epidemic; it needed to be quarantined. On the other hand, the sight of convicts being whipped, pilloried, or weighed down by a ball and chain while doing public labor sometimes evoked public sympathy, not antipathy. Spectators showered admiration on convicts who exemplified fortitude; they showed compassion for men suffering obvious distress; and they expressed disdain toward penal officials who inflicted the distress. Critics wanted criminals condemned and officials honored.[20]

Redemptive State Coercion

Reformers' main alternative to severe public punishments was imprisonment in a new institution called a penitentiary, or "house of repentance." Michael Meranze observes, "In the colonial period, the prison had been a minor support of the scaffold, whipping post, and pillory. Now the scaffold and whipping post were infrequent supplements to the prison."[21] Reformers' emphasis on incarcerating convicts for prolonged periods was based on Enlightenment optimism that, under proper conditions, prisoners could experience feelings of penitence, welcome rehabilitation efforts, redeem their manhood, and be restored to their freedom and families.

The dominant norms of manhood were central to the idea of the penitentiary as an institution of deterrence, punishment, and rehabilitation. If a mature man was an independent agent of his destiny and master of his family, then imprisonment was a frightful punishment that deprived him of his manhood. Italian criminologist Cesare Beccaria put it this way: "It is not the terrible but fleeting sight of a felon's death which is the most powerful brake on crime." Rather, it was "the long-drawn-out example of a man deprived of freedom." A male who was subordinated to his captors and separated from his family was less than a man. He suffered the psychic pain of knowing that he approached the dreaded condition of a slave. Benjamin Rush spread Beccaria's message in America. Writing against capital punishment, Rush argued, "The death of a malefactor is not so efficacious a method of deterring from wickedness as the example of continually remaining . . . a man who is deprived of his liberty."[22]

A man deprived of liberty was less than a man. He lost his independence and his family. Rush wanted to push emasculation as far as possible. He suggested that convicts be sent to distant, isolated penitentiaries: "Let a large house . . . be erected in a remote part of the state. Let the avenue to this house be rendered difficult and gloomy by mountains or morasses. Let its doors be of iron; and let the grating, occasioned by opening and shutting them, be increased by an echo from a neighboring mountain, that shall extend and continue a sound that shall deeply pierce the soul." Within soul-piercing penitentiaries, older convicts would be isolated from young ones and vicious criminals would be locked in isolation cells. Rush reasoned that isolation from family and friends "is one of the severest punishments that can be inflicted upon a man," because "attachment to kindred and society is one of the strongest feelings in the human heart."[23]

During an age when individualism was still identified with selfishness, most founders felt that a man's isolation was truly terrible. James Otis Jr. called "solitude" an "unnatural" state in which men "perish." John Dickinson declared "that to be solitary is to be wretched." Thomas Jefferson wrote that isolation from loved ones "is worse than death inasmuch as [death] ends our sufferings whereas [isolation] begins them," transforming a man into a "gloomy monk sequestered from the world." Samuel Quarrier put it best. Petitioning to be released from a debtors' jail, he wrote to President Jefferson, "This ignominious imprisonment unmans the heart."[24]

The idea that isolation "unmans" the heart implied that incarceration could be promising as well as painful. Isolated men suffered a degrading loss of manly freedom and dignity. Officials locked them up and treated them like dependent slaves, or women, or children. Simultaneously, penitentiary officials provided criminals with a chance to regain their manly independence and patriarchal prerogative. Quaker reformers encouraged convicts to use prison solitude as an opportunity to search their souls, reorder their faculties, experience penitence, and cooperate with officials who taught them to discipline their passions and learn useful trades in preparation for repatriation to society. Benjamin Rush rhapsodized at the prospect of a rehabilitated convict returning to his freedom and family: "I already hear the inhabitants of our villages and townships . . . running to meet him on the day of his deliverance. His friends and family bathe his cheeks with tears of joy; and the universal shout of the neighborhood is, 'This our brother was lost and is found—was dead, and is alive.' "[25] A redeemed prisoner was a born-again man.

The possibility of prisoner rehabilitation was intimately connected with whether penitentiaries could motivate men to discipline desire, especially symbolically charged sexual desire. Meranze reports, "The threat of sexual contact obsessed prison reformers." The September 26, 1787, *Pennsylvania Gazette* reported that a Philadelphia grand jury and the Philadelphia Society for Alleviating the Miseries of Public Prisons complained of "a general intercourse between the criminals of the different sexes" resulting in "scenes of debauchery." They condemned overcrowding and "inadequate provision of bedding" as conducive to same-sex contact among male inmates. When an old jail was transformed into a penitentiary, officials enacted rules to separate male and female convicts so that they "shall have no intercourse with each other." They also sought to improve prison cleanliness and sleeping conditions to reduce disease and eliminate sodomy. Aspiring to create a strictly controlled environment, reformers were confident that male criminals could learn to discipline desire.[26]

If most men could learn to discipline desire, then even sexual criminals could be reformed. Early American penal codes mandated hanging for convicted rapists. After the Revolution, Pennsylvania eliminated the death penalty for rape and substituted a maximum penalty of property forfeiture and ten years in prison. Because reformers believed that rape stemmed from frenzied desire, they considered it an "atrocity" that should be punished but an atrocity rooted in excessive passion, not "incorrigibility of the criminal." A rapist did not suffer "irreclaimable corruption." With solitude, he could repent and be rehabilitated to manhood, family, and community.[27] Similarly, sodomy in early America was usually a capital offense. Bradford opposed the death penalty for "the crime against nature." America was "a country where marriages take place so early, and the intercourse between the sexes is not difficult." With females abundant and accessible, no man had a real motive to engage in a same-sex relationship. Indeed, "the wretch who perpetrates [sodomy] must be in a state of mind which may occasion us to doubt whether he be *Sui Juris* at the time; or whether he reflects on the punishment at all." Sodomy was a sort of temporary insanity manifested in a man enslaved by sexual impulse.[28] He too could be rehabilitated by solitude, penitence, and fortified self-restraint.

By 1805, Pennsylvania's experiment with penitentiaries had spread to New York, New Jersey, Connecticut, Massachusetts, and Virginia.[29] What made penitentiaries innovative, and ostensibly progressive, was the idea that they employed state coercion not simply for social control but for male reformation. Theoretically, state coercion was a benign application of power to liberate disorderly men from slavery to desire and thereby clear the way for them to exercise manly freedom. Penitentiaries forced men to be free.

Black Male Incorrigibility

In actuality, the rehabilitation theory was applied to white men. Reformer optimism about male rehabilitation did not extend to the belief that *black* convicts could regain manly freedom. The founders did not attribute to black males a clear gender identity. They were seen as outsiders who lacked the manly ability to discipline their passions and the manly freedom to govern, provision, and protect their families. Essayist J. Hector St. John de Crèvecoeur's American Farmer was typical of Euro-Americans. He praised liberty and abhorred slavery, but he could not imagine including Africans among the rich mixture of immigrants who could "become men" within the new race "called Americans."[30]

Most white leaders saw blacks as "outcasts from humanity." Revolutionary officials sometimes sought to humiliate disorderly white men by associating them with black men. A duplicitous Tory might be publicly degraded by being handcuffed to a black man for a period of time or by being whipped by a black man before being banished from the vicinity. What made this juxtaposition so humiliating as to render the Tory "impotent" was white America's belief that black males were lower-order creatures such as cattle.[31] Not surprisingly, then, the founders had difficulty imagining that the two races could live together in freedom and equality. Jefferson's well-known assertions about inherent racial differences were adopted by followers such as Tunis Wortman, who argued that interracial mingling and marriage were tantamount to a "universal prostitution" that would produce "a motley and degenerate race of mulattos." Other white leaders ranted against "the infamy of such a mongrel coalition," condemned "the disgraceful and unnatural" evil of interracial unions, and proclaimed that a "free nation of black and white people [will] produce a body politic as monstrous and unnatural as a mongrel half white man and half negro."[32]

Why were the founders fearful of race mixing? Many founders saw black males as inherently impassioned and incorrigible. They viewed them as oversexed creatures whose uncontrollable desires threatened to pollute and debase the white race. Jefferson observed that black males were "more ardent after their female" but lacked "a tender delicate mixture of sentiment and sensation." This combination of black lust and coarseness stemmed from black inferiority in "body and mind" as well as "imagination," where blacks were "dull, tasteless, and anomalous." Jefferson portrayed black males as promiscuous and mindless. He wrote, "Never yet could I find that a black had uttered a thought above the level of plain narration; never see even an elementary trait of painting or sculpture." Frank Shuffelton observes that Jefferson was quite blind to the diversity of African cultures and the creativity of the black artisans in his own household.[33] This blindness allowed him and other founders to view black males as less than men.

Whereas whites occasionally perceived black women to be "remarkable for their chastity and modesty," they nearly always saw black males as immutably lustful. A white rapist suffered a redeemable abuse of natural passion but a black male's character was defined by irredeemable lust. New England rape narratives centered on black lust. A 1768 narrative entitled *The Life and Dying Speech of Arthur* was typical. Arthur was a black slave who discarded piety and industry for a "licentious liberty" that included drinking, promiscuity, running away, theft, and ultimately the rape of a white woman, for which he was hung. Daniel Williams suggests that Arthur's story helped to solidify the white stereotype of the African male as an "immoral, hypersexual black wildly pursuing women to satisfy his prodigal lusts." Indeed, the stereotype was already well established. It was manifested at least as early as 1682, when Pennsylvania Quakers briefly eliminated the death penalty for white rapists but retained hanging for black rapists, apparently because they believed black males were beyond rehabilitation.[34]

One reason the founders felt that black male slaves were beyond rehabilitation was that they were not true family patriarchs. Slave status meant that black males could do little to start families, keep them together, prevent wives' victimization, or protect children. Many male slaves lived in small, isolated households and had little or no contact with potential brides. Often, slave traders forced married male slaves to separate from wives and children, and slaveholder wills required the distribution of slave family members among various heirs. Meanwhile, owners and overseers might force slave husbands "to prostitute their wives and mothers and daughters to gratify the brutal lust of a master." The result, according to Benjamin Rush, was that slave husbands had little confidence "in the fidelity of their wives" or certainty that their wives' children were their own. Thus, male slaves showed little regard "for their posterity." Even when slave fathers were confident of their paternity, they could not "partake of those ineffable sensations with which nature inspires the hearts of fathers" because "paternal fondness" was compromised by the fact that their children would be "slaves like themselves."[35]

For many founders, then, black males could not be "men," because they lacked human status, manly independence, and family mastery. Worse, these hypersexual, coarse creatures carried a grudge against white society that threatened to escalate into racial violence. Jefferson spoke out against slavery, but he opposed combining emancipation with integration, lest free blacks act on "ten thousand recollections . . . of the injuries they have sustained." Similarly, John Taylor detested slavery, but he also hated the abolitionism that encouraged the "black sansculottes" to cut their masters' throats.[36] For the indefinite future, disorderly blacks would have to be controlled by coercion, because it was unlikely that they could be rehabilitated.

How did the founders hope to control incorrigible black males? First, the founding generation was more likely to prosecute, convict, and hang blacks for their crimes. Traditional capital and corporal punishment was by no means obsolete or exceptional for black male criminals. Second, blacks who were not executed or tortured were likely to be sold away from their families and banished from the vicinity. Finally, many black criminals were sent to prison. In the 1790s, for example, blacks constituted one-third of the prisoner population in Philadelphia's Walnut Street penitentiary. For black convicts, however, the penitentiary was not a substitute for traditional state coercion or an innovative institution for rehabilitation. Instead, it was one more option for detaining, disciplining, and controlling a select population of men whose putative passions and licentious behavior were believed to be incurable.[37]

Two-Tiered Criminal Justice

The American founders considered themselves republicans who defended liberty as a basis for men to act virtuously. After the Revolution, however, most founders worried that many men were investing their liberty in licentiousness that resulted in an "epidemic of crime," or an "unprecedented crime wave."[38] The founders' first line of defense against criminality was to encourage males to adhere to the dominant norms of manhood. Young men were enjoined to fortify individual independence with self-discipline, settle down into patriarchal family responsibilities, and become law-abiding citizens. The founders' next line of defense was to apply the dominant norms of manhood to the criminal justice system. They developed innovative ideas and institutions for deterring and punishing crime and for rehabilitating criminals.

Enlightenment criminology proposed two major principles that American reformers adopted and adapted. First, the certainty of punishment, not its severity, best deterred criminal behavior. American elites used this principle to justify replacing traditional punishments such as hanging, branding, and whipping with ostensibly lesser penalties such as incarceration. Second, rehabilitation, not retribution, was the proper goal of punishment. Civic leaders did not support prisoner isolation because it was painful (although they believed it was painful) but because it provided prisoners with opportunities for rehabilitation. The penal road between lesser penalties and rehabilitation was paved with manhood. Convicts were stripped of manhood as a motivation for them to reform, and reformed convicts were promised renewed manly freedom and dignity. The outcome was crucial to the republic. William Bradford explained that when "the offender becomes humbled and reformed, society, instead of losing, gains a citizen."[39]

Of course, the founders did not consider all men eligible for citizenship. White men who owned real property fit the English freeholder tradition. They qualified for citizenship. When a potential or actual citizen engaged in criminal activity, leaders generally assumed that he could be rehabilitated and restored to manhood and citizenship. However, the founders thought that males who lacked the attributes of manhood and citizenship were unlikely candidates for rehabilitation. In particular, they saw black males (along with libertines, lower-class mechanics, immigrants, itinerants, orphans, regular soldiers, backwoodsmen, and Indians) as licentious characters who exhibited a "sordid ferocity and savageness of spirit."[40] They doubted that these "creatures" could learn manly self-restraint, honor family responsibility, or show respect for the law. They had to be controlled because they could not be redeemed.

In conclusion, the founders' conjuncture of manhood and liberty legitimized a two-tiered criminal justice system. The founders applied state coercion to white male criminals in the service of benevolent rehabilitation and restoration to manhood and liberty. Simultaneously, their new penitentiaries functioned as coercive custodial institutions for warehousing disproportionate numbers of blacks and other males whose ostensible unmanly conduct excluded them from liberty and justified severity and subordination to control them. Penitence was for the privileged.[41]

Notes

1. Benjamin Franklin, "The Autobiography," in *The Autobiography and Other Writings,* by Benjamin Franklin, ed. L. Jesse Lemisch (New York: New American Library, 1961), 18; Thomas Paine, "Common Sense," in *The Life and Major Writings of Thomas Paine,* ed. Philip S. Foner (New York: Citadel Press, 1945), 40; John Adams, "Dissertation on the Canon and Feudal Law" (1765), in *The Political Writings of John Adams,* by John Adams, ed. George Peek (Indianapo-

lis: Bobbs-Merrill, 1954), 16; Thomas Jefferson, "Declaration of Independence" (1776), in *The Portable Thomas Jefferson,* ed. Merrill D. Peterson (New York: Viking, 1975), 236, 240.

2. Bernard Bailyn, *The Ideological Origins of the American Revolution* (Cambridge, Mass.: Harvard University Press, 1967), 305; see also Mark E. Kann, "The Bachelor and Other Disorderly Men," *Journal of Men's Studies* 6, no. 1 (Fall 1997): 1–27.

3. Susan Juster, *Disorderly Women: Sexual Politics and Evangelicalism in Revolutionary New England* (Ithaca, N.Y.: Cornell University Press, 1994), 35–38.

4. Marybeth Hamilton Arnold, "'The Life of a Citizen in the Hands of a Woman': Sexual Assault in New York City, 1790 to 1820," in *Passion and Power: Sexuality in History,* ed. Kathy Peiss and Christina Simmons (Philadelphia: Temple University Press, 1989), 41–42, 47; Christine Stansell, *City of Women: Sex and Class in New York, 1789–1860* (Urbana: University of Illinois Press, 1987), 23–27; William Bradford, *An Enquiry How Far the Punishment of Death Is Necessary in Pennsylvania,* in *Reform of Criminal Law in Pennsylvania: Selected Inquiries, 1787–1819* (New York: Arno Press, 1972), 29.

5. Arnold, "The Life of a Citizen," 35; Stansell, *City of Women,* 25; Josiah Quincy quoted in Jay Fliegelman, *Declaring Independence: Jefferson, Natural Language, and the Culture of Performance* (Stanford, Calif.: Stanford University Press, 1993), 75; Bradford, *An Enquiry,* 29.

6. "Davis vs. Maryland, 1810," in *Gay American History: Lesbians and Gay Men in the U.S.A.,* ed. Jonathan Katz (New York: Harper and Row, 1976), 26 and pt. I; Carl Degler, *At Odds: Women and the Family in America from the Revolution to the Present* (Oxford: Oxford University Press, 1980), 157; John D'Emilio and Estelle Freedman, *Intimate Matters: A History of Sexuality in America* (New York: Harper and Row, 1988), 30.

7. David Ramsay, *The History of the American Revolution,* 2 vols. (1789; reprint, Indianapolis: Liberty Press, 1990), 1:199, 2:504–5, 624, 637; James Dana, "The African Slave Trade" (1791), in *Political Sermons of the American Founding Era, 1730–1805,* ed. Ellis Sandoz (Indianapolis: Liberty Press, 1991), 1049.

8. See Mark E. Kann, *A Republic of Men: The American Founders, Gendered Language, and Patriarchal Politics* (New York: New York University Press, 1998), chap. 1; E. Anthony Rotundo, *American Manhood: Transformations in Masculinity from the Revolution to the Modern Era* (New York: Basic Books, 1993), chap. 1; Michael Kimmel, *Manhood in America: A Cultural History* (New York: Free Press, 1996), chaps. 1–2.

9. Gary Nash, *Race, Class, and Politics: Essays on American Colonial and Revolutionary Society* (Urbana: University of Illinois Press, 1986), 248; Judith Shklar, *American Citizenship: The Quest for Inclusion* (Cambridge, Mass.: Harvard University Press, 1991), 2, 15, 17; see also Joan Gundersen, "Independence, Citizenship, and the American Revolution," *Signs: Journal of Women in Culture and Society* 13, no. 11 (1987): 59–97.

10. Benjamin Franklin, "Reply to a Piece of Advice" (1735), in *Writings,* by Benjamin Franklin, ed. J. A. Leon Lemay (New York: Library of America, 1987), 249.

11. Thomas Jefferson to Edmund Pendleton, August 26, 1776, in *The Portable Thomas Jefferson,* 356–57; George Mason quoted in James Madison's "Notes from the Constitutional Convention," in *The Anti-federalist Papers and the Constitutional Convention Debates,* ed. Ralph Ketcham (New York: New American Library, 1986), 147.

12. Jacob Rush, "The Nature and Importance of an Oath—the Charge to a Jury" (1796), in *American Political Writings during the Founding Era, 1760–1805,* ed. Charles Hyneman and Donald Lutz, 2 vols. (Indianapolis: Liberty Press, 1983), 2:1020–21.

13. Bradford, *An Enquiry,* 7–8.

14. Louis P. Masur, *Rites of Execution: Capital Punishment and the Transformation of American Culture, 1776–1865* (New York: Oxford University Press, 1989), chap. 2; Michael Meranze, *Laboratories of Virtue: Punishment, Revolution, and Authority in Philadelphia, 1760–1835* (Chapel Hill: University of North Carolina Press, 1996), 19, 72.

15. Ann Fairfax Withington, *Toward a More Perfect Union: Virtue and the Formation of American Republics* (New York: Oxford University Press, 1991), xiii–xiv, 16–17, 55, 134, 184, 208, 212, 215, 217, 224, 229, 242.

16. Kermit L. Hall, *The Magic Mirror: Law in American History* (New York: Oxford University Press, 1989), 34.

17. Quoted in Meranze, *Laboratories of Virtue,* 69–70; see also Benjamin Franklin, "The Trial and Reprieve of Prouse and Mitchel" (1729), in *Writings,* 140.

18. Mercy Otis Warren, *History of the Rise, Progress and Termination of the American Revolution,* ed. Lester H. Cohen, 2 vols. (1805; reprint, Indianapolis: Liberty Press, 1988), 2:404–6; George Washington to John Laurens, October 13, 1780, in *Affectionately Yours, George Washington: A Self-Portrait in Letters of Friendship,* by George Washington, ed. Thomas J. Fleming (New York: Norton, 1967), 143; A. J. Langguth, *Patriots: The Men Who Started the American Revolution* (New York: Simon and Schuster, 1988), 508; Alexander Hamilton to John Laurens, October 11, 1780, in *Alexander Hamilton: A Biography in His Own Words,* by Alexander Hamilton, ed. Mary-Jo Kline (New York: Harper and Row, 1973), 91–92.

19. Benjamin Rush, *An Enquiry into the Effects of Public Punishments upon Criminals and upon Society* (1787), in *Reform of Criminal Law,* 5.

20. Meranze, *Laboratories of Virtue,* 88, 122–23, and chap. 3; Caleb Lownes, "An Account of the Alteration and Present State of the Penal Laws of Pennsylvania" (1793), in *Reform of Criminal Law,* 77.

21. Masur, *Rites of Execution,* 80; Meranze, *Laboratories of Virtue,* 167.

22. Cesare Beccaria, *On Crimes and Punishments and Other Writings,* ed. Richard Bellamy, trans. Richard Davies (Cambridge, England: Cambridge University Press, 1995), 67; Benjamin Rush, *Considerations on the Injustice and Impolicy of Punishing Murder by Death* (1792), in *Reform of Criminal Law,* 12.

23. B. Rush, *An Enquiry in the Effects of Public Punishment,* 4, 8, 10, 14; see also John Howard, *The State of Prisons* (1777), cited in Samuel Walker, *Popular Justice: A History of American Criminal Justice* (New York: Oxford University Press, 1980), 42.

24. James Otis Jr., *The Rights of the British Colonies Asserted and Proved* (1964), in *Pamphlets of the American Revolution, 1750–1776,* ed. Bernard Bailyn, 2 vols. (Cambridge, Mass.: Harvard University Press, 1965), 1:425–26; John Dickinson, "Observations on the Constitution Proposed by the Federal Convention, III" (1788), in *The Debate on the Constitution: Federalist and Antifederalist Speeches, Articles, and Letters during the Struggle over Ratification,* ed. Bernard Bailyn, 2 vols. (New York: Library of America, 1993), 2:409; Thomas Jefferson to Maria Cosway, October 12, 1786, in *The Portable Thomas Jefferson,* 403, 408; Samuel Quarrier to Thomas Jefferson, February 13, 1802, in *To His Excellency Thomas Jefferson: Letters to a President,* ed. Jack McLaughlin (New York: Avon Books, 1991), 150.

25. Joseph M. Hawes, "Prison in Early Nineteenth Century America: The Process of Convict Reformation," in *Law and Order in American History,* ed. Joseph M. Hawes (Port Washington, N.Y.: Kennikat Press, 1979), 41; Walker, *Popular Justice,* 42; B. Rush, *An Enquiry into the Effects of Public Punishment,* 14; see also Masur, *Rites of Execution,* 80–84.

26. Meranze, *Laboratories of Virtue,* 177–79, 184–85; *Pennsylvania Gazette* quoted in Negley K. Teeters, *The Cradle of the Penitentiary: The Walnut Street Jail at Philadelphia, 1773–1835* (Philadelphia: Pennsylvania Prison Society, 1955), 132.

27. Walker, *Popular Justice,* 33, 48; Bradford, *An Enquiry,* 29–30.

28. Bradford, *An Enquiry,* 20–21.

29. Masur, *Rites of Execution,* 87.

30. J. Hector St. John de Crévecoeur, *Letters from an American Farmer* (New York: Penguin, 1981), 68–69, 168–71; see also Doreen Alvarez Saar, "The Heritage of Ethnicity in Crévecouer's

Letters from an American Farmer," in *A Mixed Race: Ethnicity in Early America,* ed. Frank Shuffelton (New York: Oxford University Press, 1993), 245, 251–53.

31. Withington, *Toward a More Perfect Union,* 235.

32. John Witherspoon, "The Dominion of Providence over the Passions of Men" (1776), in Sandoz, *Political Sermons,* 537; Robert Gross, *The Minutemen and Their World* (New York: Hill and Wang, 1976), 94, 96; James Dana, "The African Slave Trade" (1791), in Sandoz, *Political Sermons,* 1049; Tunis Wortman, "A Solemn Address to Christians and Patriots" (1800), in Sandoz, *Political Sermons,* 1508–9; Anonymous, "Rudiments of Law and Government Deduced from the Law of Nature" (1783), in Hyneman and Lutz, *American Political Writings,* 1:584; David Rice, "Slavery Inconsistent with Justice and Good Policy" (1792), in Hyneman and Lutz, *American Political Writings,* 2:874; John Taylor, *Arator: Being a Series of Agricultural Essays, Practical and Political in Sixty-Four Numbers* ed. M. E. Bradford (1804; reprint, Indianapolis: Liberty Press, 1977), 178.

33. Thomas Jefferson, "Notes on the State of Virginia," in *The Portable Thomas Jefferson,* 94–95, 187–89, 192–93; Frank Shuffelton, "Thomas Jefferson: Race, Culture, and the Failure of the Anthropological Method," in Shuffelton, *A Mixed Race,* 268–70.

34. Rice, "Slavery Inconsistent with Justice," 2:861; Daniel Williams, "The Gratification of That Corrupt and Lawless Passion," in Shuffelton, *A Mixed Race,* 198–200; Walker, *Popular Justice,* 33–34.

35. Levi Hart, "Liberty Described and Recommended: In a Sermon Preached to the Corporation of Freemen in Farmington" (1775), in Hyneman and Lutz, *American Political Writings,* 1:314; Benjamin Rush, *An Address to the Inhabitants of the British Settlements on the Slavery of Negroes in America* (1773; reprint, New York: Arno Press, 1969), 16; Benjamin Rush, *Vindication of the Address to the Inhabitants of the British Settlements, on the Slavery of Negroes in America in Answer to a Pamphlet entitled, "Slavery Not Forbidden in Scripture; or a Defence of the West-Indian Planters from the Aspersions Thrown Out against Them by the Author of the Address,"* in *Reform of Criminal Law,* 41–43; Crévecoeur, *Letters from an American Farmer,* 169–70.

36. Jefferson, "Notes on the State of Virginia," 186; Taylor, *Arator,* 125, 180–83.

37. Masur, *Rites of Execution,* 39; Taylor, *Arator,* 188.

38. Hall, *The Magic Mirror,* 169; Masur, *Rites of Execution,* 59; Meranze, *Laboratories of Virtue,* 66–67.

39. Bradford, *An Enquiry,* 7; see also Lawrence Friedman, "The Development of American Criminal Law," in Hawes, *Law and Order in American History,* 7.

40. Meranze, *Laboratories of Virtue,* 106.

41. See Nancy Kurshan, "Behind the Walls: The History and Current Reality of Women's Imprisonment," in *Criminal Injustice: Confronting the Prison Crisis,* ed. Elihu Rosenblatt (Boston: South End Press, 1996), 141, where the author suggests that nineteenth-century U.S. prisons for women also emphasized reformation for white convicts but custodial control of black inmates.

Angela Y. Davis

Race, Gender, and Prison History: From the Convict Lease System to the Supermax Prison

Albert Wright Jr. is a fifty-year-old African American man who is serving a forty-year term in the Western Illinois Correctional Center. "In this prison of 2,000 men, of whom some 66 percent are Black," he wrote in an impassioned plea to readers of the black monthly *Emerge*, "there is seldom a positive response to the cries for help in combating the inhuman treatment that we are subjected to daily. Few of you know what the treatment is like. What prison administrators tell you is not anything near the truth" (1997:80). Wright makes it very clear that he is not asking for financial support or material goods: "I am talking about genuine interest in what is happening to your people. We are still people. We just happen to be in prison." But as with many of the hundreds of thousands of black men currently trapped in a proliferating web of state and privately run prisons, Wright's humanity—and that of the imprisoned youth on whose behalf he made his appeal—goes unrecognized by a penal system that has abandoned the goals of individual rehabilitation and social reintegration in favor of increasingly harsh forms of punishment and retribution. Because the racist-informed discourse on criminality goes largely unchallenged, black male bodies are treated as dispensable by communities in the "free world" that have all but forsaken those who are marked as criminal. Obviously concerned that middle-class black communities share the guilt of distancing themselves from the plight of prisoners, Wright submitted his piece to *Emerge* in an effort to simultaneously criticize and reach out to these communities.

Black men are now the primary targets of what Jerome G. Miller (1996) calls the "search and destroy" mission of a criminal justice system that, we must remember, also trains its sights on black women and other men of color, as well as on poor white people. African American males, who constitute less than 7 percent of the U.S. population, represent nearly half of the people in jail and prison (Donziger, 1996:102). I do not intend to suggest that most imprisoned people have not committed a crime of some sort. In fact, studies have repeatedly found that, at one point in their lives, a vast majority of most of these populations have engaged in some type of behavior that is proscribed by law. However, only a small percentage of these acts is ever examined within the context of the criminal justice system (Rotman, 1990:115). Considering the fact that, in the late 1990s, approximately one-third of all young black men were either in prison or directly under the control of a correctional system, it is not entirely far-fetched to argue that being a young black male results in a greater chance of going to jail or prison than does actually committing a crime. Although most young black men who are imprisoned may have broken a law, the fact of their race and gender more than their guilt or innocence is what tends to bring them into contact with the criminal justice system.

The staggering numbers of imprisoned black men should not, however, eclipse the fact that black women—a majority of whom are arrested for drug-related offenses—constitute the most rapidly expanding of all imprisoned populations. According to John Irwin and James Austin, "African-American women have experienced the greatest increase in correctional supervision, rising by 78 percent from 1989 through 1994" (1994:4). This phenomenon is attributable to the fact that poor black women, like poor black men, are increasingly targets of police surveillance for reasons of race and economic status, as well as for reasons of gender. The dismantling of welfare, for example, and the attendant demonization of single black mothers—who are represented as procreators of crime and poverty—contribute to a process that is leading large numbers of poor black women into prison. Moreover, differential criminalization of drug use means that those unfortunate enough to become addicted to crack can be arrested and thrown in jail, while their middle-class counterparts, who have access to licit drugs such as Valium or Prozac, are free to indulge their drug habits.

In fact, the current rise in the numbers of imprisoned black men and women can hardly be justified by any recent increase in the crime rate among black people. Steven Donziger points out that "there are so many more African Americans than whites in our prisons that the difference cannot be explained by higher crime among African-Americans—racial discrimination is also at work, and it penalizes African-Americans at almost every juncture in the criminal justice system" (1966:99). Yet black people and people of color in general are increasingly the main human raw material with which the rapid expansion of the U.S. penal system is being accomplished. I suggest that it is, in fact, the peculiarly racialized and gendered history of punishment in the United States that has, in part, facilitated the structural and ideological transformation of the penal system into a Prison Industrial Complex that imprisons, dehumanizes, and exploits ever-increasing numbers of people, the vast majority of whom are poor and black.

It is not a coincidence that rehabilitation, the historical goal of the prison, has receded theoretically and practically as U.S. prisons have come to house spiraling numbers of black men. The current notion that the "criminals" with whom prisons are overcrowded are largely beyond the pale of rehabilitation—that is, that "nothing works"—is very much connected with the fact that, in the contemporary era, the combined terms "black" and "male" have become virtually synonymous with "criminal" in the popular imagination. This is not to ignore the complex historical evolution of the rehabilitative ideal, from a moral and religious to a medicalized framework, nor the problematic category of recidivism, which has figured prominently in measurements of the success of rehabilitation.

As Richard Hawkins and Geoffrey Alpert point out:

Right now there is no uniformly accepted definition of recidivism. It generally refers to a return to crime, but in operation refers only to those detected in crime. Given that many crimes go undetected (some of which are committed by former offenders), virtually any official measure of recidivism is a conservative estimate of the failure rate among persons released from treatment. One reviewer of various recidivism definitions notes thirteen different indicators of "failure," ranging from a recorded police contact to being returned to prison. (1989:198–99)

Nevertheless, narratives of rehabilitation have been so informed by the racial assumptions that have shaped moral and religious frameworks on one hand and medical frameworks on the other that an examination of the historical specificities of these relationships may yield insights about the current construction of imprisonment as the inevitable destiny of young black men. It may also assist us in understanding why the rather small proportion of women within imprisoned populations has recently begun to rise to unprecedented heights, with black female bodies increasingly subjected to a process of criminalization paralleling that of their male counterparts.

Given the recent emergence of supermaximum-security prisons and the increasingly punitive character of prisons in the United States in general—which are being divested of educational, recreational, and other programs historically associated with rehabilitation projects—it is important to recall that, ironically, in their early history, prisons were proposed as radical alternatives to the horrendous bodily pain that then constituted the dominant mode of punishment. The penitentiary—the historical manifestation of the prison as a site for punishment (rather than as a holding facility for people awaiting trial and punishment)—was conceived architecturally and theoretically as a plan for the moral reformation of the individual. As such, it expressed the overarching Enlightenment-age assumption that reason formed the core of every human being. It also expressed modernity's vision of inevitable progress. However, as philosopher David T. Goldberg points out, the "defining of humanity in relation to rationality clearly prefaces modernity's emphasis on rational capacity as a crucial differentia of racial groups" (1993:23). In fact, modernity's construction of rational humanity was not only racialized; it was gendered as well.

Although it has been argued that the term "penitentiary" originated from a plan in England to incarcerate "penitent" prostitutes (Hawkins and Alpert, 1989:30), the penitentiary as an institution for the reformation of criminals was aimed largely at white men. In the United States, this fact acquired significance in that the birth of the penitentiary occurred during the last half century or so of slavery. This period also witnessed intense contestations over the future of women's rights.

Reflecting modernity's relegation of women of all racial backgrounds, and men of color, to reason's antithesis—nature, instinct, and the senses—the putative universality of reason masked strong racial and gendered assumptions about the bodies in which universal reason resided. During much of the nineteenth century, white women had no autonomous juridical status, and they were punished largely within the domestic sphere. Daughters were subjected to corporal punishment by their fathers, and wives were subjected to corporal punishment by their husbands. White women deemed "criminal" who were brought into the criminal justice system were considered "fallen," and, as such, beyond the pale of moral rehabilitation.

Until the abolition of slavery, most black men and women were under the authority of their slave masters, who developed punishment regimes designed simultaneously to inflict severe bodily pain and to safeguard the body as a laboring and thus profitable commodity. One example was that holes were dug in which pregnant women who were to be flogged could lay their stomachs in order to protect their unborn children, who were grist for the mills of slave labor (Davis, 1981:9). In this context, punishment was entirely disarticulated from the goal of moral reformation. Because slave laborers were largely valued in relationship to their size and strength, the worth of male slaves was generally higher than that of female slaves. A probable consequence of this was the privileging of the male body for labor and punishment. This is not to dismiss the horrors to which women were subjected under slavery, which included not only sexualized forms of punishment such as rape but also gendered forms of punishment related to the control and preservation of women's reproductive labor.

During the post–Civil War era, extralegal lynching, along with the legalized Black Codes (laws passed by southern state legislatures that severely limited the rights of blacks), constructed the bodies of black people as the loci of punishment. In this way, on the grounds of both race and gender, black men and women continued to be excluded from the moral realm within which punishment in the penitentiary was equated with rehabilitation. Black men were barred from the individuality and masculinity with which even the criminal citizen was imbued. Black women, on the other hand, were barred from the femininity that tended to protect many white women from imprisonment.

The birth of the English and U.S. penitentiaries, whose most ardent advocates were passionately opposed to harsh corporal punishment, had little impact on the punishment regimes to which slaves were subjected. Neither did they effectively alter the way white women were punished. As such, they were implicitly racialized and gendered as new and less-cruel modes of white male punishment.

The most widely publicized penitentiary design was the panopticon proposed by utilitarian philosopher Jeremy Bentham. Although few prisons were actually constructed according to the strict standards of the panopticon, its discursive impact was such that it was linked closely to the project of prison rehabilitation. Between 1787 and 1791, Bentham published a series of letters that described in detail a new architectural design for prisons and other institutions that required the surveillance and control of large numbers of people. Bentham's panopticon was supposed to guarantee the ubiquitous monitoring and the imposition of discipline he thought criminals needed in order to internalize productive labor habits. According to Bentham's plan, which he hoped would win him a contract with the government to build and operate a penitentiary, prison inmates would be housed in solitary cells situated on circular tiers, all of which would face a multilevel guard tower. Bentham suggested the use of venetian blinds, combined with a rather complex interplay of light and darkness, to guarantee that the prisoners—whose single cells were arranged so that they could not see each other—would also be unable to see the warden in the guard tower. The vantage point of the warden, on the other hand, would allow him a clear view of all the prisoners. However—and this was the most significant aspect of Bentham's mammoth panopticon—because each individual prisoner would never be able to determine where the warden's gaze was focused, each prisoner would be compelled to behave as though he were being watched at all times.

The most consistent attempt to implement Bentham's panopticon design took place in the United States. The Stateville Penitentiary, located near Joliet, Illinois, officially opened on March 9, 1925. It took shape as a direct result of a reform movement begun in 1905 that exposed the state of Illinois for maintaining "brutal and inhumane conditions" at the old Joliet prison, which had been built in 1860 (Jacobs, 1977:15–16). When a legislative committee returned from a trip to Europe to examine prison planning abroad, its members announced that they were most impressed by Bentham's panopticon. Although Stateville was built partially as a panopticon, by the time construction was entering its last phase, the state had given up on the circular panoptic plan and completed the prison with rectangular cell houses. For the first twenty-five years of its history, Stateville held a majority white prison population. However, by the mid-1950s, the prison population was majority black (Jacobs, 1977:58).

As Foucault pointed out, the prisoner of the panopticon "is seen, but he does not see; he is the object of information, never a subject in communication . . . and this invisibility is a guarantee of order" (1979:200). Moreover, "the crowd, a compact mass, a locus of multiple exchanges, individualities merging together, a collective effect, is abolished and replaced by a collection of separated individualities. From the point of view of the guardian, it is replaced by a multiplicity that can be numbered and supervised; from the point of view of the inmates, by a sequestered and observed solitude" (p. 201).

This process of individualization via the panopticon assumed that the prisoner was at least a potentially rational being whose criminality merely evidenced deviation from that potential. This architecture and regime also assumed that the individual to be reformed panoptically was, indeed, in possession of mental and moral faculties that could be controlled and transformed by the experience of imprisonment. White women were theoretically exempt from this process, since in Britain and in the United States at the turn of the nineteenth century, the overdetermining ideology of the "fallen woman" constructed female criminals as having no prospect of moral rehabilitation. Black men and women, on the other hand, were ideologically barred from the realm of morality and, unlike white women, were not even acknowledged as ever having been epistemological subjects and moral agents. Thus, they could not even fall from grace, a state they were deemed incapable of attaining in the first place.

Slaves were not accorded the social status of individuals. If they were accorded any individuality at all, it was corporal in nature, defined by their value on the market, their laboring potential, and the punishment they received. As a consequence, often they were not even subject to the gender differentiation operative in the dominant culture. Women's quotas in the plantation fields, for example, where their tasks were essentially the same as men's, were established in connection with their size and weight rather than with their gender. Women were also targets of the whip and the lash, the primary weapons of punishment during slavery.

As black people began to be integrated into southern penal systems in the aftermath of the Civil War—and as the penal system became a system of penal servitude—the punishment associated with slavery became integrated into the penal system. "Whipping," as Matthew J. Mancini has observed, "was the preeminent form of punishment under slavery; and the lash, along with the chain, became the very emblem of servitude for slaves and prisoners" (1996:25). Many black people were imprisoned under the laws assembled in the various Black Codes of the southern states. Because the Black Codes were rearticulations of the Slave Codes (which provided for perpetual, inherited servitude for Africans), they tended to racialize penality and link it closely with previous regimes of slavery. The expansion of the convict lease system and the county chain gang meant that the antebellum criminal justice system, which focused far more intensely on blacks than on whites, largely defined southern criminal justice as a means of controlling black labor. According to Mancini:

> Among the multifarious debilitating legacies of slavery was the conviction that blacks could only labor in a certain way—the way experience had shown them to have labored in the past: in gangs, subjected to constant supervision, and under the discipline of the lash. Since these were the requisites of slavery, and since slaves were blacks, Southern whites almost universally concluded that blacks could not work unless subjected to such intense surveillance and discipline. (1996:25)

Scholars who have studied the convict lease system point out that, in many important respects, convict leasing was far worse than slavery—as the title of Mancini's (1996) study, *One Dies, Get Another,* and the title of David Oshinsky's (1996) work on Parchman Prison, *Worse Than Slavery,* attest. The concern that slave owners necessarily expressed for individual slaves because of their particular value no longer applied to convicts, who were leased out en masse and could be worked literally to death without affecting the profitability of a convict crew. According to descriptions by contemporaries, the living conditions for leased convicts and county chain gangs were far worse than the living conditions for slaves. According to the records of Mississippi plantations in the Yazoo Delta during the late 1880s:

> The prisoners ate and slept on bare ground, without blankets or mattresses, and often without clothes. They were punished for "slow hoeing" (ten lashes), "sorry planting" (five lashes), and "being light with cotton" (five lashes) Some who attempted to escape were whipped "till the blood ran down their legs"; others had a metal spur riveted to their feet. Convicts dropped from exhaustion, pneumonia, malaria, frostbite, consumption, sunstroke, dysentery, gunshot wounds, and "shackle poisoning" (the constant rubbing of chains and leg irons against bare flesh). (Oshinsky, 1996:45)

The U.S. penitentiaries—as they developed according to the Pennsylvania system (which was based on full-time solitary confinement) and the Auburn system (in which prisoners worked together in total silence during the day but were housed separately at night)—envisioned labor as a rehabilitative activity. However, convict labor in the South, overwhelmingly black, was designed to reap the largest possible profits. Rehabilitation had little or nothing to do with the punishment industry as it developed in the antebellum South. Thus, the theory of punishment associated with the new U.S. penitentiaries and with the Benthamian concept of the panopticon was entirely at odds with the forms of punishment meted out to newly freed black people.

In the contemporary era, the emergent Prison Industrial Complex, which is fueled increasingly by privatization trends, recalls the early efforts to create a profitable punishment industry based on the new supply of "free" black male laborers in the aftermath of the Civil War. Drawing from the work of Norwegian criminologist Nils Christie, Steven Donziger argues that

companies that service the criminal justice system need sufficient quantities of raw materials to guarantee long-term growth. . . . In the criminal justice field, *the raw material is prisoners,* and industry will do what is necessary to guarantee a steady supply. For the supply
of prisoners to grow, criminal justice policies must ensure a sufficient number of incarcerated Americans regardless of whether crime is rising or the incarceration is necessary.
(1996:87)

Newly freed black men, along with a significant number of black women, constituted
a virtually endless supply of raw material for the embryonic southern punishment industry, in addition to providing much-needed labor for the economies of the southern
states as they attempted to recover from the devastating impact of the Civil War. Similarly, in the contemporary era, unemployed black men, along with increasing numbers
of women, constitute an unending supply of raw material for the present-day Prison
Industrial Complex.

According to 1997 Bureau of Justice statistics, African Americans as a whole now
represent the majority of state and federal prisoners, with a total of 735,200 black
inmates—10,000 more than the total number of white inmates. As the rate of increase
in the incarceration of black prisoners continues to rise, the racial composition of the
incarcerated population is fast approaching the proportion of black prisoners to white
during the era of the southern convict lease and county chain gang systems. Whether
this human raw material is used for purposes of labor or as forced consumers of commodities provided by a rising number of corporations directly implicated in the prison
industrial complex, it is clear that black male bodies are considered dispensable within
the "free world" and that they are a major source of profit in the prison world. This
relationship recapitulates in complicated new ways the era of convict leasing.

The privatization characteristic of convict leasing also has its contemporary parallels, in companies such as Corrections Corporation of America and Wackenhut Corrections Corporation, which literally run prisons for profit. In the late 1990s, the seventeen private prison companies operating in the United States (and sometimes abroad)
constructed approximately one hundred jails and prisons in which fifty thousand inmates
were incarcerated. Private prisons multiplied at four times the rate of expansion of public prisons. According to a May 10, 1997, *San Francisco Chronicle* article by Kristin
Bloomer, entitled "Private Punishment," observers of the private prison phenomenon
estimated that there would be three times as many private facilities by the turn of the
century and that their revenues would reach more than $1 billion. In arrangements rem-
iniscent of the convict lease system, federal, state, and county governments pay private
companies a fee for each inmate, which means that private companies have a stake in
retaining prisoners as long as possible and in keeping their facilities filled.

An August 26, 1997, *Washington Post* article by S. A. Presley, entitled "Texas County
Sued by Missouri over Alleged Abuse of Inmates," reports that, in the state of Texas,
there are thirty-four government-owned, privately run jails in which approximately fifty-
five hundred out-of-state prisoners are incarcerated. These facilities generate about $80
million annually for Texas. Capital Corrections Resources operates the Brazoria Detention Center, a government-owned facility located forty miles outside of Houston, Texas.
Brazoria came to public attention in August 1997 when a videotape broadcast on national
television showed police dogs biting prisoners and guards viciously stepping on and

kicking prisoners in their groins. An August 20, 1997, *Philadelphia Daily News* article by Madeline Baro, entitled "Video Prompts Prison Probe," reported that the inmates were forced to crawl on the floor and were shocked with stun guns as guards—who referred to one black prisoner as "boy"—shouted, "Crawl faster!" In the aftermath of the release of this tape, the state of Missouri withdrew the 415 prisoners it housed in the Brazoria Detention Center. Although the accompanying news reports made few references to the indisputably racialized character of the guards' outrageous behavior, the segment of the Brazoria videotape that aired on national television showed black male prisoners to be the primary targets of the guards' attacks.

The thirty-two-minute Brazoria video, which was represented by jail authorities as a training tape showing corrections officers "what *not* to do," was filmed in September 1996 after a guard allegedly smelled marijuana in the jail. Important evidence of the abuse that takes place behind the walls of private prisons, the tape came to light in connection with a lawsuit filed by one of the prisoners who was bitten by a police dog. He was suing Brazoria County for $100,000 in damages. The Brazoria jailors' actions—which, according to the facility's prisoners, were far worse than depicted on the tape—are indicative of not only the ways in which many prisoners throughout the country are treated but also the generalized attitudes toward people locked up in jails and prisons: By virtue of their imprisonment, they deserve this kind of severe corporal punishment.

An August 27, 1997, Associated Press news story, entitled "Beatings Worse Than Shown on Videotape, Missouri Inmates Say," quoted the Missouri prisoners. Once they had been transferred back to their home state from Brazoria, they told the *Kansas City Star* that "guards at the Brazoria County Detention Center used cattle prods and other forms of intimidation to win respect and force prisoners to say, 'I love Texas.'" "'What you saw on tape,'" said inmate Louis Watkins, referring to the videotaped cell-block raid of September 18, 1996, "'wasn't a fraction of what happened that day. I've never seen anything like that in the movies.'"

It is interesting that this prisoner compared what he saw during the detention center raid to cinematic representations of prison experience. One of the arguments that I make by way of historical comparisons of contemporary punishment practices with the explicitly racialized punishment regimes of the post–Civil War South is that prison experience, in popular representational practices, is a quintessentially black male experience. Whether brutal punishment within penal settings is inflicted on white, Latino/Latina, Asian, Native, or African American men or women, the typical prisoner—and the target of this brutality—is generally considered to be a black man. The gross violations of prisoners' civil and human rights, in this sense, is very much connected with the generalized equation of "criminal" or "prisoner" with a black male body.

The current construction and expansion of state and federal supermaximum-security prisons, whose purpose is to address disciplinary problems within the penal system, draws upon the historical conception of the panopticon. Again, black men are vastly overrepresented in these supermax prisons and control units, the first of which emerged when federal correctional authorities began to send to the prison in Marion, Illinois, prisoners deemed "dangerous." In 1983 the entire prison was "locked down"—that is, prisoners were confined to their cells twenty-three hours a day (Human Rights Watch, 1997). Today, there are at least fifty-seven supermaximum security federal and state prisons located in thirty-six states. A 1997 Human Rights Watch report description of supermaxes sounds chillingly like Bentham's panopticon. What is different, however, is that all references to individual rehabilitation have disappeared:.

> Inmates in super-maximum security facilities are usually held in single cell lock-down, what is commonly referred to as solitary confinement. . . . Congregate activities with other prisoners are usually prohibited; other prisoners cannot even be seen from an inmate's cell; communication with other prisoners is prohibited or difficult (consisting, for example, of shouting from cell to cell); visiting and telephone privileges are limited. The new generation of super-maximum security facilities also rely on state-of-the-art technology for monitoring and controlling prisoner conduct and movement, utilizing, for example, video monitors and remote-controlled electronic doors. [According to Craig Haney (1993:3),] "These prisons represent the application of sophisticated, modern technology dedicated entirely to the task of social control, and they isolate, regulate and surveil more effectively than anything that has preceded them." (Human Rights Watch, 1997:19)

Some of these supermax prisons house inmates in cells with solid steel gates rather than bars—an arrangement that recalls the railroad cars used to house leased convicts—so that prisoners literally can see nothing. They are unable even to see the guards who bring their food, which they receive through a slot. According to Miller, "The disproportionate percentage of black men in the general prison populations is outstripped by the much greater percentages of black men housed in supermax prisons" (1996:227). Miller refers to a study by William Chambliss, who found that, on one day in 1993, 98 percent of the inmates confined in the supermax prison in Baltimore, Maryland, were African Americans (p. 227).

The danger of supermax prisons resides not only in the systematically brutal treatment of the prisoners confined therein but also in the way they establish standards for the treatment of all prisoners. They solidify the move away from rehabilitative strategies, and they do so largely on the backs of black men. Moreover, as prisons become more repressive and as this repression becomes more remote from—and, by default, accepted within—the "free world," they promote retrograde tendencies in educational institutions that serve the populations most likely to move from schools into prisons. These educational institutions begin to resemble prisons more than schools. In poor black communities, schools tend to direct resources needed to address educational crises toward security and discipline. Rather than prepare students for college, middle and high schools in these communities are fast becoming prep schools for prison, molding black children into raw material for punishment and coerced labor.

The extent to which black men today function as the main human raw material for the Prison Industrial Complex only highlights the many ways in which the prison system in the United States in general resembles and recapitulates some of the most abhorrent characteristics of the slavery and convict lease systems of the late nineteenth century. In fact, the rampant exploitation of prison labor in an increasingly privatized context *is* a modern-day form of convict leasing. And although black men are not the only population vulnerable to this exploitation, the overwhelming numbers of black men imprisoned in the United States makes them by far the most threatened members of our society when it comes to the new form of enslavement being implemented through the prison system.

That we can so easily draw these connections between late twentieth-century/early twenty-first century imprisonment practices in the United States and various systems and practices that were in place a century ago is in large part a result of the racism that has been consistently interwoven into the history of the prison system in this country. The ultimate manifestation of this phenomenon can be found in the supermax prison, whose main function is to subdue and control "problematic" imprisoned populations— again, composed largely of black men—who, having been locked away in the most remote and invisible of spaces, basically are no longer thought of as human. Terry A. Kupers (1999) claims that entire populations are being "disappeared" from U.S. society via the prison system. The absolute authority that is exercised over these disappeared populations by supermax administrators and staff—and the lack of accountability on the part of private corporations that are in the prison business or benefit from prison labor—is reminiscent of the impunity with which slave owners, overseers, and, later, patrons of the convict lease system routinely disregarded the humanity connected with the black bodies they systematically abused.

In this sense, the supermax draws upon—even as it also serves to feed—the perpetuation of racism at every level of our society. This is true, in fact, of the entire prison system; the continued practice of throwing away entire populations depends upon the construction and perception—really the fixation—of those populations within the popular imagination as public enemies. It is precisely this relationship between racism and imprisonment that necessitates coalitional work between antiracist activists and prison activists; on the eve of the twenty-first century, these two movements are inseparable.

References

Davis, Angela Y. 1981. *Women, Class and Race.* New York: Random House.

Donziger, Steven, ed. 1996. *The Real War on Crime: The Report of the National Criminal Justice Commission.* New York: Harper Perennial.

Foucault, Michel. 1977. *Discipline and Punish: The Birth of the Prison.* Trans., Alen Sheridan. New York: Pantheon Books.

Goldberg, David T. 1993. *Racist Culture: Philosophy and the Politics of Meaning.* Cambridge, Mass.: Black Press.

Haney, Craig. 1993. "Infamous Punishment: The Psychological Consequences of Isolation." *National Prison Project Journal (ACLU)* (Spring), 3.

Hawkins, R., and G. P. Alpert. 1989. *American Prison Systems: Punishment and Justice.* Englewood Cliffs, N.J.: Prentice-Hall.

Human Rights Watch. 1997. *Cold Storage: Super-Maximum Security Confinement in Indiana.* New York: Human Rights Watch.

Irwin, J., and J. Austin. 1994. *It's about Time: America's Imprisonment Binge.* Belmont, Calif.: Wadsworth.

Jacobs, J. B. 1977. *Stateville: The Penitentiary in Mass Society.* Chicago: University of Chicago Press.

Kupers, Terry A. 1999. *Prison Madness: The Mental Health Crisis behind Bars and What We Must Do about It.* San Francisco: Jossey-Bass.

Mancini, Matthew J. 1996. *One Dies, Get Another: Convict Leasing in the American South, 1866–1928.* Columbus: University of South Carolina Press.

Miller, Jerome G. 1996. *Search and Destroy: African American Males in the Criminal Justice System.* Cambridge, England: Cambridge University Press.

Oshinsky, David. 1996. *Worse Than Slavery: Parchman Farm and the Ordeal of Jim Crow Justice.* New York: Free Press.

Rotman, E. 1990. *Beyond Punishment: A New View on the Rehabilitation of Criminal Offenders.* New York: Greenwood Press.

Wright, Albert Jr. 1997. "Young Inmates Need Help, from Inside and Out." *Emerge Magazine* (October), 80.

Marc Mauer

Crime, Politics, and Community Since the 1990s

A quick overview of developments in penal policy in the United States over the past several years reveals some of the following highlights:

- inmates in Alabama and other states being secured on chain gangs doing hard labor on roadsides
- a sheriff in Arizona "getting tough" with inmates by housing them in tents in the desert
- the federal government prohibiting inmates from receiving grant money to enable them to take college education courses while in prison

These developments cannot be dismissed as just isolated events in the field; in today's information age, they suggest more distressing consequences. With the advent of CNN, the Internet, and other technologies, policymakers and the public throughout the world can now learn of developments in the United States almost as quickly as they are implemented. Political leaders in England, for example, have recently proposed or adopted boot camps, mandatory sentencing, high-security prisons, and other harsh sanctions largely based on the U.S. model. The caning of U.S. citizen Michael Fay in Singapore several years ago received widespread publicity and much support in the United States.

These telegenic developments are of concern, but the more substantive policy changes being implemented are in many ways much more disturbing. In recent years, these have included legislation at the state and national level to lengthen prison terms, cut back on parole, prosecute more juveniles as adults, limit challenges to inhumane prison conditions, and other highly punitive proposals. The influence of U.S. business interests on penal policy can be seen in the rapid internationalization of the private prison system. U.S.-based operators, most notably Corrections Corporation of America and Wackenhut Corrections Corporation, are now global contractors, with 20 percent of inmates in Australia now being maintained in private institutions (Prison Privatisation Report International, 1997) and exploration being conducted in both eastern and western Europe.

The impact of these trends, along with the broader crime policy changes of the past quarter century, have had enormous consequences for the growing number of men incarcerated in the nation's prisons. This impact is felt most profoundly by men of color and the communities they come from, which are now experiencing rates of criminal justice control that are virtually unprecedented in the history of any free society. These effects range from the direct impact of incarceration on men's self-image and life prospects to the more subtle but equally pernicious effects on their families and communities. In this regard, the dramatic expansion of the criminal justice control apparatus can be seen as substantially more than just a response to crime; it can be seen as a blunt weapon that has exacerbated the punitive orientation of social policy in recent years.

Roots of Change in U.S. Criminal Justice Policy

None of these developments is terribly new, of course, and in order to understand the context of current crime policy in the United States, we need to look back to the early 1970s. By doing so, we can see the broad outlines of political and social change that have created the current context for public policy regarding crime.

Until the early 1970s, U.S. incarceration rates had been remarkably uniform for a period of about fifty years. Although the number of inmates fluctuated somewhat during wars and economic depressions, there was relatively little overall change. This uniformity even led criminologists Alfred Blumstein and Jacqueline Cohen (1972) to author an article that suggested a "stability of punishment" hypothesis; that is, that a nation establishes a certain level of punishment with which it feels comfortable or is prepared to tolerate and adjusts its criminal justice policies accordingly to assure this stability.

By 1972, there were two hundred thousand offenders in state and federal prisons nationally. About that time, several developments took place that would have a profound influence on criminal justice policy. First, the postwar "baby boom" brought large numbers of young males into the population. Along with increasing urbanization, this led to a significant rise in crime in the 1960s. This rise developed in conjunction with the social movements of that era, which in turn led to a political backlash. Richard Nixon's 1968 presidential campaign on a "law and order" platform was a landmark in raising the issue of crime to a national level of discussion.

Most notably, in the 1960s the rehabilitative goal of prisons came under attack from two very distinct directions. From the Left, prison activists and scholars began to question whether rehabilitation was achievable in inherently coercive institutions such as prisons and mental hospitals. They raised a challenge to the broad discretion and potential abuses contained within the indeterminate sentencing policies that had prevailed for many years. Under these systems, prison sentences were meted out with a minimum and maximum time to be served; the actual number of years served was left to the discretion of a parole board.

The rationale for the indeterminate sentence was to support the goal of rehabilitation by offering the incentive of early release to an inmate who engaged in prison-based educational and vocational programs and who generally "played by the rules" of the prison regime. The system also carried with it the potential for abuse, by granting broad discretion to judges and parole boards, leading to contentions of systemic bias based on race, gender, or political beliefs.

Coinciding with this critique of rehabilitation from the Left came an equally formidable challenge from the Right. Frustrated by rising crime rates, the liberal decisions of the Warren Supreme Court, and growing progressive dissent against government policies, conservatives took on the issue of crime as the centerpiece of a political program. Their questioning of indeterminate sentencing, though, focused on the perception that prisoners who deserved lengthy prison terms were being released early. They, too, were critical of rehabilitation, not out of a concern about the powers of an intrusive state machinery but out of a belief either that rehabilitation was not viable or that it was an inappropriate goal. The goal of the criminal justice system, they asserted, should be to impose punishment, and the most obvious means to satisfy that objective was through a definite prison sentence.

The positions of both camps were bolstered by an influential article by Robert Martinson, "What Works: Questions and Answers about Prison Reform," which was published in 1974. Basing his conclusions on an analysis of studies of a variety of corrections programs, Martinson asserted that there was no basis for the rehabilitative philosophy in practice. Although Martinson later reconsidered his broad conclusions, which were critiqued by other researchers, the study received broad attention for his viewpoint that "nothing works."

Thus, from both directions came support for a more fixed and determinate sentencing structure with decreased emphasis on rehabilitation. The only substantial disagreement among the contending parties regarded the length of prison terms to be imposed, with liberals arguing for shorter and conservatives for longer fixed terms. The stage was thus set for a shift in sentencing policy.

Change was not long in coming. By the late 1970s, states began to consider and adopt determinate sentencing systems, sometimes using the framework of sentencing guidelines to guide the discretion of judges and establish certain parameters for prison sentences and sentence length. By the early 1980s a "get tough" movement emerged in force under the guiding principles that judges were too "lenient" and that only harsh punishments might deter current or future lawbreaking. This movement has taken the form of the mandatory minimum sentencing provisions now in place in all fifty states and the federal system; "three strikes and you're out" laws in half the states; and, most prominently, a "war on drugs" that has taken a devastating toll on inner-city communities in particular. The impact of these policies on political discourse is evident in the extreme approaches taken by Democrats and Republicans alike to avoid any suggestion that they might be perceived as "soft on crime."

The Rising Prison Population

As a result of these various policy changes, the prison population has increased every year since 1973. By 1997, the national total had reached a remarkable 1.2 million inmates, nearly six times the number before the start of this historic rise. In addition, with a half million inmates in local jails either awaiting trial or serving short sentences, the overall rate of incarceration had reached 645 per 100,000 population. Only Russia and some of the former Soviet states even approach this figure. Most of the industrialized world incarcerates its citizens at one-sixth this rate or below.

Although the number of women in prison has been increasing dramatically since 1980, prisons remain overwhelmingly male institutions. Ninety-four percent of the nation's prisoners are men with an average age of about twenty. The dramatic rate of growth in the prison population has led some to speculate that prisons have now become a means of dealing with a "surplus population" of men for whom there is no room in the changing economy. Comparisons with European nations are quite intriguing in this regard.

In recent years, rates of unemployment in most European nations have been considerably higher than in the United States. Some observers have attributed this to diminished market flexibility in Europe as a result of greater support for social welfare policies and labor unions. But criminologists Katherine Beckett and Bruce Western (1997), who have examined the impact of high rates of incarceration on these trends, suggest that much of the distinction in unemployment rates reflects social policy choices. If we view the prison and jail population, which consists primarily of able-bodied young men, as a form of unemployment, the comparative picture between the United States and Europe changes greatly. We then see that unemployment rates in the United States outpaced those in Europe for eighteen of the twenty years between 1975 and 1995. By 1995, the number of prisoners in the United States was sufficient to add two percentage points to the overall unemployment rate. For black males, the change was even more dramatic: Their 11.3 percent unemployment rate in the early 1990s rose to 18.8 percent with the inclusion of prisoners.

As is true in most countries, increases in incarceration rates disproportionately affect poor and minority males. Nearly half of all prison inmates in the United States are now African American males, even though they constitute only 6 percent of the total national population. Another 9 percent are Hispanic males, also disproportionate to their percentage of the population. Overall, one of every fourteen adult black males is locked up on any given day.

If we look beyond prisons to the broader reach of the criminal justice system, the impact is even starker. Among black males in the twenty- to twenty-nine-year age group, nearly one in three is now under some form of criminal justice supervision on any given day—either in prison or jail or on probation or parole. For Hispanic males, the figure is one in eight. Thus, at a time in life when these men would otherwise be starting families and careers, they are enmeshed in the criminal justice system. As we shall see, this situation has significant negative consequences not only for the life prospects of these men but for their families and communities as well.

It is true, of course, that, in examining the high rate of incarceration in the United States, we need to recognize that rates of violent crime in the United States are considerably higher than in most industrialized nations. This is particularly so for firearms-related offenses, which is not terribly surprising, given that the United States remains the only industrialized nation that permits wide proliferation of guns among its population. If we look at the rise in the use of incarceration, though, the greatest proportional increase in recent years is not among violent offenders but among drug offenders. Between 1985 and 1995, for example, the number of violent offenders in state prisons rose by 86 percent, whereas the number of drug offenders increased by 478 percent.

The impact of drug policies can be seen in the dramatic changes that have taken place in the prison system since 1980. At that time, about 6 percent of state prison inmates were serving time for a drug offense. By 1994, that figure had reached 22 percent. In the same year, fully 59 percent of the nearly ninety thousand federal inmates were incarcerated for drug offenses. Altogether, one in four inmates nationally—about four hundred thousand offenders—is now either serving time or awaiting trial for a drug offense.

As drug prosecutions have increased, so has the proportion of African American males falling under the scope of these policies, since law enforcement agencies have tended to disproportionately target low-income, inner city communities for drug law enforcement. African Americans overall constituted 24 percent of arrests for drug offenses in 1980, but they represented 37 percent by 1995. Ninety percent of persons who are sentenced to prison for a drug offense are African American or Hispanic.

What has been the impact of the crime and drug policies of the last two decades of the twentieth century? Regrettably, despite declines in crime in the 1990s, rates of violent crime in the United States remain far higher than in other industrialized nations. And, despite the remarkable increases in the incarceration of drug offenders, hard-core drug abuse remains largely unchanged and drug use among teenagers has been on the rise in recent years. If the purpose of massive incarceration has been to "send a message" to potential offenders, the message is apparently not being heard with great clarity.

Intended and Unintended Consequences

The presumed purpose of incarceration is to control crime, and debate continues regarding the success of the institution in achieving this goal. At the same time, though, the large-scale use of imprisonment carries with it a broad array of potential unintended consequences that may undermine any legitimate crime control gains that are achieved.

These consequences are particularly severe for the minority men going through the criminal justice system. In recent years they have been dramatically affected by large-scale social and economic changes and an increasingly hostile political climate that has culminated in the growing scale of imprisonment.

Many of these changes can be traced back to the 1970s and 1980s and the confluence of economic and political change. As the U.S. economy first attempted to cope with the oil embargo of 1973 and the declining role of manufacturing, historic economic shifts took place that would have dramatic effects on urban areas. The overseas relocation of many manufacturing jobs robbed many cities in the Northeast and Midwest of the high-wage union positions that had long sustained working-class male breadwinners. In their place emerged an information economy largely dominated by well-educated Sun Belt workers and a service economy offering low-wage, low-skill jobs to the sons and daughters of those who had labored in the auto and steel plants. The growing income divide between the rich and the poor since the 1980s is but one result of these changes.

By the 1980s, a new economic alternative arose for many young men in urban areas— opportunities in the drug trade. As crack cocaine emerged as a popular drug in the middle of the decade, young entrepreneurs seized the opportunity for quick profits in the developing markets. Although media coverage often emphasized the (relatively brief) fame and fortune gained by a handful of these flashy young men, the more typical drug seller was, in fact, not so far removed from the mainstream.

Street-level research on drug sellers in Washington, D.C., and Milwaukee, Wisconsin, has demonstrated that, for most young men engaged in the business, selling drugs was a form of "moonlighting" to supplement meager wages earned in the legitimate economy. Peter Reuter, Robert MacCoun and Patrick Murphy (1990) found that two-thirds of young men in Washington, D.C., arrested for drug selling, nearly all of whom were African American, were employed at the time of arrest. They were generally working at low-wage jobs and earning a median income of eight hundred dollars a month, which they supplemented with two thousand dollars a month in drug sales.

In Milwaukee, interviews with gang members led to similar conclusions and also indicated that the values expressed by these young men were quite conventional in nature. Except for a minority who were committed to the gang lifestyle, most members shared conventional aspirations about economic security. They even shared conventional ethical beliefs about the immorality of drug dealing, but they justified their own drug sales as necessary for survival (Hagedorn, 1994).

A range of responses was possible in addressing this crisis of urban decline and the growing drug economy. The development of national economic policy that emphasized job creation and training in inner-city areas was one alternative. The coordination of efforts to interrupt the flow of gunrunners supplying weapons to teenage boys in high crime areas was another. And greater investments in expanding drug treatment as a primary option for responding to low-income substance abuse problems was yet another. But none of these policies was pursued with any vigor; instead, a "war on drugs" was waged on inner-city men and women, with devastating consequences.

We have already seen the impact of these policies on the number of young men of color caught up in the criminal justice web. By 1991, half of all state prison inmates incarcerated for a drug offense were African American and a quarter were Hispanic. Once sentenced to prison, these men had little constructive opportunity available to them. Despite the fact that an estimated three-quarters of inmates require substance abuse treatment, only 18 percent of those in need receive any form of treatment. Residential or long-term treatment is even more rare in prison; only 5 percent of prisoners are engaged in such programs.

On average, men in prison have achieved only a low level of education; two-thirds of inmates surveyed in 1991 had not completed high school. Although research has documented the positive impact of education in reducing recidivism, in 1994 a mean-spirited Congress prohibited inmates from receiving Pell grants (a financial aid program pushed through Congress by Rhode Island's Democratic senator Claiborne Pell in 1972) to enable them to pursue college education while incarcerated—despite the fact that prisoners represented less than 1 percent of all grant recipients.

Given that men going to prison often have only marginal relationships to the legitimate economy to begin with, the stigma attached to the prison experience and the limited skill training available in prison create additional disadvantages when the prisoners are released. Particularly in a tight economy, a former offender, who will have to explain to prospective employers his whereabouts over the previous several years will be at a disadvantage. A recent analysis of this relationship found that incarceration reduced employment by about one-fifth, or ten weeks per year (Beckett and Western, 1997).

Imprisonment and its aftereffects also have a potentially profound impact on men's participation in civic life through state provisions that, in effect, disenfranchise felons and former felons. All but four states prohibit inmates from voting while they are incarcerated, and thirty-one states deny a felon the right to vote while he or she is under probation or parole supervision. Of these, thirteen states disenfranchise felons for life, even if the conviction did not result in a prison term. As of 1994, an estimated 4.2 million persons were disenfranchised as a result of a current or prior felony conviction. Of these, 1.4 million were African American males, representing one in seven of all adult black males. Thus, the impact of large-scale imprisonment goes well beyond the individuals incarcerated; it affects the potential political power of the community of African American males.

Yet another unintended consequence of incarceration in minority communities concerns the ability of communities to employ their own resources to fight crime. Removing large numbers of young males from a community inevitably impacts on the ability of the community to form the human capital that is necessary to sustain social norms, provide role models, and encourage productive activities. Further, as David Courtwright has documented, the high rates of incarceration, homicide, and unemployment among African American males have greatly reduced their availability and suitability as marriage partners. This then leads to an increase in illegitimate births and the economic problems that single-income households face (1996:97).

As bleak as this situation may be, the consequences for the next generation of young men may be even more severe. Research by the Department of Justice concludes that, at current rates of incarceration, a black male born in 1991 has a 29 percent chance of doing time in prison during his lifetime. We can only begin to speculate on the profound impact that these odds have on black boys growing up. What is the effect on community aspirations when it is far more likely that young men will go to prison than to college? How do teachers, ministers, and community leaders attempt to inspire young men to achieve when so many perceive that the deck is severely stacked against them?

None of this suggests, of course, that criminal behavior should be condoned or lack consequences. Certainly, removal of serious offenders from a community has clear benefits for the community for the period of time that the offender is incarcerated. As an overall strategy for producing community safety, though, the incarceration of nonviolent offenders, at current levels in particular, now raises serious questions as to whether the unintended consequences outweigh the intended objectives.

Although it is clear that drug abuse has, in fact, exacted a substantial toll on many communities, it is equally clear that the decision to address this problem at the back end of the system—primarily through more policing and more prisons—was hardly inevitable. In the last decade and a half of the twentieth century, two-thirds of federal spending on drug abuse has been allocated to supply reduction, at a time when treatment resources are severely limited both inside and outside the criminal justice system.

Toward a More Rational and Humane Approach to Crime

Despite this rather grim situation, there are actually some hopeful signs on the land-scape of the criminal justice system. Some of these emerge from the growing recognition that enormous investments in prisons have distorted other public priorities. Many leaders in higher education, for example, are becoming increasingly concerned about what the trade-offs in spending between prisons and universities portend for the future.

Practitioners within the criminal justice system are also becoming increasingly receptive to the use of nonincarcerative sanctions for many types of offenders. For example, the movement to establish drug courts that provide treatment to addicted offenders has mushroomed in recent years and has met with wide enthusiasm among both practitioners and the public.

Also encouraging is the growing support for the concept of restorative justice, which emphasizes the interlocking responsibilities and relationships among victims, offenders, and communities. The states of Minnesota and Vermont have now incorporated this concept into their corrections planning and activities, and scores of communities are exploring the practicalities of such a system either at the time of sentencing or as an alternative to formal criminal justice processing.

The potential of these various movements can be viewed in several ways: At a basic political level, some of the alternatives being developed may prove to be more "cost-effective" than traditional incarceration. That is, they may provide sanctions for offenders that are less costly than incarceration and, at a minimum, produce recidivism rates that are at least as low as those generated by the prison system. This may, in turn, free up funds that can be used to expand prevention programs or community-based alternatives. In the long run, though, the value of various models such as restorative justice or community policing may lie in the extent to which they influence the public discussion about crime control. Transferring greater control of the problem to local communities working in partnership with the justice system may bring to light solutions to neighborhood-based crime problems that are not currently evident in the political world.

References

Beckett, Katherine, and Bruce Western. 1997. "The Penal System as Labor Market Institution: Jobs and Jails, 1980–1995." *Overcrowded Times* 8 (6).

Blumenstein, Alfred, and Jacqueline Cohen. 1972. "A Theory on the Stability of Punishment." *Journal of Criminal Law and Criminology* 64: 198–207.

Courtwright, David. 1996–97. "The Drug War's Hidden Toll." *Issues in Science and Technology* (Winter): 73.

Hagedorn, J. M. 1994. "Homeboys, Dope Fiends, Legits, and New Jacks." *Criminology* 32 (2): 197–219.

Martinson, Robert. 1974. "What Works: Questions and Answers about Prison Reform." *Public Interest* 35 (Spring): 22–54.

Prison Privatisation Report International. 1997. "Private Prospects." *Prison Privatisation Report International*, no. 6 (January): 1.

Reuter, Peter, Robert MacCoun, and Patrick Murphy. 1990. "Money from Crime: A Study of the Economics of Drug Dealing in Washington, D.C." Rand Corporation Report, June.

Anthony Thomas

Elements of Crime

Yo! is it a crime or is it elements?
trying to make a living, giving, paying the price
working hard to support two kids and a wife.
you're slaving 16 hours, no time for you to sleep,
and at the end of the week you're barely making ends meet.
bill collectors clockin' ya, the rent money is due.
you wonder what's for dinner and the baby needs shoes.
there's got to be a better way you say to yourself,
so you take your "nice guy" veneer and hang it on the shelf.
you put your "jammie"* in your pocket, all set, you're on a mission.
your program rationale is to change the condition,
or to alter the circumstance, that didn't give you a chance.
to grow or to enhance, the lives that's in your hands.
so out on the avenue you're stalking your prey,
you realize it's Friday and today is pay day.
slinking through the shadows like a phantom in the night,
without the slightest compunction of the wrong or the right,
or even the consequence of "throwing a brick,"
you're blinded by reality, so here comes "the vic."
"Yo, freeze—keep your mouth shut! this is a stick up,
you know what time it is, so just give it all up.
gimme the jewels and the green, you know what to do.
and if you got any dreams, then gimme dem too."
sirens in the distance, look out, here comes the cavalry,
a moment's indecision . . . then you decide to flee.

*A gun or weapon of choice.

running through an alley, panic-stricken with fright,
because the cops in New York are not wrapped too tight.
ya busted my man, you run into a dead end,
trapped with some jewels and some money that you'll never spend.
because you were a fool, now it's gonna cost ya,
you played the game of "gimme now, gimme done gotcha"!
sitting in a jail cell, hoping for low bail,
but that's immaterial, you're gonna do time,
for fooling with the detrimental elements of crime.

Willie London

A World Without Softness

Cell walls
one kiss blown to the wind
memories sink behind closed doors
when seen once more
summoned in time to bloom again

passing years
a chime
fading away
a tear's thought
grown in the weed of memory.

Steve Fraley

Slave Ship

Ramming sticks up brothers' asses
Stomping on naked toes
    with combat boots
Dog sniffing genitals
    he may decide to bite
Shotgun toten-women
    in case we want to fight.

Naked in the courtyard
    for seven hours
    on a warm summer night
Flexicuffs on our wrists
    much, much too tight.

Men crying
    men screaming
men lying down
Some scheming
    some pleading
    shitting on the ground

Cracking heads
    playing dead
    trying to survive
we are victims
of this war
    just staying alive.

Stripped of manhood
Stripped of dignity
   only strength can stand
There's no win
For us brothers
   in this cracker's land.

Power to the people
Who held their head
   high in degradation
Only the strongest
Will overcome
   in this type situation!

Part III

The Social Construction
of Prison Masculinities

Anyone who ascribes to the notion that, by its very nature, criminality is the same at all times and in all places has little to say about how we might reform prisons and the men who dwell within them. If there is a criminal type and criminals cannot be rehabilitated, then why try to figure out how prisons could be designed to better accomplish the aim of correcting? On the other hand, the social constructivist approach to criminology and imprisonment acknowledges that social, political, economic, and cultural forces converge within various historical settings to shape crime as well as punishment. The very notion of criminology is socially constructed, with class, race, and gender issues incorporated in the process.

As a citadel for punishment (rather than rehabilitation), the prison as an institution embodies the masculine ideal of toughness. Prisoners and guards adopt a hard-ass posture as they walk the block and do their time. But behind the hardened exterior of prison hegemonic masculinity, various and hidden forms of masculinity come into play. Some prisoners keep the softer side of their identity intact by imagining themselves back in the community with loved ones. Others form deep bonds with each other while doing their time. Some prisoners pump iron merely to signal their masculine toughness, whereas others participate in weight training and athletics in pursuit of better stress management and self-care. And still others choose to keep to themselves and engage in a course of study or a spiritual practice to sustain their sanity. The various ways that prisoners do their time mirror the many ways that men out of prison express their gender identity and their humanity within the constraints of social forces that shape masculinities.

Don Sabo

Doing Time, Doing Masculinity: Sports and Prison

I am a white, male college professor in my forties, hunched over a table in Attica Correctional Facility. My heart is pounding, my upper body is locked taut and shaking, and I am gazing into the eyes of an African American prisoner who, like so many of the men in this New York State prison, comes from what sociologists call the "underclass." We are different in most respects, but right now we are alike. Like me, he's puffing and straining, trying not to show it, sometimes cursing, and returning my gaze. We are arm wrestling, and in this case he puts me down in about two minutes, which in arm wrestling can be a long, long time.

I started arm wrestling in the joint about five years ago. I enjoy the physical connection that the contest brings. The participants initially stalk one another over a period of days or weeks, keeping their distance, evaluating each other's strengths and weaknesses. There may be some playful bad-mouthing or boasting that leads up to a bout. Eventually, they make the necessary moves that bring each to the table hand-in-hand, eye-to-eye. Even though arm wrestling is overtly combative, it can breed a closer connection with another man than is allowed for in most aspects of men's lives. It allows me to climb outside the bourgeois husk of my life and join with somebody in a way that temporarily suspends the hierarchical distinctions between free man and inmate, white and black, privileged and underprivileged, and teacher and student.

Arm wrestling also lets me pull my athletic past into the present, to enjoin youthful masculine spirits and facades. At the same time that these manly juices are resurrected, though, I try to tell myself and others that I don't take the competition so seriously. I want to learn the lesson that it is OK to be vulnerable to defeat.

Sometimes I win; sometimes I lose. It still matters to me whether I win or lose. I try hard to win, but, when I lose, I get over it quickly, accept it, and even welcome it as inevitable. Part of me is happy for the man who beat me. When I win, I savor the victories for a few days, bragging to myself, sometimes others, soothing my middle-aging

An earlier version of this essay was published in Michael Messner and Don Sabo, *Sex, Violence, and Power in Sports: Rethinking Masculinity* (Freedom, Calif.: Crossing Press, 1994).

ego with transparently masculine rationalizations that I am still strong, not over the bloody hill yet. Arm wrestlers understand that nobody wins all the time. Beneath the grit and show, we know there is more to it than winning or losing. We also know that part of what makes arm wrestling more than just a contest or pastime is that it somehow speaks to our beliefs and feelings about being a man.

I have taught in prisons for fourteen years. My experiences, observations, and discussions with inmates have revealed that prison sports have different meanings for different men. I have learned that a great many motives, messages, and contradictions are crammed into the muscles and athletic pastimes of men in prison. Like men outside the walls, however, prisoners use sports as vehicles for creating and maintaining masculine identity.

Doing Time, Doing Sports

Perhaps the most striking aspect of prison sports is their visibility. The yard is often a hub of athletic activity. Weight lifters huddle in small groups around barbells and bench press racks. Runners circle the periphery, while hoopsters spin and shoot on the basketball courts. There is the occasional volleyball game and bocce tournament. Depending on the facility and time of year, there may be football practices or games, replete with equipment and fans along the sidelines. Some prisons maintain softball leagues and facilities.

Inside the buildings, you will find a gym, basketball courts, and weight rooms. Power lifters struggle against gravity and insanity. Feats of strength produce heroes in the joint, sometimes even legends, or at least local legends. I have been told stories about Jihad Al-Sibbar, a man past his forties who weighs about 155 pounds. He is believed to be the strongest man in the New York State prison system, and I have heard it said more than once that, if given the opportunity, he could have competed at the Olympic level. I want and need to believe in these stories, not so much because they are tales of a strong man but because his triumphs say something about the potential of athletics to sustain sanity in an insane place.

Sports and fitness activities spill into the prison environment in other ways. An inmate may do daily calisthenics while in solitary. For example, Martin Sostre was an African American black power activist and inner-city bookstore owner who was framed by the police in 1967 and imprisoned for nine years. Sostre used physical exercise and yoga to survive long stints of solitary and to bolster his political struggles against prison and legal authorities (Copeland, 1970).

In almost any sector of the prison, fans may jabber about who will win the Super Bowl, the NBA finals, or the next heavyweight boxing match. The taunting, teasing, and betting that typify sports fans outside the walls are also rife among inmates and guards and other personnel. Some men gather in groups around television sets to watch the Final Four or "Monday Night Football," while others sit alone in their cells jabbing with George Foreman or soaring with Michael Jordan.

In short, sports and fitness activities in prison engage men's minds and bodies to varying degrees and, in the process, help them do their time. For some men, especially the young ones, athletics are no more than a fleeting pastime, a simple form of physical play, something to do to get to the end of another day. For others, sports and fitness activities are a crucial survival strategy, a life practice that is intended to create and maintain physical and mental health in a hostile, unhealthy place. For still others, working out or participating in sports helps them to displace anger and frustration, to get the rage out of their bodies and psyches before it explodes or turns in on them. And for some, the goal is to get big to be bad, to manufacture muscle and a jock presence in order to intimidate and dominate.

Doing Masculinity

The prison environment triggers a masculine awareness in me. I go on masculine alert. I don't walk around with biceps flexed and chest expanded, pretending to be a tough guy in front of anybody looking my way. That kind of suck-in-your-belly-and-lower-your-voice stuff faded away with my twenties. The masculinity that surfaces in the prison is more an attitude, a hazy cluster of concerns and expectations that get translated into emotion and physical movement in ways that never quite come clear. Though there are a few women around (for example, an occasional female guard, some women teachers), I see and smell the prison as an all-male domain. I sense a greater potential for danger and a heightened need to protect myself. I could get caught in a bad situation. I have been told not to trust anybody—prisoners, guards, or bureaucrats. Nobody. It sounds crazy, but the tinges of distrust and paranoia almost feel good. Indeed, there are parts of me, call them "threads" or "echoes" of a masculine identity, that embrace the distrust and welcome the presumed danger and potential for violence.

These masculine prompts are seldom uppermost in my mind. They do not emanate from inside of me; they are more like visitors that come and go, moving in and out of me like tap water gushing through an overfilled glass. Arm wrestling allows me to play out masculinity in tune with other elements of jailhouse jock culture. At the same time, the wrestling breeds familiarity with prisoners, pushes toward closeness and trust, and subverts hierarchical distinctions based on class, race, and professional status.

Like me, many men in prison deploy sports and fitness activities as resources to do masculinity—that is, to spin masculine identities, to build reputations, to achieve or dissolve status. For the men in prison, as elsewhere, masculine identity is earned, enacted, rehearsed, refined, and relived through each day's activities and choices. I'm not saying that the gender scripts that men follow in prison are reinvented each day, from moment to moment, man to man. Masculinity does not unfold inside us as much as it flows through us. It is not a strictly individual or psychological process. In doing gender, each individual participates in the larger prison culture, which scripts masculinity by supplying direction, role models, props, motivations, rewards, and values (Messerschmidt, 1993; West and Zimmerman, 1987). For many men, sports are a part of the formula for shaping gender identity.

Softness and Hardness

In prison, the manly injunction to be strong is evident not only in the bulk or bearing of many men's bodies but in everyday speech as well. I have often heard prisoners describe other men as "hard" or "soft." Over the years, I have learned that there are many guises of hardness, which, inside and outside the prison culture, illustrate a variety of masculine expressions that stretch between the honorable and the perverse.

Being hard can mean that the individual is toned, strong, conditioned, or fit, rather than weak, flabby, or out of shape. A hard man cares for and respects his body. Life in prison is extremely oppressive, and it is extraordinarily difficult to eke out a healthy lifestyle. Cigarette smoke is everywhere. The noise on the blocks can jam the senses. Most inmates will tell you that the chow stinks, and, for those who think about such matters, a nutritionally sound diet is impossible to scrape together from the available cafeteria fare. For some men, then, the pursuit of sports and fitness activity is a personal quest to create a healthy body in an unhealthy environment. Those who succeed build a sense of accomplishment and garner the respect of others. Some men strive to be hard in order to build self-esteem. Being in prison is a colossal reminder of personal failure. A regular fitness regimen helps some men center mind and identity in the undeniably tangible locus of the body. For others, getting good at basketball or being recognized as a leading athlete earns the respect of peers. Damaged egos and healing psyches drink in the recognition and repair themselves.

Being hard can also be a defense against prison violence. The hard man sends the message that he is somebody to contend with, not a pushover, not somebody to "fuck with." The sexual connotations of this last phrase take on particular significance in the prison subculture, where man-on-man rape is part of life. The act of prison rape is tied to maintaining the status order among a maze of male groups. Blacks may rape whites or vice versa in order to establish dominant status. Older prisoners may use rape to enslave newcomers. Guards or prison administrators have been known to threaten to expose prisoners to greater threat of rape in order to evoke good behavior, to punish, or to squeeze out information. As Tom Cahill, himself a victim of prison rape, observed, "Once 'turned out'—prison parlance for raped—a survivor is caught in a bind. If an inmate reports a sexual assault, even without naming the assailant, he will be labeled a 'snitch,' a contract will automatically be placed on him, and his life expectancy will be measured in minutes from then" (1990:32).

Men's efforts to weave webs of domination through rape and physical intimidation *in prison* also reflect and reproduce men's domination of women in the social world beyond the walls. In the muscled, violent, and tattooed world of prison rape, woman is symbolically ever present. She resides in the pulpy, supple, and muted linguistic folds of the hardness/softness dichotomy. The prison phrase "make a woman out of you" means that you will be raped. Rape-based relationships between prisoners are often described as relationships between "men" and "girls" who are, in effect, thought of as "master" and "slave," victor and vanquished.

The hardness/softness split also echoes and fortifies stereotypes of masculinity and femininity (Bordo, 1999). To be "hard" means to be more manly than the next guy, who is said to be "soft" and more feminine. It is better to be hard than soft in prison. To be called hard is a compliment. To be labeled soft can be a playful rebuke or a serious put-down. The meanings around hardness and softness also flow from and feed homophobia, which is rampant in prison. The stigma of being labeled a homosexual can make a man more vulnerable to ridicule, attack, ostracism, or victimization.

Conclusion

Prison somehow magnifies the contradictions in men's lives, making them palpable, visible. For many prisoners, the pursuit of manhood was closely linked to their efforts to define masculine identity and worth—for example, robbing in order to be a good provider or husband, joining a gang in hopes of becoming a "big man" on the street, being a "badass" or "gangster" as a way of getting respect from peers, braving the violence of the drug trade, raping or beating on women in order prove manly superiority, or embezzling to achieve financial success and masculine adequacy. The irony here is that these scripted quests for manly power led, in part, to incarceration and loss of freedom and dignity. For lots of prisoners, and countless men on the outside, adherence to the traditional pathways to masculinity turned out to be a trap.

Men's participation in prison sports is fused with yet another contradiction. On one hand, sports and exercise provide prisoners with vehicles for self-expression and physical freedom. On the other hand, prison officials know that involvement in sports and exercise activities helps make inmates more tractable and compliant. Therefore, the cultivation of the body through sports and fitness activities is simultaneously a source of personal liberation and social control.

It is easy for men in prison or on the outside to get trapped by the cultural mandate of hardness. The image of the male athlete as a muscled, aggressive, competitive, and emotionally controlled individual dovetails the prevailing definition of masculinity in sexist culture. Conformity to this model for manliness can be socially and emotionally destructive. Muscles may remain "*the* sign of masculinity" (Glassner, 1988:192) in the male-dominated culture and the gender hierarchies that constitute the North American prison system. And yet my observations tell me that prisoners' relationships to muscle and masculinity are not simple or one-sided. Men cultivate their bodies in order to send a variety of messages about the meaning of masculinity to themselves and others. Whereas conformity to the credo of hardness for some men feeds the forces of domination and subordination, for others athletics and fitness are forms of self-care. Whereas many prison jocks are literally playing out the masculine scripts they learned in their youth, others are attempting to attach new meanings to sports and exercise that affirm health, sanity, and alternative modes of masculinity.

Perhaps the greatest contradiction pervading prison sports is that, despite the diversity of gendered meanings and practices that prisoners attach to their bodies through sports and exercise, the cultural mandate for hardness and toughness prevails. Men's soft sides remain hidden, suppressed, and underground. The punitive and often violent structures of prison hierarchies persist, breathing aggression and fear into men's bodies and minds. The same tragic contradiction informs men's lives in sports outside the prison walls, where structured gender inequality and sexism constrain efforts to reform gender relationships toward equity and healthful affirmation of the body.

Arm wrestling teaches me that the cages in men's lives can be made of iron bars, muscles, or myths. The harder I wrestle, the more I dream of escape.

References

Bordo, S. 1999. *The Male Body: A New Look at Men in Public and in Private*. New York: Farrar, Straus and Giroux.

Cahill, T. 1990. "Prison Rape: Torture in the American Gulag." In *Men and Intimacy: Personal Accounts Exploring the Dilemmas of Modern Male Sexuality,* ed. Franklin Abbott. Freedom, Calif.: Crossing Press.

Copeland, V. 1970. *The Crime of Martin Sostre*. New York: McGraw Hill.

Glassner, B. 1988. *Bodies: Why We Look the Way We Do (and How We Feel about It)*. New York: Putnam.

Messerschmidt, James W. 1993. *Masculinities and Crime: Critique and Reconceptualization of Theory*. Lanham, Md.: Rowman and Littlefield).

West, Candace, and Don H. Zimmerman. 1987. "Doing Gender." *Gender and Society* 1 (2): 125–51.

James W. Messerschmidt

Masculinities, Crime, and Prison

Masculinity is never a static or finished product. Rather, men construct masculinities in specific social settings. The situation of men in prison provides an obvious example. Behavior by men is obviously considerably more complex than is suggested by the idea of a universal masculinity that is preformed and embedded in the individual prior to social action. In contrast, the study of masculinities shows that men are involved in a self-regulating process whereby they monitor their own and others' gendered conduct.

These practices do not, however, occur in a vacuum. Instead, they are influenced by the gender ideals that we have come to accept as normal and proper and by the social structural constraints that we experience. In prison, the constraints are stark and identifiable. Because men reproduce masculine ideals in socially structured specific practices, there are a variety of ways of doing masculinity. Although masculinity is always individual and personal, specific forms of masculinity are available, encouraged, and permitted, depending upon one's class, race, sexual preference, and social situation.

Masculinities in Prison

Among inmates, varieties of masculinities emerge. There are "rats" (those who convey information to officials), "merchants" (those who deal in illegal commodities inside the prison), and "gorillas" (those who use violence or the threat of violence to advance their own interests) (Sykes and Cullen, 1992:456). Further, socially organized power relations among men are constructed within prison. There are power relations not only between prison staff and inmates but among inmates as well. For example, one way that power relations are constructed among inmates is through rape. Rape is a widespread practice in male prisons. It is estimated that in U.S. prisons approximately one in five male inmates has been raped (Beirne and Messerschmidt, 1995). Young men in prison must often seek protection from stronger and more powerful inmates, and many become sexual slaves to their "protectors." Indeed, as Don Sabo argues, "In the muscled, violent, and tattooed world of prison rape, woman is symbolically ever-present. The prison phrase 'make a woman out of you' means that you will be raped. Rape-based relationships between prisoners are often described as relations between 'men' and 'women' and in effect conceptualized as 'master' and 'slave'" (1992:6).

In other words, although there is a complex interlocking of masculinities in prison, these masculinities are quite clearly unequal, and prison rape is one practice for constructing masculine power hierarchies. But the story does not begin or end in prison. The forms of criminality that send certain men to prison are also constructed and institutionalized. Understanding the gendered construction of crime is a critical ingredient in understand the interlocking masculinities found in prison.

Crime as Situated Accomplishment

From the street to the suite, crime is clearly a male-dominated social practice. Why? Many investigators have turned to "sex-role theory" in an attempt to answer this question. But, as numerous sociologists have shown (Connell, 1987; Messerschmidt, 1993; West and Zimmerman, 1987), sex-role theory often reduces complex social behavior to simplistic biological explanations, distorts gender variability among men and among women, ignores social action, and masks questions of power relations between men and women as well as among men. Because of such problems, the concept of gender as sex role has been increasingly supplanted in the sociological literature by a concept of gender as an active, behaviorally based, situated accomplishment.

Social conditions shape the character and definition of sex categories. Sex and its meaning are given concrete expression by the specific social relations and historical context in which they are embedded. Moreover, in specific social situations, we consistently engage in sex attribution—identifying and categorizing people by appropriate sex category as we simultaneously categorize ourselves to others (West and Fenstermaker, 1995).

In this view, therefore, gender is accomplished systematically, rather than imposed on people or settled beforehand, and it is never a static or finished product. Instead, people construct gender in specific social situations. In other words, people participate in self-regulating conduct whereby they monitor their own and others' social actions.

Men, Masculinities, and Crime

How does this notion of masculinity help us understand crime by men? When men enter a social setting, they undertake social practices that demonstrate that they are "manly." The only way that others can judge their conduct as masculine is through their behavior and appearance. For many men, crime may serve as a suitable resource for showing that they are "manly." Because types of criminality are possible only when particular social conditions present themselves or when other masculine resources are unavailable, specific types of crime can provide an alternative resource for accomplishing gender and, therefore, affirming a distinct type of masculinity. Although men are always doing masculinity, the significance of gender accomplishment is socially situated and an intermittent matter. That is, men enter situations always as men, yet gender may or may not be central to the configuration of the interaction. Indeed, certain occasions present themselves as more salient for showing and affirming masculinity. The taken-for-granted "manliness" of a man can be questioned, undermined, and threatened in certain contexts—those situations in which he lacks resources for masculine accomplishment.

In such predicaments, sex category is particularly conspicuous. It is, as David H. J. Morgan (1992:47) rightly declares, "more or less explicitly put on the line," and doing masculinity necessitates extra effort, generating a distinct type of masculinity. Under such conditions, performance as a member of one's sex category is subjected to extra evaluation, and crime is more likely to result. Crime, therefore, may be invoked as a practice through which masculinities are differentiated from one another. Moreover, crime is a resource that may be summoned when men lack other resources to accomplish gender.

The contrast between two incidents can serve to illustrate the point. One evening in New York City when Ron Santiago and a few other friends were "hanging out," they decided to rob a Kentucky Fried Chicken restaurant:

> We went inside and there were two customers and one guy behind the counter. Alvin grabbed the guy behind the counter and he stuck the gun to his head. I took the two customers and pushed them to the side and held the gun on them; the other guy just stood by the door. Alvin jumped over the counter and made the guy give up the money out of the safe, and threatened him, which was standard: don't call the police, don't use the phone, don't touch the alarm, or anything. (Hills and Santiago, 1992:34)

Santiago and his friends escaped with twenty-seven hundred dollars.

The second incident occurred one evening in Utah. Jerry Mason and three other vice presidents of Morton Thiokol repeatedly ignored warnings from their own engineers that the rubber O-rings that the company produced for the space shuttle *Challenger* were defective. During a "caucus" of vice presidents and engineers, Bob Lund, vice president of engineering, was the sole holdout among the managers committed to launch. Mason then turned to Lund and instructed him to "take off his engineering hat and put on his management hat" (cited in Messerschmidt, 1997:97). The managers then agreed they had to make a management decision. At this point, the engineers were excluded from the decision-making process and a final management review was conducted. The managers then, with Lund concurring, approved the launch for the next morning (Maier, 1993; Messerschmidt, 1997). All seven crew members—including New Hampshire elementary school teacher Christa McAuliffe—perished in the explosion that occurred just seventy-three seconds into flight.

How can we understand the significance of robbery in the lives of Santiago and his friends as well as the socially harmful decision by Mason and the other corporate executives at Morton Thiokol to launch the space shuttle? Clearly, personal profit making is a motive for robbery. Within the collective setting of the street, robbery is a means of getting money when other resources (a job) are unavailable. Yet robbery entails more; it provides a public ceremony of domination and humiliation of the victim. Because young boys on the street are denied access to the labor market and are relegated to a social situation (the street group) where gender accountability is augmented, participating in robbery provides an available resource with which to accomplish gender. "Doing robbery" then is simultaneously "doing masculinity."

Similarly, for the corporate executives within the collective social setting of the corporate boardroom, profit making played an important role in the decision to carry out the launch. Thiokol had an exclusive contract with the National Aeronautics and Space Administration—worth over $1 billion—that was in jeopardy if the launch did not occur (Messerschmidt, 1997). Yet, as with the robbery committed by Santiago and his friends, there is more to this crime than simply economics. Given that corporate executives measure their success—and therefore their masculinity—through profit making, the space shuttle case presented a social situation in which not only profits but also executive masculinity were threatened.

An additional similarity becomes obvious. In the specific social settings of the restaurant and the corporate boardroom, each man had to be a "team player" and go along with "the guys." Santiago put it this way: "You know, you can't show fear in front of the guys. Either you're down or you're not down. And if you're not down, you can't hang out" (Hills and Santiago, 1992:26). And as Mark Maier points out in his investigation of the shuttle disaster, "To *belong* to the 'team,' you had to prove your loyalty by voting to launch; to continue to resist resulted in ostracism and conformity pressure" (1993:40–41). In both situations, the importance of gender is heightened—masculinity was explicitly put on the line, and crime became a masculine solution to the problem of accountability.

Constructing Masculinities in Prison

Connell's (1995) notion of "hegemonic masculinity," which is constructed in relation to "subordinate masculinities," best exemplifies in prison the variety of masculinities as well as the power relations among them. Hegemonic masculinity is neither transhistorical nor transcultural; it varies from society to society and changes within a particular society over time. In any specific time and place, then, hegemonic masculinity is culturally honored, glorified, and extolled at the symbolic level, such as the mass media, and is constructed in relation to subordinated masculinities. Hegemonic masculinity is the dominant form to which other forms of masculinity are subordinated.

The concepts of hegemonic and subordinate masculinities permit investigation of how men experience their everyday world in prison from a particular position in that prison and how they relate to the cultural ideals of hegemonic masculinity. Gresham Sykes and Francis Cullen describe one example of "inmate hegemonic masculinity": "Somewhat aloof, seldom complaining, enduring the rigors of imprisonment with dignity, ready to fight if necessary but not aggressive, loyal to other inmates and willing to share whatever he may have—the real man is a respected figure accorded the deference that flows to those who match a group's ideals" (1992:457).

According to Sykes and Cullen, the hard, silent stoicism of inmate hegemonic masculinity "has its roots in a vision of manhood and integrity that transcends the prison: self-restraint, reserve, toughness, emotional balance, and loyalty" (1992:457).

Masculinity is based on social action that reacts to unique circumstances and relationships, and it is a social construction that is renegotiated in each particular context. In other words, inmates self-regulate their behavior and make specific choices in specific prison contexts. Consequently, inmates construct varieties of masculinity through specific social interaction inside the prison milieu.

Prison can also be a site for changing one's masculine practices. The case of Malcolm X is a good example. Malcolm entered prison as "Detroit Red," a "zoot-suited hipster hustler" (Malcolm X and Haley 1964) from Harlem. However, during his years in prison (1946–52), Malcolm underwent significant change. Malcolm's prison interaction connected him with the political ideology of the Nation of Islam and helped launch him on a program of reform. Malcolm reformulated his masculinity within the context of specific race protest. Confined to the walled refuge of prison, where living the "fast life" of the hustler did not constitute a resource for doing masculinity, Malcolm constructed a new "Muslim masculinity" for the African American separatist struggle. As Malcolm stated, "I still marvel at how swiftly my previous life's thinking pattern slid away from me, like snow off a roof. It is as though someone else I knew of had lived by hustling and crime. I would be startled to catch myself thinking in a remote way of my earlier self as another person" (Ibid., 170)."

Socially situated masculine discourse and practices, then, are not merely adaptive and incorporative; authentic transgressions within and beyond them occur under specific social conditions. Men in prison provide many examples.

In summary, men produce specific configurations of behavior that can be seen by others within the same immediate social setting as masculine. These different masculinities emerge from practices that utilize different resources. Boys in youth groups, corporate executives in the boardroom, and inmates and prison staff generate situationally accomplished, unique masculinities by drawing on different types of resources indigenous to their distinct positions in society. Because men experience their everyday world from a uniquely individualistic position, they construct masculinity in different ways.

References

Beirne, Piers, and James W. Messerschmidt. 1995. *Criminology*. 2d ed. Fort Worth, Tex.: Harcourt Brace.

Connell, R. W. 1987. *Gender and Power*. Stanford, Calif.: Stanford University Press.

———. 1995. *Masculinities*. Berkeley and Los Angeles: University of California Press.Hills, Stuart, and Ronald Santiago. 1992. *Tragic Magic*. Chicago: Nelson-Hall.

Maier, Mark. 1993. "'Am I the Only One Who Wants to Launch?' Corporate Masculinity and the Space Shuttle 'Challenger' Disaster." *Masculinities* 1 (1–2): 34–45.

Malcolm X and Alex Haley. 1964. *The Autobiography of Malcolm X*. New York: Ballantine.

Messerschmidt, James W. 1993. *Masculinities and Crime: Critique and Reconceptualization of Theory*. Lanham, Md.: Rowman and Littlefield.

———. 1997. *Crime as Structured Action: Gender, Race, Class, and Crime in the Making*. Thousand Oaks, Calif.: Sage.

Morgan, David H. J. 1992. *Discovering Men*. New York: Routledge.

Sabo, Don, and Willie London. 1992. "Understanding Men in Prison: The Relevance of Gender Studies." *Men's Studies Review* 9 (1): 4–9.

Sykes, Gresham, and Francis Cullen. 1992. *Criminology,* 2d ed. Fort Worth, Tex.: Harcourt Brace.

West, Candace, and Sarah Fenstermaker. 1995. "Doing Difference." *Gender and Society* 9 (1): 8–37.

West, Candace, and Don H. Zimmerman. 1987. "Doing Gender." *Gender and Society* 1 (2): 125–51.

David Denborough

Grappling with Issues of Privilege:
A Male Prison Worker's Perspective

Working in prisons has meant having to grapple with issues of privilege and question many aspects of my life and experience. I grew up in Canberra, the capital city of Australia, and attended an all-boys private school. It was an institution saturated in particular messages of masculinity: competition, winning, and dominating others. Fate and my white, middle-class privilege allowed me to largely succeed at those markers of identity that were required for "manhood": football, academic success, and lying about sexual endeavors. At the same time, the loneliness and cruelty of men's culture left me baffled and disillusioned. Largely through relationships with women whom I loved—my mother, sisters, friends, and partners—space opened up for me to step into ways of being that were forbidden in a masculine world. And through the challenges of my older sister and the writings of feminist women, I was able to start to make sense of the culture of men. At the same time, my father's antinuclear protest challenges to the status quo and his questioning, caring mind always invited me to think that there must be other ways forward.

Beginning to see the real effects of men's ways of being but also finding excitement in talking and working with men differently led me back into the schools to work with young men on issues of gender and violence (Denborough, 1996). And later, my work in prisons offered me an opportunity to try to give back some of the hope that these young men had once offered me. In many ways, choosing to work in a men's maximum-security prison was the result of wanting to know more about the most masculine institution in our culture. My first crucial learning was that men like me—white, middle-class men—are generally not found in the prison system.

Construction of Masculinity

There are particular crimes that result in imprisonment and particular communities and groups of men that are policed and imprisoned for these crimes. It is not only overwhelmingly poor and dispossessed men who are imprisoned but also *young* men from those communities—at least at the time of their first sentence. The ages from fifteen to twenty-four are the peak years for committing the sorts of crimes that result in imprisonment (Mauer, 1995:33).

The dominant constructions of masculinity in our culture that I experienced myself, and have witnessed in schools throughout cities and country towns, privilege the importance of dominating and controlling others, climbing hierarchies, and obtaining possessions. At the same time, as feminist writers have documented since the 1980s, these dominant ways of being a man also justify the use of coercion, force, and in many cases even violence to achieve such control and power.

Young men receive these messages in a context of relative powerlessness. Most young people in our culture are without financial independence; have little control over their own learning; and often spend much of their waking hours within rigid, hierarchical institutions (schools). Young men receive the dominant gender messages that they ought to dominate and control others in this context. In this atmosphere, the messages are understandably powerful and seductive. If young men are able to position themselves within the dominant ways of being a man, they gain attention, air space, and a greater say (power) over their lives and those of others. At the very least, they are less likely to be targets of abuse and will themselves have easy targets to pick on.

The options available for young men to create particular ways of being men are enormously influenced by issues of class and race. As a white, middle-class young man in a private school, I had not only a clear line to status and prestige through future study but also opportunities for wealth. Within an individualistic and highly competitive climate, both academically and athletically, I could compete and stand a very good chance of winning. For white, middle-class boys like me, where school achievements are not enough to shore up a masculine identity, minor outside acts with peers—such as drinking, doing pranks, or engaging in vandalism—often suffice (Messerschmidt, 1993). In the white, middle-class, masculine culture from which I come, attitudes toward power and sexual conquest led to sexual coercion and date rape of young women. At the same time, interpersonal physical violence was largely contained to the sporting field.

In many ways, we were being trained to commit forms of crimes other than those that usually result in imprisonment—crimes in the stock markets, in the boardrooms, and in the bedrooms. We were being trained and given access to other opportunities for control and domination—through the power of industry, finances, media, bureaucracies, and armed forces and the law. In the public arena, we were offered open doors to realms of power and therefore had little need to prove ourselves on the streets. Similarly, with access to resources, our drug taking or risk taking was unlikely to be noticed by the police. Even if it had been, with our connections, the likelihood of imprisonment would have remained small.

For other young men, these doors to power are hidden or firmly locked. Young men from working-class communities and communities of color receive similar overriding cultural messages in relation to the need to achieve individually, to climb the hierarchies, and to obtain the possessions, but they have little or no possibility of fulfilling these forms of masculinity. They must find other forms of identity, of power, of excitement, and of pleasure. With no access to property, the street often becomes the focus for activity. For many, street crime and drugs become two of very few options available in order to achieve status, control, and a sense of masculinity and acceptance. And street crime, unlike other crime, is stringently policed.

At the same time, being locked out of the mainstream can bring outrage, especially for young men of color, who find themselves constantly confronting racist institutions and individuals. Quite apart from these factors and their contribution to some forms of crime, many young men from poor communities become involved in crimes of property purely and simply for the money that there is little hope of obtaining in any other way.

A substantial amount of street crime that results in imprisonment is in many ways resistance to social inequities. These inequities affect young, working-class men and young men of color, who often resist in highly visible ways. Their actions are subsequently policed and result in incarceration. Without access to so-called "legitimate" (middle-class) ways of being men, some young from marginalized communities create powerful identities of resistance in which street crime plays an important part. In this way, without the access to resources that might otherwise be necessary, they can achieve the sense of excitement and adventure deemed crucial to masculine ideals.

Becoming Squarehead

Working in prisons has meant coming in contact with communities that are not my own. To find myself teaching a welfare/sociology class to long-termers in a maximum-security prison was to find myself transported into a culture very different from the white, middle-class world to which I am accustomed. One morning I naively asked the group what they would have called me if we had met as children. Without a moment's hesitation and with a deadpan expression, one guy replied, "A squarehead." Unfazed, I asked what this meant. With a large grin, he explained, "A stuck-up poof who can't fuck." My lessons had begun. Far from sounding like an insult (or a challenge to explore issues of sexuality or homophobia), it seemed a generous, if rather blunt, invitation to explore our differences and my privilege.

At this stage, in hysterics and with laughter filling the room, I managed to articulate that I would have thought of them as "westies" (from the western suburbs) but that I would not have dared call them this to their faces, as I would have been terrified of being beaten up by the violent, ugly, and stupid young men that I have believed them to be. Believe it or not, this was the beginning of ongoing attempts to build partnerships across a class divide. It was also the beginning of an ongoing process of rewriting and understanding my life through the experiences of working-class people.

What Does It Mean to Be Middle Class?

One of the first things that was absolutely clear was that they were much more familiar with the term "westie" than I was with the term "squarehead." To be middle-class means that one's culture is rarely the "object" of analysis. We "professionals" too often maintain our invisible privilege or our privilege of invisibility. Every day in prisons, "professionals" like me deny the impact of class relations by mystifying the process of imprisonment, by calling prisons "corrections centers," by claiming that self-harm is "manipulative," by diagnosing those who challenge professional practices as "difficult" and unworthy of "help," and by understanding crimes as caused by individual pathology.

By naming me a squarehead, the men with whom I work were inviting me to acknowledge the ways in which I have benefited from class relations and to realize that they had often been on the other end of these dynamics. They were demanding that I resist the common middle-class assumption that people in prison are in some way more racist, dominating, or sexist than those who are not in prison. There is no doubt that prisons breed violence, racism, and sexism, but, when people enter them, they are likely to be doing so because they have less money or darker skin than others rather than because of some deficiency or oppressive characteristic. The most invigorating, open, and honest discussions I have ever had with men about gender and sexual violence have occurred in prisons, whereas the most difficult, frustrating, and maddening conversations have occurred with middle-class men like me who profess to be "profeminist."

Becoming aware of these issues of class has similarly altered my views on crime. Where once my perception of crime involved stereotypical views of working-class men committing property offenses or street crimes, now the first image to flash into my mind is the crime that is prison. I think of the crime that the middle class commit by allowing those who live in poverty to be criminalized and brutalized. I realize now that the use of prisons does not reduce violence; instead it both creates it and moves it around so that it occurs behind prison walls, among working-class people. It was a further shock to my squarehead consciousness to discover that many people who commit armed robberies understand their actions through sophisticated analyses of capitalism and that some are knowledgeable about whole histories of which I am completely unaware, histories of worker or prison movements.

Perhaps more profound, however, has been the recognition of the specific practices or emphases of my middle-class culture, how they differ from working-class cultures, and the effects of these differences. The very conversation that began my process of becoming a squarehead would never have occurred in the adult, middle-class culture from which I come. The directness, honesty, and burly sense of humor that were essential to challenge my middle-class experience are important aspects of working-class cultures. The emphasis on politeness and reserve that characterizes my middle-class culture profoundly supports the maintenance of the status quo. Whenever a member of an oppressed group expresses his or her outrage, the claims can be disregarded simply because they are not expressed in middle-class "adult" ways.

Toward the Future

Working in prisons means that I now witness injustice that once I did not see. It is a part of privilege to have the option to be cocooned from the results of injustice, including poverty and incarceration. Being a witness brings further responsibilities: to reach out to my own kind, my people.

Finding ways to talk with other squareheads, finding ways to support each other in facing the challenges of confronting racism and middle-class privilege will, perhaps, be starting-points. Where once my life was consumed and emptied by the constant competition and isolation that is necessary to maintain privilege, now it is enriched by the sharing of stories and the search for ways to resist. The challenges of those with whom I work have opened up new ways for me to understand my life. Entire histories and landscapes that were once invisible are now available for me to draw upon.

The conversations, friendships, and relationships that have been a part of my life behind prison walls have greatly shaped the person I now am. I hope these processes will continue. I hope they lead to action. From me, and others like me, I hope they lead to acts of redress. And together, across differences, I hope they lead to acts of creation—the creation of new histories and new futures.

References

Denborough, David. 1996. "Step by Step: Developing Respectful and Effective Ways of Working with Young Men to Reduce Violence." In *Men's Ways of Being*, ed. C. McClean, M. Carey, and C. White. Boulder: Westview Press.

Mauer, M. 1995. "Americans Behind Bars: One Year Later." In *With the Power of Justice in Our Eyes: A Handbook for Educators and Activists on the Crisis in Prisons*, ed. E. Rosenblatt. Berkeley: Prison Activist Resource Center.

Messerschmidt, James W. 1993. *Masculinities and Crime: Critique and Reconceptualization of Theory.* Lanham, Md.: Rowman and Littlefield.

Carl Bryan Holmberg

The Culture of Transgression: Initiations into the Homosociality of a Midwestern State Prison

In mid-July 1972, I was interviewed for a teaching position at a new prison in a mid-western state. The buildings were mostly deserted except for a full complement of guards and a small cadre of honor prisoners—"trustees"—whose records or general compliance to the ways of prison awarded them perks, such as more time outside the walls (thoroughly supervised), better job assignments, and often better treatment and food. As it turns out, from my first appearance, the prisoners kept careful watch over the novelty of me—a hippie with Fu Manchu facial hair and long coif, compact and intense—and they broadcast all sorts of information about me among themselves, long before I showed up to inhabit the job.

The interview was daunting, first conducted in a local restaurant and then on the facility's grounds. At the entry building, for the first time in my life, I was frisked. Then I was run through two security devices. More talk in the front area, then a tour. The bars behind me, closing at each checkpoint, rendered in me a falling sense of giving control over myself to others, to strangers, to men I would have to rely upon if anything threatening were to go down. That was a new feeling, unexpected, unwelcome. At the time, I did not think of it this way, but now I do: I had been in charge of my life since high school, the privilege of a white, middle-class male. The job I sought gave that status away, on a daily basis, to other men, even though I would still have a titular persona of privilege as a teacher, someone who also could "write up" anyone who crossed me or broke the rules. Despite it all, I elected to take the job when it was offered. Until the first day of work, I looked upon it as just another job, but then, upon arrival, I quickly factored the maleness of the situation into my presentation of self (Goffman 1959), adjusting to the continual sense of being initiated into a ritualistic society of men. At first, although I had no conscious awareness of this, I did know that the job I had taken was something unusual, something special. I kept a log of my thoughts, feelings, and experiences. This later permitted expansion as a series of narrative accounts of various events coded masculine, which led to the ethnography presented in the "Interpretation of Prison Homosociality" section of this essay.

My "log" consisted of taking notes at work, then later, at home, in private, fleshing out the notes to produce an expanded version, which completed the handwritten documents that I filed away. Most note taking was easily covert. As a teacher, I frequently carried pads, paper, notebooks, index cards, and other writing implements. However, I rarely wrote anything in prison corridors, as it aroused suspicion from guards and convicts. In the year that I worked in the prison, I wrote expansions—or more complete versions of hastily written notes—only at home, again to prevent calling attention to my ongoing observation of everyday life in prison. Field notes employed the verbatim principle and recorded differences of language level between notes on specific persons and constituencies as well as my own comments. Both the verbatim and language-level principles ensure retaining the emic, or insider, characteristics of a culture's or subculture's language performance. Thus, the narratives I now present are basically reports of events and conversations initially recorded in the field notes. Analysis—I use the term "interpretation"—then follows the narratives, entitled "Initiations," "First Contact: Bobbie," "The Cult of Muscularity," "The Hat," and "Breaking Bread with Conan the Barbarian." I also kept notes on my own feelings, a feature that too rarely receives serious attention in ethnographies and that was and is crucial for my own sense making and for interpreting the initiations into the masculinities found in a prison. I was, after all, a neophyte to prison mores. Keeping track of feelings documented my growing acculturation, my learning, my acceptance into status beyond foreigner.

Initiations

My first real initiation involved filling out paperwork for the state that employed me. The assistant warden—I will call him Bert, a fictive name like those that I use for the other people discussed in this essay—was a big man who bristled gruffness. I figured it was his way. Later, I realized that, in the armed services, he had acquired a fondness and realized a true talent for acting like a dick twenty-four hours a day. He handed a group of us new teachers various forms with the sneer, "Fill these out." Basically, he tossed them on a table, then ignored us, pretty much the way he treated prisoners, as it turns out, maybe worse. He did not trust us; we had degrees and did not take authority seriously. His sense of threat showed, and most of us teachers laughed about it among ourselves but did not push it otherwise. We filled out the forms with stubby pencils that had been counted. We were cons, evidently keen on killing someone with a pencil. Not that that has never happened.

That was the easy part of the first day. Whereas subordination was implicit in filling out the forms, it soon became overt in the guise of acclimatizing us new teachers to the sorts of experiences the convicts encountered as prisoners. Getting fingerprinted was a trip. We were told we had to take a test. We waited almost fifteen minutes, not knowing what the test was for. "Go through that door." A guard stood in front of it, waiting. We crowded over, and then the guard looked sternly at us. We made a line. We went through the door one by one. All the equipment was laid out, ready to go. We waited another fifteen minutes, but we grouped in twos and threes, talking about teaching plans. Our lapse into nonmilitary grouping made the guards nervous. Finally, one of the guards who had been present the whole while stepped forward and announced, "Get in line for fingerprinting," which we did. He proceeded to ink and print us. There was no apparent reason that it took a quarter hour to begin. The guard was unnecessarily rough about it and did not seem to derive any satisfaction from taking our hands and directing our fingers for the best prints. No towels or other method of cleanup was offered to us. Clearly we did not have free run of the place, even though technically we were still in the least-secure area of the facility where men and women worked in the administrative offices, people like us, who had freedom of movement. We knew where a bathroom was, but none of us felt free to go use it. Once dried, the black goo stuck on our fingertips for the rest of the day, an indelible marker that clearly made some of the convicts smile. In between the printing and lunch, we were given many instructions, one of which made us laugh and another of which made us groan silently. The facility psychologists and sociologist met with us to present background about the situation, some history, and their plans. They told us quite sincerely that we were to call "the men" "clients." That was funny, as if "the clients" had shopped around for our services. Our laughter earned disdainful looks. At the close of the informative session, the assistant warden returned briefly to inform us that we would be traveling to the state capital after lunch; there were more tests to take. Then lunch was served in the employees cafeteria, muffins and sausage gravy. Apparently something the guards took as a delicacy, it was what one of the black convicts later called "redneck soul food." Using inky fingers to eat food that we perceived as strangely unappealing demoralized more than just a few of us. We would have no other opportunity for food until evening, so we ate inky fingered. We were ushered to waiting state station wagons, and in about an hour we were on the state police firing range.

It was a memorable day. Still, none of us realized at the time how important it was in the order of things at the prison. Our fingerprints were checked by the FBI, and our other test results would become known to the whole facility, either through the grapevine or officially or both. I passed all tests. My fingerprints were clean. My record was cleaner, so clean that it earned me a security rating almost as high as the warden's. Thankfully, that and the fact that I was a registered conscientious objector were kept secret. What was not kept secret, however, was my marksmanship score. I may have been a pacifist, but I had been no stranger to BB guns and air rifles as a boy. I tied the police academy's record score for nonuniformed personnel and beat by at least two hits everyone else at my facility. Thus, a few days after the test, the captain of the guards told me candidly that if a riot took place, I would immediately be assigned a gun and put on duty to pick off any exposed con. That was not a fun thought—and suddenly they were "cons," not "clients," which signaled to me the seriousness behind his words. To my credit, I refrained from laughing aloud at the irony. However it happened, the word about my weapon skills and the expectation that the screws had about them also got around among the cons. But instead of instilling fear, it evoked admiration. Among the guards, by contrast, it evoked jealousy. The day after the information leaked, and for weeks thereafter, I was more carefully frisked upon entering and leaving the facility than any other worker. It turned out that one of the guards' unions frowned upon the gun proficiency of a nonguard—read: nonunion worker—surpassing that of union members. Naturally, the information that I, a nonunion member, would be issued a gun before union members did not sit right with them. Their way of dealing with it was to try to get the goods on me—-anything, to get me fired. I had violated the macho order of the workers, only to the glee of the cons.

First Contact: Bobbie

We had shown up for work for almost four days without spending much time at all in the part of the facility that was called "the high school" or "the school." Even though there were briefings of all sorts to attend, and meetings, some of us began to suspect something was up, that, for whatever reason, there would be a delay to our inhabiting that space. That was the first of many suspicions about control over our time and space that the teachers shared. But the fourth afternoon all our skepticism was alleviated, when the warden himself led us to the school, chattering away like Monty Hall, all effusive, excited, and proud. He left as we settled in. There were desks and chairs for our offices, but there was, as yet, no other equipment, including tables, chairs, and the like for students. Although the rest of the facility was spartan at best, the home of our doings was even more bleak. As it turns out, this was mainly because the wardens figured we would not be security conscious, and they feared that the area would otherwise easily provide usable items for all sorts of mayhem.

The initial gloom returned once the warden left, but it did not remain for long. We heard the far door to our area open and close quietly, followed by steady steps. We had a group office, where most of us were gathered. A black man in regular prison garb, except for a dark blue cardigan sweater and a cloth band, like a librarian's, fastened to his glasses, stood in the doorway smiling. He was five feet six inches or so and shaped like a medicine ball. He was huge. He made a direct line to my desk, sat in the chair beside it, and said, "You're the one who does philosophy." That was not a question; it was a statement, and it was true. "Bobbie," he added, offering his hand for a shake. I reciprocated, playing along. "Well, a lot of us do philosophy," and I nodded around the room, indicating the others. Bobbie ignored them, diving in with questions about Georg Hegel and Immanuel Kant, Aristotle and Plato, asking what was the deal with Friedrich Nietzsche and did I think that the Black Panthers were on par with these philosophers? As I answered as best I could, it became plain that the FBI was not the only group that had conducted background checks. Bobbie stopped a moment, cocked his head, then whispered confidentially, "Friend Joey's a clerk up front, looked in all your files, just curious for me, y'know?" I smiled, and we chatted some more before Bobbie left. I took the time on the way out that evening to peek at Bobbie's file, knowing full well that one of the clerks would spread the word that I had checked some files: double life plus seventy years; crime of passion; pled guilty.

Bobbie was waiting for me the next morning and said nothing about his file. He took me on a tour of the new library, with its old books, indicating what he had read, what he liked, and what he did not like. It was clear he liked me, and it was clear he wanted something. I guessed correctly. As we walked to my school office, I offered, "Y'know, I get to order books for the library and, until someone tells us there's a budget we can't go over, I can order as much as I like—what do you want to read?" "M'man!" he said.

That pretty much sealed it. We went back up to my office and drew up a list. We accepted one another in each of our ways. For Bobbie, I—a new teacher—was someone to talk with but also someone to order books. After the first weekend, in the first two days of the next work week, Bobbie and I spent lots of time discussing the ins and outs of Kant, Jacqueline Susann, and metaphysics. A few other would-be students showed up too, and of course Bobbie picked the brains of the other teachers, but he spent most of his time with me.

Other "clients" began to show up; we were assigned trustee clerks to assist us with paperwork. That made ordering books all the quicker. I kept supplying the forms, and my clerk, Mack, kept typing them up on a daily basis. The second day that Mack worked for me, on my way out for the day, he walked me through the facility to the front, as far as he was allowed to go. We passed the visiting area that was also used to process new inmates.

"Give it two days, three tops, and that one will be taken," Mack said. "What?" I asked. "You know," he waited until we rounded a corner, out of sight of cameras, screws, and other inmates, and then thrust his crotch forward with a grunt, "Taken." I just kept walking, keeping myself from reacting as best I could. "He's just too pretty." Ah, he was referring to the new "client" who had arrived earlier that day, who we had just passed in the holding area. The new con was young, roughly good looking, maybe in his late teens, early twenties. He seemed rather defiant to me, tough, but Mack was presenting me the gender order of sexual dominance. "Mack, that happen oft—" "All the time, fact of life, one way or another." I thought about it. Finally, in the last, long, unmonitored corridor, Mack confided, "I want you to be careful, Teach." I kept walking, waiting. "Someone you know is protecting you, big time." At first I thought he meant himself, but I quickly revised that thought. "How're the book orders going?" Mack smiled, confirming my thought. "Protecting?" Mack got as nervous as he ever got, which is not much, "Contract. You're too pretty." For the next fourteen, fifteen hours, I frequently puzzled through being considered "pretty" and what "protection" might mean. I decided not to mess with it, this knowledge that, by some of the cons' standards, I was attractive, even winnable that way, which was no small indicator of how homosocial subordination works, particularly with those of us—workers—who were technically untouchable. Technically, the men were untouchable to each other too, but that was the public appearance of it. Over the months, it did not seem to matter either if I dressed formally, butched it up, or not. One look or another always got someone going, and I, unlike my fellow workers, varied my attire almost on a daily basis, which earned me my first inmate nickname, "The Chameleon."

The Cult of Muscularity

The very next day after Mack's disclosures to me, I walked into the office and found a new guy processing order forms at my desk. Mack had been replaced by another clerk, "Joe." Joe was a little over six feet and filled his prison browns with a truly awesome musculature. "Hi," he said. "Mack's sick. Got anything for me to do?" I gave him some stuff and then touched base with the assistant principal in his single office. I just wanted to know if Mack was OK, but I did not want to upset anything or anyone by asking publicly. I got the runaround. The a. principal (the other teachers and the cons called him the "a. principal," so it is proper to retain in this narrative the emic nomenclature used in the culture; one and all considered him to be a pompous ass anyway, so the "a." represented an open violation of his person as much as his pomposity violated ours) did not know any more than I at that point. But Joe's size and strength seemed a calculated presence after what Mack had told me.

That day, on the way out, I checked more "client" files, including Mack's and Joe's—both, petty larceny. But Joe's picture stunned me. It had been taken three and a half years prior, revealing a skinny, gawky boy. A string bean, as we used to say. I factored what Mack had told me the day before together with this new revelation. The way some of the men dealt with the subordinating sexual order was to get as big and buff as possible. In two more days, Mack returned, apparently having been genuinely taken by some flu, but he smiled when I asked about Joe. "That was my suggestion," he said. "Oh?" I inquired. "You're smart," he replied, "but you're pretty naive." His choice of the word "pretty" did not escape me.

Not long after that, during yet another in-service training to sensitize us to the needs and quirks of our "clients," we visited a television room that was in use. Next door was a fairly complete set of free weights and a few weight machines. Joe was one of the guys hunkered in, using maximum weights. We visited other areas, and then, while we were going through a cell block, we passed an open shower. Who was showering? None other than Joe. He was totally naked, with two guards watching him closely. As I passed, he turned around—looking quite serious, even mean, or so it seemed to me—to give us a full view. If nothing else, it was an unexpected, awkward moment for me. I had seen men shower before, of course, but not when everyone else present was fully clad. This contrast only emphasized the prohibition of privacy in prison. Joe was already monitored, discretely, by guards. But to be approached by three men while naked was a scenario fraught with danger in prison. It had the trappings of attack. Surprised to see me, Joe purposely exposed his cock and balls and his hypermuscularity to underline his displeasure about the situation, causing me to avert my eyes immediately. I had learned through my own growing grapevine that Joe and Bobbie were two of the most mild, loyal, kind men in the facility. But if crossed, they could be pretty deadly. That was a cosmic ten-four.

One other matter I also noted after some time in my early stint as a prison teach: The new convict, the young one Mack had pointed out to me, was no longer defiant. In fact, he was quiet and introverted. The wax was gone from his walk. I learned later that he had indeed been quickly passed around by the most manly of the cons until they settled on whose property "the boy" would be.

In those days, there was a hat I wore, a felt hat that I had acquired at J. C. Penney's for three dollars. It was shapeless by the time I arrived at the prison, and after only a few weeks it had become identified with me. Among the prison population, it was an object of desire.

The first manifestation of this occurred as a game of keep away between the clerks. It was nearing Thanksgiving, and I was dressed in warm overclothes. When I removed them, I threw my hat on my desk. A friend of Mack's plucked it up and proceeded to toss it among the convict guys. I ignored them, did not participate. But eventually, I picked up the phone and punched in a four-digit number, which they monitored. I entered into a fake conversation, which I directed away from them, facing into the corner. They persisted in their high jinx, not knowing whether I had snitched on them or not. After a while, they ceased. Later, the rumor circulated that I had called someone but apparently had not snitched.

The next day, when I was alone in the common office, in walked a "resident" I had not seen before. He walked the cocky "fly" walk to my desk, where he pointed at the hat and produced five hundred-dollar bills from one pocket, saying, "For the hat, you can have this or this." From the other pocket, he produced a knife.

This was a novel situation. My three-dollar hat was worth five hundred dollars! That loopy economy crashed against practicality—everyone, and I mean everyone, would have sooner or later known where this guy had gotten the hat and under what circumstances. I could lose my job for dealing in black-market contraband within The Wall. Reason also told me that this guy could be a plant, a test, to get me to screw up. Maybe it was latent hippie paranoia, but I had already heard of instances in which prison workers had duped cons into entrapping other workers for them. Both realizations collided with my sinking feeling that I could not really defend myself if the knife was used and that this guy just might be a little nuts, taking this risk. But what decided the matter was what I had already observed about the gender/sexual order of the can: An article of my clothing in the possession of one of the cons would be a symbol of ownership— this guy was hitting on me in as macho a manner as possible, with the choice of paid prostitution, fear, or both.

Registering my thoughts in less than a second's time, I figured I had only one course of action, and I took it. I said, quietly, "Just turn around and I'll forget this ever happened." I stood, holding the lip of my desk in preparation for overturning it, just in case he "offered" me the knife for my hat. To my relief and surprise, he backed off and exited. True to my word, I said nothing to anyone, though I was supposed to rat on any con who had money or knife, neither of which was allowed.

My capital among the inmate population went through the roof. They had found an honest man. Without hearing a word about it from me, my clerk told me that afternoon, "The dude will be taken care of." I thought about that statement and knew I could ask about it only elliptically. So I checked the file cabinet nearby and pulled out a file of completed equipment order forms that Mack had typed up for me. "Did you submit these contracts?" I asked. Long inured by the double-talk necessary within prison walls, he understood perfectly and answered, "Nah, those were sent in by the janitor."

The only janitor I knew was Bobbie, the double-life-plus-seventy-years murderer. Word moves fast among The Men, and as I discovered later through the grapevine, my would-be assailant? hat fetishist? lover? had boasted that I had been fool enough to snatch my hat away when he entered the office, stereotyping him as an instant threat. The boast was his form of preemptive strike in case I "put him on report" for his misbehavior. The boast would have worked if (1) some of the cons did not already know me better and (2) he had not already stashed the money and knife with a trustee con who had immediately informed Bobbie of his suspicions.

I did something unheard of at the time. I left the school area, walked through four cell blocks and went directly to Bobbie's cell. The guards were noticeably apprehensive, but I acted as if I were following orders. No one challenged me. With a protective contract out on me, even though what I was doing was foolish, I felt pretty safe, safer than I did among the guards anyway. My fake confidence and its efficacy told me a lot about how interactions work among men in a prison. Bobbie smiled and made a big deal about seeing me: "My man! What can I do for you today?" I shook the cell door like a monkey, which earned a barked expletive from the guard and all sorts of commotion from the cell block. And under that cover, I said, in what I hoped would be a voice loud enough for only Bobbie to hear, "Thanks for the protection, but I can't afford it." Bobbie smiled still: "Then it'll only be the first coat." This meant a layer of paint primer, a warning to the Hat Man to stay in line or a thicker layer would come. Before the din faded, I said, "Just don't put me on Front Street." This was prison talk for ratting on me by calling attention to me. I had, after all, not reported the incident. By that time, a guard had arrived to escort me from the place, back to my office, where I got chewed out by my supervisors, the captain of the guards, and the warden. My only answer was, "Just visiting my prize pupil." And that earned me my first and only "report," which was eventually "lost" by a clerk, never again to be seen in my personnel file.

The polysemous nature of the event, that the initial offer of money or knife for my hat could have been motivated in different ways, underscored the everyday, lived experience of life at the can: This was an artificially induced environment in which the dominant bully of the moment determined meaning, life, and death and in which any individual was necessarily tyrannized by having to monitor multiple environmental signs just to survive, let alone achieve any quality of life. The fact that justice is hidden was a given. The fact that standard operating procedure could be flaunted once, but flaunted nonetheless, was another violation of the paramilitary order of the prison. The fact that I had a knack for stretching the rules and got away with it with relative impunity earned me the nicknames that stuck, "Threeballs" but most often "Means It." "Means It" stood for my honesty and treatment of cons as equals, even when they proved undeserving of such treatment. I never wore my felt hat to work again.

Breaking Bread with Conan the Barbarian

This is not to say I was hipper-than-thou. I *was* pretty naive in a jaded world of betrayal, suspicion, and violence. After my little visit to Bobbie to clear matters up—with the ruse of making it so obvious that that could not be what was happening—I, along with everyone else, was given a new, explicit order: We were not to go anywhere in the can without obtaining permission first. I had heard all sorts of stories about the bad quality of the prisoners' food, and, judging by the quality of the meals served in the workers' cafeteria, which was pretty bad, I suspected that the stories were true. So, after letting the aftermath of my unauthorized visit to Bobbie die down, I determined to visit the guys during a meal at least once a month. I submitted my request to the warden, which my clerk made known to the cons, just as I thought he would. This leak of information made it difficult for the warden to refuse to approve the request, at least on a trial basis. It was innocuous enough, and arguably even necessary, considering that we teachers were supposed to recommend and implement new programming. Two weeks later, I was granted one-time permission, with no promise of continuation.

I did not know what I was getting into. My clerk and two of his buddies picked me up at my office and escorted me to their cafeteria. No one paid any attention as we entered, which should have clued me in right then and there that something was up. My escorts showed me the kosher line and the regular line, asking me to choose whichever I wanted to stand in for supper. Now I knew enough that this was a test, because the Muslims ate from the kosher line, and most everyone else ate from the other. Whichever line I chose, I would alienate half the prison population. The choice turned out to be a ploy. When I hesitated, looking back and forth between lines, a group of men gradually surrounded us and then an instant crowd gathered so silently, unobtrusively, and quickly that I had no escape and no guard—even if he had cared to—could have done much about it. It was a classic prison scenario. The cons could do anything to me they wanted, and I could do nothing about it. I had been put in my place. This was the way to punish or even kill someone who was out of favor with the cons. Not even Bobbie's protective contract could help, since no one remembered about that any longer, or so I thought as my life passed before me. Mack giggled and said, "So, whaddah yuh think?" Doing my best to stand firm and await whatever would happen next, I mumbled, "Sometimes I *don't* think."

Without any visible or audible sign that I was aware of, the men dispersed as quickly as they had gathered. A few of them acted disgruntled, as if I had been no fun, not worth it. I was ready to jump out of my skin, but once again, it was as if I had passed some test. Mack later confirmed this back at my office: "We told 'em you was cool, but they had to see for themselves." I said nothing, but Mack persisted: "That's what I gotta put up with every day." I nodded acknowledgment. "You never know," he finished. "You never know," I repeated.

One recurrent theme in both my daily notes and the expansions I worked up at home in private appeared to be unconnected to most of the other participant observation. There was a small group of prisoners who almost never interacted with me; in fact, I rarely saw these people interact with anyone. I knew their names and asked Mack about them when we were alone in the office. I said, "How come Randy never comes around?" Mack immediately held up his right hand in a policeman's "stop" gesture and shook his head: "We don't deal with them." I puttered with some papers and then persisted: "Cal—" "Same thing," Mack said flatly. "They don't exist." More than an hour later, after a meeting I had to attend over lunch, I got back to my desk to find Mack lying in wait. I sat and looked at him. We were alone again. "Make sure you stay away from them," he said. "They're the lowest of the low." I was totally clueless and must have looked that way—not that the strange ways of prison life did not repeatedly evoke signs of cluelessness from me. Mack concluded: "Scum. Rapists, child molesters. They don't exist." This explained why, although observation of them appeared in my notes and expansions, I had previously made no sense of them. They were physically present but put in a vacuum in which neither I nor anyone else could observe interactions. They were shunned and therefore had severely limited possibility for any sort of ongoing culture at all. They also avoided each other. As we shall see, this behavior consolidates wickedly in an interpretation of masculinities in prison based upon my participant observation.

Among the many other events that occurred in my presence, the following occurrence graphically illustrates the masculine prison dynamic. After months of preparation, classes in our high school had finally begun. For my junior (eleventh-grade) English classes, I had remedied the fact that most textbooks had not yet arrived by purchasing forty copies of the latest edition of the comic book *Conan the Barbarian*. That act alone gave my classes the best, most consistent attendance. One afternoon, in the middle of discussion, with every chair occupied, the door to the classroom opened, and there stood Mr. Vic. With a slight tilt of his head, he motioned for a chair. Immediately, one of the young cons vacated his seat and left without saying a word. Mr. Vic sat and smiled for me to continue. Then he added, "I apologize for being late." This was bizarre. He wasn't one of my students, but I played along, intrigued. He had sat next to the very young con whom Mack had indicated to me months earlier as "pretty." On the surface, a tension in the room mounted, and a few of the more talkative students became suddenly more talkative and animated. Beneath the surface—literally under the table at which Mr. Vic and Little Pretty sat—Little Pretty was masturbating Mr. Vic oh so quietly and unobtrusively. Three of the students declared that they wanted to act out a particular fight scene of Conan's—again. As they cursed and came to blows with one another, though I paid them strict attention, unquestionably Mr. Vic came. When the bell rang a few minutes later, no one stood until Mr. Vic stood. He smiled and commented mildly, "I thoroughly enjoyed your class, Mr. Holmberg." Only after he exited did anyone else move. In the common area, a janitor was already waiting with mop and bucket to clean up. Not surprisingly, it was the only room cleaned that day, presumably to remove any trace of Mr. Vic's visit. Barely ten minutes later, back in my office, Mack slapped me on the back, saying, "Hear y'all just had a good time with Conan!" I did not know what to think; I suspected I might get into trouble for not having tried to stop Mr. Vic and Little Pretty. But there were no recriminations. Mr. Vic never visited my class again, and he did not attempt anything of the kind with the other teachers. It was as if it had never happened.

Interpretation of Prison Homosociality

Although most of the narratives I have reported thus far constitute expansions and verifications of field notes taken in real-world prison circumstances, I have done my best to avoid interpretive comments other than those that occurred to me at the time. To this point, I have provided an account of my participant-observation experience as a teacher in a prison. Now however, it is time for what Clifford Geertz (1973:6–7) calls "thick description," an interpretative statement that retains the facticity of the reported events but goes deeper than mere surface reportage.

A men's prison is a societally sanctioned domain of compulsory homosociality. By "homosociality," I mean simply to identify the domain as a social location in which only same-sex interactions take place. Homosociality does not automatically mean or imply homosexuality, though, in the case of male prisons, there is a definite, masculine connection. In "normal," everyday life outside of prison, homosocial relationships between men are usually freely chosen; men associate with other men because they want to do so. The mainstream assumption ordains, however, that participants in homosocial relationships—such as buddies, drinking pals, and the dudes I watch football with— share something in common because they are guys. One significant mainstream assumption that "guys" share is heterosexuality. Thus, the homosocial environment of a prison is in no small way a punishment, a limiting of sexuality. In mainstream society, heterosexuality is presumed compulsory. Being limited to exclusive association with men is literally a punishment by inversion of mainstream values. Thus, prison homosociality becomes compulsory but in a different way; it is part of the punishment of precluding "normal" male sexual expression.

Please note at this point that I still speak emically, from the insider perspective of convicts whose masculine, macho world ordains highly sexist domination and exploitation of women and each other—particularly since women are not physically present. The assumption that heterosexuality is "normal" in prison culture is enforced by the very withdrawal of heterosexual options. One matter to consider etically—from an outsider perspective— is the fact that there *are* sexual components to homosociality, though between men they are not necessarily anywhere close to a sex act at all. Many men reported to me, even in the late 1990s, that, after they had a good time with the guys, they felt sexier, more ready for their woman or women. The support of men by means of ritualized interactions that delimit sexual expression between them still affirms solidarity between them and "sexes them up." As Eve Kosofsky Sedgwick (1985) claims, friends or rivals for the same woman's affection enhance their sense of self, their sense of desirability, of potency.

Thus, when I speak of the homosocial prison environment as compulsory and punitive, I speak from the prisoners' cultural assumption that heterosexuality is the insider, cultural norm for manhood and that the prison environment itself is a punishment of the "normal" equation of manhood with heterosexuality. Neither heterosexual options nor the sorts of freely associative homosocial bonding that heats a man up for sex or interaction with women exist. I do not agree, however, that heterosexuality is the norm for everyone. And it is not necessarily preferable either, particularly in its sexist aspects. I do note this: The culture-wide presumption of heterosexuality sees homosexuality itself as a punishment—a crime, a disease, a moral taint. Therefore, putting men in an exclusive homosocial environment is tantamount to saying that they are being treated as if they were homosexuals or that the most forbidden expression of sexuality is their only option, one that they would not seriously consider.

One might expect, therefore, that, since sexual acts are forbidden in prison (and since there are no heterosexual possibilities and no real man would do *that* with another man), masculinity would remain punished, subdued, and sexually unexpressed. Far from it. Sexuality, and its secondary expression, has forcibly been excorporated from mainstream culture, but it still lives. "Excorporated" means exported, borrowed (Fiske 1989). When something is excorporated from mainstream culture, in this case sexuality, it becomes transformed, and the subcultural domain's participants must make the excorporation their own; by so doing, it becomes oppositional to the mainstream. Indeed, the enforced, compulsory homosociality of prison gets transformed by being accepted and "worked"—masculinity in extremis.

Prison homosociality magnifies masculinity, taking it to the extremes of hypermasculinity, as in the cult of muscularity. The ongoing surveillance (Foucault 1977) additionally magnifies all performance of self, putting all action under a microscope of scrutiny or the perceived magnification that one is constantly *watched*. In fact, identifying and knowing physical areas and ephemeral situations in which less surveillance takes place or in which it is physically less possible is itself a surveillance activity necessary for survival. New convicts are almost instantly sized up as dominant or submissive, penetrator or penetrated. And they themselves know to look for signs of being treated one way or another, instantly scouting out physical locales where they can more readily be approached or approach others. Thus, a prison's culture manifests itself as what Stanley Fish (1980:14) calls an "interpretive community," one that has recognizable social markers that insiders readily acknowledge, maintain, and use and that outsiders must learn to negotiate if they are to become acculturated at all. Furthermore, the gestures of comportment—walking, standing, sitting, hanging out—become communicative inventories for conveying a person's sense of masculinity. If a man is perceived as submissive, a likely lay, then sooner or later he will manifest submissive comportment, even to the length of diverting eyes, sticking close to the wall, sagging his shoulders. Sharing another convict's attire is a sign of relationship if not possession; hence my leeriness about relinquishing my hat. The classroom incident in which Little Pretty masturbated Mr. Vic was a dramatic intersection of hypermasculinity and submissive compliance. Mr. Vic was so extreme in masculinity that his status among the prison population was preeminent. If he wanted something, no one messed with him. Little Pretty did not hesitate to "service" him during class, and no one interfered; in fact, some of the students conspired to cover up the activity in various ways. In this way, all of us—including me—were submissive to Mr. Vic's desires. For his part, he acted like a true gentleman, thereby reinforcing his act by providing a protective, socially acceptable mask to his extreme behavior.

Thus, another factor in the compulsory and excorporated men's homosociality was the esteem awarded to exploitive behavior. If a situation arose in which the rules could be worked or broken with impunity, the man or men who did so rose in coinage. Mr. Vic's foray into my class is a prime example; the situation was entirely novel and took place literally "under the table." On another occasion a group of prisoners made use of the school's new Xerox machine after hours, spending three days immersed in heavy "publication." By the time they were discovered, they had gone through hundreds of reams of paper and an enormous amount of money in copying fees—and suddenly, within just two days, their group recruited dozens more new members. I proved to be intuitively cognizant of the exploitive norm. Particularly during the first couple months, I violated all sorts of norms. Though I did not commit these violations fearlessly and usually got away with them by just plain luck, the incidents—my marksmanship score and its impact on the union guards; the books I ordered endlessly until, months later, the bills were processed and someone higher up started putting limits on purchasing; and my handling of the hat incident–earned me admiration and protection from the convicts.

Although some exploitive behavior inscribed the limits of masculine excess, however, oddly enough the behavior and the prisoners' reaction to it may seem anomalous to the hypermasculinity. Rapists and child molesters were shunned. They were not shunned because of something they did *in prison;* they were shunned for something they did *outside.* Unlike the other cons, who would listen to each other's narratives of "I was framed," the rapists' and child molesters' guilt was not questioned. Given that rape is one of the more difficult crimes to prosecute, the fact that these men had been convicted at all automatically awarded them a presumptive guilt that the other convicts could not and would not rationalize. A rapist violates the normative, heterosexual order—is not able to "get some" in acceptable ways. Because of his crime, therefore, inside prison, he can be neither considered a man nor treated as submissive. Indeed much of the rapists' nonverbal behavior signified a wide range of otherwise radically stereotyped gesture. Just as an example, a rapist or child molester may have walked "like a man" but did so alone, eyes diverted, thus commingling hypermasculine and submissive presentation of self. These sexual criminals, having taken to extreme sex in the outside world, were treated as outside the interactive social and sexual order inside prison. In comparison, men who were either made to be submissive or who embraced their own submissiveness were accorded status, and, depending on partner and circumstance, that status and esteem could be quite high.

As an ethnography of men in prison, these interpretations have their limitations. I myself was not a prisoner; therefore, my outsider status may influence both the data collected and the interpretation. However, having available to me convicts such as Mack, who were often candid, helped me acquire somewhat of an insider viewpoint and verification of that viewpoint. In addition, ethnographers commonly look to the level of acceptance in a culture as a sign that they are performing the cultural markers correctly, emically. My "protection" and other events that I have reported demonstrate some level of acceptance. In addition, I knew I was accorded a closer insider status when convicts treated me like one of the new first timers, showing me the ropes—particularly who to avoid among the cons and staff and how to perform various flimflams (such as the quick-change artistry of turning a small amount of cash into a large amount through friendly fast talk, their mail scams on pen pals, and pitching pennies). This insider status was always tentative, as was the rarely immutably fixed status of the men whose residence accorded them full insider standing.

Yet I was privileged to leave the prison daily, unlike my "clients." This reality flavored everything, like a touch of bitter herb that, though the recipe called for it, had to be treated with respect, carefully, cautiously. My awareness of the cookery at the time was inchoate for the most part; I was in the kitchen and had to put meals on the table, and I was making it up as I went along. Thus, I learned the culture of that particular prison haphazardly, with the personal drive of necessity but measured in eight- to nine-hour portions. If my prison experience had been twenty-four hours a day, especially considering my emic prettiness, I am sure that I would have consciously wised up sooner. By the conclusion of my work at the prison, I could articulate a good deal of what I have written here and did just that in a journal. Now that I have long been apart from prison culture—or so I fancy, living in northwest Ohio as a single man with bills and obligations—I can describe, in my own terms, what that culture is, what its demands of acculturation are, what its masculinity consists of.

The Culture of Transgression

Prison is the culture of transgression. The physical place houses transgressors who were caught in their transgression—an important nuance, iterated constantly among the cons: They had been caught, whereas thousands of others had not, or had been ignored, or had weaseled their way out of punishment by means of privilege or luck. The cons were convicted, compulsorily dedicated to incarceration. By choice or chance, they were dedicated. This ritualistic notion of their scapegoating as innocents was no illusory matter; they lived it to the hilt. It was the reason they were there, the way to get through, the way to get out. Oddly enough, not many actually seemed to "buy" this explanation, yet they voiced it often, lived it as if it were inexorably true.

Thus, the inmates constantly tested the boundaries of procedure in order to garner whatever momentary advantage might be attainable in an otherwise disadvantageous situation. The guards transgressed, sometimes feeding the black market, sometimes looking the other way, always finding ways to feather their nest, as long as they could avoid getting caught.

However, the contextualization of denying male prisoners heterosexuality works to emasculate them. In many cases the compulsory homosociality also sets the boundaries and invitations to transgress the enforced emasculation. In this hypermasculine plight of constant surveillance, if men choose or are forced to have sex with one another, homophobia and other forms of stigmatization come into play as they are put down—punished further—by other prisoners, prison workers, and the general public. To resist the compulsory emasculation requires the acquiescence to further censure and punishment of various kinds. Paradoxically, *among the prisoners themselves,* any transgression and particularly transgression of heterosexual norms earns cultural capital, personal credibility, a place within the convicted hierarchy.

As for me, I succeeded in transgressing all sorts of procedures and customs, sometimes by design but more often by dumb luck, for obedience in a paramilitaristic subculture is everything, within the letter of the law at least. My personal status did not require heterosexual emasculation, and I was in charge of implementing and interpreting many of the official rules and procedures. In the case of this new prison facility, there were new procedures; new architectural environments; and thus new, previously unregulated, unlegislated opportunities. For as long as they could do so without interference by the turnkeys or by each other, the men and the workers jockeyed for the very little freedom afforded. The major cause for curtailment of the convicts' transgressive exploitation of situations and others within the prison was their own boasting. Yet the safe place of equality, of someone *not* taking advantage of them, was so prized that it too eventually became a commodity of transgression, something to vie for, to protect, to disbelieve.

I quit my job suddenly when I received the news that my dad was dying. I had to be near him even though we had never really been close. I had no unused sick days at that juncture, but I had accumulated two weeks of vacation days, which I was permitted to take only *before* I quit. So my only option was to quit; give two weeks' notice; and, if approved, take my final two weeks as vacation days with pay. This was commonly done; a denial of this request would have been the first of its nature. Granted. Three weeks later I received a brief letter from one of my former teaching colleagues at the prison. At the time his news of the talk about my departure bothered me; now I see it for what it was, a logical extension of the male order at the prison, one that dismisses that which it most desires, honesty. What was the rap among the prisoners on my leaving? "I knew he'd never last." Considering the context, I got off easy.

References

Fish, Stanley. 1980. *Is There a Text in This Class? The Authority of Interpretive Communities.* Cambridge, Mass.: Harvard University Press.

Fiske, John. 1989. *Understanding Popular Culture.* Boston: Unwin Hyman.

Foucault, Michel. 1977. *Discipline and Punish: The Birth of the Prison.* Trans. Alan Sheridan. New York: Pantheon Books.

Geertz, Clifford. 1973. *The Interpretation of Cultures.* New York: Basic Books.

Goffman, Erving. 1959. *The Presentation of Self in Everyday Life.* Garden City, New York: Doubleday.

Sedgwick, Eve Kosofsky. 1985. *Between Men: English Literature and Male Homosocial Desire.* New York: Columbia University Press.

Nancy Levit

Male Prisoners: Privacy, Suffering, and the Legal Construction of Masculinity

Sometimes—rarely—discrimination results from a malicious prejudice buried deep in our soul. Sometimes—much more often—it results from unconscious biases, the assumptions of competence or incompetence, aptitude or ineptitude, a "fit" that is good or not. But sometimes—perhaps most often—discrimination is not rooted in the biases of any individual at all. Discrimination results simply from bureaucratic practices, from the unthinking repetition of the ordinary ways of operating in the world.

Robert L. Hayman Jr.

The purpose of examining the various ways in which legal doctrines and the legal system disadvantage men is not to thrust men into victimhood. Victimhood presents a dilemma. On one hand, failure to acknowledge victimization can allow forms of oppression to go unchecked. On the other hand, speaking in terms of victimization may promote passivity, helplessness, and blaming behavior on the part of victims.[1] If we learn to examine gender role stereotypes as evidential facts rather than mere opportunities for blame, we may be able to sidestep parts of the dilemma.

This chapter explores the ways legal doctrines disadvantage men through gender role stereotypes. It considers the ways these stereotypes construct masculinity: in particular how legal decisions require men to suffer certain types of harms without legal redress and to endure these harms silently. These features of how legal decisions construct masculinity in prison are intricately tied to models of masculinity outside the prison walls.

The Legal Architecture of Male Aggression

It is empirically clear that male aggression is neither mythical nor insignificant. Women in the United States suffer approximately "two million rapes and four million beatings"

An earlier version of this essay appeared in *The Gender Line,* © NYU Press.

every year; they are more likely to be injured by men they know than by car accidents, rapes by strangers, and muggings combined.[2] It is equally clear that, until institutional structures and cultural norms that perpetuate male aggression are exposed, there is little hope of eradicating it. Tracing the origins of male aggression entails exploration of a complex web of social beliefs, behavior patterns, learned interactions, and psychosocial theories.[3] However, even this approach is a relatively modern departure from the traditional view that male aggression is an inescapable part of male physiology.[4]

Only recently have scholars begun to direct attention toward the ways that law may reinscribe stereotypes of male aggression. For example, social acceptance of male aggression may be reinforced by rape laws that presume a woman's consent to intercourse in the absence of her resistance.[5] Dorothy E. Roberts notes the effect of legal decisions on assumptions about male aggression: "The stereotype of the aggressive, 'macho' Black male legitimates the massive incarceration of young Black men."[6] Similarly, labor arbitrators and judges create standards to distinguish acceptable from impermissible levels of picket line violence based on traditional assumptions about male aggression: "Assumptions about the 'animal exuberance' of male workers are used to defend and rationalize a tolerance for a minimal level of violent behavior in the 'rough and tumble' of labor activity."[7]

The U.S. Supreme Court has given official imprimatur to the stereotype that males are aggressive. In *Michael M. v. Superior Court*,[8] the Court held that criminalizing consensual sexual conduct for underage males, but not underage females, does not violate the Equal Protection Clause because only women become pregnant, and, therefore, the genders are not similarly situated with respect to sexual intercourse. Expanding on its justification for upholding the males-only statutory rape law, the *Michael M.* Court depicts females as victims and males as aggressive sexual offenders. In fact, chastity protection was the state legislature's asserted purpose, a fact that the *Michael M.* majority ignored in its analysis.[9] Instead, the Court viewed the matter as one of biology, noting that "males alone can 'physiologically cause the result which the law properly seeks to avoid'" and holding that the "gender classification was readily justified as a means of identifying offender and victim."[10] This assumption of male sexual aggression, along with its twin assumption of female passivity, not only offers a legal basis for criminalizing the conduct of only one gender; it also "construct[s] sexuality in limiting and dangerous ways."[11] The Court's ruling in *Michael M.* perpetuates commonly held perceptions about male sexual aggression, and its analysis fosters the belief that this aggression is biologically based.

Just as society has historically tolerated aggression by men, it has also tolerated aggression *against* men. The majority of male violence is directed against other men.[12] Men are almost twice as likely as women to be the victims of violent crime[13] and are treated more harshly in the criminal justice system. Men receive more severe criminal sentences than do women, even when men and women commit precisely the same substantive offense.[14] The percentage of men on death row exceeds the percentage of death-eligible offenses committed by men. In California, of 1,164 defendants convicted of first- or second-degree murder between 1978 and 1980, 5.5 percent were female, but of the 98 defendants sentenced to death, all were male.[15] Of the "16,000 lawful executions in the United States, ... only 398 (2.5%) [of those executed] have been females."[16] Some of this violence may be turned inward: Men commit suicide in much more significant numbers than do women.[17]

Consider also the exclusion of women from military combat. Banning women from military combat positions sent distinct messages about the capabilities and appropriate social roles of women. The combat exclusion for women also sent explicit messages about social expectations of and appropriate roles for men. War is a gendered construct: Just as women could not be combatants, men were not afforded the option to be noncombatants.[18] In *Rostker v. Goldberg*[19] the Court held that selective service registration for men but not women did not violate equal protection, deferring to Congress's determination that women were not suitable for combat positions and its implicit determination that men were the only appropriate warriors. Men possessed the strength to throw the grenades, the psychological wherewithal to suffer the indignities of war, and the social authorization to be killed first.[20] These are not simply the antiquated decisions of a bygone era; they are the archaic decisions of modern society, as the lower court holding in the Virginia Military Institute litigation attests.[21] Although later reversed on appeal, the lower court decision relied on biological differences between men and women on average to hold that women could be excluded from an all-male military college.

Links between gender and aggression are institutionalized and "locked in" legally. Courts seem to both accept and endorse the notion that men are militaristic, that they are society's criminals, victims, and warriors. Men possess the psychological capacity for aggression as well as the physical abilities for combat, whereas women lack both. The civic obligation of men is clear: The concept of citizenship for men is intricately tied to fighting.[22] The casualties of this legal expression of personhood are not only the subordination of women but also the construction of a rigid social order in which men have the exclusive sociopolitical obligation to engage in violence, to be the killers.

Male Toughness, Resilience, and Diminished Expectations of Privacy

One other area of legal decisions suggests the stoicism that society has come to expect of men as it protects the "vulnerability" of comparably situated women. Since the 1980s, male and female inmates have filed suits complaining about cross-sex monitoring by prison guards. These are not cases of deliberate humiliation. Female inmates simply do not want to be observed by male guards, and male inmates simply do not want to be observed by female guards as the prisoners dress and undress, shower, and use toilet facilities. Granted, this is the prison setting, in which inmates have diminished privacy expectations generally. However, as one court observed, it could not "conceive of a more basic subject of privacy than the naked body. The desire to shield one's unclothed figure from [the] view of strangers, and particularly strangers of the opposite sex, is impelled by elementary self-respect and personal dignity."[23] Perhaps central to the problem is this construction of *opposite* sexes,[24] but even leaving that issue aside for the moment, consider how courts have treated parallel claims of privacy infringement by male and female inmates.

Courts have consistently held that, if male guards routinely watch female inmates engage in personal activities, this violates their constitutional privacy rights.[25] In *Jordan v. Gardner*,[26] the Ninth Circuit Court of Appeals, sitting en banc, issued a thoughtful opinion discussing a prison policy that required male guards to conduct random, clothed-body, pat-down searches of female inmates. The court determined that the policy violated the Eighth Amendment's prohibition against cruel and unusual punishment and thus constituted the unnecessary and wanton infliction of pain. Because of the high incidence of prior sexual abuse among the inmates, the court found that women prisoners might be particularly vulnerable to the emotional impact of cross-sex body searches. In a parallel case, *Grummet v. Rushen*,[27] involving female guards conducting pat-down searches of male inmates, including the groin area, the court decided, "These searches do not involve intimate contact with an inmate's body." Other courts have held that, out of deference to the privacy interests of female prisoners, male guards can be excluded from the women inmates' living areas.[28]

On the other hand, most courts have been much more reluctant to recognize that male inmates might suffer dignitary invasions if female guards frisk, strip-search, or observe them while they are bathing, dressing, or defecating.[29] In *Johnson v. Phelan*,[30] a pretrial detainee made the equal protection claim that female guards monitoring male prisoners could observe them naked in their cells and while they showered and used the toilet. This embarrassed him and offended his sense of "Christian modesty." The Seventh Circuit Court of Appeals came close to sneering as it rejected Johnson's claims:

> Johnson's complaint (and the brief filed on his behalf in this court by a top-notch law firm) [does] not allege either particular susceptibility or any design to inflict psychological injury. A prisoner could say that he is especially shy—perhaps required by his religion to remain dressed in the presence of the opposite sex—and that the guards, knowing this, tormented him by assigning women to watch the toilets and showers. So, too, a prisoner has a remedy for deliberate harassment, on account of sex, by guards of either sex. Johnson does not allege this or anything like it.

Far more important to the *Johnson* court was the prison's interests in efficiency: "It is more expensive for a prison to have a group of guards dedicated to shower and toilet monitoring . . . than to have guards all of whom can serve each role in the prison." And the court counterposed the male inmate's privacy interests with job opportunities for women as guards, which the court characterized as a "clash between modesty and equal employment opportunities." "A prison," said the court, "could comply with the rule Johnson proposes, and still maintain surveillance, only by relegating women to the administrative wing, limiting their duties (thereby raising the cost of the guard complement), or eliminating them from the staff." Other courts have not seen the choices as so stark, and some of them have, quite sensibly, adjusted the physical structure of the facilities, job duties of the guards, or surveillance possibilities to accommodate the privacy interests of the inmates, the employment interests of the guards, and the security interests of the prisons.[31]

Reading between the lines, the majority opinion not only failed, as Judge Richard Posner noted in dissent, to recognize the essential humanity of prisoners (and Albert Johnson was a detainee, who had been only charged with, not convicted of, a crime) but also diminished male interests in privacy. Cross-sex surveillance was not an unreasonable intrusion into male detainees' privacy.

Other courts, similarly, have diminished the harms suffered by incarcerated males. In *Somers v. Thurman*,[32] Keith Somers alleged that female prison guards "subjected [him] to visual body cavity searches on a regular basis," monitored his showers, and "made 'jokes among themselves.'" These searches "violated prison regulations prohibiting unclothed body inspections by correctional employees of the opposite sex." Despite these contentions of intrusive, demeaning, and unprofessional behavior violating institutional rules, the court held that the guards were entitled to immunity. Discounting some of the female inmate/male guard precedents, the court emphasized the psychological "differences between men and women," concluding, "To hold that gawking, pointing, and joking violates the prohibition against cruel and unusual punishment would trivialize the objective component of the Eighth Amendment test and render it absurd." If the same allegations had been made by a female inmate, the decision most likely would have looked much different.

Other courts have placed the onus on male prisoners to shield themselves from view: "There are alternative means available for inmates to retain their privacy. The use of a covering towel while using the toilet or while dressing and body positioning while showering or using a urinal allow the more modest inmates to minimize invasions of their privacy."[33] None of the female prisoner/male guard cases obligated the women inmates to cover themselves to protect their privacy. Only one court even attempted to explain the difference between the privacy protection afforded to men and women. The differences in privacy protection were explained by the conclusion-begging statement that "male inmates and female inmates 'are not similarly situated'" and by the confusing bit of non sequitur reasoning that different security risks (which may or may not relate to gender) justify the differences in treatment.[34]

In short, female guards can view male prisoners in various stages of undress, but male guards cannot view female prisoners similarly disrobed. Women in custody are afforded more privacy than are men in custody. Simmering under the surface are assumptions about the motivations of the viewer: Female guards would not view men as sex objects, but male guards might be inclined to lascivious leering. The tacit assumption is that male guards would perform their jobs with malevolent motives, whereas female guards are more likely to gaze benignly. Male prisoners have diminished expectations of privacy relative to similarly situated women prisoners. Again, the cultural assumptions about characteristic features of males—men are invulnerable, autonomous, and they can build their own walls—are reflected in legal doctrines determining their rights.

Suffering in Silence

From infancy, men learn to endure suffering silently and in private. Emotional stoicism is ingrained in many and varied ways. Author William Styron says, "Women are far more able and willing to spill out their woes to each other. Men, on the other hand, don't have that. Men are fatally reticent."[35] In describing the "rules of manhood," sociologist Michael S. Kimmel explains, "Real men show no emotions, and are thus emotionally reliable by being emotionally inexpressive."[36] Various legal constructs reinforce this silent stoicism. Consider the law regarding sexual harassment of men. This is not the only area in which courts accept pervasive social stereotypes, either explicitly or implicitly, in ways that diminish the harms suffered by males,[37] but it provides an important lens through which we can view the legal construction of gender.

Sexual harassment suits by men (which constitute approximately 10 percent of all such suits)[38] often face ridicule from and diminution by society. A Minnesota attorney, who successfully represented a male city council aide in a sexual harassment suit against a female city council member, reported that radio talk show hosts were mocking his client "to the hilt."[39] When eight men sued Jenny Craig International, they complained of both sex discrimination and sexual harassment: They claimed that female coworkers had taunted them with demeaning remarks and anatomical comments about their "tight buns" and that, based on their gender, they had been assigned unfavorable tasks and denied promotions in the predominately female corporate structure. Columnists derided the suit, sarcastically referring to the workplace isolation suffered by "the Boston eight" as "harrowing," suggesting that a number of recent sexual harassment claims by men are "guffaw-engendering," and concluding, "It is far too late for judges to laugh this stuff out of court . . . that shouldn't stop the rest of us."[40]

If men were sexually harassed by other men, until the 1998 Supreme Court decision in *Oncale v. Sundowner Offshore Services, Inc.,*[41] that permitted such claims, federal appellate courts were split on whether victims of same-sex sexual harassment had a legally cognizable injury. (And even Justice Antonin Scalia's *Oncale* opinion cautioned "courts and juries" "not [to] mistake ordinary socializing in the workplace—such as male-on-male horseplay or intersexual flirtation—for discriminatory 'conditions of employment.'")

Often when men are sexually harassed by women, no one believes them. The assumptions that the typical perpetrator of sexual harassment is male and the typical victim is female are not unwarranted. The vast majority of workplace sexual harassment consists of men harassing women: Approximately 90 percent of victims are female.[42] Yet this prototype of male perpetrator and female victim can be transformed into a stereotype about sexual harassment that admits no other victim. The incidence of sexual harassment of men may be greater than people believe: Of the total number of sexual harassment cases, between 9 and 15 percent involve male victims.[43]

The underreporting of sexual harassment by either gender is not surprising. "Sexual subjects are generally sensitive and considered private; women feel embarrassed, demeaned, and intimidated by these incidents."[44] Importantly, just as women vastly underreport sexual harassment, so may men. A British Institute of Personnel and Development Survey "found that men were less likely than women to take legal action if harassed."[45] And just as women feel ashamed and humiliated by this harassment, men may feel absolutely silenced. Women fear that people will not believe their sexual harassment claims.[46] Men may fear both that people will not believe their claims and that people *will* believe their claims but will regard them as effeminate.[47] Because society equates being the target of sexual harassment with being something less than male, men may not want to admit that they experienced sexual harassment.[48] This sentiment among individual men is not unrelated to the social level of denial that males may be victims of sexual harassment. Treating a problem as nonexistent helps keep it that way.

When courts held, as they did for decades until the turn of the twenty-first century, that same-sex sexual harassment was not an appropriate basis for a Title VII employment discrimination claim, courts sent a powerful message about gender roles: When men sexually harass other men, the victims do not suffer legally cognizable injuries. More simply, perhaps the message was that men do not suffer or that "real men" do not suffer. Courts reveal a general unwillingness to believe that men could be offended by instances of sexual harassment. They trivialized men's complaints about vulgar and insulting comments and endorsed employers' messages that men who complained about these workplace incidents are providing appropriate grounds for their own termination. This approach reinforced social stereotypes of men as tough, sexually aggressive, and impervious to pain. Furthermore, it contributed to a cultural climate in which men cannot express their humiliation, their sense of invasion, or their emotional suffering.

Conclusion

This chapter has explored several ways that legal precedents reflect and feed constructions of masculinity in stereotypical directions: courts' treatment of privacy claims by men in prison, legal decisions regarding citizen soldiers, and sexual harassment suits by men. The discussion did not address the intersections of some of these areas: specifically, the claims of same-sex harassment and rape among prisoners and between guards and prisoners. It is an area of life that is basically hidden and an area of law that remains unresearched by theoreticians and blatantly ignored by politicians.[49]

The focus of legal decisions is typically individualistic: The cases of single individuals are considered by courts in different parts of the country, isolated in time, space, and history from others with similar experiences. What is often lost in the myopia of separate decisions—even those built on precedent—are the larger social patterns that these cases both reflect and promote. The indignities inflicted on men in prison are part of the larger pattern of a society that permits (and perhaps at some level has come to expect) the abuse of men and the endurance of that abuse in silence. This is the dark side of patriarchy, yet it is one with the toleration of abuse of women.

Notes

Epigraph: Robert L. Hayman Jr., *The Smart Culture* (New York: New York University Press, 1998), 133.

1. Martha Minow, "Surviving Victim Talk," *UCLA Law Review* 40 (August 1993): 1411, 1430–31, 1444.

2. See, for example, Elizabeth A. Pendo, "Recognizing Violence against Women: Gender and the Hate Crimes Statistics Act," *Harvard Women's Law Journal* 17' (Spring 1994): 157, 164.

3. See, for example, James V. P. Check, "Hostility toward Women: Some Theoretical Considerations," in *Violence in Intimate Relationships*, ed. Gordon W. Russell (New York: PMA Publishing, 1988), 29, 34.

4. See, for example, Gerda Siann, *Accounting for Aggression and Violence* (Boston: Allen and Unwin, 1985), 16–17.

5. See, for example, *State v. Rusk*, 424 A.2d 720, 733 (Md. 1981) (Cole, J., dissenting) (arguing that a woman "must follow the natural instinct of every proud female to resist, by more than mere words, the violation of her person by a stranger or an unwelcomed friend").

6. Dorothy E. Roberts, "Deviance, Resistance, and Love," *Utah Law Review* 1994 (1): 179, 188.

7. Dianne Avery, "Gender Stereotypes, Picket Line Violence, and the " 'Law' " of Strike Misconduct Cases," *Ohio State Journal on Dispute Resolution* 8 (1): 251, 274.

8. 450 U.S. 464, 471 (1981).

9. Sylvia A. Law, "Rethinking Sex and the Constitution," *University of Pennsylvania Law Review* 132 (5)): 955, 1000 n. 175.

10. 450 U.S. at 467.

11. Katharine T. Bartlett, "Feminist Legal Methods," *Harvard Law Review* 103 (February 1990): 829, 840.

12. "Men are three times as likely as women to be [homicide] victims" (Bernie Zilbergeld, "Is Male Violence Inevitable?" *San Francisco Chronicle*, June 23, 1991, 6).

13. See Bennett Roth, "Most Women Know Their Attacker, Research Finds; Study Explores Crime Victims in U.S.," *Houston Chronicle*, January 31, 1994, A1.

14. See, for example, *Wark v. Robbins*, 458 F.2nd 1295, 1298 (1st Cir. 1972) (holding that imposing a six- to twelve-year sentence on a male prisoner for escape but only an eleven-month maximum sentence on a similarly situated female prisoner was justified by the different "risks of violence and danger to inmates, prison personnel, and the outside community"); *United States v. Redondo-Lemos*, 817 F. Supp. 812, 815 (D. Ariz. 1993) (finding an equal protection violation in sentencing from [1] probation office statistics showing that male drug offenders were sentenced to an average of thirty-six months, whereas similarly situated female drug offenders were sentenced to an average of thirty-two months and [2] data that showed that 11 percent of males and 35 percent of females received probation), *rev'd*, 27 F.3d 439 (9th Cir. 1994) (holding that data relied on by the district court established disparate impact but not disparate treatment); U.S. Sentencing Commission, "Special Report to the Congress: Mandatory Minimum Penalties in the Federal Criminal Justice System," 76 (1991) (finding that, nationwide, 50.4 percent of women who committed crimes subject to mandatory minimum sentences received such a sentence, whereas 61.5 percent of men did). See also *Rodgers v. Ohio Parole Board*, No. 92AP-709, 1992 WL 341382 (Ohio Ct. App. Nov. 17, 1992); Charles J. Corley et al., "Sex and the Likelihood of Sanction," *Journal of Criminal Law and Criminology* 80 (2): 540, 541; Michael E. Faulstich and John R. Moore, "The Insanity Plea: A Study of Societal Reactions," *Law and Psychology Review* 8 (Spring 1984): 129, 132. But see Leslie G. Street, "Despair and Disparity in Florida's Prisons and Jails," *Florida State University Law Review* 18 (Winter 1991): 513, 520 ("women are generally imprisoned for less serious offenses than men, but serve longer sentences for their lesser offenses"); Kit Kinports, "Evidence Engendered," *University of Illinois Law Review* 1991 (2): 413, 421 (women who "offend judicial expectations" of appropriate gender roles, such as women who commit crimes of violence, receive longer sentences than their male counterparts).

15. *Harris v. Pulley*, 692 F.2d 1189, 1198–99 (9th Cir. 1982), *rev'd*, 465 U.S. 37 (1984).

16. Victor L. Streib and Lynn Sametz, "Executing Female Juveniles," *Connecticut Law Review* 22(Fall 1989): 3, 4.

17. See E. T. Loometsa et al., "Suicide in Major Depression," American Journal of *Psychiatry* 151 (April 1994): 531.

18. Lucinda J. Peach, "Women at War: The Ethics of Women in Combat," *Hamline Journal of Public Law and Public Policy* 15 (Spring 1994): 199, 208.

19. 453 U.S. 57 (1981).

20. See, for example, *United States v. Yingling*, 368 F. Supp. 379, 386 (W.D. Pa. 1973) (justifying selective service registration for males based only on "innate [physical] characteristics").

21. See *United States v. Virginia,* 766 F. Supp. 1407 (W.D. Va. 1991), *rev'd.* 518 U.S. 515 (1996).

22. *Selective Draft Law Cases,* 245 U.S. 366, 368 (1918) ("the highest duty of the citizen is to bear arms at the call of the nation").

23. *York v. Story,* 324 F.2d 450, 455 (9th Cir. 1963).

24. On this issue, see the thoughtful concurrence and dissent by Judge Posner in *Johnson v. Phelan,* 69 F.3d 144, 151 (7th Cir. 1995), *cert. denied,* 117 S. Ct. 506 (1996).

25. See *Lee v. Downs,* 641 F.2d 1117 (4th Cir. 1981); *Forts v. Ward,* 621 F.2d 1210 (7th Cir. 1980); *Dawson v. Kendrick,* 527 F. Supp. 1252, 1316–17 (S.D. W.Va. 1981).

26. 986 F.2d 1521, 1522–26 (9th Cir. 1993).

27. 779 F.2d 491, 492 (9th Cir. 1985).

28. See *Tharp v. Iowa Department Corrections,* 68 F.3d 223 (8th Cir. 1995); *Torres v. Wisconsin Departmentof Health and Social Services,* 859 F2d 1523 (7th Cir. 1988).

29. See, for example, *Madyun v. Franzen,* 704 F.2d 954 (7th Cir. 1983) (dismissing free exercise and equal protection claims of an Islamic male prisoner who refused to submit to a frisk search by a female guard–even though the state prison regulations allowed only female guards to frisk female prisoners). See also *Cookish v. Powell,* 945 F.2d 441 (1st Cir. 1991) (prison officials' reasonable but mistaken belief that an emergency existed justified a visual body-cavity search of a male inmate in the presence of female guards); *Michenfelder v. Sumner,* 860 F.2d 328, 334 (9th Cir. 1998) ("assigned positions of female guards that require only infrequent and casual observation, or observation at distance, and that are reasonably related to prison needs are not so degrading as to warrant court interference"); *Griffin v. Michigan Department of Corrections,* 654 F. Supp. 690 (E.D. Mich. 1982); *Bagley v. Watson,* 579 F. Supp. 1099 (D. Or. 1983). But see *contra Canedy v. Boardman,* 16 F.3d 183 (7th Cir. 1994); *Fortner v. Thomas,* 983 F.2d 1024, 1030 (11th Cir. 1993); *Cornwell v. Dahlberg,* 963 F.2d 912 (6th Cir. 1992); *Cumbey v. Meachum,* 684 F.2d 712 (10th Cir. 1982).

30. 60 F.3d 144 (7th Cir. 1995), *cert. denied,* 117 S. Ct. 506 (1996).

31. *Id.* at 147.

32. 109 F.3d 614, 624 (9th Cir. 1997).

33. *Timm v. Gunter,* 917 F.2d 1093, 1102 (8th Cir. 1990).

34. Ibid., 1103.

35. Quoted in Bill St. John, "Authors on Stage: William Styron on Styron, His Darkness and American Male Suicide," *Rocky Mountain News,* May 1, 1994, 74A.

36. Michael S. Kimmel, "Issues for Men in the 1990s," *University of Miami Law Review* 46 (January 1992): 671, 674.

37. For instance, the circuits split regarding whether male plaintiffs suing for sex discrimination, so-called "reverse discrimination," are required to establish the additional element "that the defendant is the unusual employer who discriminates against the majority." Compare *Lanphear v. Prokop,* 703 F.2d 1311, 1315 (D.C. Cir. 1983) and *Livingston v. Roadway Express, Inc.,* 802 F.2d 1250, 1251–52 (10th Cir. 1986) with *Loeffler v. Carlin,* 780 F.2d 1365, 1369 (8th Cir. 1985), *rev'd* on other grounds, 486 U.S. 549 (1988).

38. See Martha Chamallas, "Writing about Sexual Harassment: A Guide to the Literature," *UCLA Women's Law Journal* 4 (Fall 1993): 37, 38 n. 3.

39. Colleen O'Connor, "Films Distort Reality of Sexual Harassment," *Dallas Morning News,* January 5, 1995, D2.

40. Daniel Seligman, "The Follies Come to Boston," *Fortune,* April 3, 1995, 142.

41. 118 S. Ct. 998 (1998).

42. See David S. Hames, "An Actionable Condition of Work-Related Sexual Harassment," *Labor Law Journal* 1992 (July): 430.

43. See Barbara A. Gutek, *Sex and the Workplace: The Impact of Sexual Behavior and Harassment on Women, Men and Organizations* (San Francisco: Jossey-Bass, 1985), 54 (noting that sexual harassment of men is "common" and estimating its incidence at perhaps up to 9 percent of the total cases occurring); Office of Merit Systems Reviews and Studies, U.S. Merit Systems Protection Board, *Sexual Harassment in the Federal Workplace: Is It a Problem?* (Washington, D.C.: U.S. Merit Systems Protection Board, Supt. Of Docs, U.S. GPO, 1981), 98 (the results of an Equal Employment Opportunity Commission survey found that "42% of all female federal employees but only 15% of male employees reported being sexually harassed"); Bradley Golden, Note, "*Harris v. Forklift:* The Supreme Court Takes One Step Forward and Two Steps Back on the Issue of Hostile Work Environment Sexual Harassment," *Detroit College of Law Review* 1994 (Fall): 1151, 1173 ("although less common, the instances of female supervisors harassing male employees seems to increase with the number of female supervisors").

44. Catharine A. MacKinnon, *Sexual Harassment of Working Women: A Case Study of Sex Discrimination* (New Haven: Yale University Press, 1979), 27. See generally *Snider v. Consolidation Coal Co.*, 973 F.2d 555, 558 (7th Cir. 1992) (expert testimony that 95 percent of victims do not report sexual harassment because of "a fear of reprisal or loss of privacy"), *cert. denied*, 506 U.S. 1054 (1993).

45. Andrew Bolger, "Sexual Harassment of Men Highlighted," *Financial Times,* March 3, 1995, 11.

46. See generally Sarah A. DeCosse, "Simply Unbelievable: Reasonable Women and Hostile Environment Sexual Harassment," *Law and Inequality Journal* 1992 (10): 285.

47. See Michael B. King, "Male Sexual Assault in the Community," in *Male Victims of Sexual Assault,* ed. Gillian C. Mezey and Michael B. King (Oxford: Oxford University Press, 1992), 1, 5–7.

48. See, for example, Jane L. Dolkart, "Hostile Environment Harassment: Equality, Objectivity, and the Shaping of Legal Standards," *Emory Law Journal* 1994 (43): 151, 181.

49. See *United States v. Bailey,* 444 U.S. 394, 421-22 (1980) (Blackmun, dissenting) (citations and footnotes omitted): "A youthful inmate can expect to be subjected to homosexual gang rape his first night in jail, or, it has been said, even in the van on the way to the jail. Weaker inmates become the property of stronger prisoners or gangs, who sell the sexual services of the victim. Prison officials either are disinterested in stopping abuse of prisoners by other prisoners or are incapable of doing so, given the limited resources society allocates to the prison system. Prison officials often are merely indifferent to serious health and safety needs of prisoners as well. Even more appalling is the fact that guards frequently participate in the brutalization of inmates. The classic example is the beating or other punishment in retaliation for prisoner complaints or court actions." See also Stacey Heather O'Bryan, "Closing the Courthouse Door: Impact of the Prison Litigation Reform Act's Physical Injury Requirement on the Constitutional Rights of Prisoners," *Virginia Law Review* 1997 (83): 1189; James E. Robertson, "Houses of the Dead: Warehouse Prisons, Paradigm Change, and the Supreme Court," *Houston Law Review* 1997 (34): 1003.

Horace Bell

Boyz II Men

Living the street life
trying to hang
To impress the girls
and the gang _ _ _

Bumping fist
Slapping five
Talking smack
Copping jive _ _ _

Stealing cars
or selling crack
You're going to jail
that's a fact!

They're building pens
and county jails,
To make your life
an utter Hell!

When you snap
you're in the pen,
Here it's called
from Boyz II Men!

Horace Bell

Devil's Den

Once inside
a state prison,
The time has come
for a quick decision _ _ _

You can be yourself
or you can be a fool,
you can educate yourself
by going to school _ _ _

Or you can walk the yard
playing tough,
then bowing down
when times are rough

You can change
or be a punk,
your man there with you
in your bunk _ _ _

So much can happen
within the pen,
it's often known
as the Devil's Den

Willie London

My Mother Death

O Mother Death
I'm forever the son you bore
this living death tears me more
than your tender arm that I adore
when pain and suffering is a festering sore
Mother Death! I cry out loud
take my hand and make me proud
to live amongst a peaceful crowd.

O Mother Dear, I'm their living kill
thinking wrong my faith and will
as I wait out this living still
come take my hand and make me new
peaceful and calm just like you
to live amongst a peaceful crowd.

In you, your hands kind and gentle
must take me from this living death mental
let me not live this half torment
let me be whole and out of this cement
to live amongst a peaceful crowd.

O Mother Death I cannot stand
to take my life with my own hand
to take me from this living pain
which drives me wild far from sane
O Mother Death
Let me live amongst a peaceful crowd.

Derrick Corley

Prison Friendships

Prison is not an environment conducive to building friendships. It is risky to develop friendships with other prisoners, riskier to make friendships with prison personnel, and extremely difficult to have friendships with people from the street.

Men in prison form relationships with other prisoners for two main reasons: for protection, being part of a group or "crew" is stronger and safer than being alone; and for convenience, to pool resources and connections so that they can do a better "bid."

Two codes also generally shape men's relationships in prison: The manly code says carry yourself like a man, be hard and tough, and don't show weakness. The prison code says mind your own business, defend yourself and those you hang out with, and don't snitch. The practical underpinnings of prisoner relationships and the seeming harshness of the codes do not exactly make it easy for genuine and lasting friendships to evolve, but occasionally they do. A good analogy is to think of friendship as a seed and the blacktopped prison yard as the field it must take root in to live and grow. Unless the seed finds its way into a crack in the asphalt to sink its roots through, it is not going to find soil to grow. And even if it does take root, its growth will be stunted, its claim on life precarious.

Prison is a negative, hostile environment filled with people trying their best to survive. Prisoners must constantly be on the alert for someone trying to take what little they have or trying to better his situation by informing on them. Prisoners must guard their property, reputation, and body from assault. Paranoia is healthy in prison life, because a little but not too much can keep a person alive and lower his chance of becoming a victim.

Prison makes it hard to develop trust, a necessary ingredient for friendships. Prisoners feel that it is better to keep one another at arm's length, not to get too close, for to get close opens up the possibility that somebody might be in a position to cause them harm. For that reason, most prison relationships are shallow and short-lived. A friend is someone you can let down your guard around, tell your secrets to, show the *real* you and not the tough front you project in order to protect yourself. Without trust or letting someone know at least some of your weaknesses, no strong bonds can develop. Prisoners develop friendly *associations* rather than true friendships. They keep a wary eye on their relationships, always ready to sever them at a moment's notice, at the first sign of threat or trouble.

A prisoner cannot get close to prison personnel for lots of reasons. A close tie might cause other prisoners to suspect him of being an informer to the administration. Most prisoners, for example, talk to prison guards as little as possible, and, if they must talk to them, they try to do so when other inmates are present, or they talk loudly so that everybody can hear the conversation. Getting too friendly with guards or other personnel draws suspicion and, if this occurs, serious trouble can ensue.

Prison friendships are basically against official policy. Prison policy prohibits guards and other personnel from developing friendships with prisoners. A guard can lose his reputation if he gets too close with a prisoner and, in certain circumstances, he may even lose his job. A common belief is that friendly prison personnel may be smuggling contraband or, even worse, may aid a prisoner in an escape. Just as prisoners have their reasons for being paranoid about making friendships, prison authorities have security reasons for their paranoia. Firm lines are drawn, therefore, and they are seldom crossed.

Meeting new people from the street while incarcerated is extremely difficult, though not impossible. For any friendship to develop is not likely at all. The news media, books, movies, and political rhetoric have painted negative pictures of prison and prisoners—much of which is simply not true. If it is true that healthy people have healthy relationships, and, if these relationships are systematically denied prisoners, then how can we be expected to eventually live in society as normal, law-abiding, productive people?

Without contact or interaction, most relationships weaken, whither, and die. Prisoners are often jailed far from where their family and friends reside. Visits are possible, but, for many family members or former friends, the distance and travel costs are too great to bear over time. Collect telephone calls made from prison can place a heavy financial burden on the family members or friends who receive them. Telephone rates for calls made by prisoners to the outside world are higher than those on the street, and, as a result, most prisoners cannot handle the cost outlay. The results are isolation and frustration.

As for correspondence, writing is the most common vehicle used by prisoners to maintain their ties with family and friends. Unfortunately, many prisoners either lack the basic literacy to put their thoughts into words or they just don't feel they write well enough to get out their feelings and ideas. Access to prison education programs is often blocked, so there is little opportunity for prisoners to learn more writing skills that would help them get across some of these barriers to communication.

Prisoners are human, and they need friends and family in their lives. They also need to grow and maintain friendships inside prison in order to better their chances of successfully reentering society upon release. I believe that the released prisoner with strong and healthy family and friendship relationships is less likely to return to prison. Yet the prison system does little to encourage and support these relationships and plenty to discourage and hinder them. The cards are stacked against us as we move from day to day, year to year, and the weight of them presses many of us more deeply into isolation. Without friends, it's hard to find the way out.

Part IV

Sexualities, Sexual Violence, and Intimacy in Prison

Sexuality is a key locus through which domination and subordination are constructed in prison. Weak men are dominated and raped. Sexual "deviants," such as openly gay men, bisexuals, transvestites and transgendered people, are ridiculed and reduced to lower status positions. Homophobia is rampant. Even the fact that men who rape other men still think of themselves as "straight" and their victims as fags, bitches, or women reveals the confounding malleability of human sexuality and social definitions of gender.

Feminists argue that rape is more about power and violence than it is about sex. While most feminist writing on rape focuses on women's victimization by men, the reality of weaker male prisoners being controlled and raped by stronger male prisoners contains similar elements of domination and subjugation.

There is another dimension of man-on-man prison rape that links it to heterosexual sexual politics. Despite the prevalence of prison rape, prison officials and civilians often deny or fail to recognize it. The cultural silence surrounding man-on-man prison rape sustains common definitions of rape as a sexual act rather than an act of personal and political domination. It can also be argued that, just as the extent and severity of men's sexual violence against women are often tolerated or tacitly condoned in our dominant culture, so too is men's sexual violence against men in prison often denied or avoided by policymakers, reformers, and social scientists.

Rape in prison can be partly viewed as an institutional outcome of current corrections policies and their attending patriarchal cultural practices. The threat and reality of rape complicate the efforts of prisoners to forge intimate relationships with one another. Prisoners who attempt to develop or maintain romantic or sexual relationships with people from outside the prison must struggle to overcome the many institutional obstacles that the prison system places in the way of intimacy. Enforced and prolonged celibacy and the absence of emotional ties can trigger a terrible erosion of prisoners' sanity, dignity, and sense of emotional connection to others.

Despite the oppresive conditions of prison life, many prisoners manage to create intimate relationships that last long after they are released. Yet others buckle under the deprivation, violence, or loneliness. In the end, the sexual and emotional lives of prisoners display a diverse array of sexual identities and relationships, ranging from the lovingly resilient to the violently perverse.

Terry A. Kupers

Rape and the Prison Code

A prisoner is in "the hole" of a high-security unit in a state prison. He is a slight, gay man in his early twenties who does not display any of the posturing and bravado that is characteristic of so many prisoners. Convicted of drug dealing, he was consigned to a high-security prison because he carried a gun. But in prison, without a gun, his physical size and inexperience in hand-to-hand combat make him an easy mark. He explains to me that, since the time he arrived at the prison, he has been brutalized and raped repeatedly. His overt homosexuality seems to pose a threat to tough prisoners, and they regularly single him out for abuse. And he was told that, if he snitched to a guard, he would be killed. He tried talking to a seemingly friendly correctional officer about his plight, but the officer only insisted that he reveal the name of the prisoner who had raped him. He seemed more interested in busting a guilty tough than in helping this man figure out a way to be safe "inside."

This prison does not have a protective custody unit, a "safer" cell block where potential victims might be placed for their own protection—a place for child molesters, policemen who are serving time, snitches, and others who would not survive on the main line. After suffering rape after rape and multiple injuries from beatings, this man determined that the best way to stay alive while serving his time was to be locked up in the hole. So he hit a guard and, as predicted, he was placed in solitary confinement. He cries as he tells me in private how lonely he feels and how seriously he is contemplating suicide.

The rate of occurrence of rape behind bars is unknown, because many cases go unreported. The Federal Bureau of Prisons estimates that between 9 and 20 percent of prisoners become victims of sexual assault (Polych, 1992), and Daniel Lockwood (1980) writes that 28 percent of prisoners in two New York prisons report that, while in custody, they have been the victims of sexual assault. But these figures do not include the huge number of men who "consent" to having sex with a tougher con or consent to having sex with many other prisoners only because they are very afraid that, if they do not, they will be repeatedly beaten or perhaps even killed. In my view, this kind of coerced sex also constitutes rape.

The prevalence of AIDS in prison is also very high, and it is rising (Polych, 1992). Considering how much crime is drug related, this is not surprising. But this problem greatly magnifies the damage done by rape and multiplies the terror connected with sexual assault.

The New Prisoner's Dread

Hans Toch interviewed prisoners who had suffered emotional crises as they entered the prison world and discovered that, in many cases, concerns about the violence of prison initiation rites was a major precipitant of their psychological stress. According to one man, "When you're a new fish you're nothing. So you've got pressure coming from all sides. When you first come in, anyway, their first intention when they look at you is that they're going to make this man my pussy, my girl and shit. . . . They aggravate you. They say, 'We're going to test this motherfucker.' " This prisoner assumes, with good reason, that the prisoners aggravate him specifically to lure him to the back of the cell block where they can beat him and sodomize him. "So you come along back from the cell and shit, and you lock in [each prisoner is permitted to remain in his cell and lock the door during certain periods when prisoners are being let out to the day room or the yard] and see these guys, big guys, running down" (1992:82–83).

The Problem with Snitching

For the victim of rape, reporting the assault to security staff is not a simple matter. Even if the victim asks to lock up—to be transferred to a protective custody unit—the perpetrator may retaliate by killing, or by arranging for another prisoner to kill, the snitch. In addition, Toch (1992) describes prisoners' need to appear as "manly men." They must not display any sign of weakness lest other prisoners attack them. According to the code, snitching is the worst offense, but being a punk (the victim of rape or the voluntary passive partner of " butt fucking") or displaying weakness of any kind is not much better—and all are punishable by repeated beatings, rapes, or even death. Moreover, it is not at all clear to the violated male prisoner that the staff will maintain confidentiality, much less protect him if he snitches.

I have spoken to many prisoners who report that, when they have told correctional officers that they were raped, the officers have insisted that they reveal the name of the assailant. The situation is even sadder for the victim who suffers from a serious mental illness and does not really understand the code or the possible ramifications of snitching. These prisoners are especially vulnerable to victimization and rape. And when an officer demands that they give the name of the rapist, they are very likely to comply without realizing that they are violating the code and putting themselves in grave danger. I have talked to several mentally disturbed prisoners who were raped, went to a guard to ask what they should do, and ended up answering the guard's questions about who committed the rape. Once the word gets out that they have snitched, there is no way for the authorities to protect them.

Systemic Factors

Conditions of confinement are very important factors. A recent lawsuit illustrates how overcrowding and relative understaffing can lead to rape. I was asked to give an opinion about a young man who was raped by two gang members in a protective custody unit of a county jail. He was suing the county for not providing adequate protection. I examined the man and reviewed his file, including school reports and past psychiatric records. There seemed to be a pattern of vulnerability. For example, he had on occasion been the victim of mean pranks by classmates who first "suckered" him into engaging in behaviors at school that would lead to punishment and then laughed at him for being stupid enough to give in to their goading only to get caught. This hapless young man was clearly a potential victim. And after examining him, I concluded that he was suffering from severe post-traumatic stress disorder secondary to rape while he was in jail.

How was it possible, in a protective custody unit, for two gang members who had spent many years in prison to rape a vulnerable man who had never been to prison and never committed a violent crime? The victim, who had given the police the names of his accomplices at the time of his arrest, had asked to be placed in the unit because he feared he would be killed if other prisoners found out he had snitched. The two men who raped him, who were bigger and stronger than he was, had been returned from state prison to this jail only because they had to go to court to stand trial for gang-related violence inside prison. But they had been "outed" by their gangs (perhaps they were perceived as snitches). In other words, because they were in trouble with their gangs and therefore in grave danger anywhere in the correctional system, they had been placed in the protective custody unit.

At the time of the rape, a single officer was responsible for observing a day room, a dining area, and two floors of cells with open doors. It was not possible, at any given time, for that officer to observe the entire unit. In fact, the victim told me that the rape took place over a forty-five-minute time span, in a second floor cell, while the officer was in the day room, where she was unable to see inside the cells on the second floor.

The victim should not have been housed with the men who raped him. But in an overcrowded system, it is unlikely that prisoners of different security levels who are identified as being in need of protective custody will be further segregated—staff members are so far behind classifying the new prisoners that the assignment to protective custody is considered classification enough. And this is just one of the many ways that overcrowding can lead to heightened violence and mental decompensation in correctional settings.

The Code

Rape is not an isolated event in prison. It is part of a larger phenomenon: the hierarchical ranking of prisoners by their fighting ability and manliness. Jack Henry Abbott, who has spent most of his teen years and adult life behind bars, describes the process: "This is the way it is done. If you are a man, you must either kill or turn the tables on anyone who propositions you with threats of force. It is the custom among young prisoners. In so doing, it becomes known to all that you are a man, regardless of your youth. I had been trained from a youth spent in gladiator school (juvenile detention hall) for this. It was inevitable then that a youth in an adult penitentiary at some point will have to attack and kill, or else he most certainly will become a punk—even though it may not be well known he is a punk. If he cannot protect himself, someone else will" (1982:94).

The code, with some changes over time, permeates prison culture. Thus, Irwin and Austin point out that, in the first half of the twentieth century, the prisoners essentially operated prisons in the United States. They cooked, served meals, landscaped, performed building maintenance, and worked in prison industries. "Collectively, prisoners developed their own self-contained society, with a pronounced stratification system, a strong convict value system, unique patterns of speech and bodily gestures, and an array of social roles. . . . Importantly, their participation in this world with its own powerful value system, the convict code, gave them a sense of pride and dignity. It was them against what they perceived as a cruel prison system and corrupt society. . . . However, society was more accepting of the ex-convict than it is now and apparently most did not return to prison" (1994:66).

The situation is very different today. The "war on drugs" that rages in the inner cities; society's "law and order" sensibility; harsher sentences, including state and federal "three strikes legislation"; huge racial disparities in arrests and sentencing; the waning of prison rehabilitation programs; massive overcrowding of jails and prisons; racial and gang tensions in prison; and high recidivism rates have combined to change the code significantly. For instance, the prisoners no longer operate the prison, and there is less solidarity among prisoners of different races and ages. Still, some parts of the prison code remain the same.

One commandment continues to stand out: "Thou shalt not snitch!" Snitching can be a capital offense in prison. "And you had better not show any signs of weakness, or else others will pounce on you and rape or kill you!" The rules go on and on. For example, if a weapon is found in a double cell, each of the cellies is interrogated separately and encouraged—better, coerced—to snitch on the other in order to receive a pardon for having the weapon in the cell. In other words, the security officers manipulate the code to put teeth in their interrogations. They know that a prisoner who snitches and beats the rap will be attacked by other prisoners. Staff members use the code to maintain order in the prison.

Prison is an extreme environment. The men have to act tough, lift weights, and be willing to fight to settle grudges. Any sign of weakness leads to being labeled a victim, and weaklings are subject to beatings and sodomy. Of course, in this milieu, prisoners do not talk to each other about their pains, their vulnerabilities, or their neediness—to do so with the wrong man could lead to betrayal and death. Consequently, a lot of men choose to spend their time in their cells. Touring a high-security prison in the middle of the day, one is struck by the large number of prisoners lying in their bunks with the lights out—just trying to "do the time and stay alive."

This aspect of the code is not ironclad. I cite here some of the worst-case scenarios. In fact, in my tours through prisons and my interviews with prisoners, I have been impressed by a certain warmth and friendship in spite of the danger. For example, it is not rare for a prisoner to report that he was only able to survive in prison because another prisoner offered him the support and help he needed.

Politically conscious prisoners and activists in the growing prison movement on the outside are trying to build on the camaraderie and feelings of solidarity among prisoners. The goal is to help all prisoners understand that animosity toward other prisoners is misguided and that they must stand together against their real oppressors. The male dominance hierarchy, interracial animosities, and intergang battles are the obstacles that must be overcome in this organizing and consciousness-raising project.

There is even consensual sex in prison. Many men find partners, have sex as a sexual outlet in an all-male world, and do not consider themselves gay before or after release. Sex between mutually consenting prisoners can be quiet and unproblematic. There is even affection—sometimes great affection—but this kind of innovation in male intimacy does not attract the kind of media attention that rape receives. In contrast, prison rape is not about affection at all. It is about domination. A prisoner is either a "real man" who subdues and rapes an adversary, or he is a "punk."

There are four obvious structural elements of the prison code:

1. There is a hierarchy of domination wherein the toughest and the most dominant men rule those who are less dominant. Of course, the hierarchy does not begin or end with the prisoners. The security officers wield power over the prisoners; the warden dominates the security officers; and at the other end of the hierarchy, more than a few prisoners have been known to rape women or beat them and their children. Every prisoner knows his place in the hierarchy and maintains his place by proving himself when challenged.

2. There is a sharp line between those at the top of the hierarchy, the dominants, and those at the bottom of the heap, the weaklings and punks. The rape victims I have described are at the bottom.

3. The bottom is defined in terms of the feminine. Whether a man is known as a loser, a weakling, a snitch, a faggot, or a punk, he is accused of being less than a man—in other words, a woman. Jean Genet describes a man he knew at Mettray reform school: "Bulkaen, on the other hand, was a little man whom Mettray had turned into a girl for the use of the big shots, and all his gestures were the sign of nostalgia for his plundered, destroyed virility" (1966:144). When one man beats up another and sodomizes him, the message is clear: "I, the dominant man, have the right and the power to use you, the loser, sexually, as if you were a woman and my slave."

4. There is a narrowing of personal possibilities, as if the only way to survive is to conform to the rigid hypermasculine posturings of the prison culture. Sanyika Shakur, also known as Monster Kody Scott, a leader of the Crips of South Central Los Angeles, tells the story of a vicious fight between two cell mates that occurred at the beginning of his first prison term. Fat Rat began punching B.T. B.T. tried pleading with Fat Rat to stop; after all, they were both Crips from South Central. Fat Rat would not listen, and the more B.T. pleaded, the more Fat Rat gloried in his dominance—calling B.T. "bitch" and "pussy" and proceeding to humiliate him. According to Shakur, "Fat Rat, like me, was uncut street, straight out of the bush. The only language Fat Rat knew or respected or could be persuaded by was violence. Everything else was for the weak. Action and more action—anything else paled in comparison" (1993:295).

Notice that, in these four elements, the structure of masculine domination in prison mirrors the outside world. This is why films such as *An Innocent Man* and *The Shawshank Redemption* strike such resonant chords in many free men's minds. In both films a successful, middle-class man is framed for a crime he did not commit, sent to prison, and forced to fight in order to avoid rape. In *An Innocent Man,* Tom Sellak avoids rape by killing another prisoner. Middle-class male viewers shudder as Tim Robbins is repeatedly raped in *The Shawshank Redemption.* Of course, on the outside, especially among middle- and upper-class men, dominance is not based solely on physical prowess or gang affiliation. It depends more on one's level of affluence or status in the corporate world, in academia, or in the professions. And the literal threat of "butt fucking" is not as omnipresent as it is in prison; rape is more of a symbol. (Of course, for women the threat is literal.) Thus, men on the outside keep their cards close to their chests in order to avoid "being shafted" and try to avoid giving other men the impression that they might be womanly or gay. A man needs a friend who will "watch his back." And on the outside, there are women to play the role of underdog, so men can rape and oppress women instead of raping each other. But there is also, just as in prison, the ever-present hierarchy, the sharp line between winners and losers, the perpetual fear of being betrayed or defeated and falling to the bottom of the heap (this is one reason that so many men become workaholics), the castigation of those at the bottom as womanly or queer, and the narrowing and constricting of men's possibilities in the interest of maintaining the image of a "real man."

In prison, the penalty for falling to the bottom of the heap is literal. The trick for someone who is not a tough guy is to find a "third alternative," neither "pitcher" nor "catcher," neither king of the mountain nor bottom of the heap. For example, some frail intellectuals make themselves invaluable to other prisoners by becoming knowledgeable about law and learning their way around the law library. They become immune to gladiatorial battles because they have a commodity to sell—law is an invaluable resource in a correctional setting, where many prisoners are very involved in attempts to win habeas corpus motions and appeals of their convictions—so the prison toughs leave them alone.

There are other ways to create a third alternative. I met a slim, blond, effeminate man in a maximum-security prison in the Midwest. He was wearing a flowing red gown that reached to the floor, and he had a shawl draped across his chest in a way that did not allow assessment of the size of his breasts. He wore makeup and sported a very seductive female pose. He explained that, because he had been beaten and raped several times upon arrival at the prison, he decided to become the "woman" of one prison tough. He performed sexual favors for this one man, so that all other prisoners would leave him alone for fear of retaliation by his "sugar daddy." There was coercion involved, so his sex acts were not exactly performed by mutual consent. But at least there were no more beatings and rapes. Still, the exceptions to the "top dog"/"punk" dichotomy merely serve to prove the general rule of domination.

Isolation

Shakur writes, "Fat Rat had a reputation for being a 'booty bandit,' and thrived on weak men with tight asses" (1993:293). The booty bandit, the rapist on the prowl for potential victims, preys on isolated prisoners. This is one reason that prisoners are so intent on joining a gang or a group that eats together and lifts weights together. The loner is a potential victim, especially if he cannot defend himself. Men who lack social skills, for instance mentally disordered and timid prisoners, are easily victimized. And after they are raped, they keep it secret. The tendency on the part of these prisoners to isolate themselves thus works against their recovery from the violation and the resulting post-traumatic stress disorder.

Shame plays a big part not only in victims' refusal to report rapes but also in maintaining their isolation. When a boy is shamed, for instance by an alcoholic father or critical mother, he goes to his room. He does not seek the support of other members of the family. In the school yard, the boy who loses a fight or "chickens out" does not seek the support of his friends to heal his wounds; he keeps to himself, and the wounds fester. Shame leads to isolation, and in isolation there is little hope of transcending shame. In prison, it can be dangerous to speak frankly to others about one's pains—again, the code. After being defeated in a fight, especially if a man is raped, he keeps to himself; perhaps he remains in his cell all day in the dark. But this is precisely the kind of response that deepens depression or leads to chronic post-traumatic stress disorder (Pelka, 1993).

It is not only the individual's shame that makes life in prison unbearable. There is also the prisoners' contempt for a weakling. If a man tries to take his own life and fails, and there are visible scars on his wrist or neck, he is labeled a weakling and is likely to be victimized and possibly raped. Many prisoners suffering from mental disorders are raped.

The code in prison is based on intimidation. Positive outlets for the need to feel powerful are scarce. The demeaned of the land are willing to demean those who are even lower in the hierarchy than they are. And even some of the most demeaned of the prisoners, when eventually they leave prison, find themselves acting abusively toward others.

References

Abbott, Jack Henry. 1982. *In the Belly of the Beast: Letters from Prison.* New York: Vintage.

Genet, Jean. 1966. *Miracle of the Rose.* New York: Grove Press.

Irwin, John, and James Austin. 1994. *It's about Time: America's Imprisonment Binge.* Belmont, Calif.: Wadsworth.

Lockwood, Daniel. 1980. *Prison Sexual Violence.* New York: Elsevier Horth Holland.

Pelka, Fred. 1993. "Raped: A Male Survivor Breaks His Silence." *Changing Men* 25 (Winter/Spring): 41–44.

Polych, C. 1992. "Punishment within Punishment: The AIDS Epidemic in North American Prisons." *Men's Studies Review* 9 (1): 13–17. Quoting T. Hammet, *Update: AIDS in Correctional Facilities* (Washington, D.C.: National Institute of Justice, 1989).

Shakur, Sanyika. 1993. *Monster: The Autobiography of an L.A. Gang Member.* New York: Atlantic Monthly Press.

Toch, Hans. 1992. *Mosaic of Despair: Human Breakdowns in Prison.* Washington, D.C.: American Psychological Association.

Stephen "Donny" Donaldson

A Million Jockers, Punks, and Queens

The prisoner subculture fuses sexual and social roles and assigns all prisoners accordingly. Feminist analysis would note this as a patriarchal trait, and I would add that in my experience confinement institutions are the most sexist (and racist) environments in the country, bar none. As R. W. Dumond noted last year, "prison slang defines sexual habits and inmate status simultaneously" (1992) This classification system draws a rigid distinction between active and passive roles. The majority, which in this case is on top in all senses, consists of the so-called "Men," and they are defined by a successful and continuing refusal to be sexually penetrated. A single instance of being penetrated, whether voluntary or not, is universally held to constitute an irreversible "loss of manhood." The "Men" rule the roost and establish the values and behavioral norms for the entire prisoner population; convict leaders, gang members, and the organizers of such activities as the smuggling of contraband, protection rackets, and prostitution rings must be and remain "Men."

It is important to realize that whether a Man is sexually involved or not, his status is sexually defined. A Man who is sexually active (in both senses) is called a "jocker." (Note: although the term "Man" is universal in prisoner slang, other terms vary considerably from one region to another and, in some cases, with time. Since it would be too time-consuming to go into linguistic usage here, I have picked the most commonly understood prisoner term, and I use it here to the exclusion of all others. The term "jocker" was well established at San Quentin in 1925.) If a jocker is paired off, he is a "Daddy." If he engages in sexual coercion, he is a "booty bandit." Men almost always identify as heterosexual (in a few cases bisexual), and the majority of them behave heterosexually before and after confinement.

The following description is a generalization, and it should be kept in mind that exceptions to these patterns exist, but variances from one institution to another tend to be quantitative—meaning that they involve higher or lower levels of coercive pressure, sex-

Excerpts from a lecture delivered at Columbia University on February 4, 1993.

ual involvement, couple formation, gang influence, and official disapproval rather than other paradigms or patterns of sexuality.

The sexual penetration of another male prisoner by a Man is sanctioned by the subculture, is considered a male rather than a homosexual activity, and is seen as a validation of the penetrator's masculinity. "Manhood," however, is a tenuous condition, as it is always subject to being "lost" to another, more powerful or aggressive, Man; hence, a Man is expected to "fight for his manhood." Before the AIDS crisis, Men (especially blacks and Hispanics) under middle age were traditionally expected to be jockers; if they showed no inclination to demonstrate their manhood through sexual conquest, their status as men would be questioned, which would make them targets for demotion. Certain groups, such as mafiosi and the devoutly religious, could escape such suspicion. Since AIDS awareness has become widespread, Men who are not inclined to be jockers have acquired another excuse for exemption.

Below the class of Men in every way is the very small class of "queens." These are effeminate homosexuals. In jails, many are street transvestites charged with prostitution. They seek and are assigned the role of females and are referred to exclusively with feminine pronouns and terms. They have "pussies," not "assholes," and they wear "blouses," not shirts. They are always sexually passive and are unlikely to make up more than 1 or 2 percent of prison populations. They are highly desirable as sexual partners because of their willingness to adopt "feminine" traits, and they are highly visible, but the queens remain submissive to the "Men" and, in accordance with the prevalent sexism, may not hold positions of overt power in the prisoner social structure. They are often scapegoated, involved in prostitution, and viewed with contempt by the Men and by the staff. As a result, they are frequently assigned to the most undesirable jobs, kept under the closest surveillance by guards, and harassed by homophobic keepers and homophobic kept alike. In some institutions, including Rikers Island, queens are segregated from the general population and placed in special units, often called "queens' tanks." There they are often denied privileges given to the general population, such as recreation hall attendance, exercise and fresh air in the yard, library visits, chapel attendance, and hot food. Jails may put them in full-time lockdown, the equivalent of solitary confinement.

At the very bottom of the structure is the class of "punks," to which I was assigned. These are, to use Wayne S. Wooden and Jay Parker's definition, prisoners who "have been forced into a sexually submissive role," (1982) usually through rape or convincing threat of rape. Most frequent in urban jails and in reformatories but still common in prisons, gang rape (and the common threat of it) is the principle device used to convert Men into punks, and thus rape has an important sociological aspect. The vast majority of punks are heterosexual by preference and history, though some are gays or bisexuals who rejected the "queen" role but were forced into a passive role anyway. They are, for all practical purposes, slaves and can be sold, traded, and rented or loaned out at the whim of their "Daddy." The most extreme forms of such slavery, which can also apply to queens, are found in the maximum-security institutions and in some jails.

Punks tend to be among the youngest prisoners, small in size, inexperienced in personal combat, first timers, more likely to have been arrested for nonviolent or victimless offenses, middle class, and white. Given the jockers' unrelenting demand for sexual catchers and the small number of queens available, the proportion of punks tends to rise with the security level of the institution: The longer the prison term, the more risks will be taken by a booty bandit to convert a Man into a punk. Big city jails and juvenile institutions are also considered to have relatively high populations of punks. The total population of queens and punks is rarely high enough to meet the demand for sexually passive prisoners, however. This imbalance of supply and demand is thus a key to understanding the social dynamics of relentless competition among the Men in rough joints, who are in danger of "losing their manhood" at any time.

Although both groups suffer at the hands of both the Men and the keepers, relations between queens and punks are often tense: The queens tend to look down on the punks as weak, but they try to recruit them into their own ranks, a process that the punks resent, though some may succumb to it over the years. Punks, desperately trying to hang onto vestiges of their original male identity, resist the feminizing process promoted by both the Men and the queens; upon release they usually revert to heterosexual patterns, though often with the disruptions associated with severe male rape trauma syndrome. Longtime punks undergo an adaptation process, which may leave them functionally bisexual after release; some "come out" or surrender to the feminizing pressure and become queens. An umbrella term that encompasses both queens and punks is "catcher."

A macho gay male who comes into this system with considerable fighting ability may attempt to pass as a heterosexual jocker, since the only evidence of heterosexuality required is a pinup on the cell wall. If it becomes known that he is "gay," however, he will immediately be consigned to the queen role, and if he resists that, he may fall into the punk category. There is no niche in the prisoner structure for a sexually reciprocal or masculine-identified gay man such as we see in our androphilic communities. In a rural jail or minimumm-security prison, he may succeed in fending off such pressures, but in any other confinement environment, the entire institution would be against him and he would have to survive repeated combat.

In ongoing sexual relationships, a Man is paired or "hooked up" with a catcher; no other possibilities, such as a reciprocal gay pair, are tolerated. However, this one relationship is not only tolerated but sanctioned by the prisoner subculture, and virtually all catchers are required to pair off for their own protection. Vulnerable prisoners commonly learn this fact of life in jails or juvenile institutions before they first arrive at prisons and seek to "hook up" as soon as possible after arrival in order to preempt gang rapes. This fact is vital to interpretations of incidence studies of rape in prisons. These relationships are taken very seriously, as they involve an obligation on the part of the Daddy to defend his partner at the cost of his life if necessary and on the part of the catcher to obey his Man. Catchers are required to engage in "wifely" chores, such as doing laundry, making the bunk, keeping the cell clean, and making and serving coffee. Because of the shortage of catchers, only a small minority of jockers succeed in entering into such a relationship, and the competition for available catchers is intense, sometimes violent.

The impetus manifested by the jockers to form pairs is remarkable in light of the many disadvantages to doing so. For the Daddy, these include not only the risks of having to engage in lethal combat on behalf of someone else and having to suffer for his catcher's blunders, seductiveness, or good looks but also the heightened vulnerability to administrative discipline that comes from raising his profile and increasing the predictability of his prohibited sexual activities. The fact that so many jockers seek to form pairs rather than find sexual release through rape, prostitution, masturbation, and so forth is strong testimony for the thesis that such relationships meet basic human needs, such as the need for affection or bonding, which are related but not identical to the sexual need.

Prisoners serving long terms are often looking for a companion to "do time" with; such jockers tend to rely less on aggression and more on persuasion in their search for someone to "settle down" with, but often they are not above arranging for a confederate to supply the coercion needed to "turn out" a punk for this purpose.

Sometimes the Daddy role is actually a collective, so that a catcher may belong to a group of jockers or to a whole gang. Ownership of a catcher tends to give high status to the Daddy and is often a source of revenue, since the jocker, who is often without substantial income, can then establish himself in the prostitution business. These relationships are usually but not always exploitive, and they often result from aggression on the part of a booty bandit, though the Daddy is often a third party. The catcher may or may not have consented before the jocker "puts a claim" on him, though often he is able to choose from among jocker suitors if he acts quickly.

"Freelance" or unpaired catchers are uncommon, since they are usually unable to protect themselves and are considered to be fair game for any booty bandit. Usually, a rape or two is sufficient to persuade an unattached catcher to pair off as soon as possible. A catcher who manages to break free from an unwanted pairing is called a "renegade," and he is usually quickly claimed by another jocker.

Pair relationships are based on an adaptation of the heterosexual model, which the prisoners bring with them from the Street; the use of this model also validates the jail relationship while it confirms the sense of masculinity of the jocker and undermines that of the catcher. The Men tend to treat their catchers much as they habitually did their female companions, so a wide range of relationships, ranging from ruthless exploitation to romantic love, exists.

The Daddy's emotional involvement with his catcher is less common than with his women "on the Street," but it is far from rare; long-term prisoners may even "get married" in an imitation ceremony in the chapel attended by the whole cell block. One little-noted emotional significance of the relationship for most Daddies, however, is that it becomes an island of relaxation away from the constant competitive jungle, with its continual dangers and fears of exposing anything that might be considered a "weakness," which mark social relations among the Men. Confident in his male role, the Daddy can allow himself to drop the hard mask that he wears outside the relationship and express to his catcher the otherwise suppressed aspects of his humanity, such as caring, tenderness, anxiety, and loneliness.

The punk's total dependence on his Daddy for protection and social interaction induces psychological dependence, which can also facilitate emotional involvement. Thus, long-term prisons exhibit the remarkable phenomenon of two men, both heterosexual by preference and identity, involved in sexually expressed love affairs with each other. Incidentally, this aspect of sexuality led Peter C. Buffum to one of the all-time howlers in the literature, when he suggested that "the line officer might serve to reduce prison homosexuality by providing one outlet for inmate affectual needs" (1972). When prisoners love guards, there will be parties for the Ku Klux Klan in Harlem, and Pat Robertson will write a column for The Advocate. That is almost as good as the woman who read about quasi-familial relationships in women's prisons and looked to see whether there were similar nonsexual relationships in men's prisons. And in a 1989 article published in the *Prison Journal,* she found them, citing as evidence for "father/son" relationships equivalent to the "mother/daughter" dyads in the women's prisons the male prisoner slang terms "Daddy" and "sweet kid" (a common synonym for "punk"). Sexual reciprocation in these relationships is rare, and when it does occur, it is kept very secret. Some Daddies will go so far as to masturbate their punks, but even that is uncommon.

Another noteworthy variance from the heterosexual model is that the Daddies tend to be considerably more casual about allowing sexual access to their catchers than they would be about allowing such access to their women on the Street. The catchers are frequently lent to other jockers out of friendship or to repay favors or establish leadership in a clique or gang, and they are commonly prostituted. Unlike women, the catchers will not get pregnant by another man. It is very important, however, for a Daddy to retain control over such access to his catcher.

The punks, who retain a desire for an insertive role (which they cannot find in sex with jockers), sometimes reciprocate with one another in a mutual exchange of favors, giving each a chance to temporarily play the "male" role that is otherwise denied them. These situations account for most of the cases in which a survey shows both active and passive behavior by the same person. The queens ridicule such exchanges as "bumping pussy," revealing an incidental disdain for lesbianism.

Only a small minority of the jockers succeed in obtaining possession of a partner; these tend to be the highest-ranking Men in the prisoner power structure, so possession of a catcher is a status symbol. The remainder make use of prostitution if they have resources, join in gang rapes, borrow catchers from friends who control them, use a catcher belonging to their gang, or do without.

Many of the reasons for such involvement go beyond the necessity of relieving the sex/intimacy drive, though I should add before leaving the subject that those armchair theorists who claim that sexual deprivation is not one of many factors in prisoner rape, as distinguished from rape in the community, are mistaken. One major reason for jockers' involvement is that aggressive sexual activity is considered to validate masculine status and hence tends to protect the Man from attempts to deprive him of that status. In many institutions, there is considerable peer pressure to engage in "masculine" sexual activity because it also validates such activity on the part of other jockers, who are defensive about the fact that (even though they themselves reject the notion) the U.S. establishment and many staff members consider their behavior homosexual.

Other motivations are not as directly sexual. Deprived of power over his own life by the regime of incarceration, a jocker often seeks to stake out a small arena of power by exerting control over another prisoner. The existence of such an island of power helps the jocker retain a sense of his own masculinity—the one remaining social asset that he feels the administration cannot take from him—because of his identification of power and control with masculinity. For an adolescent prisoner, this motivation is often even stronger, as he has few other means of acquiring "manhood." Furthermore, involvement in prohibited sexual activity is an act of rebellion against the total institution and thus a demonstration that the institution's control over the person is less than complete, that he retains some measure of autonomy. Finally, sexual activity serves to demarcate other power issues: A gang or ethnic group wishing to assert its dominance over another may do so by seizing one of its rival's members and turning him into a punk for their own use. This is most commonly done by blacks against whites, as a symbolic attack on the manhood of all whites, who are said to be "unable to keep their bitches." It is thus the source of much of the racial conflict and tension in confinement.

Researchers have yet to examine the effects of the AIDS crisis on prison sexuality. By my own before-and-after observation of federal prisons, homophobia has risen, especially among whites; the status of queens has fallen; virgin heterosexuals are more highly prized; fewer jockers are hooking up; and much of the sexual behavior has become more covert. Daddies are getting more possessive about their catchers, particularly when it comes to anal sex, and prostitution is down. One would expect rape to increase under these circumstances. Growing numbers of institutions are circumventing their bans on condoms. But in all but a few systems, they remain contraband and most administrators refuse to allow them, on the grounds that to do so would be to "condone homosexuality," something they apparently consider worse than the death of prisoners.

Sexual activity in confinement may take place nearly anywhere; the expectation of privacy that prevails in other circumstances gives way to necessity. Furthermore, it is often to a jocker's advantage for other prisoners to see him engaging in "masculine" sexual activity, thus enhancing his reputation as a Man. For these reasons, sex is often a group activity, with participants taking turns standing "lookout" for guards or shooing away uninvolved prisoners from the area being used.

Although disciplinary codes in U.S. confinement institutions are unanimous in outlawing all sexual activity, the major effect of these codes is to ensure that sex takes place outside the view of the guards. A secondary effect is often to discourage protective relationships as an alternative to rape. Furthermore, these codes inhibit catchers from enlisting the aid of administrators in avoiding rape situations, given the fact that such avoidance usually requires pairing off with a protector. The furtive nature of consensual activities and pairings necessitated by the disciplinary codes also works to dehumanize them and favor quick, mechanical relief rather than an affectionate relationship.

The severe sanctions against informers that the informal prisoner code provides protect even rapists from being reported to the administration by their victims, who fear retaliation from the perpetrators or their allies. Officials usually have a general idea of what is going on, based on reports from informers, but informers cannot make these reports openly enough to provide a basis for disciplinary action.

One promising strategy against sexual assault that, so far, has yet to be tried would be to legalize nonassaultive sexuality and encourage the formation of stable, mutually supportive pair bonds in that context, while reserving the full weight of administrative attention and punishment for instances of coercion. With administrators continuing to regard both rape and consensual sexuality as problems to be equally ignored or, when acknowledged, eliminated, such suggestions have produced only the standard reply: "We can't condone homosexuality."

The openness of jailhouse sexuality, in spite of disciplinary codes, is one of its more remarkable features. The institution of "hooking up," which is the heart of the system and which specifies that any catcher who is "hooked up" may be "disrespected" only at the risk of violent retaliation from his Daddy, is utterly dependent on general awareness of the details of such pairings among the entire prisoner population. Virtually the first result of a successful claim being laid on a catcher is its announcement to the prisoners at large; sex is the number one topic of conversation, and the news that a new punk has been "turned out" spreads like wildfire throughout an institution. Often such hooking-up announcements are visual, taking the form of a jocker's continually eating and walking around the yard or block with a catcher until everyone has seen them together consistently and often enough to conclude that a pair has been formed.

Under such circumstances, guards and administrators with their eyes open can hardly fail to be aware of pairings. Often, in fact, housing moves are made to facilitate keeping the pair together; practical experience has shown that this tends to minimize fights and therefore keeps the general peace, which is the first priority of officials. Thus, when a jocker in a double cell acquires a catcher, he "persuades" his current cell mate to request a move out, the new catcher requests a move in, the catcher's current cell mate is prompted to request that he be moved out, and the administration approves it to keep the peace among all concerned. Other, more homophobic administrators seek to keep a pair as far apart as possible. A particularly dangerous situation is one in which a catcher is bunked with a jocker other than the one he is hooked up with. For this reason catchers are sometimes celled together.

There is, as may be expected, a wide range of administrative attitudes toward both violent and consensual homosexuality in these institutions. Consensual activities are accepted as inevitable by some and hunted out and seriously punished when discovered by others, but most tend to look the other way so long as the behavior does not become disruptive or too open. There are, unfortunately, all too many reports of administrators who are indifferent to or even supportive of coercive sexuality; some even use it to recruit informers.

The uniformed guards, who are more likely to come from the same economic class as the prisoners, often have a different set of attitudes from the civilian staff. Some of them consider all participants in sexual activity to be homosexuals; some display considerable homophobia and engage in private witch-hunts, trying to catch someone "in the act." Others, especially those with long experience as guards, may encourage a jocker whom they consider disruptive to get "hooked up" with a catcher, on the theory that paired-off Men are less likely to cause trouble. Guards are also involved in setting up some rapes and sexual encounters, in exchange for payoffs or for such diverse purposes as the destruction of the leadership potential of an articulate prisoner.

The application of middle-class concepts of homosexuality to prisoners produces much absurdity and little understanding. It leads writers who ought to know better to designate males who rape males as "aggressive homosexuals" and to argue that conjugal visiting programs would have no effect on prison rape, because these "aggressive homosexuals" would obviously have no interest in sex with women. It causes writers to engage in fruitless theorizing over the astonishing number of homosexuals in prison. It produces verbal atrocities such as the term "homosexual rape" for an offense that virtually no incarcerated homosexuals commit. It leads even such a supposed authority as Buffum to lament the damage inflicted on young inmates who are, and I quote, "the victims of aggressive, sex-driven prison homosexuals" and to later even go on to call these punk victims "made homosexuals" (1972).

The salient fact that the overwhelming majority of young males in confinement, freed from the fetters of social disapproval, will seek sexual gratification from members of the same sex strongly implies that the capacity for male homoeroticism is nearly universal, its suppression a matter of cultural mores and the availability of women. If this is so, and there is abundant data from outside confinement to support this conclusion, what are its implications for our understanding of sexual orientations and their causes? For concepts of gay identity and homosexuals as a minority group? These questions remain on the table even if we choose to ignore them as too uncomfortable for our currently fashionable ideas.

For the majority of prisoners, penetrative sex with a punk or queen remains a psychologically heterosexual and, in the circumstances of confinement, normal act; the relationships involved are also psychologically heterosexual to them (as well as to most of their partners, willing or not). These prisoners, who are perhaps focused more on the physical and less on the psychological dimensions of sexual activity than are members of the middle class, insist that the difference between the experience of entering a female mouth and of entering a male mouth is not significant, that the experiential difference between entering a vagina or female anus and a male anus is not significant. In all of these cases, they are aggressive, thrusting, dominating, stimulating the nerves in their own penis in quite similar fashion, inserting their energy and themselves into another body, and obtaining orgasms for themselves. A wide gulf, they insist, exists between such behavior and becoming passive, taking someone inside their own body, providing pleasure and orgasm to someone else's penis instead of their own. If one is to draw a line dividing sexual behavior into two categories, they argue, it is much more logical to separate these two radically different experiences than to draw the distinction based on whether one partner happens to have an unused, uninvolved, and ignored penis. The fact that these arguments are made by prisoners rather than by professors and that they do not advance a political agenda does not make them one whit less valid. Until academics recognize and address them, one can only conclude that current religiously based concepts of sexual orientation prevail only because their advocates are afraid to debate them.

Another area where current dualistic concepts based on legal distinctions fail to address actual prisoner sexuality is that of coercion and consent. Writers divide all sexuality into that which is coerced—rape and other forms of sexual assault—and that which is "voluntary." But for the passive prisoner in most acts and relationships, the punk, usually neither term applies. I have coined the term "survival driven" as an intermediate category, and I suggest its applicability in other contexts, including heterosexual ones, as well. From the typical punk's point of view, none of his passive sexual activities is truly voluntary, since, if he had his own way, he would not need to engage in them. Many continuing and isolated liaisons originate in the aftermath of gang rape or to counter the ever-present threat of gang rape. Prison officials and researchers label such behavior as "consensual." I, too, would treat it legally the same as consensual activity, but fear on the part of the passive partner is certainly the prime motivation. On the other hand, when a punk hooks up with someone, forming a long-lasting relationship with a protector, often selected by the punk from among multiple contenders, we are clearly dealing with something other than rape or sexual assault, something that exists only because to the punk it is dramatically different from, and greatly preferable to, rape and sexual assault.

For this reason, we need a third category. Wayne R. Dynes and I (Dynes and Donaldson, 1992) developed a typology of same-sex relationships that we presented to you at the very first meeting of this university seminar. The application of this schema to prisoner sexuality is not obvious, though clearly androphilia is not present. The relationships with queens at least are gender differentiated, and some of the characteristics of that type are applied to punks as well. But since the punks are generally the youngest prisoners and the jockers somewhat older, there are elements of age differentiation involved. Unlike in pederasty, the punk is not expected to mature out of his passive status and become active as he gets older. The preferred age group for punks suggests ephebophilia, but other significant traits of that type are reversed. Certainly, the question of situational homosexuality arises, since, for the jockers and the punks, the same-sex activity is a product of a particular situation characterized by the absence of the opposite sex. Reflecting the preoccupation of academics with questions of identity, however, the situational type has not been examined in any systematic manner. And although the possible commonalities of prisoner sexuality with that of sailors, students in boarding schools, monks, and so forth are in some cases obvious, they have not been explored.

The type that fits most generally, however, is that found to prevail in ancient Rome: The dominance-enforcement model where the sexual element expresses and symbolizes a previously imposed power relationship, the desires of the passive partner are irrelevant, the rulers are prohibited from taking a passive role, and sexual penetration of an adult male is viewed as the natural fruit of conquest. Prisoner sexuality also raises the thorny issue of socially assigned gender. This phenomenon is well known to anthropologists and can be observed wherever heterosex raises messy boundary questions for feminists and others and is therefore usually ignored by U.S. academics.

It is a cliché of academic presentations to conclude by urging further research and theoretical exploration. But in few fields is this standard appeal so richly justified as in that of sexuality in confinement. A million jockers, punks, and queens demand an explanation, and their numbers continue to soar with every year.

References

Buffum, Peter C. 1972. *Homosexuality in Prisons.* Washington, D.C.: U.S. Department of Justice. Reprinted in R. R. Mickley, *Prison Ministry Handbook,* 3d ed. (Los Angeles: Universal Fellowship of Metropolitan Community Churches, 1980).

Dumond, R. W. 1992. "The Sexual Assault of Male Inmates in Incarcerated Settings." *International Journal of the Sociology of Law* 20: 135–57.

Dynes, Wayne R., and Stephen Donaldson, eds. 1992. *Homosexuality and Government, Politics, and Prisons.* New York: Garland.

Wooden, Wayne S., and Jay Parker. 1982. *Men Behind Bars: Sexual Exploitation in Prison.* New York: Plenum.

Anonymous

The Story of a Black Punk

June 24, 1982

"I'm a 35 year old Black man, married and an ex-offender—and an ex-punk. I got busted the first time when I was just a kid and they sent me to a 'Youth Facility,' which is just another fancy way of saying 'Reform School.' My first night there 6 dudes took me off and from that night until I was released I was forced to give it up to anyone that wanted me. . . . Whenever I'd hit one joint there would be dudes that had had me in other joints and my reputation would be passed around. I have been forced to be a punk for 17 years (all of them figuratively behind me now that I'm doing well), but the years of sexual slavery weigh heavily on my mind occasionally.

"The first time I got raped I didn't know anything about sex and was too ashamed to ask my father for comfort. No matter where I was or who raped me, they always referred to me as a 'girl,' which messed with my sexual identity. . . .

"You isolated the important thing: 'Even though we are constantly subjected to homosexual rape we remain heterosexual.' I was able to get my identity straightened out with the help of a Black psychologist who patiently worked with me for three years. I also had some racist problems to deal with. Since I'm light skinned the first dudes that raped me were Blacks who thought I was white. After word got out that I was Black they left me alone but then the whites took me off. After that I was a 'Black' punk and passed on to whites.

"You were so right when you wrote about the misery, humiliation, isolation; and shame involved in our shared experience. I'm totally ashamed to admit this even to you, and we are 'Brothers' in experience. Possibly what our Brothers in misery must be brought to understand is that we remain heterosexual and have NOT lost our manhood with the rape. Sexual relations with women are still possible and our painful experiences don't physically change us in any way. . . . Another thing I personally have had to deal with is my heavy hostility as a result of my victimization for 17 years. I have dealt with my hatred by pushing myself to go back to school and acquire my . . . degree in psychology.

"The one thing, to this very day, that I can't admit to anyone is that I was ever raped. . . . My wife, a tender and understanding Black woman, is supportive and our relationship is beautiful . . . and healthy. I sublimate my hostility by working hard to save our people from going back which, in my imagination, is a way of starving the system which I believe is responsible for my years of humiliation.

"I would avoid contact with homosexuals since they seem to view our painful experiences as 'titillating' and 'exciting.' It has been my experience that the gays just want to hear about the actual rapes and then move on, leaving the speaker ashamed and lonely.

"Well, my Brother, take care and for God's sake don't let anybody in the joint know what you're up to or they'll mess you over."

September 15, 1982

"Many Whites got turned on seeing a Black dude getting raped and joined in where perhaps they might not have if the victim was White. I have been raped and beaten by Blacks as a punishment for permitting myself to be raped by Whites. The racial politics is a very real thing as you already know[,] my brother.

". . . The racial crap makes things so much more rotten for folks like us. Blacks are 'homo-phobic' (perhaps that is my personal prejudice showing) and not too serious about abolishing evil that affects them.

"I had the same response from my wife about me being a better lover behind my prison experiences and she says it made me more thoughtful in bed.

"I pretended to go with the whole thing for fear of death, but the shame to me was terrible. Still, I have to confess that getting fucked by a tender, gentle jock was better than the vicious gang-bangs and there was pride in making my man happy in bed. . . . The s & m freaks . . . always scared the hell out of me and were the worse [sic] of all the jocks in any joint I was in."

October 7, 1982

"I haven't done too much thinking about these things and to my surprise, they are still painful. It's hard to put them down on paper and to tell someone who is a stranger to me (even though you have suffered the same things).

"I got busted on a silly theft rap (stole a toy . . .) and they sent me to the . . . Youth Facility for ten days. The first night three older teens raped me for two hours. The second night the three dudes came back with three friends and they all took turns raping me again. It was the first experience I ever had with white folks and the other Black kids didn't lift a finger to help me out. They just turned away. The next day I was accosted by two custodians who told me they had heard I was turned into a girl by some of the other dudes—they raped me orally. I spent the rest of my time there servicing the three dudes that took me off the first night and depending how they felt, their buddies as well. I remember how my insides hurt but I was too ashamed to even report it, and then when I finally got out I was too scared to even go to a doctor.

"When I was 14 I got busted for 'joy-riding' in a 'borrowed' car (smile) and sentenced to a year at [a reform school]. The first day there I was put into a dorm and one of the three dudes who initially took me off in the youth house was on the same dorm. He told the rest of the inmates that I got turned out and then beat me badly in front of the other guys. He topped his beating off by raping me and established my identity in the dorm as the 'nigger punk.' I spent that year servicing the boys in the dorm and any of their friends that wanted sex. Donny, that was when I realized that my position wasn't too different from my ancestors and that for the rest of the year I wasn't any different from a plantation slave.

"Would you believe that as I typed the above I started to get all choked up and actually felt like crying? Talk about actual catharsis (smile).

"When I was about 15½ years old I ran away from home. . . . My sex with girls was terrible and I couldn't always get hard. Lots of times, if I got hard then I couldn't cum. This scared me and I began to think that I really got turned into a freak or something. So, I ran off. . . . [I] tried to call home but I didn't have any money. So, I broke into a car and stole a camera and some petty shit that was in the glove compartment. Got busted and did a year in . . . county jail. I remember the second night when a Puerto Rican dude paid the hack to leave my cell door unlocked.

"Donny, this dude was BIG and he just walked right into my cell and told me he was going to fuck my sweet ass. I got up real fast and tried to run out of the cell but he grabbed me by the hair and punched me in the face. I remember that I was bleeding from the nose and suddenly I was on the bunk, pants off and my legs were on his shoulders.

"He told me that he liked his girls Black and that he wanted me to be his girl. I agreed to the arrangement and was his punk for the whole year I was there. He was into s & m, which was my first experience with that shit. It was my first experience with 'ride the whip' too. He would invite his buddies (Whites and Puerto Ricans) to his cell where I would be forced to sit on his lap with his dick up my ass. Then he would masturbate me while his friends would take turns raping my mouth. God, even now I'm humiliated telling anyone about that. . . . I learned that I had to do everything a wife did and my existence depended on his contentment. If I resisted his little torture scenes, he would beat me and I would wind up doing it anyway.

"Donny, you wrote . . . about how you couldn't escape the sense that they . . . had conquered you and I could relate to that feeling too. This Puerto Rican jock just walked up and there wasn't anything I could do to stop it. He just took possession of me and for one year I belonged to him. This again took on the aspects of slavery which I guess is what all of us punks experience. Still, with a Black punk it takes on certain connotations. . . . I felt totally humiliated when my rapists were White and terribly sad when Blacks took me off.

"My bids at the State level were for armed robbery. . . . My first night out of quarantine I was gang raped in the shower and the word went into population that I was fully turned out. I got raped a few more times until a Black Brother offered to be my man, which I accepted right away to avoid getting killed. He wasn't too bad but he got into heavy debt and 'sold' me to this other Black dude for swag to get him off the hot seat. By this time, Donny, I was beginning to identify with slaves and took it with a grain of salt. I became terribly depressed suddenly and my new man ignored my feelings and moods. It got real bad and I began to withdraw into a fantasy world. It was this time that I started to get psychotherapy which helped me deal with my self-conflicts.

"I met my wife when I was back on the streets and she helped me out sexually. Thank God for her patience, Donny. I got back some of my old confidence thanks to her. Still, in a short period of time I was back in prison. My reputation as a punk before was still fresh in the minds of the men who had raped me earlier, and before long I was getting offers. Two Italian dudes raped me in very much the same way. I started to get depressed again and the way they treated me (and all the other punks too) began to mess with my head. I was terribly scared all the time and humiliated by the things they would yell as I walked by. . . .

"My first year back in . . . they had the riot and that probably did the trick. I remember it like it was only one minute ago—a straight dude (also Black) and I were walking near the school when a huge gang of crazy cons came running up the stairs screaming and yelling. They saw us and started yelling 'Get the queers' (at this time I didn't know what was jumping off). They grabbed us and dragged us into the t.v. room, stripped us and draped us side by side over the back of a sofa. They took turns raping us anally and orally simultaneously. I don't know how many there were but they were lined up all the way to the stairs to get at us. I passed out and woke up in the hospital with both my arms broken. As soon as I got out of the hospital one of the Italian dudes that raped me came up and offered to be my man and I accepted. I was thankful for the protection and greatful *[sic]* that he didn't force me to wear drag. However, I played the total woman and for three years I became the perfect punk in every way. The young man that was raped with me in the t.v. room went on a shooting spree two years ago and was shot to death by the police.

"This has proven to be weird and I'm not too sure that I've actually dealt with my feelings as well as I originally thought. I feel very humiliated that you should know what happened to me, even though I know you understand."

November 28, 1982

". . . After the t.v. room incident I spent time in the hospital. . . . After gettinq released from the hospital I was gorillared *[sic]* into becoming this Black dude's punk. He made me work the joint for him, turning tricks for swag and drugs. Come to think about it[,] Donny, I never was courted. They just put their claim on me or sold me. I never was good with my hands and I guess I'm easily intimidated, which worked in their favor. I've been beaten so many times that I hate the thought of fighting—when I know I don't have a chance. They always got what they wanted anyways so why go through the extra pain.

"There is a dude that just moved into the project where we're living. He was one of the dudes in the t.v. room incident and we met on the elevator the other day. He recognized me and I'm wondering what trouble this will cause—you mentioned once not being able to avoid the feeling of being conquered and now I can dig what you mean. I was intimidated immediately."

December 5, 1982

"I didn't have relationships with the gays in the joints I was in. My time was totally taken up by the dudes who had me and I was usually working for them in one way or another. As for other punks, occasionally we would cry on each others' shoulders or just share our company since nobody really would allow us in their presence except to use us for their pleasures or clean up after them. My relationships were always very superficial, Donny, and I was usually on my guard against anybody.

"The one fear I had when I got out was that I couldn't relate to anybody[,] especially a woman. I actually believed for a while that I had lost my male identity and couldn't sexually satisfy any girl. It took many efforts and one hell of a lot of patience on my wife's part for me to conquer my fears. Another thing was guilt and that still haunts me just a bit. It hangs in there but I'm dealing with it. There was a feeling of self-loathing that fucked with my head for a while too.

"Being held by another man would be very comforting. Inside, nobody ever showed me compassion, friendship or gentleness. Nobody ever held me except to use me, Donny.

"You asked me about 'water sports.' [In] my first encounter with that . . . some white dudes had me on my knees and the leader of that pack was mocking me out to the other jocks when he forced my mouth open and then pissed into it. I was shocked at first but I had to keep on swallowing it. The other dudes all laughed at me and then they started to piss all over me while making racial remarks. It was the most humiliating experience I could remember behind the fact it was connected with my inferiority as a Black man and a punk.

"Occasionally my man would use my mouth to relieve himself instead of making the effort to go to the toilet. . . . During the mass rape . . . many of the dudes who were fucking my mouth would cum in me and then follow it up with a stream of piss to wash it down. That I remember very clearly. The dudes who were fucking my ass sometimes pissed over me after they had cum in me.

"You hit it right on the head when you wrote about total surrender bringing with it a feeling of relaxation. I found that happening . . . when I was [in prison] for that year. . . . It was also true of my reactions in [another joint]. My Puerto Rican man was crude, to put it mildly, but there was never any doubt I belonged to him and that took ALL responsibility for what was being done to me out of my hands. . . . 'Riding the Whip' was terribly humiliating for me, but even that got to be just another experience. I came to take the jokes and the laughter from the spectators as a part of the experience, and they didn't bother me so much after a while. Hell, Donny, if we let the cruel remarks and the ridicule we experience get to us we would all go crazy. Christ, so many punks I saw took the jokes and the humiliations to heart and got seriously depressed to the brink of suicide."

January 28, 1983

"I remember only one dude that was kind to me, a Brother . . . named 'Doc' who worked in the pharmacy. I was his 'wife' and he always treated me nicely as long as I continued to play that role. 'Doc' insisted that I be as feminine as it was possible for me to be, but if I ever got into my 'male bag' he would get very rough. Still, he was gentle and kind. He shared his (and my) packages with me and we were friends when I got paroled. We send cards at Christmas and I still like the man. My response to his kindness was to do whatever I could to make his (our) time easier and I feel a warmth towards him (to this day) for taking care of me so I didn't get hurt badly. When he sent me out to turn tricks for him, Donny, he actually split everything fifty-fifty, which I found thoughtful and a sign of his affection, which I reciprocated. 'Doc' seems at this time to be the only kind man I ever met in the joint. . . .

"My wife was shocked when I told her. She helped me with patience and kindess, which brought me out of my intense fear—that I could never satisfy a woman. Before that I suffered from impotence that almost drove me to suicide. She takes a lot of convincing (smile) and wouldn't give up on me. Now we have a wonderful sex life together . . . thank God."

Susanne V. Paczensky

The Wall of Silence:
Prison Rape and Feminist Politics

I was shocked when I heard for the first time about men being raped, and I did not quite believe it. I had been a feminist for over twenty years, and I had been involved with the rape crisis center in my hometown of Hamburg, Germany. I had lectured and written about sexual violence, and I had never heard of sexual violence being directed against men. In all the books I had studied in feminist literature and in sociological research, rape was always described as a symptom of patriarchy, as the essential act of male domination over women. Even the laws in most countries describe the crime of rape as committed against women.

How could rape possibly be directed against men? Wasn't that allegation one of the chauvinist backlash arguments, such as "battered husbands" or "harassed males in the workplace," that antifeminists like to hold up—arguments that are used only to discredit women's demands?

But once I started to dig into the topic more deeply, I could not ignore the data: All over the United States, mostly in prisons and jails but also in other institutions, men are being raped, boys are being abused, thousands, even tens of thousands, every year. A wall of silence hides these crimes from public attention.

As a journalist, I am used to collecting little pieces of evidence and pasting them together. I listened to the painful memories of former inmates and to the testimony of psychologists; I learned from the experiences of people involved with rape crisis centers. I was deeply impressed by the publications put out by the organization "Stop Prisoner Rape," by the work of Wilbert Rideau and Ron Wikberg (1992) and Gilligan (1996), and I realized that the revelations in these writings were not new. Every few years, for more than half a century, reports have been published about the shocking amount of sexual violence in prison, and each time they are quickly put aside.

The latest such study by psychologist Cindy Struckmann-Johnson (1996) reports that 22 percent of the male prisoners in the peaceful plains of Nebraska have been victims of sexual coercion, mostly by their co-prisoners. But no public outcry, not even a discussion, followed her publication. The prison authorities were upset; they announced plans for an orientation program for their staff. But that was all.

"If it is happening in Nebraska, it is happening everywhere," said Struckmann-Johnson when I asked her in a spring 1997 telephone interview about the consequences of her study. "But I did not expect the general public to be interested. Homosexual acts are so abhorrent to most men that they fear to even talk about it. It is easier for a woman to be connected to this field of taboos."

The longer I worked on the subject of prisoner rape, the more I realized that the wall of silence has different layers: Prisoners could not report what happened to them, because they feared other inmates. "Snitching" could be dangerous, even fatal. They could not count on help from the staff, because prisons are not equipped to treat victims of sexual assault; some staff members even consider the climate of intimidation necessary for prison discipline. Prisoners do not seek help outside, because they are ashamed of the acts they have submitted to; they try to hide their degradation from family and friends, often from themselves. Even after their release, they are unlikely to report what happened to them. And even if they wanted to do so, to whom should they report it?

There seem to be no ears to hear the complaints, no media reports, no court cases, no public place to get justice or revenge or even pity.

Churches, human rights organizations that usually stand up for prisoner rights, and other benevolent institutions have shown little interest in prisoner rape. In at least some of the groups involved in the men's movement, efforts are made to fight against male violence that is directed against women or children, but there seems to be less concern when the violence is directed against men.

Every big city has a rape crisis center, sometimes a gay help line as well. But these services are focused on women or homosexuals. It takes a lot of courage for a young man who is insecure about his manhood to seek help from these groups, even if they might be willing and able to counsel him. It takes a lot of courage and self-confidence to overcome rape. Most victims are young, nonviolent, first offenders; they have been beaten and frightened and shamed until they have little courage and confidence left. We cannot expect them to initiate the fight against prisoner rape. So who can do it?

Thinking back over to the 1970s, to the beginning of the women's movement, I remember how difficult it was to raise consciousness about sexual violence against women. Victims were not willing to speak out, and public opinion was against them. True rape was considered a very rare occurrence and probably the woman's own fault. We can still hear an echo of these prejudices; it is still very painful to go to court against your attacker, as the trials of Mike Tyson and William Kennedy Smith both demonstrated; and rape is still one of the most underreported crimes. But there is a strong body of public opinion against sexual violence against women: Social scientists and city officials, public prosecutors and novelists have agreed to consider it a public outrage, and almost every female victim of sexual violence in every Western country can find a place to be helped and consoled. This change has not been accomplished by the efforts of the victims alone but by the political and practical work of a powerful social movement.

What is the difference between the victimization of men and the victimization of women? The experience of being raped, invaded against one's will, hurt and humiliated, made to participate in abhorrent acts—all are probably comparable for women and men. Perhaps it is easier for women to complain, because society has always allowed them to weep and suffer. Perhaps it is easier for the general public to accept women as victims and come to their aid because they have always held a subordinate position. There is obviously not so much sympathy for men who go to pieces; they are expected to take care of themselves. Even less compassion seems to exist for men in prison. It is their own fault that they are incarcerated. They are different. Although it would seem that the campaign to be "hard on crime" should apply to both sexes, there is more protest against sexual and other abuse in women's prisons than in men's prisons. In 1996, for example, when Human Rights Watch exposed cases of female inmates being assaulted, the organization made no mention of the larger number of male prisoners who suffer repeated rapes.

The wall of silence that surrounds the topic of prisoner rape is built of many different components: the shame of the convicts that they could not defend themselves, prisoners' fear of the possible reprisals, and the general public's radical lack of concern for prison conditions. But the glue that holds the wall together is homophobia. Even the enlightened liberal or Christian who might be willing to fight for prisoners' rights, to expose brutal guards or rotten food, seems to shy away from the embarrassing topic of sexuality. Even to think about homosexual acts, to consider the possibility that men can be forced to take part against their will, and to identify with those who have been violated must be so painful for most men that they prefer to deny what goes on in prison. Whoever dares to speak out may even risk being considered a pervert himself.

If men cannot protest against the rape of men, must women take over?

When I started discussing this proposal with female friends, their reaction was largely negative. At a meeting of German feminists, I met the same aversion as in a group of Berkeley academics (both groups consisted of mostly middle-aged, educated, well-to-do women). "Let men clean up their own mess" was the general opinion. "We are tired of being nurse to every sickness of society." Other women whom I tried to interest in the topic did not even listen. They reminded me that feminists had been fighting to get out of the traditional roles of mother and helpmate. Only a small number of women, mostly those who worked in social professions, considered the fact that violence concerns all of us and must therefore be fought regardless of sex.

In the late 1980s, when male victims started to turn up on the feminist rape help lines, female counselors greeted them with great reluctance. Many volunteers had had terrible experiences with violent men, and they refused even to consider them as clients. For a number of years, the help line volunteers were torn apart by violent disagreements about their function and about the best way to get men to look after their own.

Since then, the situation has changed. Many women are tired of trying to teach men nursing and caring skills. Sexual abuse has become a much larger problem than originally imagined: After the initial campaign against rape (believed to be committed by strangers), society became aware of date rape and marital rape; after the first revelations about child abuse, society learned about incest and abuse by close relatives or caretakers. Every step was painful and met public resistance. And most of these steps were taken by women, who fought for recognition of the fact that violence is much more frequent than we want to know.

Male victims were included, for the first time, in studies of child abuse. For many years interest had been concentrated on the violation of little girls. It had been presumed

SUSANNE V. PACZENSKY

that boys were not sexually molested, and even if they were, it did not harm them to the same degree that it harmed little girls. Only in recent years has it been acknowledged that a large number of boys and male adolescents have been sexually abused. The therapeutic community has had to adapt to a new circle of clients, the survivors of sexual violence.

The next step will have to include adult males and their victimization, and women will have to bring their own skills to this task. I talked to some of them in the spring of 1997 from very different perspectives: "It is easier for a woman," said a psychologist, "because women are less handicapped by homophobia." "It is our job," said the director of a rape help line, "because the violence that is brewed in prisons comes out to hurt all of us."

"Mothers against Prisoner Rape" is a group of four middle-aged women in Illinois who started to fight for their sons and ended up being the comforters and confessors for hundreds of inmates who have been sexually assaulted and have no one to confide in. "Sometimes we can help by appealing to the prison authorities and having the boy transferred to some safer ward, but most of the time all we can do is listen," said one mother by phone from Gary, Indiana, in spring of 1997. This woman, whose son committed suicide shortly after being released from a prison where he had been raped repeatedly, impressed me as very courageous. She corresponds with many inmates, visits them, and writes letters to the local newspapers to alert them about prison conditions. Many former friends and neighbors and even her church have ostracized her for speaking out against prisoner rape, but she continues with what she considers her mission.

The wall of silence has proven to be very solid. It will crumble only when many mothers, wives, and sisters become worried about their incarcerated family members and start to act. Feminist groups that have done so much in the past to fight violence will have to include men in their agendas, not only for humanitarian reasons but, above all, in their own interest. Most of the men who have been brutalized in prison will be released only to act more violently against women and children.

The task that I set for myself was to look at prison rape from a feminist point of view. This is only a limited angle; other segments of society will have different perspectives. I can only hope that men and women, gay and straight, can come together in an effort to enlighten the general public on the dark side of their prisons and to denounce all forms of violence. This book can help us take a step in that direction.

References

Gilligan, James. 1996. *Violence: Reflections on a National Epidemic.* New York: Grosset/Putnam.
Rideau, Wilbert, and Ron Wikberg. 1992. *Life Sentences: Rage and Survival behind Bars.* New York: Times Books.
Struckmann-Johnson, Cindy. 1996. "Sexual Coercion Reported by Men and Women in Prison." *Journal of Sex Research* 33 (1): 67–76.

O'Neil Stough

A Moment

Imagine for a moment, cement blocks stacked on one another forming a fifty-foot wall. Interspersed in this wall, steel doors on cells, with cement walls, cement floors, iron trap slam! slam! slamming! three times every day if you're lucky, more if you're not. These cells sweep up one side, a double tier, with open space to the other side, where yet another double tier rises, two-story madness in this horseshoe, with open area, space to space. In these cells men are buried alive twenty-four hours a day, except the two days that it's only twenty-three hours, country club holidays. Hot, humid, dank— swamp coolers straining in monsoon season, moans, sweaty curses, simmering rage.

And imagine if you will for one moment a young man in his early twenties, frail, scared, shimmering in the heat, "high yella" confusion, springs from his cell when door cracks, scurries to center of horseshoe, drawing all eyes. With a courage that could be born only of pure terror, he takes a stand, faces off with the state, all their chains, pepper spray, clubs, guns, troops. He demands a cell change, refuses to say why, though all, including the guards, know it's because a darker man is screwing him, making him do unspeakable things, bringing out all the bitch in him. Good-ol'-boy beefy guard approaches, pepper can at eye level, "You gonna lock down, asshole!" he hollers, bellowing for the crowd, canister of chemical hell only inches from the eyes, ready to maim and beat, knowing, like the kid's cell mate, how vulnerable and easy the kid is, all eyes watching now.

"He scaird, man, can't you see that?" voice screeches under steel door. "Lock down now, you piece of shit," said as only guards can. Behind the kid, another guard approaches, stealthlike, creeping chains wrapped in beefy fists, leg irons. Control room guard gets the rabble going over the speaker, artfully: "Now, you piece of shit! Return to your cell now, you son of a bitch!" All cells alive now, screams and hollers, scent of blood in the air. "You're going NOWWWW, you fucking asshole. You're going to live there AND LIKE IT!" Guard getting into it now, letting it all hang out, knowing denials will be made from this point on, cloud of confusion.

Just as he gets ready to spray the eyes, then rush in hard, and just as the creeper from behind gets ready to pounce and strike with excessive force on the defenseless and fearful, just as we all know a bloody stomping is coming down, suddenly, like a sharp breeze, the kid, at center stage fright, his hands held at sides in passive posture, and with all looking on, begins to cry openly. Tears flood down his cheeks, body trembles with giant sobs, convulsions of despair, hopelessness, terror. The guard creeping from behind is frozen in step—guard with spray ready and anxious to harm, wanting to like a good piss, freezes.

The entire cell block falls silent as a tomb. In a quarter of a century of dwelling in this house of the damned, in all the madness and anguish, where mercy is on extended vacation, I've never seen such a moment. All watch spellbound as he is led away, as his former cell mate screams obscenities. All return in silence to their solitude, as do I.

I feel for both the savage beast and its frightened prey.

Mumia Abu-Jamal

Caged and Celibate

For hundreds of thousands of men imprisoned across the United States, in all but seven state jurisdictions, life behind bars is one of state-enforced celibacy. In prison, one's sexuality is locked in a cocoon of ice or diverted into myriad survival strategies.

The seven U.S. jurisdictions that provide some degree of conjugal visitation are California, Connecticut, Minnesota, Mississippi, New York, South Carolina, and Washington. Indeed, many national governments expressly provide for conjugal visits—for example, Canada, Belgium, Denmark, Germany, Great Britain, Holland, Russia, Sweden, and numerous Asian and Latin American countries. The reluctance on the part of the United States to broaden conjugal visitation appears to be out of step with the progress of many other nation-states.

Origins

Any historical discussion of prison takes one to the early American colonies, which, ironically, were the cradle of not only political liberty from the British Empire but also the systematic institutionalization of the penitentiary as a tool of state power and social control. All roads to long-term incarceration lead back to Philadelphia, where the "Philadelphia System" originated: one prisoner per cell; imprisonment as repentance; and large, regional institutions.

In 1790, Philadelphia was the, albeit temporary, capital of the newly minted nation. Quakers, then part of the elite, proposed a sane alternative to grisly "old world" European practices, such as drawing and quartering and disembowelment. In the waning days of the Age of Reason, they instituted the practice of confining persons in total institutions—prisons. Prisons, by design, were to be dark and foreboding places where prisoners were to be held in strict silence in solitary cells and deprived of visitation, letters, or any kind of external influence, save the Bible that each man possessed. Not surprisingly, this regimen drove men literally insane; thus, it was tempered, lest the state lose to the grave or the abyss of madness those it sought to teach penance.

Today the enforced silence of yesteryear is no more, but one feature of the Victorian Age remains. The assumption that sex is sinful and bad, as opposed to natural and good, remains operative through the denial of conjugal visits.

Sexuality Shackled

Imprisonment, with all that it entails, is as much, if not more, an act of state violence than the silent violence of poverty. Prison officials often speak loftily of the rehabilitative benefit of family relationships in the lives of the men in prison. In practice, however, the family is decimated as a side effect of imprisonment. The tangled web of human relationships between fathers and children, sons and mothers, and husbands and wives is atomized and ripped asunder by transfers from urban to rural facilities, severe encroachments on interpersonal communication, noncontact visitation, and the curbing of conjugal visits.

Prison reformers missed a valuable opportunity in the 1980s, when a Gallup poll revealed strong support for conjugal/family visitation. A May 1982 poll[1] asked Americans to react to the statement, "In some nations, and in some states in the U.S., in order to keep families together, wives are permitted to spend some weekends each year with their husbands in special weekend guest houses within the prison grounds." The majority of respondents expressed support of the idea.

While widespread public support for conjugal visits has been allowed to wane and remain a policy whisper, politicians and prison officials have exploited public attitudes toward capital punishment. The nation has ignored a life-affirming option and magnified a dark, death-centered option.

Sexuality Gone Awry

Deprived of meaningful outlets for sexual expression, men in prison develop myriad coping techniques. Prison's secondary staple, after cigarettes, is pornography or "paper pussy." Smut books circulate and become a coveted commodity and currency. Some men assign personalities to the porn stars and invent names in order to augment masturbatory fantasies. Severed from relationships with the living, the mind seeks its shadow through projection.

It should be no surprise that prison is a hotbed of homosexuality, which, in turn, is intricately linked to a system of dominance among men. Although all prisons have rules that prohibit homosexual sexual contact, it continues unabated, fanned by bans against conjugal visitation and implicit administrative acceptance. At one level, homosexual relations reflect and reproduce pecking orders of dominance and submission among the prisoners themselves. At another level, savvy administrators look the other way on such couplings, because they can utilize these relationships to extend their control. For example, as in any macho subculture, homosexuality is extremely stigmatized. An official may threaten a closeted homosexual with exposure, thus triggering certain violent retribution and potential rape. To avoid such threats, the gay prisoner may inform on other inmates, thus enlarging the web of interprisoner conflict and distrust while solidifying centralized administrative control.

The following two cases show that sexual fantasy sometimes spills over into delusion, complicating relationships among fellow prisoners and between prisoners and professional staff. One prisoner, struck by a nurse's gentle manner, badly misinterpreted a simple smile for genuine affection, and in his mind there arose the belief that she was his wife. He went so far as to argue with and threaten follow prisoners who dared to talk with her. This grew into a fixation so pointed that, after several suicide attempts, which were probably staged in order to gain her sympathy or access her nursing skills, he was committed to a regional mental facility for several weeks. After his return, he no longer claimed that the female staffer was his wife, but his fingers fidgeted constantly and his tongue perpetually darted in and out of his mouth. These are telltale symptoms of tardive dyskinesia, the permanent side effects of psychotropic medication that is used to "treat" some psychiatric patients.

Another prisoner, imprisoned for more than a decade, since his midteens, developed a jailhouse reputation for flashing au naturel whenever a female staffer, usually a nurse, came to his cell. Orders and repeated misconduct reports failed to deter his practice. At one point the husband of the female staffer responded by assaulting him. The administration finally assigned a male nurse to attend to his medical needs. The flashings and many of his illnesses ceased.

Both of these cases, though anecdotal, reflect the tortured and maddening lengths that some prisoners go to in order to give some, albeit twisted, expression to their sexuality. Both situations might have been mitigated by a conjugal visitation program. Both men, and tens of thousands like them, spend their twenties, an age of peak sexuality, in shackles—unable to touch and be touched and barely able to dream. Upon their inevitable release, what will be unleashed upon the world?

Diversions

Many prisons wisely provide organized sports programs, which serve to channel the omnipresent tensions within the joint. Athletic programs help maintain social control, but, at the individual level, many prisoners use exercise as a coping strategy for dealing with emotional and sexual frustrations.

Prison jocks bring a level of intensity and involvement to their athletic pursuits that most outsiders would find impossible to sustain. It is possible that some of the world's best boxers, basketball players, and weight lifters are largely anonymous and behind bars. Unfettered by free-world diversions, many men devote hours each day to honing their athletic skills. A prisoner, who is on the bottom rung of the social ladder, owns only himself (that is, his body—and that, only barely), and it is for this that he works. Further, by burning energy through athletic endeavor, he better manages his sexual tensions.

Keeping People Whole

In Alkmaar, Holland, prison officials have operated "sex cells" for long-term convicts. They laud this innovation as a correctional program that works. Deputy Governor Joseph Poelman of Schutterswei Prison has stated, "We try to keep people whole; no worse at least when they leave than when they arrive. If you keep people in prison too long or too repressed or too crowded, you can break them mentally and leave them less intact than before."[2]

The policy of keeping men whole seems to be a reasonable alternative to shattering their personalities, sexualities, and family relationships. The seemingly simple recognition that men have a human need for sexual intimacy should, in part, underpin thinking about prison reform. The bar against conjugal visitation should be terminated in order to keep people whole.

Notes

1. George H. Gallup, *The Gallup Report*, report no. 200, Princeton, New Jersey, May 1982, 14. Quoted in U.S. Department of Justice, Bureau of Justice Statistics, *Sourcebook of Criminal Justice* (Washington, D.C.: U.S. Government Printing Office, 1983), 267.

2. *The Economist*, February 6, 1988.

Michael Keck

The Phone

(Image: Bars; Text: Struggle; Sound: Cell block.)

Hey baby. What's up? You know you on my mind. Can't do nothin' without thinking 'bout my baby. Know what I'm saying baby? *(Singing)* I've got those mean ol', low-down, wall-climbing, nail-biting, teeth-gnashing, heart-breaking, mind-bending, tear-jerkin', lord-I-miss-you, gotta-have-your-body . . . BLUES. You like it when I sing to you don't cha? You know how much I love singing to you. You still my best fan right? Right? You been cool? Keeping the dogs off? You know I don't want nobody sniffing 'round my baby now. Know what I'm saying?

So where's my lil man at? I got a song for him too. Yeah I wanna sing happy birthday to him. Did he like the card I sent? Made it myself.

(To another inmate waiting in line for the phone) Yeah one minute OK?

Yeah I know when his birthday is. There were seven guys in front of me yesterday. I would have called from a direct line in my suite but they were reblocking the drapes and shampooing the carpets. So why didn't you just pack him up and bring him out? You know I just can't walk outta here and come see him.

(To inmate) Just a minute, OK?

What's wrong with you bringing him to see me? He's not too young. . . . When you gonna tell him? What's wrong with the truth? . . . He has to know the truth. He knows who his daddy is.

I ain't got nothin from you this week, last week neither. So what's been happening wit-chu? Un huh . . . so where's the kid at, what he up to? Put him on. . . . I wanna sing to him anyway. . . . Better late than never.

(To inmate) I just told you I'll be off in a minute!

I don't care what ya'll doing. . . . Get him on the phone, bitch, NOW! OK, OK,! I apologize. Yeah right so you gonna hang up? I said I'm sorry, whaddaya want from me? Look we don't have to go through this shit if you just put him on the phone.

(To inmate) Back off! I ain't bullshittin'!

Hey lil man ... hey buddy ... that you? You ain't nuttin' but a peanut head ... yes you are, you peanut head. OK, OK, wait a minute and listen ... listen ... Happy Birthday to you, Happy Birthday to you ... Happy Birthday ...

(To inmate) Motherfucker, if you don't get outta my face ... *(Black out)*

Alice

Be Not So Quick to Judge

They asked why I loved him
A man so flawed, they
Thought, "how could she?"
But they didn't see the honesty
Or the ramrod straight steel
Of a soul tested by adversity
In their polite little world
There was little risk and
Lots of scorn which they
Hurled at me obliquely
Causing me to wince and wonder
Which was the worst sinner
Them or the tender prisoner
Who knew the depths of his
Aching wound and used it
To nourish me daily
Who was the better person
The middle class pretender
Or the tortured, denied man
Forced to feeling and compassion
On his knees in isolation
Robbed of everything except
The only values that matter–
True friendship, love, respect,
An unbroken spirit, dignity intact,
The love of a merciful God
Who alone did not desert him

And knowing that, he commenced
To share with me so generously
That I finally knew male richness
Which opened my heart
Encircling me, meeting me
Full blast, brazenly, I was
Weak kneed at the conquest,
Finding myself invited to the dance
With a brave and gentle warrior
Who knew himself deeply
As most men never do
Bringing that and little else
He claimed me as his bounty
With lusty, loving sexuality
As no other had or would
At the same time that he
Shared his fears and tears
So openly, fearlessly
That I too began to trust

Still they asked, "What is she doing?"
When I answered, "falling in love"
Their eyes turned downward
They were so full of judgment
They couldn't comprehend
I might be enlarging myself
They couldn't see the beauty of
His taut and tensile strength
Nor know his gentleness
And the raw hunger with which
He approached life and me
Spontaneous, open-hearted, unspoiled
How dare they judge my need
To move in new directions
Essential to my soul journey
They wanted me the same, I guess
So as not to disturb their boat
Nor could they see the
Tenderness that passed between
These two abandoned children

Who knew better than many
What it meant to be unloved
And the persistence it took
To confront their darkness
In pursuit of a sinewed Self
But most of all they
Could not fathom how
Two souls could come from
Many lifetimes to travel
Such different paths
Offering the other, in this one,
Solace, comfort, caring
Laughter, friendship, romance
Across class barriers
Through prison bars
Beyond ordinary considerations
Pity they could not imagine
The mirror and magic of a
Deep and abiding LOVE
They shunned me as
I walked into his arms
I knew them once
I called them family
I think of them sometimes
But mostly with sadness
They were too quick to judge

Carlos Hornsby

Reflections

In his cell, he sat on the edge of his bed and reflected upon a past that could only be called ugly. A career criminal who didn't have much of a career. He paid his money, took his chances, and lived his life. Now, he is collecting the full benefit.

All the memories were there; they just weren't in any order. Hearing Gene Chandler sing "Duke of Earl" almost thirty years before on an old AM radio, smoking his first joint, robbing parking meters, going to clandestine Coney Island meetings, using drugs, robbing banks, dealing with dope dealers, becoming involved in shoot-outs, and ending up in prison. Step right up; pick one. See yourself. He sat on his bed looking for a memory of happiness. He couldn't find one.

He was tired. Lying down, he pulled a cigarette from his pocket, lit it, and inhaled deeply. He looked at it. It was a Pall Mall. Taking another drag, he thought about getting cancer, and in the silence his mind said, "Fuck it. Get it in both lungs." Behind closed eyes, faces appeared as if shot from a projector. Mother, father, parking lot attendant, people he knew and people he didn't know, some still alive somewhere, but most of them long dead. People he cared for, people he had terrorized, and people who had cared for and terrorized him. Each had a place in his life, and each had come and gone, remaining only as an image in his mind. The only child of parents who were the only children of his grandparents, he was the last of his line, and he carried with him the loneliness of all men who live lives of uncertain destiny. Taking a final drag off his cigarette, he flicked it toward the open grillwork that made up the front of his cell. It hit a bar, bounced back, and came to rest on the concrete floor by the foot of his bed. It was still lit. Turning his head slightly, he muttered a single word: "Figures." Closing his eyes again, he didn't move as the cigarette burned itself out.

Leaving yesterday, he sped forward. He didn't mind looking at his past, but he refused to stare at it. That took too much out of him, and he didn't have much left. Looking at the present was no bargain either, but he was more comfortable with himself in the present. At least now, the denial was over and the bullshit discarded. Opening his eyes, he took another cigarette from his pocket, lit it, and blew smoke rings at the ceiling. This time there were no thoughts of getting cancer; there were just the idle musings of a man suffering the pain of being in love at the wrong time of his life.

His mind went from point to point like a train, stopping at some stations, passing through others. Meeting her, talking with her, telling her about himself without pretense and with an honesty that could often be called brutal. She was a prison volunteer, and she had listened to every word. There was no "I'm sorry" or pity in her eyes when they talked, and for that he was grateful. He already knew who and what he was; he just wanted someone to talk to.

They saw each other once a week for over a year and came to know each other well. When she would hear him say, "If I get out of here . . ." she would smile and correct him by saying, "It's not 'if' you get out; it's 'when' you get out." They came to trust each other, and with that trust came a deep and mutual respect. Then one day, as the convicts and volunteers were forming a circle to say the Lord's Prayer just before parting, she looked at him and held out her hand. He stared at her; she knew he didn't believe in God. As he started to walk away, he heard her say in a soft voice, "Fake it." He turned around and looked at her; their eyes met. With her hand still extended, she smiled. He went to her and joined the circle. With the last smoke ring, he again flicked his cigarette toward the front of his cell, and again it hit a bar and bounced back, still lit. He didn't move or say anything. He just let it burn.

The locomotive in his brain continued to speed along, and he remembered how four weeks later she had stopped coming into the prison as a volunteer, and a week after that he received a letter from her asking him to put her on his visiting list. His world was changing. For the first time in over twenty years, he could actually say he was in love, and as far as he could tell, he was happy. He pulled another cigarette from his pocket and lit it. As the smoke curled slowly upward, he reviewed his life in the visiting room. The stories, the laughter, the hope. The memories made him feel better, but they didn't change reality.

As he finished the cigarette, he again flicked it toward the front of his cell. This time, it sailed through the open grillwork and out onto the tier. It was still burning out there when his cell door opened. He was transferring from the cell block to the back ward in the hospital. That was where the AIDS patients went. As he left, he looked down at the cigarette on the tier and grinned. He had been aiming at one of the bars.

And so it was as told to me, by a convict in the Attica Correctional Facility.

Dan Pens

Skin Blind

I did not know what I was missing. That's what struck me the hardest. I had had *no idea* that there was a gigantic hole in my life. Not until it was again partially refilled.

Then the yawning emptiness of that hole revealed itself to me. And I was struck dumb.

This happened in 1987. I had been imprisoned for six years. During those half dozen years, I had come to appreciate the loss of my freedom. So many things I missed: wet sand between my toes along an ocean shore, the cool shade of tall elms on a crackly warm summer day, the cuddly joy found only in a bundle of floppy-eared puppies. These and many other things I dreamed of. But there was one thing I missed and did not even know it.

A hug.

Over a three-day period in 1987, I attended an "Alternatives to Violence" conflict resolution workshop at the Washington State Reformatory. The workshop was facilitated by several volunteers from the community. On the third and final day of the workshop, after an extended weekend of growing, sharing, and learning, it was time to say goodbye. One of the volunteers approached me to say how much she had appreciated my participation. I smiled; said, "Thanks"; and extended my hand. I thought she would shake it. Instead, she took hold of my fingers and pulled me toward her, wrapped her arms around me, and engulfed me in what has to be the second most memorable hug of my life.

It felt like warm, honeylike energy was being poured into the dusty, dry, empty tank of my soul.

There was nothing sexual about these feelings and certainly nothing sexual about the hug. But my skin sang. I felt more alive—more human—than I had for years. I think I cried. With joy. And then with sadness as the realization of the yawning emptiness that had been strip-mined out of my psyche by six years of prison life descended upon me.

There is no touching allowed in prison.

It is one of the few rules that The Man does not need to enforce with disciplinary tickets or loss of good time. To be sure, at least in this prison, there are "no-touching" rules on the books. (I kid you not.) But there is no need for such rules. The no-touching taboo is a self-reinforcing phenomenon in an all-male prison.

For six years I had lived in very close proximity with a thousand men. Without touching. Oh, there was the occasional accidental bump or brush of shoulders in a crowded breezeway. You can be certain, though, that these chance encounters were swiftly followed by an "Excuse me." To fail to acknowledge quickly that the touch was unintentional and offer an apology was to plant the seed of resentment at the very least—and possibly to trigger an immediate eruption of violence.

These brushes, and maybe a few bumps on the basketball court, were the only experience of human touch that I had had in six long years.

For two of those years, I had lived in a nine-foot-by-six-foot cage with another man. Fifty-four square feet. There was no room for both men to move about the cell at the same time. If one was up and moving, the other had to be tucked away on a bunk.

It is possible to live in closer proximity to another human than (unless you have been in prison) you can possibly imagine and yet not touch.

These thoughts tumbled in my head for days after that hug. I wondered whether I had been deprived of touch on the streets. Maybe I had. But I had never consciously missed it. Whatever sensitivity I may have had to such things was numbed through daily drug and alcohol use.

I had quit the drugs and alcohol in prison. I was clean and clear of mind when that hug knocked my life off balance. And so, for the first time ever, I understood something that I have not forgotten since: Touch is life. It is vitality. It is the music of the skin. It is the color that a blind man cannot see. To be deprived of touch can wreak devastation upon the psyche. To touch is to be human. To live without touch is to wander alone in a wasteland.

In 1989 I met my wife-to-be. She, too, was a community volunteer who had come to the prison to share our world. We met. We talked. We were each surprised when we discovered a mutual attraction. And I was scared. Almost pushed her away. I had time to do. I did not need to bring her into my life. Not this life.

But I called myself on that, recognizing my fear for what it was, and took a risk. I wrote her an eight-page letter. I spelled out everything to her. The crimes I had been convicted of and the many more that I had not. I wanted her to know the truth, to base our relationship—if there was to be such a thing—on honesty and openness. I mailed the letter to her. And waited. For three weeks. Nothing. No reply.

Then I saw her again at the monthly meeting, which we both attended. And when the meeting was over, I walked up to her. My heart was in my throat. Did she think I was a beast? Would she judge me harshly? Was I forever condemned by my past?

"Did you get my letter?" I feebly asked.

I do not remember ever feeling more vulnerable, waiting for her reply. But she said nothing.

Instead, she pulled me toward her and enveloped me in what—hands down—has to be the most memorable hug of my life. Not a word slipped through her lips. Yet that hug was all the reply I needed. I was loved! Accepted! Appreciated!

About a year later, Heather and I were married in the prison chapel. She drives up to the prison two or three days a week for a visit. And during each visit, we hold hands. We both talk. Words. But beneath the words, our hands communicate a deeper language.

Our skin sings the song of life, of human touch. And our souls are filled with that honey-warm energy of humanity.

I live in a two-man cell with a man I care about. He is the best "cellie" I have ever had. A good man and a good friend. He has been imprisoned for twelve years. And he is not married. He has few visits.

I asked him about touch several weeks ago, whether he misses it. "Yes," he said without hesitation, "and I'm a touchy-type of person, too."

I have not forgotten how starved I was for touch after six years. His hunger must be double that. Since our conversation, I have considered how I could offer some touch to him. A back rub? A hug every now and again?

But the prison wraps itself around me and screams, "NO WAY, DUDE!" What if somebody saw us? What would they think? What if he thought I was crazy to suggest such a thing? Would he feel threatened? Homophobic?

And so I do nothing. We go on living together in this tiny cage. And never do we touch. Not even accidentally.

And that, my friend . . . *that* is prison.

Stephen Wayne Anderson

Once More I Dream

Last night I dreamt of her again,
a dream which comes every few days;
sometimes in the night she appears
with her strange and haunting ways.
Who she is I do not know,
this lady dressed in mystic lace,
a woman who smiles at me
as I reach out to touch her face.

For a moment she stands with me
or we sit together side by side;
what we say I do not recall,
but when she left I know we cried.

It seems to be but a dream,
this image of a woman so dear;
yet each dawn when I awake
my heart feels her spirit near.

Surely she is not real at all,
just a phantom of my prose,
a memory of my mind somewhere
where only the dreamer goes.

Part V

Men's Health in Prison

Under the banner of the women's health movement, feminists investigated gender bias in the diagnosis and treatment of women, sex discrimination in the health care professions, and key women's health issues. This early work on gender and health, however, focused almost exclusively on women's health needs and ignored those of men. Although participants in the 1980s U.S. men's health movement had some awareness of men's health issues, the field of "men's health studies," which consciously integrated critical feminist theory and research, did not emerge until the mid-1990s (Sabo and Gordon, 1995).

Today men's health researchers study ways in which various constructions of masculinity put boys and men at risk for illness and early mortality (Courtenay, 2000). They address key men's health issues, including prostate cancer, testicular cancer, coronary heart disease, occupational hazards, suicide, and accidents. They also identify groups of males for whom aspects of work, lifestyle, economic circumstances, or cultural practices are associated with elevated risk for illness—for example, low-income men, adolescents, the unemployed, athletes, those who are HIV positive, and gay and bisexual men. The writings in this section deal with the physical and mental health status and needs of prisoners, who are among the most marginalized men in North America.

Men's health advocates also preach prevention (Sabo, 2000). Mainstream magazines that focus on men's health and fitness have become popular media staples. Recent public health initiatives encourage men to exercise regularly, forego fatty foods, check their blood pressure, stop smoking, and have regular prostate examinations. However, prisoners have fallen through the cracks of these public health initiatives, and too often their needs lie buried under corrections policies geared to punish at the expense of promoting preventive health.

References

Courtney, Will H. 2000. "Constructions of Masculinity and Their Influence on Men's Well-being: A Theory of Gender and Health." *Social Science and Medicine* 50 (2): 1385–1401.

Sabo, Don. 2000. "Masculinities and Men's Health: Moving Toward Post-Superman Era Prevention." Pp. 285–98 in *Men's Lives,* 5th ed. Ed. M. S. Kimmel and M. A. Messner. Boston: Allyn and Bacon.

Sabo, Don, and David F. Gordon, eds. 1995. *Men's Health and Illness: Gender, Power and the Body.* Thousand Oaks, Calif.: Sage.

Will H. Courtenay and Don Sabo

Preventive Health Strategies
for Men in Prison

This chapter explores the health risks of men in prison and identifies preventive strategies that prisoners can use to improve their health. There is compelling evidence that practicing preventive behaviors favorably influences health and longevity in the larger population (Ratner et al., 1994; U.S. Preventive Services Task Force, 1996). Little is known, however, about its effects among men in prison. Furthermore, recent studies show that preventive health behavior is a gendered practice. Women are more likely than men to adopt health-promoting beliefs, behaviors, and lifestyles (Courtenay, in press; Kandrack, Grant, and Segall, 1991; Lonnquist, Weiss, and Larsen, 1992; Ratner et al., 1994; Rossi, 1992; Walker et al., 1988). Although the underlying assumption in much of the medical literature is that what it means to be a man has no bearing on men's health, emerging theories and research are examining and identifying health risks associated with masculinity and the daily practice of being a man (Courtenay, 1998a, 1998b, 2000a; Sabo and Gordon, 1995). The gendered aspects of health among prisoners have just begun to be investigated (Polych and Sabo, 1995; Sabo and London, 1992).

Although there is a need to address prevention in prisons (Weisbuch, 1991), applying a preventive health model within the prison context is a complex matter. There is significant variation not only in prison conditions (which range from maximum-security institutions to "so-called country clubs") but also among prisoners (in such areas as personality, health beliefs, intelligence, and educational background). Moreover, the concepts of *health promotion* and *preventive health* often contradict the institutional mandate of prisons to surveil and to punish their inhabitants. The overall philosophy and day-to-day operations of many prisons revolve around hurting prisoners, not coddling them. Preventive health proponents urge individuals to take personal responsibility for making decisions and developing habits that lower their risk of disease. However, prisons are total institutions that limit personal autonomy, regiment behavior, and discourage individual initiative. Simply put, prisons are generally not about wellness, and health care delivery in prisons is designed primarily to treat illness after—not before—it occurs.

The institutional limits that prison imposes on men's health are further compounded by external factors (Marquart et al., 1996). A majority of prisoners come from poor and working-class communities, where educational opportunities and high-quality health care are usually not readily available and where people are apt to be more concerned with day-to-day survival than with planning a healthy future. Furthermore, the proportion of young men in the prison population has grown in recent years, and these younger men are less likely to be emotionally or educationally prepared to practice preventive health behaviors or to be responsible for their own health.

The observations and conclusions presented in this chapter grew out of a college-level seminar in sociology of health and medicine conducted at a northeastern maximum-security prison. The twenty-two students/prisoners agreed to work collectively with the instructor (Don Sabo) to study the concept of health risk, to identify the health risks of prisoners, to articulate realistic prevention strategies for prisoners, and to explore the influence of masculinity on health. This endeavor was facilitated by the self-administered health-risk assessment for men developed by Will H. Courtenay (1996). The assessment tool consists of fifty-four items that assess ten areas of risk, such as diet, drug use, safety, sexual health, social support, and attitudes about manhood. Each student completed the assessment and determined his level of risk in each category and his overall level of risk. In order to summarize the students' health-related experiences, the authors then systematically analyzed term papers in which each student discussed his individual health history, identified health risks that he faced in prison, and specified preventive strategies that he found effective.

This study draws upon standpoint epistemology, which holds that disadvantaged and less-powerful members of a society have unique and useful knowledge to offer others (Nielsen, 1990). It is exploratory and speculative. The insights and interpretations that are presented were developed from the perceptions and voices of the students who participated in the seminar. The seminar participants, as a group, were probably unrepresentative of the larger prison population. They were racially and ethnically diverse, and their social and educational backgrounds were varied. About two-thirds came from impoverished inner-city or rural backgrounds, and about one-third grew up in working- or middle-class communities. Although two men held college degrees, for the rest of the group, the prison college program was the first higher education they had received.

Men's Health Risks in Prison

The students identified many factors that are commonly known to increase the health risks of prisoners and nonprisoners alike, including the use of tobacco, drugs, and alcohol; sexual health risks; being overweight; biologic influences and genetic predispositions; and physical inactivity. The student-identified health risks that are relevant to the prison context are examined here in detail.

Violence

Violence was the most frequently cited health risk. Stab wounds and cuts inflicted by fellow inmates and beatings inflicted by guards were described as common occurrences. Risk factors for violence among prisoners include gambling, involvement in the drug trade, stealing, reneging on debts, "snitching," and "not showing respect." Prisoners use razors, can tops, Plexiglas, and bedsprings to "slash," "rip," "stab," and "touch" fellow inmates. Two students implicated harassment by guards as risk factors for violence among prisoners and suggested that inmates "displace their anger [at the guards] toward one another."

Environment

The students expressed concern about high levels of noise; secondhand smoke; inadequate fire safety precautions; and a general lack of sanitary conditions, especially with respect to food safety. They specified unsterilized utensils, poor hygiene among food handlers, and birds and bats in food areas. The environmental risks most often cited, however, were overcrowding and close quarters. These factors, students argued, increased the risk of infectious and communicable diseases, including HIV and AIDS, tuberculosis, hepatitis, colds, and flu, illnesses that constituted one of their primary health concerns. Prisoners are, in fact, among those at highest risk for tuberculosis, hepatitis, and HIV (CDC, 1992; Hammett et al., 1994; MacIntyre et al., 1997—see also the essay entitled "Sentence—Death by Lethal Infection: IV-Drug Use and Infectious Disease Transmission in North American Prisons" in this volume).

Health Care

Half of the students considered the prison health care system itself to be a risk factor, citing "inadequate," "substandard," inconsistent, and noncomprehensive care. They described delays in treatment, infrequency of exams, inadequate staffing, and inferior medications. They spoke of the withholding of treatment and denial of prescribed medication as forms of punishment. They also cited inadequate access to care, such as the inability to receive emergency treatment at night. The students leveled similar criticisms against prison dental care. They also reported that their distrust of prison medical care prevented some prisoners from seeking help or sustaining treatment. However, a Federal Bureau of Prisons study contradicts these claims. According to this study, 89 percent of inmates experienced no change in their overall health status during incarceration, 4 percent improved, and 7 percent deteriorated (Wallace et al., 1991).

Health Knowledge

Many students identified their own limited health knowledge and lack of health information among inmates as key risk factors. A study of the health knowledge of prisoners in a maximum-security prison in Washington State found that most were not aware of the causes of common health problems or ways to prevent them (Kruzich et al., 1984). Men in prison are not alone in their lack of knowledge about health matters. A consistent finding among civilian populations is that men in the United States are far less knowledgeable than women about health in general (Courtenay, 1998a, b) and about risk factors for specific diseases, such as heart disease (Ford and Jones, 1991), cancer (Bostick et al., 1993; Polednak, 1990), and sexually transmitted diseases (STDs) (EDK Associates, 1995).

Diet and Nutrition

Most students cited inadequate diet and poor nutrition as potential health risks. Specific risks included limited nutritional choices, poor food quality, and improper preparation—such as overcooking vegetables and meats. Students also criticized the diet for offering inadequate portions in general and insufficient amounts of fresh fruits and vegetables in particular; for comprising foods that are high in cholesterol and sodium, and for including spoiled or "deliberately tampered with" foods. They cited the lack of money to purchase healthy dietary supplements through the commissary as a risk as well.

Mental Health

Some students considered psychological problems, such as chronic stress and depression, to be a daily health risk. One indirect index of depression that substantiates this claim is the rate of suicide among prisoners, which is nearly twice that of the general population (Salive, Smith, and Brewer, 1989). According to the students, depression undermines prisoners' ability to practice preventive care. Sources of stress and depression that they cited included the lack of close contact or communication with family and friends, tension and conflict with guards, and violence.

Prison Culture

Several students identified negative health impacts of the prison culture. They considered the general lack of social support in prison, the prevalence of "type A" coronary-prone behavior, and the demonstration of aggressive forms of masculinity to be health risks. For example, they described displaying scars—especially facial scars from fighting or attacks—as "almost stylish," particularly among young prisoners who have grown up in urban gang subcultures. Many students lamented the lack of social support from family, society, or fellow inmates. As one man put it, "Here in prison I have yet to recognize anyone whom I can go to for real support. Sure I have a few fellow inmates I can depend on for help, but there is a limit to how much. Most inmates have their own problems and they surely are not too interested in helping others. And . . . the employees here, from what I've observed and experienced, have no concern for inmates' well-being."

Preventive Health Strategies for Prisoners

The assignment to identify preventive health strategies for men in prison challenged the students. Some initially reacted negatively to the health risk assessment, complaining that it was designed primarily for "men on the street." Many of the lifestyle factors that were covered, they argued, simply did not pertain to prisoners. Some scoffed at dietary items such as "eating fresh fruits and vegetables," which they described as scarce in prison. They criticized items that pertained to seeking social support and help for failing to recognize that self-disclosure and socializing with others in prison can be both impractical and dangerous. Some laughed at the items assessing safer sex practices, because it had been years since they were sexually active with women.

Other prisoners in the seminar eventually rebutted these initial claims. They spelled out and defended counterarguments: Even if the prison diet was generally unhealthy, there were healthier options on the menu, and they could purchase fresh fruit from the commissary in lieu of potato chips; it was possible to make friends in prison and to be more diligent at maintaining family ties; some inmates have sex with women through the visitation programs, and some have sex with other inmates. The consensus conclusion was that, even though prison conditions create unique obstacles to well-being, preventive health choices can still be made. Students also recognized that, despite some marked differences, there are similarities between the health options of prisoners and those of men on the street. Both, for example, can choose to refrain from using tobacco, alcohol, and drugs. A summary of the preventive health strategies that students later identified in their papers follows.

Practice Self-Care

Students recommended that prisoners practice self-care and take personal responsibility for their health. However, they viewed this largely as a way to compensate for the perceived inadequacies of prison health care. This perspective is reflected in comments such as these:

> Prisoners are given the bare minimum when it comes to adequate health care. Basically the only real care is self-care.

> In here, it's up to me to take responsibility for my own state of health and expedite an organized plan of self-maintenance.

> Prevention is difficult but is of paramount importance because cures are a rarity with the limited efforts put forth by the Department of Corrections.

The fact that these students, as well as other inmates, take personal responsibility for health matters out of necessity does not diminish the value of the practice. Research among civilians indicates that an individual's active involvement with health care is associated with a variety of positive outcomes (Deber, 1994; Meichenbaum and Turk, 1987; O'Brien, Petrie, and Raeburn, 1992). However, it is unlikely that most men in prison are provided with the information, basic skills training, and institutional support that make self-care feasible.

Reduce Violence

The students identified a variety of ways to address anger and to reduce violence. Many felt that individual inmates should take responsibility for their own safety rather than rely on the prison system for protection. Strategies included being vigilant to potential violence, "resisting harmful influences," and avoiding dangerous activities—such as gambling and drug use—that could instigate aggressive reprisals. Students also recommended meditation and breathing exercises as techniques for reducing frustration. One student suggested that prisoners "confront the danger they pose to each other" and recognize that safety from violence is a "reciprocal right" that is granted to those who give it to others. Students recommended a variety of interpersonal techniques that were consistent with this notion, including "practicing good social habits," being "prudent" in developing relationships, keeping anger to oneself, being "polite to everyone even [those who] are abrasive," and refraining from responding to guards or prisoners who act offensively or try to instigate conflict. They also suggested participation in prison programs to reduce violence and foster positive feelings. In fact, one prison study, supporting this notion, found that anger management training resulted in a reduction of inmates' vengeful and hostile emotions and actions (Holbrook, 1997).

Lower Environmental Risk Exposure

Students suggested a variety of strategies for lowering the risk of contracting communicable and infectious diseases. Strategies included washing hands with soap before eating or handling food and encouraging others to do so; refraining from sharing eating utensils, including refraining from drinking out of another person's cup; greeting others by touching closed fists, rather than by shaking hands; resolving not to get tattooed; keeping windows open and fans operating for ventilation; and spending time outdoors when weather and routine permit. One student suggested staying away from smokers to lower the exposure to secondhand smoke.

Reduce Sexual Risks

The students put forth several strategies for reducing sexual risks in prison. Most recommended complete abstinence from sexual contact with other prisoners. Additional suggestions included resolving to have only protected sex, promoting safer sex, and participating in prison HIV- and AIDS-education programs. One man cautioned against participation in the conjugal visitation program in order to avoid risks associated with "unfaithful wives." Finally, students proposed masturbation as a safe and viable sexual outlet for prisoners.

Increase Health Knowledge

Students frequently cited education as a means of reducing risks and improving health. One student said that prisoners have "a willingness to gain good knowledge and information about how to maintain one's health" and added that, in so doing, they "avoid the unnecessary worry and stress that come with rumor, myth and falsehood." Students suggested that prisoners need to learn more about disease as well as about their family health history in order to identify potential health risks. This "learn more" strategy appears warranted in light of research findings that health knowledge is positively associated with seeking care for cancer symptoms (Love, 1991), practicing safe sex (EDK Associates, 1995), and avoiding risky behaviors associated with the transmission of AIDS (Carmel, 1990). According to one student, "Education has played a major role in my adopting these new life habits." Another student said, "As I become more knowledgeable about my health and the various factors that affect it, I am taking steps to improve my overall physical, mental, emotional, and spiritual condition."

Improve Diet and Nutrition

Most students described strategies for improving diet and nutrition. A primary goal was to be selective at meals whenever possible and to choose foods that are low in saturated fat and high in fiber, protein, and complex carbohydrates. Additional recommendations included supplementing the prison diet with fresh fruits and vegetables; requesting healthy foods from home; purchasing healthy foods and vitamin supplements from the commissary; consuming protein drinks; limiting consumption of "junk food," salt, and processed sugars; and drinking eight to ten cups of water each day.

Reduce Stress and Emotional Conflict

Some students recommended reducing stress through mental, physical, and breathing exercises. One man described a strategy that consisted of reading magazines and books. Others suggested channeling stress through the use of humor and activities that increase positive feelings. Some recommended involvement in enjoyable activities—such as participating in sports, reading, watching television, and listening to the radio—as a means of decreasing boredom. Some students cited religion, spiritual practice, and meditation as strategies for reducing stress and improving health. One prisoner described the benefits that his own experience with spiritual practice offered: "Active involvement in church activities . . . [has] led to a more stable emotional state, which in turn has led me to a healthier physical state."

Increase Social Support

Several students suggested that prisoners could improve their health by increasing their social support. Specific strategies for creating stronger social bonds included forming support groups, getting married, becoming involved in religious organizations, maintaining family ties, and attending school. These recommendations are well advised in the context of research that indicates that men generally have much smaller social networks than women do (Broadhead et al., 1983; Burda, Vaux, and Schill, 1984; Kandrack, Grant, and Segall, 1991; Verbrugge, 1985) and that, especially for men, the lack of social relationships can be a risk factor for mortality (Kandrack, Grant, and Segall, 1991; Seeman et al., 1987; Shye et al., 1995; Umberson, 1992). We know of no research that examines the relationship between social support and health or health behavior among prisoners, although some of the students' remarks suggest that there is such an association. "I am quite able to pull myself out of the blues using my immediate family as support and one or two close associations with fellow inmates," one man said. "Social support from fellow inmates . . . allows you to cope with daily strains," another student remarked.

Adopt Healthy Attitudes and Beliefs

Many men utilize their cognitive skills to approach health matters intellectually (Courtenay, 1998c). Incarceration fosters self-reflection, and men in prison spend much of their time thinking. It is not surprising, then, that half of the men identified cognitions that would favorably influence their health. One student recommended being "mindful" of personal health, making healthy decisions, and remaining "consciously aware of the environment and its negative aspects at all times." Others pointed out the importance of "thinking through" the consequences of one's behavior before taking action. Some discussed strategies for managing cognitions, such as "restructuring" the meaning of imprisonment to reduce the effects of its emphasis on deprivation. In one man's words, "Mental thoughts ... and how I cope with them, is a prerequisite for achieving and maintaining proper physical and mental health."

Several students emphasized the importance of clinging to hope and thoughts about life after release from prison. These cognitions may help foster positive health behaviors in some prisoners. As one man stated, "The strong desire to not only survive my prison term, but to also live my remaining years in a good state of health, drove me to reevaluate my health and examine what I could do to reduce my health risks." Some studies of civilian populations indicate that future-oriented people are more likely than present-oriented people to adopt positive health behaviors (Mahon and Yarcheski, 1994; Mahon, Yarcheski, and Yarcheski, 1997), to engage in safer sex practices (Rothspan and Read, 1996), and to avoid intravenous-drug use (Alvos, Gregson, and Ross, 1993). Some researchers have also associated future orientation with reduced risk for depression and suicide among nonprisoners (Breier-Williford and Bramlett, 1995). We know of no similar research among prisoners, but students' comments suggest that their health behaviors are linked to a future-time perspective. "It is in my best interest to guard against sickness and disease so that when I am released I will not be debilitated physically and will thus be able to enjoy my remaining years in a productive and fulfilling manner," one student said. Another commented, "If I had no hope for the future, why bother to watch what I eat? Why not extract all the pleasure I possibly could by eating all the junk food I desire?"

Prison Masculinities and Preventive Health

Women and men use health-related beliefs and behaviors as resources in demonstrating femininity and masculinity. In many North American cultural settings, positive health beliefs and behaviors are constructed as forms of idealized femininity (Courtenay, 2000a). So when a man brags, "I haven't been to a doctor in years," he is simultaneously describing a health practice and situating himself in a masculine arena. Men can also use unhealthy or risky behaviors to negotiate their status in relationship to women and other men. A man who adopts a "tough guy," "I don't care if I work myself to death" persona—or who dismisses pain or symptoms as "sissy stuff"—may be positioning himself within the hierarchy of men and distancing himself from both "feminine" characteristics and women. Therefore, the constructions of masculinity and some health behaviors can be linked to relationships of power as well as to identity construction (Courtenay, 2000b; Pyke, 1996; Kaufman, 1994; Sabo, 1995). In this way, the social actions that individuals demonstrate when they enact gender and health simultaneously sustain and reproduce broader structures of power and inequality.

Prison Masculinities and Health Behaviors

Upon entering a maximum-security prison, a man is stripped of much of his identity. Subsequently, as one student explained, he "constructs an identity that is consistent with his new hardcore environment." The institutional structures of prison life dramatically restrict the variety of resources and social actions available to men to "do" gender (West and Zimmerman, 1987). As C. Newton points out, "The prisoner's masculinity is in fact besieged from every side: through loss of autonomy and independence, enforced submission to authority, lack of access to material goods, all of which are central to his status as a 'man'" (1994:197).

The narrowing of prisoners' options for constructing masculinity can foster the adoption of hegemonic forms of masculinity that pervade prison cultures—that is, the acceptance of hierarchy, toughness and stoicism, physical dominance, aggressiveness, heterosexism, and homophobia. The forms of hegemonic masculinity that some prisoners adopt differ from the forms of masculinity they practiced on the outside as loving fathers, supportive spouses, or workers. For other prisoners, however, the pursuit of hegemonic masculinity is consistent with their former identities as gangsters, abusive husbands, street fighters, or con men. Newton has concluded that prisoners generally adopt "a tough, hypermasculine ideal, an abhorrence of femininity and aggressive homophobia" that are more extreme than the hypermasculinity adopted by subordinated men outside of prison (1994:198).

We speculate that pursuit of hegemonic masculinity undermines the health of many men in prison. As one student put it, inmates learn to adopt prison values that "actually go against the message of preventive health." Many codes of "manly" conduct require stoic denial of pain, physical dominance, and personal risk. One middle-aged student said, "When you got stabbed you usually bandaged yourself up and dealt with the guy when you saw him. To go to the doctor would appear that you are soft." Others observed that "'real' prisoners are tough, stand-up guys," or that "prisoners conceive of themselves as tough, fearless, and hard and they have a 'don't take any shit' attitude and are always ready to prove their 'manliness.'" Violence and physical dominance are central to the structuring and sustaining of hierarchical relationships in prison (Sim, 1994), as the comments of one student illustrate:

> I have been shot and stabbed. Each time I wore bandages like a badge of honor. . . . Each situation made me feel a little . . . tougher than the next guy. . . . Being that I had survived, these things made me feel bigger because I could imagine that the average person couldn't go through a shoot out or a knife fight, survive and get right back into the action like it was nothing. The perception that I had constructed in my mind was that most people were discouraged after almost facing death, but the really bad ones could look death in the eye with little or no compunction.

For some men, incarceration itself was a means of negotiating masculinity and status in the hierarchy of men. As one student explained, "Jail was seen as a rite of passage for young Black boys into manhood. If we could survive prison . . . then we would have greater standing among our peers and be harder and tougher men."

Like the failure to engage in physically risky behavior, the adoption of health-promoting behavior can undermine a man's ranking among prisoners and relegate him to a subordinated status. As one student put it, "If you told the officer that you had been stabbed, then you were a punk and possibly a snitch, so you had to handle it." Students described prisoners as openly criticizing fellow inmates who "complained too much" about sickness or pain. Excessive complaining was seen as a sign of personal inadequacy or "softness." Fellow inmates considered some prisoners who made frequent visits to the health clinic to be malingerers, or they suspected them of hustling medications in order to "handle their bid." Students' comments suggested that prison personnel and health care providers held similar attitudes.

At least one-third of the students debunked "macho" definitions of manhood as naive and dangerous. Some reminisced about how, as boys and younger men, they had considered themselves to be "invincible," or "invulnerable to serious injury," or "immune to physical harm." Now older and wiser, they saw that these "Superman" images were unrealistic. As the semester progressed, they discussed their personal experiences with aches and pains, surgery, prostate problems, hypertension, impotence, and other illnesses as a means of conveying their dawning awareness of their vulnerability to aging, illness, and death. These classroom discussions were sometimes startlingly frank and compassionate, and to some extent they expressed changes in the ways the men were perceiving their bodies, their health options, and their identities of manhood.

It is relevant that the students could critically assess the links between masculinity and their health risks. A growing body of research indicates that men who adopt traditional beliefs about manhood have greater health risks than men who hold less traditional beliefs (Courtenay, 1998a; Eisler, 1995; Eisler and Blalock, 1991; Good and Mintz, 1990; Pleck, Sonenstein, and Ku, 1994). Men who rigidly adhere to traditional notions of masculinity have more anxiety and poorer health habits than their less traditionally minded peers (Eisler, Skidmore, and Ward, 1988), and they have greater cardiovascular reactivity in stressful situations (Lash, Eisler, and Schulman, 1990). Men who adopt traditional beliefs about manhood also experience higher levels of depression and greater vulnerability to psychological stress and maladaptive coping patterns (Eisler and Blalock, 1991; Good and Mintz, 1990; Sharpe and Heppner, 1991; Good, Dell, and Mintz, 1989; Oliver and Toner, 1990).

Finally, although the topic of homosexuality came up during the seminar, detailed discussions about risks such as rape and same-gender sex did not occur. We can only speculate about the experiences and health beliefs of men who have sex with men in prison, gay and bisexual prisoners, and those men who have been "enslaved" through prison rape. Their perceptions of and approaches to both health risk and prevention are no doubt very different from those of other prisoners.

Obstacles to Preventive Health in Prison

Official and public indifference to prisoners' health, combined with harsh conditions and long sentences, makes many prisons desolate places in which to live and work—and especially difficult places to practice preventive health. We have identified four specific obstacles that prisoners face in their attempts to take personal responsibility for their health and to adopt preventive health behaviors.

First, they must overcome the sense of powerlessness and the lack of self-efficacy that many prisoners experience. Among civilians, the perceived lack of control over one's life and health has been associated with risk-taking behaviors and poor preventive health practices (Courtenay, 1998a). Among prisoners, there are a number of factors that undermine a sense of control and self-efficacy. Many prisoners come from low-income and underclass backgrounds, where fatalism is often a way of life. Poverty and harsh, unhealthy social conditions breed this fatalism and foster the belief that much of what happens in life is beyond an individual's control. In a wealthy economy and status-driven class system, low-income people do not exert as much control over their lives as middle-class or professional people do. For many of the low-income men who make up the majority of the prison population, fatalism is, in fact, realism.

Institutionalized powerlessness and stigmatization may further undermine prisoners' self-efficacy in practicing preventive health strategies. Goffman (1961) describes the prison as a "total institution" in which individuals are systematically stripped of autonomy and efficacy by routinization, surveillance mechanisms, and depersonalization. The inculcation of obedience, subservience, and conformity is unlikely to foster self-efficacy among prisoners. Indeed, many of the students were reluctant to recognize that they actually had an investment in, or a responsibility for, their own health. After being institutionalized, prisoners often construct identities as victims of the economy or the criminal justice system. Consequently, they internalize both the stigma and the powerlessness associated with prisoner status. A prisoner's identity as victim—and his very real powerlessness in relationship to guards, the prison bureaucracy, and the health care system—do not promote the motivations and ambitions necessary for practicing preventive health.

Second, if men in prison are to adopt preventive health measures, they must embrace social practices and self-care strategies that have been in some ways culturally constructed as "feminine" (Courtenay, 2000a). Because prison life tends to promote hegemonic masculinity and devalue forms of femininity that are associated with self-care, a prisoner's pursuit of preventive health practices and philosophies may present personal and social contradictions. Furthermore, even if prisoners are willing to risk undermining their demonstrations of hegemonic masculinity, they may be unfamiliar with specific self-care practices. Whereas girls often learn self-care during adolescence, through regular physical and reproductive health examinations, boys are not typically taught this skill (Courtenay, 2000b). For most prisoners, generally their wives, girlfriends, or mothers monitored their health and scheduled any medical appointments that they had. Prisoners who want to take greater responsibility for their health will need not only to cross gendered boundaries but also to learn new skills. As one student pointed out, "It is up to the inmate to take initiative and take advantage of available resources and to keep track of annual exams or check-ups."

Third, social support represents something of a health paradox for prisoners. One strategy for reducing health risks in prison that a few students suggested was to "stay to yourself." This recommendation contradicts the decades of research among civilians cited previously, which conclusively links social relationships with health and longevity. Other students, however, described the importance of social support and the benefits that they gained from group, gang, or organizational affiliations. The potential health rewards of these affiliations are evident in the remarks of one student who described his group's goals: "To enhance Latino pride; a group bent on self-improvement; the main goal was to give its members a direction to change the negative traits that got us in prison and to become better and productive members of society; to be a positive role model for the younger generation to look up to." However, this student also acknowledged the potential risks associated with this affiliation, noting that it could lead to involuntary participation in gang violence: "The problem of one member is the problem of all the members. I don't go around looking for trouble, but many of my so-called brothers do. . . . As it stands, I am at a very large risk of losing my life because of someone else's bad judgment."

Social support is further complicated and made contradictory as a health strategy by what inmates learn through their social relationships in prison. One student described the influence of these associations on his construction of masculinity: "As a result of my incarceration, . . . I've accepted [many of my peers] as role models, I've developed the same masculine identity traits in myself, and they represented a major [unhealthy] influence in my life and my health." How prisoners can overcome these particular obstacles in negotiating gender and preventive health remained unclear to students.

And finally, for some men, incarceration itself can represent a health paradox. Several students described prison as a protective and healthy environment compared to their lives on the outside:

> I'm almost certain that had I not been arrested all the times I ended up in prison, I would have been dead a long time ago from a drug overdose, a deadly STD such as AIDS, or someone preventing me from stealing their property could have killed me.

> In prison I got healthier than I had been in years. I ate regularly three meals that are not nearly as high in fat, calories, and cholesterol as the fast foods I lived on.

Indeed, some men have greater access to health care in prison than they have in their communities outside of prison. The previously cited study of Federal Bureau of Prisons inmates found that the health of some inmates actually improved during their incarceration and that, for most inmates, health at least does not worsen (Wallace et al, 1991). This raises the question of whether men who are released from prison need transitional, supportive services for living healthy lifestyles.

Conclusion

Men in prison are among the populations at highest risk for disease, injury, and death (see the chapter entitled "Sentence—Death by Lethal Infection: IV-Drug Use and Infectious Disease Transmission in North American Prisons" in this volume). Despite these high risks, little is understood about their health. The preventive health practices of prisoners have never before been examined. By examining preventive health from the perspectives of the twenty-two prisoners/students in this college-level sociology of health seminar, we were able to identify risks and preventive practices that are particular to men within the prison context. More important, when given the opportunity to explore their own health concerns, the students produced insights and preventive agendas that are unique to men in prison.

The seminar provided a structure that enabled the students/prisoners to take the first steps toward improving their health. They developed a working understanding of how basic preventive measures can lower their risk for illness and death. They learned that health is not something that just happens to men's bodies; rather, it is something that men can often control and influence. Over the course of the semester, they also came to view health not simply as the absence of disease but more holistically, as a state of being intimately related to emotions, attitudes, personal relationships, institutional conditions, and changing social and historical patterns.

The students identified seven general areas of risk. They recommended ways for prisoners to address these risks, offering very specific strategies for practicing self-care, reducing violence and environmental or sexual risks, increasing health knowledge, improving diet and nutrition, reducing emotional problems, increasing social support, and adopting healthier attitudes and beliefs. These strategies are in many cases supported by research that demonstrates their effectiveness among civilian populations. Future research is needed to substantiate the risks identified by these prisoners and to assess the effectiveness of the recommended strategies.

Although we have briefly addressed the influence of masculinity on men's health, we conclude by emphasizing the complexity of its influence on the health of prisoners in particular. Negotiating masculinity presents prisoners with a unique health paradox. Although the students acknowledged that endorsing hegemonic masculinity increased their risks, they also suggested that the failure to enact a degree of manliness in the prison hierarchy would invite trouble. Although most agreed that belligerent or confrontational behavior was dangerous, they were also willing to resort to aggression "if necessary." The students/prisoners thus faced a challenge: They must renegotiate masculinity in ways that not only protected their health but also reinforced some of the exploitive and violence-prone power structures in the prison hierarchy. Thus, they continually grappled with tensions and contradictions between the definitions of manliness that pervaded the institution itself and their personal feelings and thoughts as men. Additional research is needed to better understand how prison masculinities influence the health risks of prisoners.

Although we have focused on prisoners' personal health practices, it is important to reiterate that structural influences can either facilitate those practices or inhibit them. To the extent to which the prison system erodes men's ability to embrace preventive health values and practices, their collective prognosis remains poor. The continuing institutional failure to give millions of U.S. prisoners the educational tools and support they need to practice preventive health will only increase the future burden on the public health system.

References

Alvos, L., R. A. Gregson, and M. W. Ross. 1993. "Future Time Perspective in Current and Previous Injecting Drug Users." *Drug and Alcohol Dependence* 31 (2): 193–97.

Bostick, R. M., J. M. Sprafka, B. A. Virnig, and J. D. Potter. 1993. "Knowledge, Attitudes, and Personal Practices Regarding Prevention and Early Detection of Cancer." *Preventive Medicine* 22 (1): 65–85.

Breier-Williford, S., and R. K. Bramlett. 1995. "Time Perspective of Substance Abuse Patients: Comparison of the Scales in Stanford Perspective Inventory, Beck Depression Inventory, and Beck Hopelessness Scale." *Psychological Reports* 77 (3): 899–905.

Broadhead, W. E., B. H. Kaplan, S. A. James, E. H. Wagner, V. J. Schoenbach, R. Grimson, S. Heyden, G. Tibblin, and S. H. Gehlbach. 1983. "The Epidemiologic Evidence for a Relationship between Social Support and Health." *American Journal of Epidemiology* 117 (5): 521–37.

Burda, P.C., A. C. Vaux, and T. Schill. 1984. "Social Support Resources: Variation across Sex and Sex Role." *Personality and Social Psychology Bulletin* 10 (1): 119–26.

Carmel, S. 1990. "The Health Belief Model in the Research of AIDS Related Preventive Behavior." *Public Health Review* 18 (1): 73–85.

Centers for Disease Control (CDC). 1992. "Tuberculosis Transmission in a State Correctional Institution—California, 1990–1991." *Morbidity and Mortality Weekly Report* 41 (49): 927–29

Courtenay, Will H. 1996. *HEALTH MENTOR Health Risk Assessment for Men™*. Berkeley, Calif.: Men's Health Consulting.

———. 1998a. "Better to Die Than Cry? A Longitudinal and Constructionist Study of Masculinity and the Health Risk Behavior of Young American Men." Ph.D. diss., University of California, Berkeley. Abstract in *Dissertation Abstracts International* (Publication number 9902042) 59 (08A).

———. 1998b. "College Men's Health: An Overview and a Call to Action." *Journal of American College Health* 46 (6): 279–90.

———. 1998c. "Communication Strategies for Improving Men's Health: *The 6-Point HEALTH Plan.*" *Wellness Management* 14 (1): 1, 3–4.

———. In press. "Behavioral Factors Associated with Disease, Injury, and Death among Men: Evidence and Implications for Prevention." *Journal of Men's Studies.*

———. 2000a. "Engendering Health: A Social Constructionist Examination of Men's Health Beliefs and Behaviors." *Psychology of Men and Masculinity* 1 (1): 4–15.

———. 2000b. "Constructions of Masculinity and Their Influence on Men's Well-Being: A Theory of Gender and Health." *Social Science and Medicine* 50 (10): 1385–1401.

Deber, R. B. 1994. "Physicians in Health Care Management: The Patient-Physician Partnership: Changing Roles and the Desire for Information." *Canadian Medical Association Journal* 151 (2): 171–76.

EDK Associates. 1995. *The ABCs of STDs*. New York: Author.

Eisler, R. M. 1995. "The Relationship between Masculine Gender Role Stress and Men's Health Risk: The Validation of a Construct." In *A New Psychology of Men*, ed. R. F. Levant and S. W. Pollack. New York: Basic Books.

Eisler, R. M., and J. A. Blalock. 1991. "Masculine Gender Role Stress: Implications for the Assessment of Men. *Clinical Psychology Review* 11 (3): 45–60.

Eisler, R. M., J. R. Skidmore, and C. H. Ward. 1988. "Masculine Gender-Role Stress: Predictor of Anger, Anxiety, and Health-Risk Behavior." *Journal of Personality Assessment* 52 (1): 133–41.

Ford, E. S., and D. H. Jones. 1991. "Cardiovascular Health Knowledge in the United States: Findings from the National Health Interview Survey, 1985." *Preventive Medicine* 20 (6): 725–36.

Goffman, Erving. 1961. *Asylums: Essays on the Social Situation of Mental Patients and Other Inmates*. Garden City, N.Y.: Anchor Books.

Good, G. E., D. M. Dell, and L. B. Mintz. 1989. "Male Role and Gender Role Conflict: Relations to Help Seeking in Men." *Journal of Counseling Psychology* 36 (3): 295–300.

Good, G. E., and L. B. Mintz. 1990. "Gender Role Conflict and Depression in College Men: Evidence for Compounded Risk." *Journal of Counseling and Development* 69 (1): 17–21.

Hammett, T. M., L. Harrold, M. Gross, and J. Epstein. 1994. *1992 Update: HIV/AIDS in Correctional Facilities—Issues and Options*. Washington, D.C.: National Institute of Justice, Department of Justice.

Holbrook, M. I. 1997. "Anger Management Training in Prison Inmates." *Psychological Reports* 81 (2): 623–26.

Kandrack, M., K. R. Grant, and A. Segall. 1991. "Gender Differences in Health Related Behavior: Some Unanswered Questions." *Social Science and Medicine* 32 (5): 579–90.

Kaufman, M. 1994. "Men, Feminism, and Men's Contradictory Experiences of Power. In *Theorizing Masculinities,* ed. H. Brod and M. Kaufman. Thousand Oaks, Calif.: Sage.

Kruzich, J. M., R. L. Levy, J. Ellis, and D. G. Olson. 1984. "Assessing Health Education Needs in a Prison Setting." *Journal of Prison and Jail Health* 4 (2): 107–16.

Lash, S. J., R. M. Eisler, and R. S. Schulman. 1990. "Cardiovascular Reactivity to Stress in Men: Effects of Masculine Gender Role Stress Appraisal and Masculine Performance Challenge." *Behavior Modification* 14 (1): 3–20.

Lonnquist, L. E., G. L. Weiss, and D. L. Larsen. 1992. "Health Value and Gender in Predicting Health Protective Behavior." *Women and Health* 19 (2/3): 69–85.

Love, N. 1991. "Why Patients Delay Seeking Care for Cancer Symptoms: What You Can Do about It." *Postgraduate Medicine* 89 (4): 151–58.

MacIntyre, C. R., N. Kendig, L. Kummer, S. Birago, and N. M. Graham. 1997. "Impact of Tuberculosis Control Measures and Crowding on the Incidence of Tuberculous Infection in Maryland Prisons." *Clinical Infectious Diseases* 24 (6): 1060–67.

Mahon, N. E., and T. J. Yarcheski. 1994. "Future Time Perspective and Positive Health Practices in Adolescents." *Perceptual and Motor Skills* 79 (1): 395–98.

Mahon, N. E., T. J. Yarcheski, and A. Yarcheski. 1997. "Future Time Perspective and Positive Health Practices in Young Adults: An Extension." *Perceptual and Motor Skills* 84 (3): 1299–1304.

Marquart, J. W., D. E. Merianos, S. J. Cuvelier, and L. Carroll. 1996. "Thinking about the Relationship between Health Dynamics in the Free Community and the Prison." *Crime and Delinquency* 42 (3): 331–60.

Meichenbaum, D., and D. C. Turk. 1987. *Facilitating Treatment Adherence: A Practitioner's Guidebook.* New York: Plenum.

Newton, C. 1994. "Gender Theory and Prison Sociology: Using Theories of Masculinities to Interpret the Sociology of Prisons for Men." *Howard Journal of Criminal Justice* 33 (3): 193–202.

Nielsen, J. M. 1990. Introduction to *Feminist Research Methods: Exemplary Readings in the Social Sciences,* ed. J. M. Nielsen. Boulder, Colo.: Westview Press.

O'Brien, M. K., K. Petrie, and J. Raeburn. 1992. "Adherence to Medication Regimens: Updating a Complex Medical Issue." *Medical Care Review* 49 (4): 435–54.

Oliver, S. J., and B. B. Toner. 1990. "The Influence of Gender Role Typing on the Expression of Depressive Symptoms." *Sex Roles* 22 (11/12): 775–90.

Pleck, J. H., F. L. Sonenstein, and L. C. Ku. 1994. "Problem Behaviors and Masculinity Ideology in Adolescent Males." In *Adolescent Problem Behaviors: Issues and Research,* ed. R. D. Ketterlinus and M. E. Lamb. Hillsdale, N.J.: Erlbaum.

Polednak, A. P. 1990. "Knowledge of Colorectal Cancer and Use of Screening Tests in Persons 40–74 Years of Age." *Preventive Medicine* 19 (2): 213–26.

Polych, Carolyn, and Don Sabo. 1995. "Gender Politics, Pain, and Illness: The AIDS Epidemic in North American Prisons." In *Men's Health and Illness: Gender, Power, and the Body,* ed. Don S. Sabo and David F. Gordon. Thousand Oaks, Calif.: Sage.

Pyke, K. D. 1996. "Class-Based Masculinities: The Interdependence of Gender, Class, and Interpersonal Power." *Gender and Society* 10 (5): 527–49.

Ratner, P. A., J. L. Bottorff, J. L. Johnson, and L. A. Hayduk. 1994. "The Interaction Effects of Gender within the Health Promotion Model." *Research in Nursing and Health* 17 (5): 341–50.

Rossi, J. S. 1992. "Stages of Change for 15 Health Risk Behaviors in an HMO Population." Paper presented at the thirteenth annual scientific sessions of the Society of Behavioral Medicine, New York, March.

Rothspan, S., and S. J. Read. 1996. "Present versus Future Time Perspective and HIV Risk among Heterosexual College Students." *Health Psychology* 15 (2): 131–34.

Sabo, Don. 1995. "Caring for Men." In *Nursing Care in the Community,* 2d ed., ed. J. Cookfair. St. Louis, Mo.: Mosby.

Sabo, Don, and David F. Gordon, eds. 1995. *Men's Health and Illness: Gender, Power and the Body.* Thousand Oaks, Calif.: Sage.

Sabo, Don, and Willie London. 1992. "Understanding Men in Prison: The Relevance of Gender Studies." *Men's Studies Review* 9 (1): 4–9.

Salive, M. E., G. E. Smith, and F. Brewer. 1989. "Suicide Mortality in the Maryland State Prison System, 1979 to 1987." *Journal of the American Medical Association* 252 (2): 365–69.

Seeman, T. E., G. A. Kaplan, L. Knudsen, R. Cohen, and J. Guralnik. 1987. "Social Network Ties and Mortality among the Elderly in the Alameda County Study." *American Journal of Epidemiology* 126 (4): 714–23.

Sharpe, M. J., and P. P. Heppner. 1991. "Gender Role, Gender Role Conflict and Psychological Well-Being in Men." *Journal of Counseling Psychology* 38: 323–30.

Shye, D., J. P. Mullooly, D. K. Freeborn, and C. R. Pope. 1995. "Gender Differences in the Relationship between Social Network Support and Mortality: A Longitudinal Study of an Elderly Cohort." *Social Science and Medicine* 41 (7): 935–47.

Sim, J. 1994. "Tougher Than the Rest? Men in Prison." In *Just Boys Doing Business? Men, Masculinities and Crime,* ed. T. Newburn and E. A. Stanko. New York: Routledge.

Umberson, D. 1992. "Gender, Marital Status and the Social Control of Health Behavior." *Social Science and Medicine* 34 (8): 907–17.

U.S. Preventive Services Task Force. 1996. *Guide to Clinical Preventive Services,* 2d ed. Baltimore: Williams and Wilkins.

Verbrugge, L. M. 1985. "Gender and Health: An Update on Hypotheses and Evidence." *Journal of Health and Social Behavior* 26 (3): 156–82.

Walker, S. N., K. Volkan, K. R. Sechrist, and N. J. Pender. 1988. "Health Promoting Life-Styles of Older Adults: Comparisons with Young and Middle-Aged Adults, Correlates and Patterns." *Advances in Nursing Science* 11 (1): 76–90.

Wallace, S., J. Klein-Saffran, G. Gaes, and K. Moritsugu. 1991. "Health Status of Federal Inmates: A Comparison of Admission and Release Medical Records." *Journal of Prison and Jail Health* 10 (2): 133–51.

Weisbuch, J. B. 1991. "The New Responsibility for Prison Health: Working with the Public Health Community." *Journal of Prison and Jail Health* 10 (1): 3–18.

West, Candace, and Don H. Zimmerman. 1987. "Doing Gender." *Gender and Society* 1 (2): 125–51.

Carol Polych and Don Sabo

Sentence—Death by Lethal Infection: IV-Drug Use and Infectious Disease Transmission in North American Prisons

The prison system acts as a whirlpool of risk for many men who, upon arrest, reside in structurally disadvantaged communities, where poverty, unemployment, and racial oppression already yield high rates of tuberculosis (TB), hepatitis, and HIV/AIDS. Because of unhealthy prison conditions, they are yet again exposed to heightened risk for illness (Toepell, 1992; Bellin, Fletcher, and Safyer, 1993; Kupers, 1999). This chapter argues that the corrections system is part of an institutional chain that facilitates transmission of HIV and other infectious diseases in certain North American populations, particularly among low-income, inner-city men of color. Prisons are not sealed off from their surrounding communities, and men constantly move in and out of the corrections system, oftentimes carrying physical or mental illness with them. The average prison sentence in the United States is less than five years, and about 95 percent of all prisoners are eventually released, despite the trends toward longer sentences (Kupers, 1999). Upon release, many infected male prisoners return to communities in which low-income and racially oppressed populations of *both* males and females already exhibit disproportionately high rates of infectious disease (Zierler and Krieger, 1997).

In 1994, the Expert Committee on AIDS and Prisons (ECAP, 1994b) alerted us to impending disaster. The prison health care system, already dangerously inadequate, was being swamped by two epidemics: the spread of infectious disease in general and the transmission of HIV/AIDS as a result of the mass incarceration of poor African American and Latino drug users. Because these two epidemics are intricately related, this chapter examines some of the intersections between intravenous-drug (IV-drug) use, the conditions of imprisonment, and the spread of infectious disease in and through North American prisons to wider civilian populations.

Wedding critical sociological and epidemiological approaches, our analysis begins with a review of infectious disease transmission in North American populations by documenting the prevalence of HIV/AIDS. Next, we discuss the differential risk for HIV transmission among various subgroups of male prisoners, particularly those with histories of IV-drug use. We also outline the transmission of hepatitis B (HBV) and hepatitis C (HCV) infections and TB. Finally, we argue that current legal and correctional practices are escalating the spiral of infectious disease transmission in prisons and wider society.

The HIV/AIDS Epidemic and Prison

The HIV/AIDS epidemic in prisons is a multifaceted phenomenon, with origins and impacts that stretch far beyond the institutional confines of prisons themselves. In order to understand how the AIDS epidemic influences men's health in prisons, therefore, it is necessary to present some initial data that describe the epidemic in U.S. and Canadian societies in general.

Though white males who have sex with men were once regarded as the main group at risk for HIV infection, the disproportionate impact of HIV on nondominant races was noted years ago. About half of all intravenous drug users (IDUs) infected with AIDS are African American. Among African Americans and Latino Americans diagnosed with AIDS, 40 percent report that their infection is due to IV-drug use, and 11 percent report that it is from heterosexual sex (Lindesmith Center, 1997). Women now contract up to half of all new HIV infections in the United States, primarily through heterosexual sex, often with IDUs (Schacker, 1998). In Canada, 31 percent of new HIV infections are among women, over half of whom are mothers (Walmsley, 1998).

Overrepresentation of racial and ethnic minorities among North American prison populations has been well documented and is especially alarming in those states with a high prevalence of AIDS, such as New York and California. The increasing risk for both transmission of HIV and hepatitis and the incarceration of racial and ethnic minorities is related to the growth in IV-drug use and drug-related crime, which, in turn, has been fueled partly by widening social and economic inequalities in postindustrial capitalist societies.

The Joint United Nations Programme on HIV and AIDS (UNAIDS) recently reported that the prevalence of HIV and AIDS is often ten times higher behind bars than on the outside (testimony of Ralph Jurgens in "Witness Presenting . . . ," 1997). Violence, fear, sexual tension, tattooing, and IV-drug use support the spread of HIV in prisons (Kingma, 1997). The Canadian Task Force on HIV/AIDS and Injection Drug Use declared that incarceration is a risk factor for acquiring HIV. It pointed out that the number of known cases of HIV/AIDS in federal prisons rose 46 percent between 1994 and 1996 (testimony of O. Instrup in "Witness Presenting . . . ," 1997). Incarceration is also a known risk factor for contracting HCV, which infects inmates at a rate of 30–40 percent (van Beek et al., 1998). Epidemiologists are also concerned about the spread of HIV and other infectious diseases to the families of inmates when they return to their communities (Jurgens, 1997–98).

Since 1998, about 650,000 persons with AIDS have been registered in the United States, and about another million Americans are estimated to be carrying the HIV virus (Quinn, 1998). IV-drug users, their sexual partners, and their children now account for

36 percent of AIDS infections (CDC, 1998a). AIDS is reflective of HIV infection contracted about ten years previously. The United States sees about 41,000 new HIV infections annually (Katz and Gerberding, 1998), half of which are among IDUs (Nadelman, McNeely, and Drucker, 1997). Canada has registered 16,250 persons with AIDS, with a further 40,000 Canadians diagnosed with HIV; half of the 4,200 newly acquired HIV infections were among IDUs (Health Canada, 1999a, 1999b).

African American men represent less than 6 percent of the U.S. population, but they constitute 48 percent of those confined to state prisons (Haney and Zimbardo, 1998). Of every one hundred thousand African Americans, sixty-three hundred are inmates of prisons and jails; this rate is more than seven times greater than the rate of imprisonment of Caucasians, who see nine hundred per hundred thousand imprisoned (Drucker, 1999). The disproportionate number of African American men in prison is related to the increase in incarceration for drug-related offenses; a change of 700 percent over ten years (Haney and Zimbardo, 1998). More than 5.1 percent of U.S. adults, including 35 percent of all young African American men are under correctional supervision in the U.S. system composed of prison, jail, court, probation, parole, and compulsory treatment (Drucker et al., 1998).

In 1998 in New York, there were about twenty-two thousand drug offenders in custody, 25 percent of whom received time for simple possession—usually of small amounts of illegal drugs for personal use, such as half a gram of cocaine. Over half of drug offenders behind bars had no previous record or had only one other similar conviction, yet they served from four to seven years on average for a first offense (Sundquist, 1999). Canada, which reviewed its approach to illegal drug use in 1997, recently reaffirmed its commitment to criminal prohibition, following the lead of the United States. Through the passage of Bill C8, it ensured imprisonment of large numbers of Canadians for drug use (Davis, 1998). In Canada, about 10 percent of federal prisoners are serving time for a drug offense, and over 50 percent have a recognized problem with substances (Vittala, 1999).

New York City AIDS cases constitute 10 percent of all U.S. cases, and about 25 percent of the total number of AIDS cases are due to IV-drug use (Des Jarlais et al., 1998). In countries such as Australia, where needle exchange was set up early and has been well supported, the rate of HIV infection among IDUs is low, at about 5 percent. Partly because of restricted needle exchange in North America, in contrast, the rate of HIV among IDUs living on this continent is much higher; ranging from 30 percent in Baltimore to 50 percent in New Jersey (Beilenson, 1998) and 65 percent in Detroit (Simpson, 1998). In Canada, IDU populations show HIV infection at a rate of about 8 percent in Toronto, 20 percent in Montreal (Toronto Public Health, 1997), and 23 percent in Vancouver, where the seroconversion rate is 18.6 percent yearly (Davis, 1998). The sorry case of Vancouver illustrates how rapidly HIV can spread among drug users, often to 40–50 percent within one to four years, once it tops a prevalence of about 10 percent in a population (Strathdee et al., 1998).

During the early 1990s, two-thirds of deaths among inmates were AIDS related, but by 1998 this rate had declined sixfold as a result of chemoprophylaxis (CDC, 1998b). With almost 5,000 AIDS-related deaths of inmates by 1994, and a further 5,000 inmates diagnosed with HIV, correctional institutions have an AIDS rate six times higher than that of the general population (Stephens, Cozza, and Braithwaite, 1999).

In 1995, twenty-three thousand inmates in U.S. state prisons and about a thousand in federal prisons were known to be HIV positive, for a prison population rate of 2.4 percent and 1 percent respectively (Braithwaite, Braithwaite, and Poulson, 1998). Twenty-one percent have a confirmed AIDS diagnosis (CDC, 1998b). However, pockets of high risk exist. New York State, which harbors one of the largest prison populations in the United States (seventy thousand people) estimates that almost ten thousand of its inmates are infected with HIV. In Canadian prisons, the estimates of the HIV rate vary from 1 percent to almost 8 percent (Jurgens, 1998).

Just over 1.3 million Americans who were arrested in 185 of the largest U.S. cities were found to be illegal drug users (Hser et al., 1998). It is estimated that 1.5 million Americans inject their illegal drug (Parts, 1997), including a half million regular heroin users and another half million recreational users (Nadelman and McNeely, 1996). In Canada, it is estimated that there are almost 100,000 illegal opiate users alone, 14,000 of whom reside in Toronto (Fischer and Rehm, 1997). The CDC(1998a) estimate that an illegal drug user may make about 1,000 injections yearly, for a projected annual total of 1.3 billion injections across the United States.

Corrections Policies and Risk

How do corrections policies influence the course of the HIV/AIDS epidemic in North America and the prison system? Needle provision is one vehicle for curbing the spread of HIV transmission within a population. With adequate needle exchange, for example, the yearly rate of HIV infection in most cities decreases by 6 percent (compared to a yearly *increase* of 6 percent in cities with poor exchange) (Nadelman, McNeeley, and Drucker, 1997). Whereas Swiss prison officials are satisfied with the procedures established to conduct needle exchange behind bars, exchange does not occur in North American prisons. Correctional Services of Canada does state, however, that condoms and bleach are provided in all federal institutions (Ingstrup, 1997).

In the United States, as of 1996, even condom availability in corrections facilities was limited to New York City, Washington, D.C., San Francisco, Philadelphia, and Mississippi (Stephens, Cozza, and Braithwaite, 1999). Corrections officials generally consider sexual activity among inmates to be a disciplinary offense. Regardless, 26 percent of Canadian inmates report engaging in unprotected sex, needle sharing, or tattooing (Ingstrup, 1997). Sex with another inmate was reported by 6 percent of Canadian federal inmates, but only one-third of the respondents had a condom. Inmates who inject have been found to be six times more likely than other prisoners to report anal sex with another man while in prison; sex may constitute a means of financing drug use, or it may be the result of rape following default on drug payments (Gore, Bird, and Hutchinson, 1998). Transsexual inmates are more than twice as likely to inject their drugs while they are imprisoned, and they are three times more likely to have sex with an IV-drug user. They are also almost six times more likely to have more than one sex partner behind bars (Stephens, Cozza, and Braithwaite, 1999). All these factors put inmates who inject and inmates who are transsexual at extraordinarily high risk in an already high-risk environment.

Some corrections policies have sought to eliminate the use of drugs through random urine testing. However, such testing may bring about increased IV-drug use as inmates attempt to avoid detection by using IV drugs that have a shorter window of detection than drugs such as marijuana (Jurgens, 1998). In prison, 11 percent of federal inmates reported injecting drugs (whereas other sources estimate the rate of IV-drug use behind bars at closer to 30 percent), but only 57 percent of injectors thought that the equipment they used was clean. Needle sharing is commonly reported in prison, with fifteen to twenty inmates using a single needle without cleaning it between uses (ECAP, 1994a). Among inmates of a provincial prison in Quebec City, all those infected with HIV reported IV-drug use. Among the 9 percent who reported sharing a needle, for example, the prevalence of HIV was 14 percent, and 10 percent of the men who identified themselves as IDUs admitted to injection while in prison (Dufour et al., 1996).

The HIV virus is primarily transmitted between adults by unprotected penetrative sex or by needle sharing with an infected partner. Sexual contacts between prisoners occur mainly through consensual unions but also secondarily through sexual assaults and rape. Other sexual activity may take place as a result of submission based upon intimidation or for protection or other favors (see Part IV in this volume). The Federal Bureau of Prisons estimated that between 9 and 20 percent of prisoners become the victims of sexual assault (Hammett, 1989). Twenty-eight percent of inmates in two New York State prisons had been targets of sexual aggression while in custody (ECAP, 1994b).

Incarceration versus Prevention

The emphasis on incarceration as a solution to illegal drug use has also contributed to a disproportionately high rate of HIV/AIDS infection in prison. On any day in 1997, almost half a million Americans were behind bars for violating a drug law (Nadelman, 1998). Two-thirds of the $16 billion federal budget was spent on enforcement, an amount equaled by state and local funding (Drucker et al., 1998). Yet the U.S. General Accounting Office and the Federal Bureau of Prisons estimate that, although 75 percent of state inmates and 31 percent of federal inmates need drug treatment, only 5 percent of the state and 0.9 percent of the federal prison budget goes toward drug treatment (Belenko et al., 1998). Ernie Drucker and colleagues (1998) call for at least provision of methadone in prison, at an adequate dosage (60–100 mg), as a means of reducing sharing of injection equipment.

The situation growing in and around corrections has profound health implications for all prisoners, corrections staff, their families, and the people close to them. In 1996, there were 1.6 million people incarcerated in jails or prisons, but 10 million Americans streamed through admissions and release from these institutions. The inmates at the center of this whirlpool are at higher risk of becoming infected with not only HIV but TB, hepatitis, and other STDs as well. And upon release, these same men can carry the illnesses home with them to unsuspecting families and communities.

Additional Forms of Infectious Disease

Epidemiological data suggest that the treatment of drug offenders by the courts and prison system contributes to the spread of infectious diseases other than HIV/AIDS. Even when HIV is controlled, for example, the rate of HCV infection transmitted by IV-drug use can be high. The yearly incidence of HIV among IDUs in Seattle, for example, is under 1 percent, but the yearly conversion rate for HCV is over 20 percent (Hagan et al, 1999). It is estimated that 4 million Americans are now infected with HCV. IV-drug use has led to over half of all chronic infections and 50 percent of new infections; 50–80 percent of IDUs acquire HCV in six to twelve months of onset of injection (Spaulding et al., 1999). Joseph Tranchina (1998) estimates that 41 percent of prisoners in California carry HCV. Chronic infection will develop in about 85 percent of infected people, and cirrhosis will develop in 20 percent within twenty years. During this time of progression, 1–5 percent may come down with liver cancer, and a further 4 percent may contract cancer each year once cirrhosis is established (Spaulding et al., 1999). The threat presented by HCV may prove to be even more lethal than HIV and just as insidious.

Coinfection of HBV and HIV is common, and both infections may be transmitted at the same time in prison. The average incubation period for HBV is between three and six months, and it has been shown to be transmitted in prisons without being diagnosed or persons being aware that they are ill (Hutchinson et al., 1998). In the United States, about 18,000 new infections occur annually, with a total of about 350,000 Americans carrying HBV; the prevalence is 12 percent among African Americans (Coleman et al., 1998). About 1 percent of those infected with HBV go on to develop chronic liver disease or cancer. Even though vaccination against HBV has been available since 1982 (CDC, 1999a), many inmates have never received the vaccine even when they have spent considerable time in custody or after repeated incarcerations.

A considerable number of people diagnosed with HIV carry TB. During 1995 in Ontario, about 5 percent of those who had AIDS were also infected with TB, and about 3 percent of those who had TB were also infected with AIDS (Naus, 1997). In the United States, a median of 3 percent coinfection has been found among the general population, but the rate in some cities is inflated. In San Francisco, Miami, and New York City, for example, 28–46 percent of adults who were diagnosed with TB were also found to carry HIV infection (Weis et al., 1999).

E. Y. Bellin, D. D. Fletcher, and S. M. Safyer (1993) conducted a study in the New York City jail on Rikers Island that found that one year of jail time doubled the odds of catching TB, a figure that New York public health authorities believe seriously underestimates the risk (DiFerdinando, 1993). It is estimated that 15–25 percent of all inmates at Rikers Island test positive for TB infection, posing a risk for the 16 percent of inmates who also test positive for HIV (ECAP, 1994b). The Rikers Island facility houses 15,000 prisoners on any given day and has an average length of stay of sixty-five days, with half the inmates being released during the first week. Under prison housing conditions and given the whirlpool dynamic of infectious disease transmission linked to incarceration, TB can spread rapidly among HIV-infected inmates, their visitors, staff, and the household contacts of visitors and staff (CDC, 1999b). In urban U.S. centers, 30–40 percent of new cases of TB are due to recent transmission (Health Canada, 1996). The CDC (1993) also speculates that 25 percent of the 550,000 federal and state corrections inmates discharged annually may be carrying latent TB infection, which can activate later.

The rate of TB among inmates is generally recognized as being seven to eleven times greater than the rate in the general population. In Georgia, 70 percent of prison inmates treated for TB were diagnosed only upon entry into the prison system via county jails. This lag in diagnosis has led to concern that many inmates who are released back into the community from these jails may not know that they have been infected and may carry the infection back to their families. The prevalence of TB in these Georgia prisons was 113 per 100,000 in new admits (Bock et al., 1998). For comparison, the TB rate in Canada is 6 per 100,000 for a total of 2,000 nationwide in 1996 (Health Canada, 1998:11).

The Politics of Neglect

The increased risk of HIV infection posed by imprisonment and the attendant increase in TB and hepatitis infection may ultimately be resolved as economic constraints drive the criminal justice system to consider nonincarcerative alternatives to corrections. It is apparent that prisons cure neither crime nor the social problems that are linked to crime (Lasker, 1991).

Blacks and Hispanics are at the greatest risk of contracting HIV/AIDS infection in prisons. But, just as yellow fingers do not cause lung disease, it is not their race or ethnicity that confers risk but the behaviors that they engage in, the social circumstances of their lives (U.S. Public Health Service, 1993), and the disregard of minority health status by the authorities. HIV/AIDS, TB, and HCV are tied to a network of problems that includes community disintegration, unemployment, homelessness, eroding urban tax bases, mental illness, substance use, custom, criminalization, and poverty (Wallace, 1991).

In "Gender Politics, Pain, and Illness: The AIDS Epidemic in North American Prisons" (Polych and Sabo, 1995), we discussed the gender politics around infectious disease in prisons. Within the intermale dominance hierarchies that constitute the prison system, prisoners are being *systematically* deprived of comprehensive health education, condom and needle promotion and provision, and drug counseling. To some extent, therefore, the disproportionately high rates of infectious disease in prisons among low-income and mainly African American and Hispanic men reflect structured class and race inequalities in public health priorities (Gilbert, 1991). Two outcomes of the existing policies and structural conditions are (1) the systematic increase in the number of prisoners with HIV/AIDS and associated illnesses and (2) the ultimate spread of infectious diseases by ill prisoners who are released and return to their own communities.

The lack of comprehensive health care interventions to deal with the infectious disease epidemic in prisons, we contend, exposes the harshly punitive nature of modern corrections. Foucault's (1979) account of the historical transformation of the prison in Western society documents a trend away from overt torture to more covert forms of punishment. The new prison system is not really intended to be more humane than the "primitive" torture wheel or gallows; it is intended "to punish better . . . to insert the power to punish more deeply into the social body" (Foucault, 1979:82). The epidemic spread of infectious disease through prison populations should, therefore, be a prime phenomenon for future research and advocacy work by public health advocates.

Conclusion

Prisoners—who may be burdened with not only social disadvantage but also high rates of physical illness, mental disorder, and substance use—are entitled to protection from conditions that may jeopardize their health (Editor, 1991). When individuals are incarcerated, they are no longer able to control their own lives and bodies because they are under the supervision of correctional systems. Accordingly, their ability to protect themselves from infection, assault, and other threats is severely limited. This responsibility is assumed by the state when it imprisons inmates. Although the official power structures in prisons are put into place to control inmates, unofficial power relationships result in further rigidity and the constriction of those choices that may yet be open to an individual inmate (Reyes and Coninx, 1997).

The World Health Organization (WHO) states that all prisoners have the right to receive health care, including preventive measures, equivalent to that available in the community (Jurgens, 1998). Inmates are sentenced to serve time; they are not sentenced to death by lethal infection (Jurgens, 1998). It is the responsibility of the government and prison officials to create a safer environment in which the risk of infectious disease is decreased.

North American society needs to seriously examine its cultural addiction to the scapegoating and imprisonment of individuals to whom it has affixed the label of drug abusers. We must ask ourselves some tough cultural questions about the class and race warfare now underway in the guise of a drug war. The data presented here suggest that the interplay between punitive government approaches to the problems of drug addiction, harsh sentencing practices within the legal system, and the lack of preventive health policies in corrections institutions is increasing the rate of infectious disease among male prisoners. If prisoners are the designated captives of the so-called drug war, then the family members and residents who are infected by the movement of ill prisoners in and out of predominantly low-income communities might well be regarded as civilian casualties.

References

Beilenson, P. 1998. "Welcome Address." Paper presented at the Eighth North American Syringe Exchange Network conventions, Baltimore, April.

Belenko, S., J. Peugh, J. A. Califano, M. Usdansky, and S. E. Foster. 1998. "Substance Abuse and the Prison Population: A Three-Year Study by Columbia University Reveals Widespread Abuse among Offender Population." *Corrections Today* 1998 (October): 82–89, 154.

Bellin, E. Y., D. D. Fletcher, and S. M. Safyer. 1993. "Association of Tuberculosis Infection with Increased Time in or Admission to the New York City Jail System." *Journal of the American Medical Association* 269 (17): 2228–31.

Bock, N. N., M. Reeves, M. Lamarre, and B. DeVoe. . 1998. "Tuberculosis Case Detection in a State Prison System." *Public Health Reports* 113 (July/August): 359–64.

Braithwaite, R. L., K. Braithwaite, and R. Poulson. 1998. "HIV and TB in Prison: Increasing Incidence of Infectious Disease Calls for Aggressive Plan of Action." *Corrections Today* (April): 108–10, 180.

Centers for Disease Control (CDC). 1993. "Tuberculosis Prevention in Drug-Treatment Centers and Correctional Facilities—Selected US Sites, 1990–1991." *Morbidity and Mortality Weekly Review* 42 (11): 210–13.

————. 1998a. "Update: Syringe Exchange Programs, United States, 1997." *Morbidity and Mortality Weekly Review* 47 (31): 652–55.

————. 1998b. "Decrease in AIDS-Related Mortality in a State Correctional System—New York, 1995–1998." *Morbidity and Mortality Weekly Review* 47 (51/52): 1115–117.

————. 1999a. "Update: Recommendations to Prevent Hepatitis B Virus Transmission—United States." *Morbidity and Mortality Weekly Review* 48 (4): 33–34.

————. 1999b. "Tuberculosis Outbreaks in Prison Housing Units for HIV-Infected Inmates—California, 1995–1996." *Morbidity and Mortality Weekly Review* 48 (4): 79–82.

Coleman, P. J., G. M. McQuillan, L. A. Moyer, S. B. Lambert, and H. S. Margolis. 1998. "Incidence of Hepatitis B Virus Infection in the United States, 1976–1994: Estimates from the National Health and Nutrition Surveys." *Journal of Infectious Diseases* 178 (October): 954–59.

Davis, S. 1998. "Injection Drug Use and HIV Infection among the Seriously Mentally Ill: A Report from Vancouver." *Canadian Journal of Community Mental Health* 17 (1): 121–27.

Des Jarlais, D. C., T. Perlis, S. R. Friedman, S. Deren, T. Chapman, J. L. Sotheran, S. Tortu, M. Beardsley, D. Paone, L. V. Torian, S. T. Beatrice, E. DeBernardo, E. Monterroso, and M. Marmor. 1998. "Declining Seroprevalence in a Very Large HIV Epidemic: Injecting Drug Users in New York City, 1991–1996." *American Journal of Public Health* 88 (12): 1801–6.

DiFerdinando, G. T. 1993. "Risk of Tuberculosis and Time Spent in Jail." *Journal of the American Medical Association* 270 (8): 940–41.

Drucker, E. 1999. "Drug Prohibition." *Public Health Reports* 114: 14–29.

Drucker, E., P. Lurie, A. Wodak, and P. Alcabes. 1998. "Measuring Harm Reduction: The Effects of Needle and Syringe Exchange Programs and Methadone Maintenance on the Ecology of HIV." *AIDS* 12 (supplement A): S217–30.

Dufour, A., M. Alary, C. Poulin, F. Allard, L. Noel, G. Trottier, D. Lepne, and C. Hankins. 1996. "Prevalence and Risk Behaviours for HIV Infection among Inmates of a Provincial Prison in Quebec City." *AIDS* 10 (9): 1009–15.

Editor. 1991. "Health Care for Prisoners: Implications of 'Kalk's Refusal.'" *Lancet* 337 (March 16): 647–48.

Expert Committee on AIDS and Prison (ECAP). 1994a. "HIV/AIDS in Prisons: Summary Report and Recommendations of the Expert Committee on AIDS and Prisons." Ministry of Supply and Services Canada Catalogue No. JS82-68/2-1994. Ottawa, Canada: Correctional Service of Canada.

————. 1994b. "HIV/AIDS in Prisons: Final Report of the Expert Committee on AIDS and Prisons." Ministry of Supply and Services Canada Catalogue No. JS82-68/1-1994E. Ottawa, Canada: Correctional Service of Canada.

Fischer, B., and J. Rehm. 1997. "The Case for a Heroin Substitution Treatment Trial in Canada." *Canadian Journal of Public Health* 88 (6): 367–70.

Foucault, Michel. 1977. *Discipline and Punishment: The Birth of the Prison.* New York: Vintage Books.

Gilbert, D. 1991. "These Criminals Have No Respect for Human Life." *Social Justice* 18 (3): 71–83.

Gore, S. M., A. G. Bird, and S. J. Hutchinson. 1998. "Injector-Inmates and Anal Sex with Another Man in Prison." (Letter to the editor), 781.

Hagan, H., J. P. McGough, H. Thiede, N. S. Weiss, S. Hopkins, and E. R. Alexander. 1999. "Syringe Exchange and Risk of Injection with Hepatitis B and C Viruses." *American Journal of Epidemiology* 149 (3): 203–13.

Hammett, T. M. 1989. *1988 Update: AIDS in Corrections Facilities*. Washington, D.C.: National Institute of Justice.

Haney, C., and P. Zimbardo. 1998. "The Past and Future of US Prison Policy: Twenty-Five Years after the Stanford Prison Experiment." *American Psychologist* 53 (7): 709–27.

Health Canada. 1996. "Evidence for TB Clustering in Vancouver: Results from Pilot Study Using RFLP Fingerprinting." *Canada Communicable Disease Report* 22 (7): 49–51.

———. 1998. "Tuberculosis in Canada: 1996." Catalogue No. H49-108/1996. Ottawa, Canada: Government Services Canada.

———. 1999a. "HIV/AIDS among Injection Drug Users in Canada." In *HIV/AIDS Epi Update*. (Online [cited May 10, 1999].) Available from www.hc-sc.gc.ca/hpb/lcdc/bah/epi/idus_e.html.

———. 1999b. "HIV Prevalence and Incidence in Canada: 40,100 Living with HIV Infection and 4,200 New Infections per Year." In *HIV/AIDS Epi Update*. Available from www.hc-sc.gc.ca/hpb/lcdc/bah/epi/idus_e.html.

Hser, Y. I., M. Prendergast, M. D. Anglin, J. K. Chen, and S. C. Hsieh. 1998. "A Regression Analysis Estimating the Number of Drug-Using Arrestees in 185 US Cities." *American Journal of Public Health* 88 (3): 487–90.

Hutchinson, S. J., D. J. Goldberg, S. M. Gore, S. Cameron, J. M. McGregor, J. McMenamin, and J. McGavigan. 1998. "Hepatitis B Outbreak at Glenochil Prison during January to June 1993." *Epidemiology and Infection* 121 (2): 185–91.

Ingstrup, O. 1997. "Presentation." *Canadian HIV/AIDS Policy and Law Newsletter* 3 (2/3): 27.

Jurgens, R. 1997–98. "Task Force Calls for Methadone Maintenance and Needle Exchange in Prisons." *Canadian HIV/AIDS Policy and Law Newsletter* 3/4 (4/1): 27.

———. 1998. "HIV/AIDS and Drug Use in Prisons: Moral and Legal Responsibilities of Prison Systems." *Canadian HIV/AIDS Legal Network at Geneva 1998*. (Online [cited August 12, 1998]). Available from www.aidslaw.ca/elements/geneva98/prisons2.html.

Katz, M. H., and J. L. Gerberding. 1998. "The Care of Persons with Recent Sexual Exposure to HIV." *Annals of Internal Medicine* 128 (4): 306–12.

Kingma, S. 1997. "Prejudice Feeds Spread of HIV in Prisons." *Canadian HIV/AIDS Policy and Law Newsletter* 3 (2/3): 29.

Kupers, T. 1999. *Prison Madness*. San Francisco: Jossey-Bass.

Lasker, M. E. 1991. "American Prisons and Prisoners in 1990." *Proceedings of the American Philosophical Society* 135 (1): 30–40.

Lindesmith Center. 1997. *Syringe Availability*. (Report.) New York: Lindesmith Center.

Marcourt, J. W., V. E. Brewer, J. Mullings, B. M. Crouch. 1999. "The Implications of Crime Control Policy on HIV/AIDS-Related Risk among Women Prisoners." *Crime and Delinquency* 45 (1): 82–98.

Nadelman, E. 1998. "Commonsense Drug Policy." *Foreign Affairs* 77 (1): 111–26.

Nadelman, E., and J. McNeely. 1996. "Doing Methadone Right." *Public Interest* 123 (Spring): 83–93.

Nadelman, E., J. McNeely, and E. Drucker. 1997. "International Perspectives." In *Substance Abuse: A Comprehensive Textbook,* 3d ed., ed. J. H. Lowinson, P. Ruiz, R. B. Millman, and J. G. Langrod. Baltimore: Williams and Wilkins.

Naus, M. 1997. "Epidemiology of AIDS/TB Coinfection in Ontario—1990–1995." *Phero* (April 25): 94–98.

Parts, M. 1997. "Disease Prevention as Drug Policy: A Historical Perspective on the Case for Legal Access to Sterile Syringes as a Means of Reducing Drug-Related Harm." *Fordham Urban Law Journal* 24 (3): 475–532.

Polych, Carol, and Don Sabo. 1995. "Gender Politics, Pain, and Illness: The AIDS Epidemic in North American Prisons." In *Men's Health and Illness: Gender, Power and the Body,* ed. Don Sabo, and David F. Gordon. Thousand Oaks, Calif.: Sage.

Quinn, T. C. 1998. "Epidemiology of HIV Infections: International and US Perspectives." *Hopkins HIV Report* (May): 11–12.

Reyes, H., and R. Coninx. 1997. "Pitfalls of Tuberculosis Programmes in Prisons." *British Medical Journal* 315: 1447–50.

Schacker, T. 1998. "Primary HIV Infection: Early Diagnosis and Treatment Are Critical to Outcome." *Postgraduate Medicine* 102 (4): 143–51.

Simpson, H. 1998. "Oral Mucosal HIV Testing and Its Implications for Needle Exchange Programs." Paper presented at the eighth North American Syringe Exchange Network Convention, Baltimore, April.

Spaulding, A., C. Greene, K. Davidson, M. Schneidermann, and J. Rich. 1999. "Hepatitis C in State Correctional Facilities." *Preventive Medicine* 28: 92–100.

Stephens, T., S. Cozza, and R. L. Braithwaite. 1999. "Transsexual Orientation in HIV Risk Behaviors in an Adult Male Prison." *International Journal of STD and AIDS* 10: 28–31.

Strathdee, S. A., E. J. C. van Ameijden, F. Mesquita, A. Wodak, S. Rana, and D. Vlahov. 1998. "Can HIV Epidemics among Injection Drug Users Be Prevented?" *AIDS* 12 (supplement A): S71-79.

Sundquist, D. 1999. "Official Data Reveal Most New York Drug Offenders Are Nonviolent." (Online [cited January 11, 1999].) Available from lessharm@cwix.com; INTERNET.

Toepell, A. R. 1992. *Prisoners and AIDS: AIDS Education Needs Assessment.* Toronto, Canada: John Howard Society of Metropolitan Toronto.

Toronto Public Health, Communicable Disease Notification Unit. 1997. *1996 HIV/AIDS Annual Statistics.* (Report.) Toronto, Canada: Toronto Public Health Department.

Tranchina, J. 1998. "Hepatitis C." Paper presented at the eighth North American Syringe Exchange Network Convention, Baltimore, April.

U.S. Public Health Service. 1993. "Current Trends: Update—Acquired Immunodeficiency Syndrome—United States, 1992." *Morbidity and Mortality Weekly* 42 (28): 547–57.

van Beek, I., R. Dwyer, G. J. Dore, K. Luo, and J. M. Kaldor. 1998. "Infection with HIV and Hepatitis C Virus among Injecting Drug Users in a Prevention Setting: Retrospective Cohort Study." *British Medical Journal* 317: 433–37.

Vittala, K. 1999. "Criminal System Begins to Recognize Health Issues: Focus on Treatment vs. Punishment." *Journal of Addiction and Mental Health* (January–February): 11–14.

Wallace, R. 1991. "Travelling Waves of HIV Infection on a Low Dimensional 'Socio-geographic' Network." *Social Science Medicine* 32 (7): 847–52.

Walmsley, S. 1998. "The New Antiretrovial 'Cocktails': Is the Stage Set for HIV-Positive Women to Benefit?" *Journal of the Canadian Medical Association* 158 (3): 339–31.

Weis, S. E., B. Foresman, P. E. Cook, and K. J. Matty. 1999. "Universal HIV Screening at a Major Metropolitan TV Clinic: HIV Prevalence and High-Risk Behaviors among TV Patients." *American Journal of Public Health* 89 (1): 73–75.

"Witness Presenting before the Parliamentary Subcommittee on HIV/AIDS and Drug Use in Federal Prisons, in Response to HIV/AIDS in Prison: Final Report (November 26, 1996)." 1997. *Canadian HIV/AIDS Policy and Law Newsletter* 3 (2/3): 413.

Zierler, S., and N. Kreiger. 1997. "Reframing Women's Risk: Social Inequalities and HIV Infection." *Annual Review of Public Health* 18 (1): 401–36.

O'Neil Stough

Deliberate Indifference

It was another night of tossing and turning. I noticed every time the guard went by for the count. He didn't come by for the 2:00 A.M. count, but I'd bet he nonetheless logged it as "count made—all accounted for." At 3:30 A.M., I figured it was almost breakfast, so I got up and fixed myself a cup of coffee.

I was growing weary of these sleepless nights. Every time I thought about what had happened, and was still happening, I became more upset. I'd tried to dismiss it somehow, or accept it, or even ignore it, but I couldn't. It was one of those things that won't go away until it's fully resolved, and in some ways it never will be.

It began a little over four months ago. Roland Dotson approached me on the yard and said he had a problem he'd like to talk to me about. He's a little skinny guy, twenty-eight years of age, and he's been locked up about six years for possession of speed with intent to distribute. In general, he's not well liked and is the type of guy many take advantage of. I'd heard of several instances when he'd had store items ripped off and was swindled or pressured (extorted) by the stronger and more capable. Besides his vulnerable stature, the main reason he's been fair game for such mistreatment was because he had AIDS, and there were some wild rumors as to how he got it. Inside, like outside, there is quite a bit of prejudice against those who have HIV. And, also like outside, the emphasis is on how the person may have contracted it. The consensus is that if a person acquired it via a blood transfusion or birth, then it's a sad and awful tragedy. In all other cases, however, it's seen as getting what they deserve.

I told Roland we could walk the track and talk. I was curious about what his problem may be. I was equally curious why he had sought me out, since we'd never spoken to each other.

"I'm having some trouble with Medical," he hesitantly began as we headed around the track. He was very nervous, and I could tell he was being selective in his choice of words.

"What kind of trouble?" I asked, urging him on.

In memoriam: Mr. Rowland W. Danielson, 1965–1993

"Well, the doctor told me . . ." he stopped and then started again. "The doctor explained there wasn't anything he could do for my——for my medical problem. He just doesn't seem to care," he broke off.

Obviously, he didn't know I knew he had AIDS, and he was feeling very uncomfortable about saying it. I figured the only way we'd get anywhere was to get it out in the open.

"Look, Roland," I said as matter-of-factly as I could, "I'm aware you have AIDS, and, if that's the medical problem they're giving you trouble about, then tell me about it. You asked to talk, so let's talk—OK?"

He was quiet for a bit, and I was concerned he'd misunderstood my aim and would make an excuse to walk away. Then he looked at me, and I gave him a little nod of encouragement.

"Yeah, that's the problem," he began, and he let it spill forth. "The doctor won't give me anything to help. I read some stuff in magazines about how eating a healthy diet helps, and taking vitamins, and stuff like that. Besides the garbage they serve us, it's tiny portions. You have to watch out for stuff like colds or flu, and they only allow those two thin blankets. I asked the doctor if he'd OK it for me to have one or two more, and he said it wasn't possible. I don't know why not! I asked about some vitamins too, but he said they were expensive and only used in rare cases. The diabetic guys get a sack lunch at night. It's just some cereal and milk or sometimes a sandwich, and I asked if I could be put on the list for that. He shrugged his shoulders and said those were diabetic bags and not authorized for—for, well, for AIDS cases. I don't' get it!"

I didn't either. All of those sounded like legitimate and reasonable requests. The food served is, in fact, barely adequate for a healthy person. The blankets are tattered and thin. In the cell block, especially now that winter was coming upon us, it was often around thirty-five or forty degrees at best. The cold wind blows in through various cracks, the double-wide open doors, and the broken windows. I'd not had any experience dealing with the treatment of AIDS cases, but I was a bit shocked and angered to hear how severely lacking it was.

"What do they do for you?" I asked.

"Once a month they take a blood sample, weigh me, and take my temperature and blood pressure," he stated flatly.

"That's it?" I snapped.

"Well, sometimes when I get real bad body aches, if I can catch the right nurse, I get Tylenol or some Motrin," he answered too quickly, as if he was somehow defending them.

He was so accustomed to being intimidated that he had developed an automatic response of submissiveness toward anything that appeared remotely confrontational or that threatened to cause a disturbance. I could see why his requests to the doctor had not been very successful. No doubt the doctor had seen this in him too.

"How long have you been diagnosed?" I asked him.

"It's been about five years now."

I further discovered that, although he still had a good appetite, he was losing weight and getting body aches and feeling feverish more frequently.

"You need to file a Grievance on this, Roland, and you need to do it tonight. Outline exactly what you need, what you requested from the doctor, and his response.

Explain clearly and concisely what is going on. Do you have any Grievance forms?" I asked, looking at him.

He didn't look back. He was walking head down and quiet.

"Did you hear me, man?" I prodded.

"I don't want any trouble," he began.

"Don't worry about that, man," I quickly interrupted. "You're not going to."

"And I don't know how to write," he finished.

"Not at all?" I inquired.

"A little," he replied. "Like I can spell my name and a few things, but I have trouble putting words together."

I sometimes forget that roughly 62 percent of those incarcerated are illiterate. Roland was not only illiterate; he was also afraid to file a Grievance, or "rock the boat," as he saw it. There was no doubt, however, that his situation, as well as those of people like him, needed addressing. I explained that I would file the Grievance. He was still worried, but he agreed.

Then he asked, "Is this gonna cost me anything?"

I could sense the trepidation in his voice. Being accustomed to being used and abused, he was resigned to it. "I don't have much money," he meekly finished.

"Hell yeah, it's gonna cost, man. You know nothing is for free. I expect a hundred bucks from you!" I rigidly proclaimed.

His eyes bugged for a moment and even glazed over. Then I laughed out loud.

"No, man, this isn't going to cost you anything. Relax, OK?" I reached over and mussed his hair, and then he laughed too. Not a lot, but a little, and probably for the first time in a long time.

That night I filled out the Grievance form. Under "Description of Grievance," I wrote:

It has come to my attention that Roland Dotson-377440 is receiving less than adequate medical care. He was diagnosed as HIV five years ago. In recent months he has experienced consistent weight loss, body aches, chills and fevers. He specifically requested supplemental foodstuff such as diabetics receive, vitamins and extra blankets to combat the bitter cold. These are quite reasonable requests in my view. The quality and quantity of regular food provided is insufficient for one with such a condition as Mr. Dotson. Obviously maintaining his body strength is very important. Likewise, blankets for warmth to guard against cold or flu is essential to his health. The medical department, specifically Dr. Bernard Sorenson, denied all of these requests and in my view exhibited a deliberate indifference toward the legitimate health needs of Mr. Dotson.

Under "Proposed Resolution" I continued:

Of immediate concern, Mr. Dotson should begin to receive extra foodstuff (diabetic bag), vitamins, three extra blankets, an extra sweatshirt and any medications which may commonly be administered to those outside under a doctor's care who are HIV positive. Medical needs to develop guidelines for adequate treatment of HIV cases. These guidelines should, at the very least, include the above-requested items for Mr. Dotson and any other treatments which may be helpful. Any apathy or prejudice that may exist toward those who are HIV should not be condoned in any form. Thank you.

The following morning I read it to Roland before submitting it. As I finished reading, I looked up. He had a big smile on his face, and his eyes were misty. "You called me mister," he gasped. "No one has ever called me mister!"

By policy the authorities have forty-five days to respond to a Grievance. I had thought it was a fairly clear issue and soon Roland would be receiving what had been requested. He was not getting any better as time went on. He had lost more weight, and his body aches were getting worse. Also, winter was in full force, and already many throughout the cell block were getting colds.

On the forty-second day, I received the following response:

Regarding your Grievance concerning the Health Unit. The Grievance is being returned to you unprocessed for failure to state a proper claim. The Grievance procedure is designed to address matters personal to your incarceration. You are not affected by issues concerning other inmates and you are directed to not involve yourself in matters unrelated to you personally. You are further directed not to abuse the Grievance procedure in such a manner. Failure to comply with these directives will be considered a violation of a direct order and you shall duly be issued a IV-12 disciplinary write-up for failing to follow a direct order.

Every muscle in my entire body knotted as I read these pompous and arrogant words. Every word rang in me like a clanging bell. By dinnertime, I was fuming. I sat down at my usual table where three other regulars also sat. The chow hall was our place to discuss various events and get the skinny from each other on what was going on. Each of these guys I'd known for years. They could see I was furious.

"What's up man?" asked Freddy Boy.

I angrily responded to his inquiry. "I got a response from the Grievance Coordinator refusing to process the damn thing about Medical. He said it wasn't a personal issue! This is bullshit! That dude Roland gets sicker day by day, and they're playing bureaucratic head games!"

"What's the deal on that anyway, man?" piped in Roscoe. "Screw that dude Roland. Why you getting so jacked about that fucking weasel?"

"Because it's bullshit, man," I snapped back.

"You're gonna end up going smooth off if you don't slow down." added the Hawk. "You've been drove for weeks wondering why they haven't responded, and now they do and you're more drove! You're gonna end up rolled up to Iso' if you keep going like this."

"They can throw me in the hole if they want. I don't give a damn!" I blurted out, and I meant it. "This guy is sick for real. If they refuse to process the Grievance, why didn't they return it the first week? It's almost two months now. They're stonewalling, man!"

"You want some of that shit going around?" asked Freddy Boy, as an offer aimed at helping my stressed condition. "We still have some left—the private stuff, not what we're putting out."

"Nah, thanks, man," I responded. "I'm just venting some. I'll be all right. Besides, I'm trying to get a thing going with Nancy Reagan, you know, " 'Just Say No.' "

"Hey!" the Hawk blurted out, "do you think Frank Sinatra was really bopping her?"

"Shittttt, man," droned Roscoe, "would you?"

"You mean like right now?" Hawk shot back.

We all looked at each other. "Hell, yeah!" we chorused and then began laughing. Then we all agreed that the White House was looking a lot better now that Hillary was there.

When I saw Roland, I explained that we needed to resubmit the Grievance using his name. "Look, man, this is a legitimate issue. You have a right to proper care. You're getting worse every day. Don't worry about any retaliation, OK?"

I redid the form in his name and submitted it the next day. It was now mid-November, and Roland had developed a cold. On December 20, an announcement came over the speaker system: "Dotson—377440—report to Programs Unit for Grievance Committee hearing." I wanted to go with him, but the rules didn't allow it. I figured he'd be okay, though. At least he was getting a hearing.

About a half hour later he returned. He was walking with his head down. He'd been doing that lately from feeling nauseated.

"How'd it go?" I asked as soon as he got close.

"They said this was a medical issue that was at their discretion," he began. "I tried to ask what that meant, but they said I have to understand that this is prison and things are run differently here. Every time I tried to ask a question, the coordinator cut me off by saying I was being disruptive. He seemed real serious."

Real serious, in that context, meant intimidating. I found it unlikely, hell impossible to believe, that Roland could be or had been disruptive in any way. Besides his characteristic meekness, he was weak with illness. All they had done was manipulate the guy and put the pressure on. "Bastards!" I kept muttering, "Friggin' bastards!"

"I wish you could have gone with me," he continued. "They acted pretty upset at me. Do you think I'll get in any trouble?"

"No, man, don't even think like that," I assured him. "They wanted to scare you and make you afraid to push the issue. They're typical scumbag cowards," I said through a tightening jaw.

Roland began coughing. His cold had been getting worse lately. It might have even been the flu at that point. After clearing his throat, he said, "They're gonna get madder if it's pushed anymore. It's been almost three months now and still nothing has happened. I appreciate what you've been trying to do. I need to go lie down a little while. I feel tired."

"We'll figure something out, Roland. You just take it easy and get some rest. And don't worry about their threats, OK?"

"Okay," he said and walked away.

What could be done I wasn't sure. I thought about a lawsuit, but that could take months, even years, before it would finally be heard. I thought about a letter campaign where you write a letter about what's going on and send it to newspaper editors, TV anchors, politicians, anyone you can think of. Any exposure helps. The problem was that Roland was not looking too good. His flu was getting worse, and he looked very frail. He wasn't making it to all meals, even though he still had an appetite. It was simply too much of an effort to make the outside trek from the cell block to the chow hall in the bitter cold and wind. Plus, the food was not very appetizing.

My table buddies, even Rosco, were noticing Roland's declining condition. "We talked to a few people about the situation with Roland," he said at dinner.

I looked at him and the others and smiled. "I thought he was such a—what was it you called him a little while back, a "fucking weasel?" I chuckled.

"Well shit, man, he is, but it's wrong what is happening to him. And that could be anyone in that situation. Fucking AIDS can happen to anybody. I have a couple of bros over in Cell block Four that found out they have it too."

"Yeah," the Hawk jumped in. "There's several guys I know too that found out they have it. That's some serious shit, man, and I bet there's a whole lot more who have it but don't know it—yet! And these people here don't pass out no info about how to take precautions."

"How's Roland feeling?" Freddy Boy asked me, effectively sidestepping the way the conversation was going.

"He's got an appetite, but it's too painful for him to get to the chow hall for every meal. He's freezing at night, and he's always thirsty. He's down, man, depressed, and this is the worst place in the world to be in such a condition. It sucks, and I don't know what to do at this point. I don't think he's gonna make it."

"It's only four days till Christmas," Hawk shot out. "They usually have a pretty decent meal then," he trailed off after his feeble attempt to inject some hope into the conversation.

Over the next few days, Roland had a lot of traffic to his cell door. "Hey, Roland," said a guy named Biff. "I have some extra snacks. Here, take this bag." In it were candy bars, cookies, and pastries. Everyone knows there's no such thing as extra anything around here, and Roland was stunned by the action.

"Say, Roland, what's up dude?" said a vato (a respected man from the barrio) named Wedo. "Here's some extra sodas I had. I'll have the trustee drop off a bag of ice later. Take care, man." He had dropped off a whole case of 7-Up.

A progression of strangers and others, some of whom Roland greatly feared, stopped by as well-wishers, and all bore gifts. Candy bars, juices, cans of tuna, crackers, blankets, sweatshirts, and various magazines were passed into his cell.

For a guy whose cell was usually barren and who anytime he did get anything usually got swindled or pressured out of it, he was doing all right.

On Christmas Eve I stopped by just before lockdown. "Damn, man, look at you! You're high-rolling now," I laughed as I teased him. He was snuggled under about seven blankets and, though he was in a severely weakened state, he beamed a big, feeble smile. "You got all the big shots catering to you now—pretty heavy stuff," I joked with him.

"Yeah," he smiled, and then had a coughing spell. "It's amazing! Even that guy Roscoe stopped by and gave me a whole canned ham!"

I smiled inwardly. Besides being one of the most dangerous and feared guys on the yard, Roscoe is also a chowhound. He would kill for a can of ham, maybe even a good slice, yet he'd done that. The guy was a piece of work for sure. I stood there staring at the peacefully happy, silly grin on Roland's face. "Hey," I said, "let me get your signature on what we discussed yesterday." Just as he signed, the speakers blared.

"ATTENTION ON UNIT: FIVE MINUTES TO LOCKDOWN—FIVE MINUTES TO LOCKDOWN!"

"Well, man, I better get going." I turned to go. After a few steps, I stopped and turned around. I stepped back to Roland's cell and, looking in, I said something I haven't said or heard personally for about seventeen years: "Merry Christmas, Mr. Dotson." Unable to stop it, Roland allowed a single tear to streak down his feverish cheek.

"Merry Christmas to you too," he was barely able to utter, "and thanks, man, thanks for everything."

"LOCKDOWN ON THE UNIT—LOCKDOWN ON THE UNIT!" the speakers blared. "Gotta go buddy—later!" I made a dash for my cell.

The following morning, Christmas morning, breakfast was delayed for about an hour. Everyone was a bit anxious and wondering why we were running late. Had there been a fight? A stabbing? A disturbance of some kind in another cell block? At 8:30 A.M. a trustee stopped by my cell. "They just took Roland out of here a little while ago, out the east exit," he said in a hushed tone.

"Is he all right?" I asked.

"No, bro, he was in a body bag. Apparently he died early this morning. He was discovered sprawled on the floor at the 6:00 A.M. change of shift count."

All I could say was "Damn!"

Christmas Day was noticeably quiet throughout the complex, more than usual for Christmas. People had a lot of mixed feelings about what had happened. Irrespective of who had died, and in what manner, the prevailing view was that the administration had contributed to it.

Over the next few days, my table buddies and others told me to let it go. "It's over, man," Freddy Boy said to me at dinner.

"No, it's not over" was my only reply.

That night I wrote a Grievance. I began under "Description of Grievance:"

It has come to my attention that Mr. Roland Dotson—377440 is dead. He suffered terribly in the last few months and it is clear you, and the entire Administration, contributed to this suffering, and death, by your deliberate indifference to the legitimate requests made by me on behalf of Mr. Dotson, and by himself before the Committee concerning his need for adequate food, clothing, blankets and medication. I would like to believe there is a perfectly rational and justifiable reason for such callous disregard being exhibited. I'd like to believe that you folks who are entrusted with such power and authority were possessive of the traits worthy of leadership such as humaneness, understanding, and compassion. I would like to believe those things, but the fact is I can't, because it is untrue. You are neither worthy of the position you hold nor is there any justification for the indifference and cruelty you've exhibited. While those in your charge have committed crimes of the state, you, sir, have committed a crime against humanity, and against God. If you'd like me to "state a claim," I will, quoting Matthew Chapter 25, verses 41 through 45: "I was hungry and you gave me nothing to eat; thirsty and you gave me no drink; I was a stranger and you did not take me in; naked and you did not clothe me; I was sick and in prison and you did not look after me." The people answered, "But when did we do these things to you, Lord?" The Lord replied, "I tell you a truth, whatever you did not do for the least of people, you did not do for me. Therefore, depart from me you who are cursed, I never knew you."

Under "Proposed Resolution," I continued:

Mr. Dotson is dead. Though you had the power to contribute to his death, and did, you do not have the power to resurrect him, though at times you act like or think you have such almighty powers. There are many more Mr. Dotsons' in this complex. It is time now, immediately, to provide the proper care they deserve such as that which you denied Mr. Dotson. Maybe, sir, just maybe, you might redeem yourself with your God if you spearhead a drive to provide adequate and appropriate medical care to those who are HIV. Excuse me for doubting you will. I have therefore put into motion my own resolution. Placed in the mail two days ago were copies of all previous requests with your responses, plus a deathbed affidavit from Mr. Dotson detailing the hearing you conducted, where he was threatened and discouraged about pursuing this matter, as well as a copy of the Grievance. Numerous packets were mailed to media representatives, political offices, and the Board of Medical Examiners. If you think I have violated your earlier direct orders to not concern myself with this matter, then for once you are right. I do not personally have AIDS, and I am not personally dead like Mr. Dotson, but nonetheless, I and the rest of the world are personally affected by this issue, and whether you realize it or not, so are you.

Two days later I placed the Grievance in the Grievance box. At 4:00 P.M. five guards entered the cell block and came to my cell. I was issued two write-ups. One for "disobeying a direct order" and the other for "attempting to overthrow, or disrupt, the good government of the institution." I was placed in handcuffs and leg chains and taken to the Isolation Unit (IU), the hole.

That's where I've been for the past two weeks, and as I said earlier, I have not been sleeping well. The IU houses about five hundred prisoners. You can partially see out the meshed-screen, hard plastic window on the door into the cell block, but you can't hear anything. The doors and walls are superthick. The place is appropriately named.

Around 6:00 P.M. one evening, two guards entered the downstairs corridor pushing a laundry cart. Behind them came a trustee carrying a clear plastic garbage bag full of paper sacks. The guards looked at the clipboard and began going to various cells in the cell block. A chill shot down my spine. Each selected cell from their list received three extra blankets and two extra sweatshirts, which the trustee passed in through the door. The trustee would then pass in a sack lunch. It was surrealistic watching this scene carried out in silence. Many stood at their doors staring out through the mesh screen—faceless, nameless, unknown.

I lay down on my bunk. I released a heavy sigh. No doubt I'd get a sound sleep that night—finally! I smiled to myself. Now, I thought, it's over. My head pressed softly into the pillow. "Goodnight, Mr. Dotson," I said quietly and nodded off into the welcoming arms of deep sleep.

Terry A. Kupers

Mental Health in Men's Prisons

A massive mental health crisis exists in our jails and prisons (Kupers, 1999). There is a growing subpopulation of prisoners with serious mental disorders. Deinstitutionalization and budget reductions in the public mental health and social welfare systems, along with high unemployment and the criminalization of homelessness, cause many individuals suffering from serious mental disorders to be incarcerated. Courts are much less willing than they once were to consider a defendant's psychiatric disorder as a mitigating factor. And overcrowding, the demise of education and rehabilitation programs, and the growing reliance on supermaximum-control units inside the prisons create a very harsh environment that causes heightened violence inside and many serious psychiatric breakdowns.

Male posturing in prison has a double edge in relationship to mental health issues. On one hand, men's need to keep their cards close to their chests and refuse to disclose their needs and pains often prevents them from seeking the kind of mental health care that might help them do their time and come out of prison emotionally prepared to "go straight." On the other hand, it is actually very dangerous in prison to expose one's vulnerabilities; thus, men's tendency to refrain from expressing their feelings and inner experiences can serve to keep them out of certain kinds of trouble. For example, other prisoners pick on men who are known to be "weak in the head"; in addition, the psychiatric notes in a man's "jacket" can cause a parole board to postpone release indefinitely based on the assumption that his mental illness would make him a threat to the community.

Punitive Segregation and Male Issues

"The SHU (Security Housing Unit) Syndrome" is a little-known psychiatric disorder with a quickly increasing incidence. It occurs in supermaximum-security prisons, which house a growing number of individuals who suffer from serious and persistent mental disorders. Because correctional mental health services are vastly understaffed and lacking in outpatient and psychosocial rehabilitation services, many mentally disturbed felons, left to their own devices, get into trouble and are sent to punitive segregation or solitary confinement, where they suffer worse breakdowns.

The acronym "SHU" refers to supermaximum-security prison units, where the prisoners are locked in their cells nearly twenty-four hours per day and are cell-fed. Not all states use this acronym, but "SHU" has become the generic term for "supermax," "maxi-maxi," or "control units" such as the ones at Pelican Bay State Prison in California; Dannemora in New York; and Florence, Colorado, in the federal system.

These units are like "the hole" of the old days, except that a prisoner who misbehaved was thrown in "the hole" for ten to thirty days, whereas prisoners are sent to the SHU for years. And instead of being dark, damp dungeons, most SHUs' are very high-tech. The lights are on all night, the doors open by remote control, and prisoners are video-monitored. In other words, the prisoners have very minimal contact with guards and other prisoners and almost nothing to do.

Harvard psychiatrist Stuart Grassian (1983) coined the term "SHU Syndrome" (see also Grassian and Friedman, 1986). He examined a large number of prisoners during their stay in segregated, solitary confinement units and concluded that these units, like the sensory-deprivation environments that were studied in the sixties, tend to induce psychosis. Even prisoners who do not become truly psychotic report a number of psychosis-like symptoms, including massive free-floating anxiety, hyper-responsiveness to external stimuli, perceptual distortions, hallucinations (auditory, visual, and olfactory), a sense of unreality, difficulties with concentration and memory, acute confusional states, the emergence of primitive aggressive fantasies, persecutory ideation, motor excitement, and violent self-mutilatory outbursts. And they experience rapid subsidence of symptoms upon termination of isolation.

Between one-quarter and one-half of the prisoners in all the SHUs' I have visited or read about suffer from serious and long-term mental illnesses. They are, on average, the most severely psychotic people I have seen in my entire twenty-five years of psychiatric practice. There are two basic reasons for this: (1) Inadequately treated prisoners who suffer from mental disorders break rules (they are not known for their capacity to follow rules) and get into fights (often as victims, but that does not mean they will not be punished) and (2) they are punished with time in "lockup," or solitary confinement, of one kind or another. After they have been sentenced to enough time in solitary, they are sent to the SHU, where their psychotic symptoms and prognoses worsen.

Of course, one reason so many men run into disciplinary problems is their need to maintain a tough image so they can avoid victimization on the yard. Prison magnifies male competition and violence, and the hypermasculine posturing continues even after a prisoner is placed in solitary confinement. For instance, a young African American man in punitive segregation refuses to return his food tray after lunch one day because, according to him, "This food ain't fit for a dog!" The guard comes over to his cell and tells him he has to return the tray right now or the guard will come in and get it. The young man backs up a few paces, raises his fists in a boxing pose, and says, "Well, come on in then. We'll see how tough you really are." The guard turns, muttering something about "damn niggers" not knowing their place, and leaves the tier. Ten minutes later he returns with a "cell extraction team" composed of five guards wearing bulletproof vests and the kind of padding worn by professional ice hockey players, replete with helmets and visors, cans of mace, and electrical stun guns. The guard taunts the prisoner anew, calling him a "nigger" as the other guards laugh, and the prisoner maintains his pugnacious stance until the team bursts into the cell and roughly subdues him.

Who is to say which prisoner is of sounder mind in this situation: the one who permits himself to be subjected to endless indignities or the one who chooses a moment to take a stand even in the face of overwhelming force. But clearly the prisoner who is hearing voices and suffering from delusions in his solitary cell is not very capable of controlling his rage. And this is why so many severely disturbed prisoners wind up in punitive segregation and why so many are the objects of brutal "cell extractions."

Increasingly, prisoners are "maxing out of the SHU." Prisoners on fixed sentences have a release date, and their disciplinary infractions in prison do not extend that date, though they are sentenced to SHU time for the infractions. When their release date comes up, even if they are housed in a SHU at the time, they are simply set free. (Some states offer some prerelease programming, but those that I have reviewed are not adequate to the task of resocializing a psychotic individual who has been in solitary for a long time.)

Of course, the implications in terms of public safety are ominous. Not only are individuals suffering from severe and long-term mental illnesses being sent to prisons in ever larger proportions; they are also inadequately treated, they wind up in lockup, a subgroup is showing up in SHUs' (members of another subgroup voluntarily isolate themselves in their cells so they will not get into trouble), and eventually they "max out of the SHU." This means that they come out of prison, after spending months or years in a cell by themselves, decompensated and full of rage.

Rape and Post-traumatic Stress Disorder

Rape is widespread in men's prisons. Unlike rape in women's facilities, where the perpetrators are almost always male staff, rape in men's prisons is perpetrated by male prisoners who are obsessed with the dominance hierarchy, which demands that they rape other prisoners in a bizarre attempt to prove that they are "real men" and not "punks." But the male dominance hierarchy also dictates that, once raped, a man must not admit that he is hurting or seek help. It is not unusual for a man who has been raped to turn around and rape a weaker man—for example, a newly arrived prisoner, or "fish."

Prison rape often leads to post-traumatic stress disorder (PTSD) in the victim. Because PTSD is not on the correction department's list of "major mental illnesses," which includes such disorders as schizophrenia and bipolor disorder, it is often wrongly treated as undeserving of urgent attention. It is grossly underdiagnosed and undertreated in correctional settings. Symptoms of PTSD include flashbacks, nightmares, panic attacks, and severe constriction of emotional range and daily activities. Depression and suicide are frequently part of the clinical picture. Treatment for PTSD involves talking about the trauma in individual or group therapy (Herman, 1992). Medications are sometimes helpful as an adjunct to the verbal processing of traumas, but they are not an adequate treatment when they are prescribed alone.

The male prisoner faces overwhelming obstacles to talking through the trauma of prison rape. First, if he reports the incident to staff members, they will demand that the perpetrator be named before they will offer any help. Either the victim must identify the perpetrator and face the likelihood of deadly retaliation for "snitching," or the staff will refuse to help the victim get treatment. Even if the victim manages to get as far as seeing a psychiatrist, the therapist is very likely to disbelieve the patient's report of the rape and his symptoms of PTSD and accuse the prisoner of manipulating the system to gain attention. Or, because of insufficient mental health treatment resources, the psychiatrist may prescribe tranquilizing or antidepressant medications without any "talk therapy." And if the prisoner manages to get into group therapy, he is faced with the shame of admitting that he was raped and the prison code prohibition against exposing his vulnerabilities and pains in front of other men. Is it any wonder that so many rape victims never report the incident; never seek treatment; or, if they do reveal their plight, are denied adequate treatment? Is it any wonder that so many then become depressed and eventually commit suicide (Kupers, 1996)?

Addressing Men's Issues in the Course of Prison Reform

We need to attend to the mental health crises behind bars. It is not merely a matter of hiring more psychiatrists—that would only lead to more prisoners' being drugged into a stupor and spending twenty-four hours per day in their cells for fear of being attacked if they came out. Rather, changes are needed in the entire criminal justice system. Currently, 75 percent of newly admitted prisoners have never been convicted of a violent crime. Most of them should be diverted to noncorrectional settings where they can receive help for their problems, which often involve substance abuse and chronic unemployment. A much larger proportion of mentally ill offenders need to be diverted to noncorrectional treatment settings. We need to reinstate meaningful education and rehabilitation programs inside prisons. We need to ameliorate the racism that permeates the criminal justice system. We need to reverse the trend of recent decades to lengthen sentences and make punishment harsher. We need to put an end to the use of supermaximum-control units and other forms of cruel and inhuman captivity. We need to focus much more attention and much larger resources on youth, to keep them out of the corrections system. And we need to find effective means of helping men and women who have broken the law to reform themselves and return to the community and lead productive lives. Only in the process of achieving all of these aims will it become possible to establish quality mental health services within correctional insititutions (Kupers, 1999).

Gender is also a very important issue that is, unfortunately, rarely addressed in discussions of prison reform. We need to attend to men's issues as we reform our criminal justice system and provide adequate mental health treatment programs. Recall that two of the many ways that men's mental disorders are intensified by male proclivities in prison are (1) hypermasculine posturing and bravado, which cause many male prisoners—especially those already suffering from or prone to develop serious mental disorders—to break rules and be sent to psychosis-inducing solitary confinement, where the harsh atmosphere worsens their condition and (2) the mentally disordered prisoner's vulnerability, which leads to his being raped and then having no opportunity to process the trauma in a trust-inspiring situation.

These unfortunate scenarios are made all the more tragic by the male tendency to trust nobody, keep silent about private pains and vulnerabilities, and then act out aggressively to keep from talking about inner turmoils. Of course, these tendencies are omnipresent among men in the outside world, but in prison they are greatly magnified by the male code. Complicating the picture is the very real danger of being perceived as weak or of trusting someone only to be betrayed. Even many men who are aware that they suffer from a serious emotional disorder refuse to admit it and seek help, because they fear they will be perceived as weak and will be victimized by staff or other prisoners.

My pointing out ways that men's proclivities cause them to be vulnerable to emotional distress and make it harder for them to benefit from treatment by no means implies that male prisoners are responsible for the terrible conditions, including the deplorable mental health services, in prison. That assertion would constitute "blaming the victim." It is the uncaring, even sadistic, attitudes on the part of many (though certainly not all) correctional officers, wardens, and mental health personnel in the prisons that lead to cruel policies, inadequate mental health interventions, and vindictive punishments. For instance, I have seen many instances in which prison guards have taunted a prisoner they know to be psychotic until he takes a swing at one or throws excrement, and then the guards have gleefully rushed in, beaten the prisoner, and hustled him off to solitary confinement. Gilligan (1996) believes that prison staff members purposely ignore weaker prisoners' claims that they are being repeatedly raped in order to appease the tougher prisoners who perpetrate the sexual violence and gain their cooperation in keeping peace within the institution. In other words, guards very often consciously and malevolently use prison rape to divide the prisoners and maintain their own authority.

From well-documented efforts in the community, we have learned a great deal about preventing rape, ending men's violence, helping people end their drug and alcohol dependence, and treating trauma survivors (Warters, 1991; Kivel, 1992). But the lessons from community interventions are rarely applied very conscientiously within the prisons. For example, we know that women who have been raped are at risk of feeling that they are being raped again, or retraumatized, when they are treated gruffly during an emergency room forensic gynecologic exam or are crudely cross-examined in court about their prior sexual experiences. Yet in prison the guards are permitted to threaten with inattention those prisoners who complain of being raped if they do not identify the perpetrator. And medical and mental health staff members are likely to disbelieve them if they do seek help.

Daniel Burton-Rose (see the chapter entitled "The Anti-exploits of Men against Sexism, 1977–78" in this volume) chronicles the evolution of the group Men against Sexism, which was founded by Ed Mead in 1977 to reduce the incidence of prison rape. Ed went from cell to cell to discuss the problem with fellow prisoners, and the mere act of talking instead of being shamed into silence caused a striking reduction in the number of occurrences. This suggests that men collude in silence in the continuation of cruelty, and it is possible for caring men to get together to put an end to the worst cruelty. At the very least, the experience of Men against Sexism provides convincing evidence that something can be done to prevent prison rape.

Men's centers in the community have had great success doing group work and providing education aimed at reforming perpetrators of domestic violence. Yet even though we know that a signficant proportion of men in prison have resorted to domestic violence in the past or are likely to commit some kind of domestic violence after they are released if they do not get proper help during incarceration, there are very few prison programs modeled on the kind of group work and education that have proven successful in combatting male domestic violence in the community.

The successes of Men against Sexism inside a correctional institution and of men's centers aimed at reducing domestic violence in outside communities are two examples of how we might combine our understanding of mental health issues with our growing knowledge of men's gendered proclivities to produce an effective intervention strategy. Other examples of this general approach are provided in the following chapters in this volume: David Denborough's "Coming to Grips with Male Privilege through Prison Work," Jackson Katz's "Boys Are Not Men: Notes on Working with Adolescent Males in Juvenile Detention," Harris Breiman and T. Pete Bonner's "Support Groups for Men in Prison: The Fellowship of the King of Hearts," and Charles J. Sabatino's "Men Helping Men: Facilitating Therapy Groups for Sex Offenders." The troubling question is why so little of this urgently needed work occurs in men's prisons in the United States.

We must attend to men's issues as we struggle to improve conditions and treat mental illness within the prisons. A big stumbling block is that the same kind of tough, cruel law-and-order thinking that makes it unthinkable to provide rehabilitation programs and adequate mental health services behind bars makes it even more unimaginable to change men's attitudes and behaviors. For this reason, the political, profeminist men's movement, which was founded on the premise that men can and must change, must join the struggle to reverse the extreme cruelty and abuse that are so rampant in our prisons today.

References

Gilligan, James. 1996. *Violence: Our Deadly Epidemic and Its Causes.* New York: Putnam.

Grassian, Stuart. 1983. "Psychopathological Effects of Solitary Confinement." *American Journal of Psychiatry* 140 (11): 1450–54.

Grassian, Stuart, and N. Friedman. 1986. "Effects of Sensory Deprivation in Psychiatric Seclusion and Solitary Confinement." *International Journal of Law and Psychiatry* 8: 49–65.

Herman, J. 1992. *Trauma and Recovery: The Aftermath of Violence—From Domestic Abuse to Political Terror.* New York: Basic Books.

Kivel, P. 1992. *Men's Work: How to Stop the Violence That Tears Our Lives Apart.* Center City, Minn.: Hazelden.

Kupers, Terry A. 1996. "Trauma and Its Sequelae in Male Prisoners: Effects of Confinement, Overcrowding, and Diminished Services." *American Journal of Orthopsychiatry* 66 (2): 189–96.

———. 1999. *Prison Madness: The Mental Health Crisis behind Bars and What We Must Do about It.* San Francisco: Jossey-Bass.

Warters, W. 1991. "The Social Construction of Domestic Violence and the Implications of 'Treatment' for Men Who Batter." *Men's Studies Review* 8 (2):7–16.

Rudy Chato Paul Sr.

Night Crier

I'm working on my first novel. The night is silent and the darkness is thick. It's frightening. A cool spring breeze makes its way through the bars and the steel-wire meshing of my window. I remember when they installed the reinforced steel meshing. That was before Frog got killed, back in the summer of 87. Since then, C-Block has been made into a prisoners' prison.

The silence is broken by a scream, followed by lengthy cries and jumbled words that I can't quite make out. I recognize "god" and "c.o."* The cries swell and fade in a crazy rhythm, a mantra of pain. "Ahhhhhhhhhhh . . . ," he moans. Eventually I realize that the sound comes from the hospital. Someone is hurting, I presume.

My concentration is broken and I can no longer focus on the novel. I go to the window and see lights flicking on in the cells adjoining the hospital building. The cries are reaching ears in these cells as well.

"Ahhhhhhhhhhh . . ." This time the cries sound more agonized, and I strain to recognize the voice but fail. I don't know if I should feel sorry for the individual or not. The night crier continues his refrain. He's shrieking now, and the sentences are getting longer.

My feeling of indifference bothers me. Am I no longer able to care? Have I lost touch with human compassion entirely?

A few of my close neighbors are awake now. Some cough, some flush toilets. I wonder if they feel as I do? How do I feel?

"Ahhhhhhhhhhh . . ." No long sentences this time. No mention of c.o.'s or god. He seems to have decided to moan just for the satisfaction it provides him. I realize that it takes a great deal of courage to cry out the way he's doing. Crying in prison is taboo. In a maximum-security prison Like Attica, it's an even greater breach of the manly codes. I wonder how much pain I could endure before I cried out like he does. Or would I merely cry into my pillow instead, as I have done in the past?

A jet passes overhead. The passengers are oblivious to the misery below. The crying ceases, and the cell lights go off one by one, like stars fading into the dawn. My neighbor snores lightly. Another toilet flushes. It's 4:19 A.M., April 16, 1991.

*Editors' note: "C.o." is short for "corrections officer."

I look around my cell. The calendar I have pasted on my wall is marked off. Three years, eleven months, twelve days, five hours, eleven minutes, and twenty-seven seconds left until I see the parole board. But who's counting?

I'd better get some rest. I have a rough day ahead. I have to sleep late. Then I have to go to the mess hall, providing I want to eat. Fifty yards. Damn! That's a long fuckin' walk. If only the food was worth it. Since there is no menu on the bulletin board, I have to guess what will be served.

I really don't need a menu. I've been here long enough to know what they serve. It's been the same for the past five years. But the guessing game we play is part of our survival kit, a way to inject a little meaning into one more day. What's tomorrow? Tuesday? My guess is it'll be mashed potatoes and franks with colored greens. Colored greens? It that a tautology?

I might as well get back to my writing. The crying has stopped. Mine resumes, however, in the form of a novel.

Part VI

Prison Reform, Reforming Prison Masculinities

*Prison reform is urgent. Prison conditions that breed failure—especially the over-
crowding, the idleness, and the consignment of large numbers of prisoners to punitive
lockups for long stretches—require immediate remedy. We must also evaluate the outcomes of corrections practices that are based on the "get tough" thrust of recent criminal justice legislation and court rulings. And we must take into account the social correlates of crime, such as poverty, inadequate schooling, a lack of affordable housing,
dismal job prospects for those at the bottom of the socioeconomic ladder, and the dismantling of the social services that once served as a "safety net." These priorities have
long been on the policy agendas of liberal prison reformers.*

*Too often, however, the reformers lack any awareness of how issues of masculinity
enter into discussions of rehabilitation. For example, we know that prior physical and
emotional abuse is omnipresent in the personal histories of prisoners. The brutal punishments that men receive while incarcerated, including rape and extended solitary confinement, too often serve as traumatic reenactments of abuse that they experienced as
infants, children, or adolescents.*

*Prisoners themselves have a role to play in reforming such destructive aspects of
prison life as sexism, homophobia, and violent aspects of the male code. But they need*

help. Counseling to end substance abuse and domestic violence is proving to be quite successful in the community, yet very little of this kind of help is available inside prison. Although at least 75 percent of prisoners have a history of substance abuse, only 17 percent receive any treatment for the problem while incarcerated. And even fewer prisoners are provided opportunities to take part in health and AIDS education, counseling programs for domestic violence and sexual abuse, and workshops on anger management and healthy fathering.

Moreover, work is central to men's gender identity and sense of adequacy, whether they are employed in factories, office buildings, or prisons. Yet prison administrators and correctional staff members have paid little attention to prisoners' feelings about work, unemployment, and underemployment. Meaningful work is a primary ingredient in the making of a man, and the deprivation of satisfying job opportunities can be part of what drives men to use drugs, commit crimes, and resort to violence. Today, as a result of the dismantling of prison rehabilitation programs, most prisoners are left to their own devices when it comes to fending for prison jobs or planning reentry into the existing labor market upon release.

The lack of rehabilitation programs also affects sex offenders, who are considered the lowest of the low within the prison hierarchy. They are feared and loathed by most people in civilian society. But most sex offenders will eventually be released, and whether their experiences behind bars served to worsen or help them transcend their proclivities is a critical issue. Staff members who work with men in prison need to be part of an agenda for personal reform that at once holds men accountable for their actions and facilitates growth. Again, men's counseling programs aimed at ending violence and other destructive behaviors have achieved some successes in the community but have not been adequately applied in the prisons.

In these and many other ways, prison reformers must apply the lessons of the men's movement to reach out to and help men in prison.

Jarvis Masters

Scars

I remember the first time my eyes really witnessed the scars on the bodies of my fellow prisoners. I was outside on the maximum-custody exercise yard. I stood along a fence, praising the air that the yard gave to my lungs that my prison cell did not. I stood in my own silence.

I watched the prisoners on the yard playing basketball and handball. I watched them showering and talking to one another. John, Pete, and David, the inmates I felt closest to, were lifting weights in a corner. I began to notice the lashlike scars on their skin, which were shining with sweat from pumping iron in the hot sun. Other prisoners had similar types of scars and gashes on their legs, backs, ribs, arms, and faces.

A deep sense of sadness came over me as I watched these strong and powerful men. It shocked me to recognize that the entire yard was filled with men who were flecked and striped by the physical evidence of the violence in their lives. All the acts of abuse that had taken place in my own childhood bubbled to the surface. I remembered being beaten and whipped by my stepfather and all the lonely nights and days of abandonment by my mother, who was a heroin addict. Like an electrical shock, I felt a terrible longing for my mother, who had died less than a year before. "Wow," I thought, "I still wish I had been there when she died."

I began to connect the stark realities of the scarred men before me to my own childhood and readings I had been doing on child abuse. In the 1980s people began to uncover and understand the alarming rate of child abuse in U.S. society. They wrote books and did research studies, and they set programs in motion. Yet here, hidden in the exercise yard of San Quentin, was a cluster of America's lost children, surviving in rage and in refuge from society. Most of us were born in the fifties and sixties, when there were few laws that protected us from being victimized by child abuse. Could there be connections between the violent crimes these men committed to land in prison and the violence they experienced as children?

Talk about Scars

I set out that day in the sun to get my fellow inmates to talk about child abuse. "Am I crazy to want to get men to open up about their experiences with child abuse," I wondered. Most inmates will not even use the term "child abuse," let alone talk about it seriously. "None of these men will ever admit that their parents abused them," I thought. They looked hardened to the core as they stood around the weight-lifting bench, proud of their bodies and the images they projected. Their posture of pride symbolized the battle wounds that they had "made their bones" with; this is prison talk for "prove your manhood." In prison, shucking and jiving is the usual route men take to avoid dealing with serious or sensitive matters. If they would not talk about child abuse, I reasoned, maybe they would talk about their scars.

I approached John, a hulking six-foot, three-inch twenty-eight-year-old who is serving twenty-five years to life for murder. I first met John when we were both in youth homes in southern California. We were eleven years old. For years we traveled together throughout the juvenile systems, until the penitentiary became our final stop. While the others listened, I asked him about the scars on his face. He bragged, "These scars came from kicking ass and in the process getting my ass kicked, which was rare and few. . . . My father taught me how to fight when I was maybe five or six, and I had to learn from him beating on me."

John explained that his father had loved him enough to teach him how to fight. In a sense, he grew up with a loving fear of his father. He pointed to a nasty-looking scar on his upper shoulder. Laughing, he explained that this was where his father had hit him with a steel rod when he tried to protect his mother from being beaten by his father. Most of us had seen this scar but had never had the nerve to ask about it. As we stared, John seemed to feel ashamed. Avoiding us with his eyes, he mumbled a few words before going on to show us more scars. He had total recall of the smallest details surrounding each violent event. The childhood experiences still haunted him, as many abuse memories do. In spite of his apparent suffering, his ongoing explanations remained very rational and low-keyed. He had spent more than half his life in one institutional setting or another, and as a result he regularly projected a cold and fearsome, even boastful, smile on his face. He used smiles, jokes, and jive-talk to hide what he was feeling in his heart. In his mind, he was not talking about child abuse. The rap was on scars.

He directed our attention to a huge gash on his back that was hidden by a tattoo of a dragon. It was an ugly scar, like what I imagined a slave would have got from a severe whipping. "Rub your finger down the dragon's spine," he beckoned. As I did so, it felt like a thick string that moved jerkily like a worm beneath his skin. "Damn, John, what in the hell happened to you?" There was something in my question that made him laugh, and the others joined in. He explained that, when he was nine or ten, his father had chased him with a cord, and he had tried to hide under his bed. He had grabbed the bedsprings and tried to hang on while his father pulled him by the legs and hit his back repeatedly with the cord until he fell unconscious. He woke up later with a very deep flesh wound. Again with a smile on his face, John said that was the last time he ever ran from his father.

David and Pete told similar stories of beatings that had occurred at early ages. The stories seemed to explain, at least in part, how we had come to be in one of the worst prisons in the country.

Prison as a Painful Refuge

I believe that, for many men, institutionalization is a kind of refuge from the devastation of child abuse in their lives. Most prisoners who were abused as children were taken out of the custody of their natural parents at very early ages. The authorities placed them in foster homes, youth homes, or juvenile halls to protect them from further abuse. These settings in most cases were adopted by the children as protective shields against an uncertain world. For most prisoners abused as children, prisons are a continuation of this same process of living in a state of painful refuge.

This was the attitude that I carried unconsciously during my more than fifteen years of institutionalization. Not until I read a series of books on adults who had been abused as children did I begin to understand about healing the shame that binds persons to their past. I became committed to examining my own history of child abuse and how it had somehow led me to expect to go from one youth institution to the next. I had never really tried to stay out of these places, and neither had my friends.

The comments of the men in the exercise yard that day showed me how each of them seeks a similar kind of refuge in his denial. They could not allow themselves to admit openly the hidden truth of the pain and hurt they lived with. As for me, I spoke to them very openly about my life history of abuse. I talked about being abandoned by my parents when I was five years old. I shared some childhood horror stories about how my mother had left me and my sisters alone for days with our newborn twin brother and sister when I was only four years old. The baby boy died from crib death, and since I had been made responsible, I always believed it was my fault. I spoke of the hurt and pain that I had carried through more than a dozen institutions, and I discussed my belief that these events had ultimately entrapped me in a cycle of lashing out against everything and everybody. I never wanted to look inward to face the fact that I was hurting and crying out for help so long after the abuse and neglect from my parents took place.

Each of the men had been a victim of child abuse, yet they could not speak directly about their experiences or share their feelings in ways that went beyond bravado and false humor. My own comments seemed to sadden them, but they avoided linking my experiences to an understanding of their own. Perhaps what they heard was the voice of their own unspoken stories. We all fell silent around the weight-lifting bench as each one squatted down and stared at the men across the yard.

John and I later spoke privately. Surprisingly, he confided, "You know something, the day I got used to getting beaten up by my father and by counselors in all those group homes was the day that I knew nothing would ever hurt me again. Everything that I thought could hurt me I saw as a game. I had nothing to lose and just about everything to gain. A prison cell to me is something that will always be here for me."

It occurred to me that John was speaking for most of the men I had met in prison. Secretly, we all like it here. This place welcomes a man who is full of rage and violence. Here he is not abnormal or perceived as different. Here rage is nothing new, and for men scarred by child abuse and violent lives, the prison is an extension of inner life. We learn to abuse and reabuse ourselves by moving in and out of places like San Quentin.

Conclusion

We are all men out there on the exercise yard—muscled, mean, and manly. The prison defines us as such. But I realize that there would be much greater power in what we men see in one another if we could see ourselves as human beings first. We live with the impressions of manhood, and they leave us bolstered but hollow and lonely.

It scares me to realize that most prisoners will eventually reenter society, become fathers, and repeat their own history of abuse with their children. With no educational programs in most prisons that speak to the issue of abuse, there is reason to believe this is likely to occur. The cycle of crime and abuse will continue.

Finally, I confided in John about wishing earlier that morning that I had been there when my mother died. He asked, "Hey, didn't you say she neglected you?" He was right. But I asked myself whether I would be neglecting myself even more by wishing that I was not there, that she was not my mother, that I still did not feel love for her.

Jackson Katz

Boys Are Not Men: Notes on Working with Adolescent Males in Juvenile Detention

When I was a teenager in the mid-1970s, I thought about kids in the Department of Youth Services (DYS) in the same way that I thought about some of the menacing men with ugly tattoos that I would occasionally see on a subway trip into Boston. I was intimidated by them. I hadn't met any actual DYS kids, but I imagined they had a street toughness that I rarely encountered in my mostly white, mostly middle-class town. I was from a blue-collar family, but in my mind "juvenile delinquents" (JDs) were city kids. They lived in housing projects or run-down tenement buildings. They had weapons and knew how to hot-wire cars. I didn't see them as my peers—as immature, pimple-faced adolescent boys with problems just like my own: family problems, body image problems, gender and sexual anxieties.

Then, in my early twenties, after graduating from college, I went to work part time as a counselor at a short-term juvenile detention facility in the Boston area. It wasn't a high-security lockup, and it didn't look like a traditional prison. It was a program for adolescent male offenders, aged nine to seventeen, and it was located in a building on the grounds of an old state hospital for the mentally ill. It was funded by DYS and run by a private nonprofit agency that had been pioneering new intervention alternatives to the institutional violence of the old prisonlike "reform schools" for youngsters in previous generations. It was a staff-secure facility, meaning there were alarms on the doors but no locks, and the staff was responsible for knowing where each child was at all times.

In that setting, with the proximity and occasional intimacy that being a counselor (as opposed to a corrections officer) can offer, I began to think about "JDs" in a different way. The young thugs and criminals I had feared in my youth and had been angry with (for crimes of violence and misogyny) in my increasingly politicized young adulthood were quickly becoming real people: some likeable, others ornery, some cocky and aggressive, others shy and withdrawn. Save the occasional seventeen-year-old whose poise and wisdom belied his tender age, however, I realized early on whom I was working with. These were not, by and large, innocent kids, caught up in a Dickensian life of orphanages and cold and uncaring adult institutions. Some of them had committed serious offenses, including assault and robbery. Some had left truly innocent victims in their wake. But neither were they coarsened men. They were kids. Some of them were children. Most of them needed help, just as I had when I was their age.

Our society has finely developed mechanisms to pathologize those who exhibit bad or socially disapproved behaviors, in part because disidentifying with the transgressors is a way of distancing ourselves from their deeds, as well as from our complicity in them and the systems that produce them. This is one of the tried-and-true functions of racism in a white supremacist society: It keeps the spotlight on the dark-skinned miscreants and off the white-dominated economic, social, and political institutions that produce, in Jonathan Kozol's memorable (1991) phrase "savage inequalities."

Labeling young males "juvenile delinquents," "adolescent offenders," or the more recent "superpredators" serves to dehumanize them in the popular discourse and allows most Americans to distance themselves from the lives and crimes of these young people. This depersonalization allows class biases to shape our perceptions of who in our society has problems and who causes problems. It also allows racism to color our understanding of the "crime" problem. Moreover, the degendering of the delinquency discourse allows us to pretend that a certain percentage of "youth" in every generation becomes involved in criminal behavior, when we know that the vast majority of serious crime by "juveniles" is perpetrated by boys and young men. Acknowledging this fact might inspire a greater degree of societal introspection, because talking about what is going on in the lives of *boys* is more personal and probing than talking about what is happening to our *youth*. But self-preserving systems resist introspection almost by definition, often subtly, and so most of us continue to be diverted from looking at "youth crime" as *our* problem or a gender problem. Similarly, most "educated," middle-class white males are spared the feeling of "there but for the grace of God go I" when we hear and read about what goes on in the lives of hundreds of thousands of poor and working-class young males. The feeling is more "How could *they* do those things?" and "*We* never would have gotten into that kind of trouble."

But we might have. Who among us—especially we middle-class, college-educated white males—can say that there is no way that we would have ended up in a juvenile detention facility? How about those of us who smoked pot and used other drugs in high school? Can we honestly say that, if we hadn't been shielded by our class and race privileges, we wouldn't have been harassed more frequently by the police and prosecuted more vigorously? How about those of us who grew up in emotionally or physically abusive families? Can we honestly say that, if we had been born into poverty, we would never have acted out in ways that might have brought the attention of the police and other agents of state authority? The more I started talking with some of the scared, angry, and confused young people who came, handcuffed, through the doors of the detention center, the more I felt uncomfortable "othering" them and denying some of the similarities between my painful adolescence and many of theirs.

In the hit 1997 film *Good Will Hunting*, Matt Damon's character, Will Hunting, is a brilliant but troubled young man from South Boston who has a history of violent assaults. After a particularly brutal assault, in which he explodes in a violent frenzy during a meaningless street fight, the judge, perceiving the young man's obvious emotional problems, orders him to get therapy. Thus begins Will's personal struggle to heal the deep scars of his abused childhood.

But what about all the young boys across the country who are similarly scarred yet who receive no treatment at all, who are simply locked up and thrown into an often brutal, dehumanizing system? According to a July 15, 1998, *New York Times* article entitled "Profits at a Juvenile Prison Come with a Chilling Cost," mental health authorities estimate that 20 percent of juveniles incarcerated nationally have serious mental illnesses. Yet few, even those with diagnosable mental illnesses, receive any treatment whatsoever. Then there are all the adolescent males in detention or juvenile prison who, although not mentally ill, are untreated trauma survivors, often developmentally delayed and emotionally shut down.

The knee-jerk response of conservative politicians and public opinion shapers is often "Too bad. They did the crime; now they should stop whining and do the time." The reality is, in the mainstream media discourse, much of the conversation about juvenile justice in the wake of heinous violent crimes by boys is, predictably, about making the penalties harsher. After some of the school shootings in the spring of 1998, one Texas state legislator actually filed a bill calling for *eleven-year-olds* to be eligible to receive the death penalty. These crimes are despicable, and public safety considerations are perfectly legitimate. But lethal assaults represent only a small fraction of the crimes for which boys are committed to the juvenile system. Indeed, in 1995, person offense cases (including assault, robbery, rape, and homicide) accounted for 22 percent of all delinquency cases, and homicide accounted for less than 1 percent of these (U.S. Department of Justice, 1998).

Adolescent Masculinity and Criminality

Notably, adolescent males who are convicted of assault are often found guilty of assaulting family members. Although this is clearly criminal conduct for which there must be clear and just consequences, the assaultive behavior often speaks to underlying family dynamics. It has long been a truism in developmental psychology that girls tend to internalize and boys tend to externalize their pain and despair. That is why, at least in part, boys are eight times as likely as girls to be arrested for violent crimes and much more likely than girls to commit serious crimes of all sorts. Considering the fact that millions of boys *and* girls grow up in dysfunctional families, in poor, working-class, and middle-class communities, would it not be in the best interest of all of us, except demagogic politicians, to understand *why* so many more boys act out in criminal ways and how cultural constructs of masculinity contribute to this behavior?

Too often, boys are locked up for exhibiting behaviors that are expected of them in their immediate peer cultures, behaviors that carry benefits within their social environment. Richard Majors and Janet Billson have observed this phenomenon at work in the inner city, where the effects of racism and poverty often cause young, poor, black males to strike a "cool pose" and to exhibit "compulsive masculinity" to compensate for feelings of shame, powerlessness, and frustration: "In compulsive masculinity, typical masculine values become a rigid prescription for toughness, sexual promiscuity, manipulation, thrill-seeking, and a willingness to use violence to resolve interpersonal conflict. These values [are] perpetuated through male-to-male transmission in a tightly knit street culture" (1992:34).

But this "compulsive masculinity" is not strictly race-bound, as even a casual glimpse at the swaggering walks and outward toughness of many white, Latino, and Asian boys in detention will quickly demonstrate. Neither is it exclusively a phenomenon of the inner city.[1]

Adolescent, white males in middle-class suburbia, although not exposed directly to the racism or economic deprivation of blighted city neighborhoods, are nonetheless influenced by various cultural discourses around "manhood," some of which derive from the mean streets of urban America. Still, middle-class, white boys—including those who break the law—are far less likely than their poor and working-class counterparts to end up in the juvenile system. This is partly because the behavior of these boys is not as closely monitored as is the behavior of boys in lower-income communities and partly because boys in middle-class communities typically have access to higher-quality legal representation than do boys in lower-income communities. One result is that the juvenile system is literally overflowing with poor and working-class boys from rough urban or rural environments who have or see few legitimate means of validating their manhood or gaining the approval and respect of their peers beyond taking the tough-guy pose.

Unfortunately, for many of these kids, this constructed macho pose often leads to inexorable antisocial, criminal behavior. As Messerschmidt puts it, some middle-class, working-class, and lower-working-class young men exhibit "unique types of public masculinities that are situationally accomplished by drawing on different forms of youth crime" (1993:119). Thus, effective long-term strategies to reduce adolescent male crime would have to confront the daunting challenge of changing the patriarchal gender order, along with oppressively hierarchical class structures and their attendant masculine (and feminine) social constructions. The problem cannot be reduced simply to the need to teach children "right from wrong."

Regrettably, over the past couple of decades, the public attitude toward juvenile crime has had less to do with understanding its community, family, or gendered causes than with expressing anger and outrage and calling for more-punitive remedies. Since the presidential election of Ronald Reagan in 1980, advocates of a less-authoritarian, more treatment-oriented approach to juvenile crime and punishment have been in retreat, as legislatures pass harsher sentencing laws and millions of dollars in state and federal monies are invested in new prison construction.

What gets lost in this movement to instill "discipline" into the lives of these young boys by punishing them even more severely for their misdeeds is that subjecting them to the harsh masculine prison subculture—juvenile or adult—is more, not less, likely to exacerbate the problems that led to their criminal acting out in the first place. It is woefully naive to think that mandatory sentences and tougher treatment are a necessary wake-up call to kids whose life experiences have already left them oppositional and defiant in the face of adult authority. It is even more naive to think that a law-and-order approach will work with young boys who have been neglected or sexually or physically abused. Such boys are legion in the juvenile system, and many of them already have alcohol and other substance abuse problems or suffer from untreated mild depression.[2] The inconvenient fact is that the vast majority of boys and young men in the juvenile system, having done their time, will be back out on the streets one day, often with no greater insight into their problems and with no more effective strategies for coping than when they went in. Only now they'll be older—and angrier.

Bad Boys, Sad Boys

One of the basic feminist insights that informs profeminist men's studies is the truism that men, far from being the fixed "cultural norm" against which women should be measured, are gendered beings ourselves. Our life experiences and chances are every bit as shaped by the gender order—refracted by class and racial structures—as are women's.

Traditionally, progressive sociologists and criminologists have understood crime and delinquency by focusing mainly on conditions of socioeconomic inequality, the contradictions of commodity capitalism, and the tensions produced in a society with vast disparities of wealth and opportunity (Keller, 1992). Since the early 1970s, feminist social scientists have expanded the zone of understanding by studying the relationship between gender construction and criminal behavior, particularly in the lives of women and girls. But as basic and important as their work has been, feminists with insights into the gendered aspects of delinquency, rehabilitation, and punishment—insights that have profound implications for the lives of boys and men—have faced an uphill struggle in the male-dominated fields of sociology and criminology. In fact, until fairly recently, little attention if any has been paid to the gendered aspects of the lives of boys and men and how cultural constructs of masculinity might contribute in significant ways to their life experiences, including antisocial behavior, crime, and punishment. There is, clearly, a need for more informed and vibrant discussion in this area.

Researchers who are looking into the gendered nature of the causes and consequences of boys' delinquency might consider using as a resource the thousands of men and women who work with these boys in juvenile detention centers, community-based programs, and even secure, locked facilities. In my fifteen-year association with the detention center (I have stayed in touch), I have observed many people who know little if anything about the academic debates surrounding these issues but who nonetheless possess a great deal of personal and visceral knowledge from repeated and often powerful connections with the boys themselves. In my own experience, the two aspects were combined. Working with these boys over several years during my mid-twenties, I learned a great deal, for example, about the masks boys and men wear to hide inner turmoil and vulnerability. These insights have helped me both personally and, over the past decade, in my work in gender violence prevention.

Counselors in a staff-secure facility spend a lot of time sitting around, talking with kids, playing cards, watching TV. There are no individual or double-bunk cells with individualized locks on the doors, as in adult prisons. In the detention center where I worked, the boys live in large rooms called "dorms" with six cubes each and a counselor assigned to each dorm. It is a short-term facility, with kids rarely staying longer than several months. The task of the counselors is to supervise the youths' time, provide them with some gentle but firm adult guidance, and assist in whatever way possible in finding the right placement for them in a more long-term setting. Sometimes you meet and bond with a boy, and he is gone in a couple of days. Other times you get to know the boys pretty well, depending on how long their placement is and how well you hit it off.

A counselor in a detention center cannot possibly know all the complex factors in boys' lives that land them in the system. But sometimes, because of the special vulnerabilities that these boys experience, the counselor catches a glimpse of what real life looks like for some of the individuals that the public—in a close-minded, conservative era—sees simply as "bad kids." Consider some examples from my own experience working with boys in youth detention:

One night, one of the boys I was responsible for was on the phone in the shift area, talking with his mother. It was a half hour after lights out. The twenty-four other boys in the place were in bed, many fast asleep. I was sitting quietly near the doorway, making sure the five other boys in my dorm had settled down and stopped talking to each other across the room. I was keeping one eye on Darryl*, trying not to eavesdrop too noticeably on one of the few semi-private conversations he was allowed to have.

Quite abruptly, he put the phone down hard and ran by me to his cube, where he plopped down onto his thin-mattressed, twin-sized institutional bed and buried his head in the pillow. I could hear his muffled sobbing.

I didn't know this kid very well. He had been at the facility for only a few days, and I hadn't spent much time with him. All I knew was that he was a charismatic sixteen-year-old African American from Dorchester. I alerted one of the other counselors who knew him better, and he entered the darkened room to talk to the distraught boy.

It turned out that Darryl was upset because right in the middle of his phone conversation with his mother, her boyfriend started yelling at her and beating her. Darryl had to stand there and listen on the other end, utterly powerless in some godforsaken DYS unit twenty miles from home.

Advocates for battered women have increasingly been paying attention to just this sort of trauma. Their attention has focused not just on whether girls in abusive situations are more likely to grow up and become abused or whether boys in abusive situations are likely to become abusers. Their goal is to understand how "delinquent" and self-destructive behavior—by girls and boys—is related to the traumatic experience of growing up in a home where their mother is being abused. How does the violence done to their mother affect her children? How do they cope? What are some of the gender differences in the way children of battered women handle the abuse?

I wondered how I would have felt as a child in a situation similar to Darryl's. What if I were powerless to stop a man from assaulting my mother? How would I be able to focus on anything else—the daily routine of a juvenile facility: going to class, doing chores, playing cards? I knew Darryl was feeling guilty—if not outright responsible—for his mother's suffering.

---

*Some names have been changed to protect the privacy of individuals.

He blamed himself, because he loved her but could not protect her. He was the one who had screwed up and gotten himself locked up. When he ran a week later, foolishly, impulsively, who was surprised? I never found out what happened to him.

Another time there was a fifteen-year-old blond, white boy named Brian in my dorm. He looked as if he could have been a Laguna Beach surfer, but in reality he was from a lower-middle-class section of Lowell, Massachusetts. He had just recently been brought into the system. Again, it was 10:30 at night, after lights out, when he rushed over and urgently asked me if he could use the bathroom. Moments later I heard him vomiting. He was in the doorless stall for a full half hour. I checked on him periodically, reassuring him that he would be all right, that it was probably his stomach rejecting something he had eaten earlier at dinner.

When he felt ready to leave the bathroom, he came out red-eyed and visibly exhausted and sat with me in the shift area before heading back into his cube. "I'll never again let myself get in a situation like this," he vowed, tears in his eyes. "It sucks getting sick like that in a place like this, having to ask to go to the bathroom, not having your family around. This is the last time." Although he didn't say, "I want my mommy"—that would have rendered him far too vulnerable (read: unmanly) with me—it sure seemed that he was thinking it.[3]

Writing about second-graders, Olga Silverstein and Beth Rashbaum note that a boy gets the message that he simply is not supposed to have certain feelings, such as fear, uncertainty, or sadness. A boy gets "a very problematic message, since he's well aware that he himself does. Having got the message that he's not to be a 'mama's boy,' he knows he mustn't allow anyone, not his father and certainly not his friends, to see how strong his attachment is to his mother. What he does with his many 'unacceptable' feelings is to disguise them with shows of bravado" (1994:45).

For some eleven-, twelve-, and thirteen-year-old boys, being committed to the juvenile system pulls them away from their mothers for the first time. But they can't begin to show their pain or their longing for her (and occasionally for their grandparents, fathers, and siblings). Quite understandably, it is rare to see a boy let the facade slip, especially in front of other kids. But juvenile detention counselors, in their offices, behind closed doors, see the vulnerability, the sadness, all the time. In a personal interview in June 1988, Dick Zegarowski, the director of the center, told me that he even keeps a box of tissues on a small table in his office.

Zegarowski tells the story of one Christmas day when a fourteen-year-old boy was expecting his mother. Since the mother did not drive, a female staff member had made plans, even though she was off for the holiday, to pick up the boy's mother and take her to see her son. All the mother had to do was call, and she would be picked up. But she never called. The boy waited all day, until it became clear that she was not coming. She didn't even call her son.

A few days later, the mother came to the facility for a meeting with her son and his caseworker. As she walked into the room, she opened her arms, expecting an emotional mother/son embrace. But the boy, who presumably was no stranger to her erratic behavior, just sat there; he did not even stand up to greet her. As she was leaving, the same awkward scene played out. The mother opened her arms to hug the boy, and he slumped away, avoiding any physical contact.

Despite more than twenty years of atavistic conservative leadership at the federal and state level, our society has made progress in identifying some of the connections between child abuse and a range of other social problems, including juvenile crime. But child neglect, a phenomenon often associated with poverty, has received much less attention—even though it constitutes the largest share of child abuse and neglect cases substantiated annually by the National Center on Child Abuse and Neglect. (cited in Little, 1995). Neglect is far less sensational than abuse; moreover, according to Craig Little, "acknowledging its existence in an affluent society raises fundamental questions about the society's values and social and economic organization. Research funding to investigate such matters is hard to find" (1995:239).

But although research in the area of child neglect may be hard to find, victims—especially in the juvenile system—are easy to find. Zegarowski reports that he sees the effects of neglect all around him: adolescent boys with dramatically undeveloped social skills, flat affect, and a limited knowledge of basic hygiene. He says, "We used to say, 'misguided youth'; now we say, 'unguided youth.'" Boys who have birthdays at the center get a cake and a happy birthday song from the staff and their peers, in part to ameliorate their pain when, as often happens, they fail to get even a phone call from a parent or from anyone else.

Conservative politicians in recent years have, to a great extent, successfully manipulated public anger at adolescent male crime—especially when the crimes involve violence. But it is hard to stay mad at a fourteen-year-old boy for stealing a bike or even a car, when you sit with him on Christmas and no one calls or comes to visit—not a parent, a grandparent, or a sibling—and he waits in his chair, out of the sight of his peers, crying. It makes you wonder. Did his family give up on him at fourteen because he has gotten into so much trouble? Or did he get into the trouble in the first place because his family is so screwed up? Was he abused? Neglected? You cannot find answers to these sorts of questions by reading police logs in the daily paper. When you spend countless hours with a boy, eating meals, listening to music, shooting baskets, you begin to see him as a frightened, lonely fourteen-year-old. But to most everyone else, he's just another young thief.

Over a six-year period, when I worked at the center, I only occasionally inquired about the specific crimes committed by the boys with whom I worked. (Because I worked part time, I didn't have primary responsibility for individual cases.) But I did look into the background of one boy, another fourteen-year-old, a bright, good-looking boy, who was committed to the system for sexually assaulting a young girl. I was, admittedly, angry when I heard what he had done. But, like many of these kids, he became less of a one-dimensional ogre when I learned a little about his life.

Like many children in the juvenile system, Charles came from a poor city neighborhood. His mother had been forced into prostitution by his father, a violent, alcoholic man who terrorized his family. One time, the father came home to their fifth-floor apartment on a rampage and forced Charles over to an open window. He grabbed the boy's ankles and proceeded to hang him out the window, threatening to drop him. On numerous other occasions, the father, unprovoked, attacked both Charles and his mother. At one point he permanently disfigured Charles's mother—in front of her son—by stabbing her in the face with a broken bottle. Of course, none of this justifies for a moment Charles's assault on a girl. But it does raise questions that few people seem willing to ask: At what age do we cease to have empathy for boys who are victimized, traumatized children, badly in need of therapeutic intervention and treatment? At what point do we start feeling angry and vengeful toward them when they turn around and perpetrate violence against others?

New Approaches at the Millennium

A staff-secure detention center is not a prison, and boys are not men. Some of the adolescent males who are committed to the juvenile system are, sadly, on their way to lifetimes in and out of prison. Their armor is already too thick and strong, their anger too lethal for a "normal" life on the outside. But many more are not yet irretrievably lost. They're immature, troubled youngsters whose family and social environments—combined with the cultural pressures that demand that they measure up to impossible masculine codes—have set them up for various forms of criminal behavior. Treating fifteen-year-old boys as if they are already hardened criminals might make good media sound bites, but it defies both common sense and the daily experience of thousands of counselors across the country who work with these boys. It is also worth restating, in the frenzy to build more and more detention facilities and prisons, that high-profile murders and other heinous crimes represent only a small fraction of offenses for which boys and young men are incarcerated. As always, extreme cases make bad social policy.

Progressive reformers in the juvenile system have been arguing since 1970 that adolescent boys in detention often need nurturing more than they need punishment. This is as true today as it was then. But in designing new approaches and programs at the turn of the century, contemporary reformers have the advantage of being able to draw on the growing body of profeminist research and theory about the relationship between gender identity construction and adolescent male criminality.

There are a number of ways to incorporate this new insight into existing institutional practices. It is clear that a tiny fraction of the federal and state monies that go to new prison construction would be enough to provide in-depth in-service training to the staffs—including the administrators—of juvenile facilities. The men and women who work with these boys every day should have the benefit of exposure to some of the important new research and ideas about boys' emotional and psychological development, as well as sociological insights into the gendered nature of various delinquencies.

Similarly, criminology programs at the post-secondary level are the training ground for the next generation of law enforcement, criminal justice, and legal professionals. They, too, should be incorporating in their curricula new progressive insights into male psychology, the construction of hegemonic and subordinated masculinities, and the relationship of these psychological and sociological phenomena to adolescent male delinquency and crime. The rationale is obvious: Policy makers and others who understand the gendered aspects of crime and punishment are more likely to design effective interventions.

For now, those who seek to implement even these modest proposals face an uphill struggle. As feminists in the field have known for years, sometimes the greatest challenge is getting men in positions of influence and authority to see and acknowledge the obvious. Generational change offers hope. For example, consider the increasing presence of women in the historically male domain of juvenile (male) detention. When I worked in the detention center in the 1980s, there were only a handful of women staffers. Today, women constitute 40 percent of the staff, and the program is stronger than ever.[4] We can only hope that as more late baby boomer and Generation X men who have been influenced by modern feminism work their way into positions of leadership, they and women who have risen through the ranks will be able to help guide our institutions beyond the current fixation on outdated solutions. We are, after all, at the start of the twenty-first century.

Notes

Acknowledgment: I thank Jeremy Earp and Martha-Elin Blomquist for their valuable input and assistance on this essay.

1. For a discussion of compulsive masculinity and criminality exhibited by white, middle-class boys in a suburban setting, see Lefkowitz, 1997.
2. For a discussion of some of the connections between culturally constructed norms of masculinity and depression, see Real, 1997.
3. To cite one example of a phenomenon that has long been observed in men who are rendered vulnerable by danger or trauma: In Steven Spielberg's cinematic tour de force "*Saving Private Ryan*" (1998), which featured what many critics—and veterans–say are the most realistic battle scenes from World War II ever put on film, several mortally wounded soldiers are overheard crying out for their mothers.
4. Women working in the hypermasculine adolescent male detention environment face special challenges that need to be acknowledged and addressed. They often have to deal with not only the reluctance of some boys to respect women in positions of authority but also a lack of full acceptance as legitimate colleagues by some of their male peers. To counteract these pressures, one strategy implemented at the center is to have a regular "women's group" meeting, where female staff members raise and discuss sexism and other job-related issues.

References

Keller, R. 1992. "From 'Con' to Counselor: Changes in Gender Identity in a Prison Juvenile Awareness Program." *Men's Studies Review* 9 (1): 18–22.
Kozol, Jonathan. 1991. *Savage Inequalities: Children in America's Schools.* New York: Crown.
Lefkowitz, Bernard. 1997. *Our Guys: The Glen Ridge Rape and the Secret Life of the Perfect Suburb.* Berkeley and Los Angeles: University of California Press.
Little, Craig. 1995. *Deviance and Control: Theory, Research, and Social Policy.* 3d ed. Itasca, Ill.: Peacock.
Majors, Richard, and Janet Billson. 1992. *Cool Pose: The Dilemmas of Black Manhood in America.* New York: Lexington Books.
Messerschmidt, James W. 1993. "Varieties of 'Real Men.'" In *Masculinities and Crime: Critique and Reconceptualization of Theory.* Lanham, Md.: Rowman and Littlefield.

Real, Terrence. 1997. *I Don't Want to Talk about It: Overcoming the Secret Legacy of Male Depression.* New York: Scribners.

Silverstein, Olga, and Beth Rashbaum. 1994. *The Courage to Raise Good Men.* New York: Penguin.

U.S. Department of Justice. (1998). Office of Juvenile Justice and Delinquency Prevention. "Person Offenses in Juvenile Court 1986–1995," No. 77. April.

Harris Breiman and T. Pete Bonner

Support Groups for Men in Prison: The Fellowship of the King of Hearts

[*Editors' Note:* The two companion essays that follow lay out a pathway for men in prison to think and feel through their lives in ways that take gender into account. Harris Breiman is the founder of the Prison Council Project in Woodstock, New York. T. Pete Bonner is a former prisoner and staff writer for *Prison Life.* In order to honor the confidentiality of inmates currently in the New York State system, the editors have created pseudonyms for the prisoners cited in Bonner's essay.]

Starting a Men's Prison Council

Harris Breiman

The prison experience is one of isolation and emptiness, fear and mistrust, violence and chaos—an assault upon the soul. What can you do while incarcerated to keep your sanity, to develop your creativity, to not only survive but also realize your human potential and prepare for your return to society? Is transformation possible?

Over the past several years we have developed a men's prison council at the Shawangunk Correctional Facility, a New York State maximum-security prison. Our prison council, which we have named the Fellowship of the King of Hearts, is a successful model that any prison open to rehabilitative programs can use.

What exactly is a prison council and how does it work? The prison council at Shawangunk is a forum that addresses universal issues and concerns: the desire to heal personal wounds and overcome emotional trauma, the struggle to build communities where a sense of meaning and purpose can be shared, and the need to create a world where peace with justice reigns. These concerns have motivated people throughout history to

Reprinted by permission of Harris Breiman.

form groups or councils where ideas, wisdom, and experience can be shared; support can be offered; and decisions to bring creative action out into the world can be made. Twelve-step support groups help individuals on the difficult road from the trauma of addiction to recovery. Group therapy provides a collective setting in which members are guided to work through psychological pain and distress. Indigenous tribal cultures and modern religious communities provide ritual, mythology, and inspired teachings to help individuals appreciate the sacredness of life and to reconnect with the Earth and the Divine Spirit. Our prison council draws upon each of these pathways to personal healing and empowerment.

We focus on questions of masculine development, accountability, and responsibility. Incarcerated men often experience heightened tendencies common to all men in our culture: tendencies to become frozen into macho armor, to experience emotional isolation and numbness, to participate in cut-throat competition, and to make desperate attempts at domination. If we add to this the stress of growing up in broken families in urban war zones and the trauma of being targets of racism, poverty, and social injustice, there is great potential for the manifestation of chaos and criminal behavior. When the prison experience focuses exclusively on punishment and incarceration, a deadly cycle is perpetuated, and the result is continual escalation of violence on our streets. If prisoners are ever to return as redeemed men and creative contributors to our culture, there must be a shift of perspective in the way prisons function. The prison council can be one element in transforming incarceration into a positive rite of passage by supporting psychological health and spiritual growth. This path reduces violence and promotes desirable behavior, allowing these men to become positive role models and mentors to those who are both inside and outside the "Wall." Members of our council have encouraged other prisoners to begin or continue their academic studies, to resist negative peer pressure, to participate in therapeutic and vocational programs, and to grow in self-awareness and understanding. They challenge others to become the kind of men who command rather than demand respect—the kind of men who empower others rather than abuse them.

How does our council operate? First, all participation is voluntary. The idea to form a council was spread by word of mouth from counselors and directors of existing programs to the general prison population. We invited interested prisoners to a presentation that I developed. A core group of men formed, and these men then invited others to participate. Today, the group screens all new recruits, and consensus on each prospective member's character and trustworthiness must be reached before he can join.

The council meets every other week for approximately two hours. My colleague Onaje Benjamin and I facilitate each meeting on a volunteer basis. We provide a computer call-out list, and the prisoners are released from their cells when our arrival is announced. At any given meeting, anywhere from eight to eighteen men participate. A code of honor among those present commits each man to confidentiality and mutual respect. After handshakes and hellos, our meetings begin with several minutes of silence and slow breathing to quiet the mind. One of us then invites everyone present to come together on common ground with a sense of brotherhood and solidarity. Then a council member invokes words of prayer, asking for the grace of the Divine Spirit to guide our time together. We sit in a circle to symbolize equality of power and the desire to experience true community. One man assumes the task of calling upon others to speak. Each person is recognized and given an opportunity to share without interruption. Only when all have spoken does cross talk or conversation among us begin. The goal is to listen receptively and to share honestly. Both support and challenge are welcomed. Within this atmosphere, the men often express a diversity of viewpoints, and resentment or anger can flare up. We believe it is a sign of a mature man to have the emotional depth, the intellectual discipline, and the physical control to let such conflicts be creatively experienced, contained, and transformed, rather than destructively or violently expressed.

The issues raised in the council are far-ranging and vary from session to session. We have examined the meaning of masculinity by exploring the King, the Warrior, the Magician and the Lover—basic archetypal structures that exist in every man's psychology. We have spoken about the spiritual journey as a foundation for sanity, the necessity of ongoing education, the importance and power of family, the inner work involved in preparing for parole and release, the economics and politics of racism and social injustice, and the importance of mentoring and community service. We have also explored remorse about the past. Each man brings a unique perspective. Each participant assumes responsibility for his input, leadership, and outreach to others. We initiate specific tasks, projects, and goals as determined by collective vision and inspiration. Our council seeks to be open to the tremendous diversity of age, race, religious, ethnic, ideological, and other orientations among the men in the prison. Our only prerequisite is that each man bring an open mind and a sincere desire to initiate positive change. Although feelings of grief and sorrow are important to express, these sessions are not intended as opportunities to whine, complain, or indulge in a stance of victimization. Rather, they are opportunities to enter an oasis where personal renewal is possible and where positive actions can emerge.

Members of our council have committed themselves to mentoring younger inmates; they have helped raise funds for Rwandan relief; they have worked to promote "good time" legislation in New York State; they have taught African and Latino studies classes; they have worked as facilitators in prerelease and literacy programs and in Alternatives to Violence and innovative therapeutic process workshops. They have helped other inmates in the law library, served as mediators in disputes, become actively involved in the Christian and Muslim communities, and offered to produce for the media public service announcements to help break the cycle of violence and give something back to society.

When our sessions come to a close, we stand together in a circle and join hands. We express final thoughts, visions, hopes, and prayers, and we become silent one last time. We imagine the energy among us going out to other inmates in the facility and beyond the walls into the world. As we part, we know that we will carry each other in our hearts until we meet again. We call ourselves the Fellowship of the King of Hearts to symbolize our commitment to providing service and positive leadership and to serve as just and compassionate role models for other men.

The poet Theodore Roethke wrote, "What is madness but nobility of soul at odds with circumstance" (Roethke 1992). These men have survived the madness in the belly of the beast. They are using prison as a positive rite of passage by aspiring to the noble side of human nature and by bringing gold out of the ashes of incarceration.

We invite administrators and counselors in correctional facilities to join our efforts, to consider starting such a program or being open to inmates who want to start one on their own. Prisoners may approach their administration with such a proposal and take responsibility for helping to organize a council such as the one described here. Finally, we have created materials for prison council development, and we are available to provide consultation and assistance. Let us work together in this quest for healing, community, and justice. Let us work together to free the imprisoned soul!

For further information, contact OASIS, The Prison Council Project, P.O. Box 31, Woodstock, NY 12498; phone: (914) 679-7441.

Reference

Roethke, Theodore. 1992. "In a Dark Time." In *The Rag and Bone Shop of the Heart,* ed. Robert Bly, James Hillman, and Michael Meade (New York: Harper).

Tough Guys Open Up

T. Pete Bonner

Forty-four-year-old Jamal Smith, doing twenty-five years to life, talks about being a role model by guiding other prisoners in the right direction. He was locked up for killing two cops and discusses the "evils of manhood" and the "mechanisms of masculinity."

William "Samoa" Jones, twenty-nine, convicted of first-degree homicide, attempted murder, and robbery, speaks eloquently about young black men having no sense of direction.

And thirty-five-year-old Carlos Alejandro, who is doing seventeen years to life for possession of narcotics, quietly laments his lost youth: "I didn't know in the streets the things I know now."

Could it be? Tough guys—convicted murderers and dope dealers, macho veterans of the street—expressing their innermost feelings? They are not provoking, challenging, or insulting fellow prisoners' mothers in a high-wire game of the dozens. Instead, they're sitting in a circle, talking quietly and respectfully to each other. They're listening, connecting, relating, and opening up their minds and souls. They're honestly talking about their fears, their values, and how they screwed up their lives. In short, they are communicating.

It's happening at Shawangunk Correctional Facility, a maximum-security prison located in the peaceful rural valley of Wallkill, New York. Ten to fourteen men make up the Men's Council of Shawangunk, the first sprouting of the men's movement in a U.S. penitentiary. They are making history, not to mention creating a model for men trapped in prisons throughout the world. Ironically, it's happening in a prison where approximately 56 percent of a population of over five hundred men are serving life sentences.

The group is led by forty-year-old Harris Breiman, a holistic therapist who codirects the Mustard Seed Center for Healing in Woodstock, New York. Breiman started the group as an outgrowth of his work with men's groups at a local homeless shelter and at the Ulster County Jail. With the support of Robert Vosper, the supervisor of Shawangunk's prisoner grievance program, Breiman pursuaded the prison's superintendent to give it a try. Surprisingly, the forward-thinking administrator bought the idea.

Making the program happen took some coaxing. Getting beyond prisoner homophobia was the first step. After that, prisoners thought the idea reeked of white, middle-class values. Men of color doubted whether they could get anything out of it. Still, seven courageous men were willing to be guinea pigs. After all, they had nothing to lose. And they certainly had plenty of time on their hands.

What they found was an open forum where they could say anything they wanted without being criticized or judged. With a code of confidentiality, they learned that they could benefit from an open exchange. It became a powerful escape hatch to release psychic steam.

Breiman delights in saying that the core group still remains, the founding fathers being the base for recruiting new members. The men sit in a circle, and each man takes his turn talking about anything on his mind. The others react and freely voice their opinions. They've learned that there is no right or wrong, only healthy dissent.

The conversation moves from fighting for your manhood to the dehumanization of the prison system, from fears of resuming life on the outside to rising crime in ghetto neighborhoods, and from solutions for preventing violence to frustration with prisoners who are not motivated to improve themselves.

Since the group began two years ago, each man has become an amateur psychologist, a critical observer of himself and others. At a recent meeting, Hamed Nafron, forty-three, doing twenty years to life, asserted that black people ought to accept responsibility for their actions. "Hey, let's be honest," he says. "It's on you to change. It's not the government's responsibility. We've got to get our acts together and take a serious look at ourselves. Just look at what we're doing to each other."

James Jackson, forty-five, who has already done seventeen and a half years of a twenty-year-to-life sentence, nods his head in agreement. Jackson continues, "Black people can get on the radio and use the words 'nigger' and 'bitch.' To me, that's serious. If you think white people are going to stop us from calling us niggers and bitches, you're crazy. We've got to stop degrading ourselves."

Part of the solution depends on finding positive role models. One man explains, "We created the problems. Now it's up to us to stop them. The only way to do so is on a grassroots level. We can break the vicious cycle of crime by going back to our old neighborhoods and becoming positive role models. That's the only way to secure them. We have power, yet we don't use it."

Forty-six-year-old William Post adds, "The world only stops for courageous people. These are the people who deserve respect."

Picking up on Post's comment, another council member says, "That's right. Like myself, most young black men have no sense of direction. We must take responsibility for being men."

Robert "PJ" Parcel, serving eighteen years to life, pipes in, "My peer group is lost. They need someone to tell them what it means to be a man and a father. It's not about being macho. It's about being real."

The discussion continues, fueled by a self-propelling energy in hot pursuit of truth and self-awareness. After the two hours bolt by, the men hold hands for a closing benediction before guards escort them back to their cell block. Before leaving, a few men exchange hugs. Most are disappointed that the session is over. With little prodding, they would have continued for another two hours.

Don't get the wrong idea. This is no confessional, Breiman explains. These men are breaking ground, exploring uncharted terrain. The work they're doing at the Men's Council continues long after the session ends. "They're not whiling away their days watching TV and pumping iron," says Breiman. "They're working on themselves. They're asking intelligent questions. They're questioning conventional scripts of manhood and masculinity; they're rethinking their plight."

The nonthreatening sessions bond the men to each other. "For the first time in their lives, they can pull away their macho masks of pseudomasculinity and share common feelings," says Breiman. "They feel a sense of community and thus discover a comforting sense of support. Instead of living in isolation, distrusting other men, they're realizing they're not alone. Other men have the same fears and problems and can thus be supportive."

Elder statesman of the group James Huggins, fifty-six, agrees. "Form a group made up of intelligent men, and you can learn something about yourself and others," he says. "In the process, you can change and improve." Pausing for a moment to gather his thoughts, the philosophical prisoner serving a twenty-five-year-to-life sentence says, "Most men doing time want to change; they just don't know how."

An optimistic Breiman insists that men's groups are a step in the right direction. "If the public and prison administrators observed our program, they'd see that it is a positive way to diminish the mindless, punitive attitude perpetuating violence," Breiman proclaims. "Prison does not have to be a warehouse where bodies are stowed. It can be a place not only where rehabilitation takes place but where men can transform themselves so they can return to the community with tremendous gifts. Having a men's council like the one we created at Shawangunk is one way it can be turned around. There ought to be one like this in every prison."

The present prison system is not working, according to Breiman. "I'm not saying men shouldn't be incarcerated and punished for their crimes," he adds." But they shouldn't be discarded and forgotten."

The Shawangunk Men's Council is a small but powerful beacon of light, an oasis where minds and souls are being nurtured back to life. It offers the promise of renewal and transformation.

With any luck, prison administrators will open their eyes and realize that men's groups are a rehabilitative springboard, a powerful tool for turning men around so they can be sent back to society as positive role models capable of breaking what James Jackson described as the "vicious cycle of crime."

Daniel Burton-Rose

The Anti-exploits of Men Against Sexism, 1977–78

Once an ex-con told me i was pretty,
he said if i were in prison i'd be somebody's woman,
i'd have to obey him and be faithful to him,
if i got caught screwing with someone else,
i'd be slit with a knife or a razor blade,
slit until the blood from my faggot ass
met the blood from my throat,
bled until the redness became a poem
and then a song,
until a mute nation heard
but they haven't heard and sometimes
i realize they can't hear at all

From Tommi, "The Rape Poem," Washington State, 1976

I'll tell you what, we were tough faggots.

Ed Mead, veteran member of Men Against Sexism, 1997

The name came from a local gay men's collective: Men against Sexism (MAS). The name of the revolutionary prisoners' group captured well its melding of radical feminism and gay liberation. What the name did not reveal was one of the more unique aspects of MAS: its militant, direct-action component.

The men who loved men of MAS saw sexism as a brutal form of domination, one that twisted and destroyed the emotional and physical relationships that were potentially the most beautiful features of life. Prison compounds all the nastiest aspects of the outside world; this is especially true of the process by which tenderness is transformed into weakness—in which what is sweetest, given, becomes horrific when violently taken. From at least the early seventies, prisoner rape and sexual slavery were the norm in Walla Walla, Washington State's most notorious maximum-security prison.

The members of MAS resolved to fight them, with every means that the wartime situation merited.

Ed Mead, the intellectual leader of the group, was serving a de facto life sentence for taking up arms against the state as a member of the George Jackson Brigade, a northwest guerrilla group active from 1975 to 1978. Inside "Big Red," the brick Intensive Management Unit in which Mead was placed to contain his revolutionary contagion, Mead met up with Danny Atteberry, a radicalized social prisoner (a politically conscious individual who is imprisoned for acts of conscience) with whom Mead had an immediate affinity. On December 30, 1974, Atteberry and some of his equally riled comrades had taken possession of a sizable part of the prison, as well as several guard hostages to increase their bargaining power. Their demands focused on changing the medieval conditions of confinement at Walla Walla, and righting the sabotage of prisoner self-government in which the twenty-year warden, B. J. Rhay, was engaged.

Late on the night of May 31, 1975, as a member of the brigade, Mead had crept into the offices of the Washington Department of Corrections (DOC) in Olympia and placed a pipe bomb under the desk of the director. Members of the brigade had scoped the building earlier to make sure it was empty. The bomb exploded after several hours, as planned, doing major damage to the third-floor offices of the DOC. The bombing and accompanying communiqué aimed to draw attention to the suppression and brutalization of the men who had participated in the December 1974 takeover that Atteberry and others had staged.

Soon after Mead arrived at Walla Walla, he realized he had some friends he had never met before. This was a time when the domestic civil war was subsiding in the outside world. While many crushed and confused radical elements wondered what hit them, a state of war continued to rage behind bars. When Mead was forcibly thrown back into the volatile mix this time around—he had been in and out of prison as a social prisoner since age twelve—his radical social analysis, working knowledge of weapons, and resolve that he could not live in the world as it existed helped focus earlier, very diffuse anger.

Routine sexual assault was one of the most visibly horrifying aspects of "Concrete Mama," as the physically foreboding prison was often called by its residents. The standard cycle in the 1,750-man institution went something like this: A strong, aggressive prisoner would pick a weak, vulnerable prisoner—who was usually young and openly gay, effeminate, or simply unable to defend himself—who had just gotten off the bus, and he would inform him, "You'll turn tricks for me or I'll slit your fucking throat." The new prisoner belonged to the pimp and was now his whore. The newcomer's sexual availability was marked by such signs as lace sown onto his sleeve. All that was needed from a customer was the appropriate amount of cigarettes. The whore had no right to refuse anyone. All profits from tricks went to his owner. These were the days when "I better see shit on my dick or blood on my knife" was a popular saying. And the young and pretty were not the only ones so abused; elderly inmates and anyone else without protection were targets for sexual slavery. It was a nauseating prospect of existence for years or decades of life, and prisoners were committing suicide rather than live the nightmare.

Mead wanted to protect the rape victims. Atteberry's stance was more along the lines of "Fuck 'em if they won't stand up for themselves." Mead was bisexual, and Atteberry had always identified as straight. So Mead collected more gays, and together they began disrupting the systematic sexual exploitation at Walla Walla.

An early necessity that MAS addressed was finding shelter for vulnerable incoming prisoners. They came up with the concept of "safe cells," cells they bought from other prisoners, who would transfer out of them. MAS members would meet prisoners on the chain—those fresh off the bus and on their way to processing—and take the ones aside who seemed to meet the exploiters' target criteria. They would then explain the situation at Walla Walla to the newcomers and, if the newcomers so desired, give them a cell until they could be absorbed with less danger into the prison population.

MAS became active in developing the prison community. The group brought in anti-sexist films with such names as *Men and Masculinity,* as well as antiwar films in a general attempt to politicize the population. Twenty or thirty men, mostly gay, would show up for such events. MAS also published a newsletter called *The Ladyfinger.* The previous prison underground newsletter was named *The Bomb.* MAS intentionally opted for a move away from the macho.

MAS brought in bright cultural workers, such as members of Olympia's Theater of the Unemployed, a radical political satire troupe. MAS played host at the isolated prison in rural eastern Washington, taking new friends on tours of the prison, feeding them, and getting to know them. It was a powerful experience for many outsiders to become personally tied to the conditions under which folks were living in the prison and to begin to feel those confines themselves through human ties that they developed with prisoners. For MAS members, the contact with the outside world (which for some did include, but was in no way limited to, activities along the lines of sucking and fucking in broom closets) was a lifeline, delightful and encouraging.

MAS drew some members from the loose outside collective from which MAS had taken its name. After meeting MAS members, the collective found attacking the rape system a compelling necessity. Mead was also known to the collective because its bimonthly journal, *Morning Due,* was on the brigade's communiqué list, and the collective had published communiqués and constructive criticisms of the brigade.

In the summer of 1977, a member of MAS made contact with the Metropolitan Community Churches (MCC), a religious organization for gays based in Los Angeles that claimed thirty thousand to forty thousand members at the time. John Rowe, an MCC chaplain, served on the National Board of Institutional Services, and his only duty was to serve the institutionalized population of Washington. Rowe began making monthly visits to Walla Walla, conducting a prayer service and Holy Communion and counseling individual prisoners. (Mead's conception of communism included a steady expansion of rights—economic rights—as well as what he called the standard bourgeois rights, such as freedom of religion. The days when Rowe gave a sermon were the only time in his life he ever attended church regularly.)

The incident that spawned the gay preacher's admission into Walla Walla happened like this: One Sunday, information leaked out that the Protestant preacher who had preceded Rowe and the MCC would give a sermon focused on the evils of homosexuality. MAS sent the word out. Roughly thirty to forty queers filled the pews—a substantial number, as church was poorly attended—and when the preacher lit into his tirade, Mead stood up and denounced him for persecuting the religious freedom of gays and for being un-Christian in his hostility to tolerance and diversity. Other queers followed Mead's lead, while the straight Christian flock failed to defend its ostensible leader. Preacherman backtracked, and MAS follow-through on the incident got MCC and Rowe into Walla Walla.

A MAS support group in Seattle soon started up. Diverse in age, race, and sexual orientation, its members shared political awareness or ties with someone inside. The group organized families of prisoners—helping them overcome the shame of having a family member in prison—to come out to rallies (unless family members felt that their imprisoned relative was in imminent danger, getting the families of Native American and black prisoners seemed especially difficult to the activists). Protesting families of prisoners made good copy in those days, and the news media actually seemed to befriend the support group. Television production crews turned rallies of ten or twelve into densely packed protests of a hundred with trick-of-the-trade camera angles. Supporters also rented cars for the five-hour trek to Walla Walla and brought sewing machines fund-raised by the outside gay community. Inside queens used the machines to make pimp fashions—hats, vests—that were sold to raise funds for safe cells.

MAS obtained a quiet coup when it took over the Lifers' Club—an organization with its own office and beautiful garden. Most of MAS's members were lifers, and the previous group running the club was not, in the opinion of Mead and some others, doing with it all it could. MAS started selling candy and with the money bought a football table and a pool table. With MAS in control, unlike with the previous leadership, there was no corruption or dope dealing. The group turned the area into a retreat. Some members could even arrange to have intimate trysts with outside supporters. Twenty to thirty prisoners were showing up each week at MAS meetings. For some, it was just another club and something to do, but for a hard-core of six or so, it was a central aspect of their life.

MAS was not without threats and opposition inside the prison. One of the central elements of the philosophy of the organization was the revolutionary truism that, if you aid the weakest, the rest will rise. For this reason, they defended child abusers, a group that was routinely beaten for sport at the prison. Mead knew viscerally that, if he let anyone slide, he was no longer a revolutionary. No one can ever be thrown over the side. To direct anger where it belonged, MAS could never let prisoners vent their anger downward.

MAS soon ran into trouble with a group of bullies, a prisoner "class" that Mead, always the staunch Marxist-Leninist, referred to as the "toughoisie." MAS's defense of the lowest of the low was not widely understood. "What are you doin'? This guy, he's a fucking child molester. What are you doin'?" So went the incredulous response of tormentors.

"It's the principle," Mead and the rest tried to explain. "You can't buy and sell people, no matter who they are."

But the message did not get across. In time, MAS's control of the Lifer's Club was challenged. Resentful prisoners were calling the club "The Faggots Club," and a group of dope fiends resolved to take it back. Just as it was becoming clear that a showdown was imminent, Tommy Thomas, a member of the club who was not a member of MAS, offered to reveal the location of six shotguns that Mead and the others had stowed away in exchange for his and his lover's transfer to a less-secure prison. On the brink of confrontation, the MAS hard core found themselves unarmed. They began to fear that they might have to give up the jewel.

As MAS's situation intensified inside, Don Duffy, a Seattle supporter, began to understand both the hideousness of the situation they were confronting and the real effect they were having. Duffy let MAS members know he was with them "till the wheels fell off." Duffy's parents' had first institutionalized him at age fifteen for being queer. In and out of institutions for most of his teens, he self-medicated with over-the-counters till he was on a psychological roller coaster in his twenties. About the time MAS started up, he became a member of a gay and lesbian mental health clinic that encouraged him to change by struggling to change society rather than focusing negatively on himself. In his early thirties, Duffy felt compelled to take what might be called "a therapeutic approach" toward the society that screwed him up. One of Duffy's first small acts was to smuggle a revolver and eighty rounds of ammunition to Mead. To test the piece out, Mead went into the cafeteria walk-in refrigerator and, with sentry posted, fired into a side of beef. The demonstration helped MAS get a little space.

A crisis occurred in late 1977 when the president of the Chicano Club took a very effeminate queer prisoner as his property, saying she would dance for the club. The prisoner was in a relationship with another con at the time, a relationship that was actually loving rather than, as was more common, coercive. When MAS got word, the group called an emergency meeting for the core of six, including Mead, Atteberry, their cellmate Mark LaRue, and a prisoner who went by the name "Blue." Their feeling was that, if they permitted this sort of violence to take place in the prison, MAS might as well not exist. Someone was dispatched to try to talk with the club, and he returned with the words the Chicano Club had sputtered with hatred: "Fuck you, fuck you, fucking faggots. No sissy faggots'll tell us what to do!"

The response of MAS was, "Okay, so be it." Mead went to get the revolver he kept in his portable radio, the ammunition, and three homemade grenades. The six had a conversation. The gist was, "It's time to make our stand. We'll go in there and we'll muck out as many of these people as we need. And whatever happens we'll have sent a message." It was resolved. At this point, Blue asked for a final chance to talk with the club. He somehow conveyed to them that they were genuinely about to die. The gay prisoner was released, and the immediate situation was defused.

Pressure continued to mount against MAS. The safe cell system was crumbling because people never felt secure enough to move out, and MAS could not support the weight. More ominously, pimps were getting angrier and angrier as their livelihood became increasingly hampered and interrupted. Checking into protective custody would have been the only way to avoid the gathering storm, but the MAS hard core did not consider it an option, as it would confirm negative stereotypes about gays as weak and unable to protect themselves. And they were feeling cooped up anyway.

So Mead and Atteberry cooked up an escape plan and let their cellmates, LaRue and Joe Green, in on it. Tina Nehrling, a supporter from Theater of the Unemployed, and Duffy would rent vans and fill them with camping equipment and guns. Duffy would pin down the guard towers with automatic weapon fire while Mead, Atteberry, Green, and LaRue hopped the concertina-wire-topped fence. Once free, they would take off for Oregon's lush and dense Blue Mountains and make their way to Wolf Creek. They would be known as "the Red Dragon Unit," and there they would start the revolution. They planned the execution of the breakout for just after a Saturday morning and afternoon MAS banquet, to which all their supporters were invited.

The guests started trickling into the prison lobby at the appointed time: 10:00 A.M. on Saturday, July 4, 1978. They were told to wait. The wait stretched on, and visitors began to become apprehensive. To ease fears, prison administrators let the visitors into the meeting space. Duffy, who had a guard's uniform waiting in the van, was wearing overalls and sandals. He was pulled aside and told he had a visit with a prisoner. Nehrling was also informed she had a visit. Once isolated, each of the two was arrested. Visitors soon realized something serious was taking place and became alarmed.

There was immediate coverage of the escape attempt across the state. Much of it was highly sensational, blatantly inaccurate rehashing of police agencies' most hysterical fears: The escape was orchestrated by the George Jackson Brigade; the van used in the escape had a blazing red dragon emblazoned on the side. Most damagingly, the articles said the plot was planned for visiting hours, which could have endangered prisoners' family members. Some of those who participated in the escape attempt felt that the disinformation was a smear campaign aimed at getting them killed or maimed by other prisoners.

The escape attempt severely shook up the police, and security was intensified immediately. The prison was divided into four security quadrants, and personal clothing was banned. Mead, Atteberry, LaRue, and Green had been busted and sent to isolation. A slip-up on the prisoner side had caused their scheme to be foiled. Though Green was soon paroled, the others, with copious time added to their already deadly sentences, were soon shipped separately to other state and federal prison systems around the country. Decapitated, MAS quickly slipped into the role of social sewing club for effeminate prisoners.

When asked today about the lasting legacy of MAS, Mead—now a computer programmer living in San Francisco—replied, "We changed things. In Washington State we stopped prisoner-on-prisoner rape, and it's never gone back to the way it was." (Unfortunately, a friend in a maximum-security prison in Washington State reports that the situation has declined since Mead was paroled in 1993 and that prisoner-on-prisoner rape is a daily occurrence in several major institutions.) Walla Walla, the toughest joint in the state, set the limits of what was cool and what was acceptable. MAS permanently changed those limits. Says Mead with a strong, hard-won smile on his face, "Of all the political work that I've done, Men against Sexism is what I'm most proud of."

Acknowledgment: This account is based on interviews with Danny Atteberry, Grace Cox, Don Duffy, Ed Mead, and other active participants in MAS and MAS support work. Many thanks to them for their time, hospitality, and forthcomingness. *Northwest Passage,* the Seattle countercultural paper of the time, legal records, and mainstream media clippings were additional sources. This essay is dedicated to everyone who finds MAS's story an inspiration worth acting upon.

Charles J. Sabatino

Men Helping Men: Facilitating Therapy Groups for Sex Offenders

Since 1989, I have co-led a therapy session for a group of men who are judged by society at large, and even by themselves, as despicable. They are men on parole or probation for sex offenses such as child molestation, incest, and rape. A key reason for the deep stigmatization is that they have victimized those among us who are culturally defined as most vulnerable—children and women.

My feelings about working with sex offenders are very ambivalent. Along with most others in society, I feel a great deal of anger toward what they have done. However, I also recognize that they are human, and I have slowly come to understand that the majority of the crimes these men have committed are not rooted in a desire to harm others but in some deep pain of their own. Although I find the harm they have caused others to be absolutely unacceptable, it has been my experience that accepting these individuals without judgment, and having them accept one another in like manner, is the single most important factor in bringing them to accept responsibility for their crimes and initiate the necessary changes in behavior to ensure they will no longer victimize others.

This chapter discusses the goals and dynamics of therapy groups for sex offenders who have been released from prison. Sex offenders are prone to repeat their crimes. At a social level, the group therapy program was designed to lower the recidivism rates among the former inmates who participated. At the interpersonal level, the group was intended to provide former sex offenders with a therapeutic process that could help them to change their identities and lives in healthful, nonvictimizing ways.

Group Process: From Shame to Acceptance

Since 1989, I have worked with approximately 150 men who have committed sex offenses. The typical group consists of between ten and twelve members at any given time. It meets weekly for an hour and a half and is open-ended in the sense that individuals who enter eventually leave, each spending about twelve months. Some of the men have molested children; others have raped adults. This mix contributes to one of the important dynamics of the group: to help these men confront one another's tendencies to deny, minimize, and rationalize their crimes.

I have learned that the majority of individuals who have committed sex offenses can and do change if they commit themselves to their treatment. Only five individuals who participated in our group have offended again. Some research shows that, with treatment, less than 23 percent reoffend, though the recidivism rate for rapists is slightly higher than that for child molesters (Maletzky, 1991). I suspect our success rate has been higher because participants must first accept responsibility for their offenses before entering the group. Thus, they have already taken a major step toward change.

Sex offenders are aware that most members of society despise them. I have often witnessed the fundamental sense of shame that those who enter our group experience. Many of the men have carried the stigma of being "the lowest of the low" for years. They most likely hid the nature of their crimes while in prison, where guards and other inmates label sex offenders "scumbag" or "tree jumper." Furthermore, as several participants reported, they are especially at risk for being sexually assaulted by other inmates. The shame they feel serves to lock them inside themselves, further isolating them from others. And ironically, the feelings of rejection and the experience of social isolation were often factors that helped to trigger the development of their sex offenses in the first place.

About half of the men in group reported having been sexually abused sometime in their lives. Research indicates that about two-thirds of sex offenders experienced physical or severe emotion abuse, and slightly less than half were victimized by sexual abuse (Finkelhor, 1984, 1986). Such findings suggest that sexual abuse tends to cross generations.

I have observed that most group members demonstrate deep-seated resistance to the revelation that they were sexually abused. Some find it more difficult to discuss their own victimization than their sex offenses. Many quickly dismiss these events as insignificant or "not worth talking about." Others do not see what was done to them (especially if it was done by a female) as abuse at all; instead, they consider it an early sexual initiation into manhood. Others perceive their early victimization as an inability to protect themselves and, in gendered terms, a strike against their masculinity. At some level they believe that real men do not allow themselves to become vulnerable and controlled by others, and if they do, then it must be that they are weak, unmasculine, or somehow at fault (Levant, 1995).

It is difficult to understand how someone who was abused could become an abuser himself. John Money and Margaret Lamacz (1989) describe the process this way: The young person is enticed or forced into a sexual relationship with an adult. He is led to believe that sexual intimacy is an appropriate way to show affection, that various practices are in fact special signs of caring between adult and child. In this manner, he learns behaviors and attitudes that may be acted out later as an adult. The likelihood of engaging in sexual abuse as an adult is greater if the pleasurable feelings experienced in youth triggered the growth of haunting insecurities and self-doubts about his own sexuality. This can leave the individual feeling anxious, inadequate, or too vulnerable to attempt to negotiate relationships with same age peers.

The dynamics of shame play a major role in the crimes of those who were themselves sexually abused. Donald Nathanson (1992) showed that the victim of abuse is often left feeling inadequate, damaged. This feeling of inadequacy contributes to deep-seated feelings of helplessness that are often present in the pattern of abuse among those who molest children, and it is often the source of anger that is so common among men who rape (Prendergast, 1991). For boys and men, the shame associated with having been controlled by another while being abused is particularly problematic, because males are conditioned to maintain control at all costs. It is not unusual for abused males to interpret their experiences in terms of control and subjugation rather than in terms of sex. The abuse they later perpetrate against victims becomes a way of reversing roles, perhaps a way of reestablishing their own sense of control. Because they are left feeling helpless and shamed by the earlier abuse they experienced and incapable of engaging in a relationship with someone who is their equal, they select a child or woman who is even more vulnerable than they are.

Clinically, it is important for the healing process that the men sort through the confused feelings associated with their own victimization, feelings that they have been carrying around for most of their lives. These feelings can play a role in shaping the pattern of their sexual offenses against others (Van Der Kolk, McFarlane, and Weisaeth, 1996). At the same time, however, we constantly caution the group members against defining their own victimization as children as the cause of their sex offenses against others. This equation can too easily be translated into an excuse for their behavior, something to latch onto in order to avoid individual responsibility. The fact is that most abused children do not grow up to be abusers.

The group setting offers a temporary respite from the condemnation and stigma surrounding sex offenses that these men encounter in society. Group members frequently state that, except for the group, they have no place where they can talk with someone who is willing to help them. I have heard several members say to one another, "You are the closest thing to friends I have." In group, the men begin to experience, perhaps for the first time, some level of interpersonal acceptance in spite of their crimes. The atmosphere of acceptance encourages them to open up, not just to one another but to themselves. Nevertheless, the nonjudgmental atmosphere fostered in group is not meant to condone what has been done in any way, and it does not encourage participants to legitimate one another's offenses. Quite to the contrary, acceptance of one another is a necessary first step in helping them acknowledge and come to terms with the full implications of their offending behaviors. If the sex offenders entering the group are ever going to break out of their feelings of rejection, isolation, and shame, a climate of acceptance needs to be established.

Recognizing Patterns

Despite the differences among their crimes (molesting, incest, rape), the men share many issues in common. The ultimate goal of the group is to initiate a change in behavior, and in order to move forward, participants are first required to move backward. Soon after entering the group, each man is asked to tell his own life story, focusing on the more important experiences and events of his past. This autobiographical reflection allows the men to get to know one another, but it also helps each individual to assess his own life in a way that he has never done. Eventually, their accounts focus on the offending behavior, and to one extent or another, the men begin to come to terms with the various factors contributing to their crimes.

The men usually begin their stories haltingly, searching for words and images. Many resist the process, claiming that the "best way to get away from the past is simply to forget it." In contrast, as therapists we know that the group is designed to help them to free themselves from the past by returning to it and focusing on it. With varying degrees of speed and insight, the men eventually learn that their past sex crimes are shrouded in denial and avoidance and that the only way to get beyond them is to return to and work through them. In one man's words, "What you cannot speak about becomes bigger than yourself. The more you hide from problems, the bigger they get, and the more they control you. Being able to speak about them was a beginning to take my life back."

As group members discuss their sex offenses from week to week, it becomes increasingly clear that their crimes were not spontaneous acts occurring in a social or personal vacuum. There is a gradual realization that the offenses stem from a larger pattern of behavior, feelings, and needs that were dealt with inappropriately. For example, consistent with A. N. Groth's (1979) claim that sex offenses should not be interpreted as meeting primarily sexual needs, the men begin to understand that the underlying issues behind their crimes do not necessarily concern sex. A man can be truly shocked to realize that he has acted not so much out of a need for sex as out of a deep anger (usually the case with a rapist) or a repressed need for affection (often the case with a child molester).

The underlying motives for sex offenses are quite complicated. Even in our relatively small group, for example, a wide spectrum of issues and behaviors surrounding child abuse needs to be worked through. Whereas one member's molesting behavior stemmed from loneliness or feelings of rejection by the adult world, another acted more out of depression and frustration or perhaps out of resentment and anger at his spouse. Some men who have committed acts of incest come to understand that their spouse's unavailability as a result of death, illness, or general sexual dysfunction created feelings of rejection and anger that then slowly led them to substitute their daughters or stepdaughters as sexual partners. It is necessary to spend considerable time in group helping each member come to terms with his own personal pattern of offending, focusing especially on the feelings and needs that were being acted out through his offenses. The more this is probed, and it is seldom probed without resistance, the more aware the men become and the more capable they become of admitting how wrapped up in their own self-pity and how bent upon having their own needs met they really were.

Group members also learn to confront and analyze the patterns of interpersonal relationships that grew around their sex offenses. Contrary to much public opinion, child molestation does not tend to be aggressive or violent. Rather, as several group members clearly expressed, the man who molests children is often seeking intimacy or affection that he believes or fears he can find in no other way. It becomes important, therefore, for these men to convince themselves that the molester/victim relationship is really a "caring" one, to believe that the child was not a victim but a willing participant. In one meeting, a group member was describing the elaborate steps he took to build a relationship with certain children, which really means, as other members pointed out, to "set up" and "groom" his victims. This individual had so desperately needed to feel cared for yet was so fearful of rejection from the adult world that he would go through weeks and months of planning, enticing the child into a friendship so that *he* could believe the child was not a victim but a willing participant. "I could easily spot a child who was vulnerable and in trouble," he explained. "Then I played the role of 'special friend' and 'savior' by buying gifts, granting favors, and giving special attention in order to get the child to trust me, be grateful, and submit. Slowly, I would turn it into more of a sexual thing." Yet this same individual had criticized the rapists in the group because they used force to have sex. Upon hearing the molester's explanation, the rapists in the group challenged him, arguing that his caring words and actions were also designed to secure submission from the victim and, perhaps, to enhance the power and stature of the molester over the victim.

This is a good example of the way that group members are often more effective at identifying issues or communicating insights than are the co-therapists. A group member who easily dismisses a statement made by the therapist is often hard-pressed to dismiss the perceptions of another group member. Because the group members have had similar experiences, they are able to recognize and point out the defenses and deceptions for what they are—ploys for avoiding, denying, or at least minimizing the seriousness of the offenses. Another example involved incest: One father in the group claimed that his daughter had initiated their incestuous relationship. Another group member simply questioned him about how long he had been "looking at and taking an interest in her as sexually blossoming." The propensity for avoidance and denial has long been observed by researchers on incest (Herman, 1981; Horton et al., 1990). The longer the group works together, however, the more willing the members become to confront and listen to one another.

One of the most striking realizations to emerge from the long-range group process is the extent to which each of the men is locked into a habitual pattern of abusive behaviors. Patrick Carnes (1983a, 1983b, 1989) suggests that sexually abusive behavior, at least in certain instances, is similar to addictive and other dependency-forming behaviors, such as drug and alcohol addiction and eating disorders. He sees addictive behaviors as mood altering in nature and believes that their power derives in part from the capacity to afford an escape from experiences that individuals find too painful to deal with. This pain often involves negative feelings about oneself. The work of Nathanson (1992) on the role that shame plays in bringing on destructive behaviors supports this view.

Most of the group members exhibit what John Bradshaw (1988) calls "toxic shame," which is a fundamentally flawed sense of worth as a person. To the extent that this is so, it helps me to approach the men in group not so much from a moralistic point of view that judges how "bad" they are but more from a therapeutic perspective that interprets the offense as a symptomatic form of acting out. This therapeutic posture does not minimize the pain that sex offenders have caused others, but it does allow the abusive behavior to be understood as arising from a kind of felt pain of the perpetrators' own. I often ask myself why I have this concern for the feelings of the offender. Each has created victims and caused harm to others that may last for a lifetime. I have to catch myself whenever I begin to feel that the social and emotional difficulties that the group members have gone through somehow excuse their offenses. And yet, maddeningly, their pain is real and, for some, their own victimization as children or adolescents is also real.

In summary, the group process fosters healing by providing group members with healthier ways to deal with their life problems than through the abusive behavior. The strategy for change that we enact in the group is to help the men to recognize their patterns of offensive behavior, to identify the triggers for abuse, and to become better able to manage their lives and avoid those inner and outer forces that put them at risk for repeating their offenses. Thus, for the most part, we follow a relapse prevention program (Laws, 1989).[1]

The Issue of Responsibility

Though the sex offender is ultimately accountable for his crime, there is a question of diminished responsibility. As the men discuss their histories of abuse, it is apparent that they made many decisions about their actions along the way. One man recalled feeling lonely, walking to a school yard, allowing himself to entertain a sexual fantasy, and then making contact with one child in particular. Each step represents choices that he made, and it is essential that he take responsibility for each of these choices. It is not unusual to hear an offender say that he simply could not believe that he committed the offense or that he had allowed himself to make the choices that led up to that offense. Although such statements are a form of denial, they also represent a recognition that the sex offense itself makes no sense even to the offender. In short, such statements may be a way of saying that the offender feels driven by an obsessive chain of urges, fantasies, and behaviors over which he exercised very little control.

An important outcome of the group process is to provide these men with a growing sense of responsibility for their abusive actions. As already indicated, the men spend a good deal of time exploring one another's feelings about abuse. As their insights grow, they seem able to take on more ownership of responsibility for how they acted out these feelings. It is significant, for example, to hear a man who has abused his daughter admit that he was acting out of his own feelings of rejection, loneliness, or helplessness—or to watch a rapist begin to realize just how much anger he carried around from day to day. As these insights occur, it is apparent that the men are often quite unaware of how long or to what extent these feelings have been part of their lives and identities.

The behavior and mindset of the offenders are often fueled by a sexually charged fantasy world. Fantasy provides most of us with an escape from boredom or what we find too painful or demanding in the world. Sexual fantasies can be simply erotic or infused with aggressive or violent content. With sex offenders, a sexually charged fantasy is a very dangerous trigger. Even before he acts, the offender has learned to associate immediate relief from stress with a sexual activity carried out in his imagination. It is important for him to recognize that in his fantasy world he "gives himself permission" for his offense sometime before it occurs. If a sexually abusive fantasy is accompanied by masturbation, as is often the case, there is a strong reinforcement for developing a pattern of sexual arousal that is linked to deviant forms of behavior. Unfortunately, there is an urge for the fantasy, sooner or later, to be acted out.

Immersion in fantasies can become an escape from a reality that is experienced as threatening or overwhelming. Fantasies can thus act much like a "fix" that drives an addict. The relief that the fix promises lures the offender to seek out a real victim and encourages him to rationalize, deny, minimize, or even justify his victimization of others. Money's (1988) assertion that the fantasy world needs the reinforcement of being acted out, therefore, partly explains the compulsive, obsessive, and habitual nature of some sexually abusive behavior. Fantasy also offers an opportunity for those individuals who feel trapped in a deep sense of shame to escape into a world of their own making, a world where they can have the control or the love they really feel that they are lacking. Unfortunately, it is also a world in which the unacceptable—sex with a child or forcing oneself on a woman— first begins to become acceptable. Whatever the psychological contours of the dynamic, it runs deep within the psyche of the offender. As more than one member in the group has indicated, the group's goal that he change his identity and offensive behavior in effect requires that he change something, perhaps the main thing, that has made him feel good. The convoluted immersion in the cycle of fantasy and abusive practice explains why treatment can be so difficult, involving, and time-consuming. It should be noted that members tend to be most defensive and exhibit the most denial with respect to fantasies. Apparently, owning responsibility for one's fantasies cuts very close to home.

Sexual fantasies do not originate within the neurochemistry of individuals. They are produced by and peddled in the larger culture. However, I can only speculate on the extent to which the offenses of the men in our group were influenced by the larger culture of sexism or distorted by inequitable gender relations within the larger society. As feminist critics of pornography have argued, a great deal of pornography is geared to modeling hierarchical power relations between dominant agents and submissive pawns (Brownmiller, 1975; Dworkin, 1985). Sexual images in the media often mix displays of physical force with sexual gratification. Child pornography remains a multimillion-dollar business in the United States, and more conventionally, young girls are often sexualized by the advertisers of cosmetics or fashion. It is likely, therefore, that the soft and hard pornographic images that pervade so much of mass media shape and energize the sexually charged fantasy worlds of sex offenders. However, research shows that it is not mediated eroticism per se that leads to deviant behavior; it is its linkage to images of violence, domination, and humiliation. The media, in turn, reflect attitudes and gender expectations around sexuality that promote exploitation. I expect that this is where these attitudes and expectations can be seen as promoting fuel for what then becomes the fantasy world of offenders.

Victim Empathy

Victim empathy is the final dimension of group dynamics tied to the larger issue of responsibility. Sexual abuses inflict tremendous harm on victims (Burgess et al., 1987; Crewsdon, 1988; Forward, 1980). Sex offenders tend to use the belief that they have not really hurt anyone as a form of defense mechanism. It is a major step forward when someone in the group admits, to himself and to the group, that, in the pursuit of his own needs, he harmed another person. This realization and admission provoke a great deal of pain. In one case, a father in an incestuous relationship with his daughter realized that he had taught her to trade sexual availability for acceptance and affection. He understood that he had violated the trust she had placed in him as a father and left her confused about the meaning of love. He also knew that she would blame herself and face emotional confusion for many years to come.

The group members resist acknowledging their complicity in other people's suffering. When they do come to grips with the harmful and hurtful consequences of their actions, the realization frequently creates much inner turmoil and anguish. Group sessions are often intense and painful. I have witnessed men break down and cry. I recall that one evening a man who had raped a woman admitted, "I did not even see her face or hear her cries," and he admitted that this had been important during his assault. He had simply never been aware of the terror he had caused. It was only after viewing a video in which victims revealed what they had gone through that he began to understand. Referring to the rapist depicted in the video, he stated, "That man disgusts me, and it is me." Arousing victim empathy is a major step, because, as several offenders put it, "If I had known and felt what I was really doing, I could not have done it."[2]

Conclusion: There Is Hope in Healing

When asked how much we expect from the group, my co-therapist and I answer that success, for us, is believing that at any given time reoffense is not taking place. We have learned to take one step at a time, one week at a time. When a group member confesses that he is feeling lonely or confused and asks for help in dealing with it, we consider that a success. When a group member proudly announces that he handled a situation with a woman or with his daughter differently from how he had in the past, we consider that a success. For me, one of the best examples of the potential healing power of group therapy is evident in one member's observation: "For the first time in many years, I am finding again the good person I once was but had lost." Then he began to recall some of the devastating abuses he had received as a child at the hands of his family. He said, "During those years, I slowly lost sight of the good person I was. I was always feeling like a loser, a nobody. I was angry and started treating others the same way I was being treated, and the good person I was became all the more lost." There followed several years of drug use and abuse of others, years during which "life meant nothing and I did not care. I was a dead man, really, except, even worse, I was still able to hurt others." Yet there he was about eight years later saying, "I am beginning to find again the good person I was."

For most men who stay with their treatment plan, the group facilitates personal growth and helps them not to reoffend. It also keeps them out of prison, where, in most instances, no real opportunities for rehabilitation exist. In addition, their personal successes in the group are an asset to the community, whose members become safe from those who might otherwise have victimized them.

Notes

Acknowledgments: I acknowledge my co-therapist, Ann Zorn, C.R.C., M.S. Having Ann as a colleague and friend has been a pleasant side effect of working with the group. I also thank the other staff members of Horizon Health Services' Transitions Program for their support.

1. A discussion of the Relapse Prevention Model can be found in Laws, 1989; and Marshall, Laws, and Barbaree, 1990.

2. A discussion of the impact of sexual offenses can be found in Burgess et al., 1987; Crewsdon, 1988; and Forward, 1980.

References

Bradshaw, J. 1988. *Healing the Shame That Binds You.* Deerfield Beach, Fla.: Health Commission.

Brownmiller, S. 1975. *Against Our Will: Men, Women, and Rape.* New York: Simon and Schuster.

Burgess, J., T. Broth, M. Holmstrom, and S. Sgroi, eds. 1987. *Sexual Assault of Children and Adolescents.* Lexington, Mass.: Lexington Books.

Carnes, P. 1983. *The Sexual Addiction.* Minneapolis, Minn.: CompCare.

———. 1989. *Out of the Shadows.* Minneapolis, Minn.: CompCare.

Crewsdon, J. 1988. *By Silence Betrayed.* New York: Harper and Row.

Finkelhor, D. 1984. *Child Sexual Abuse: New Theory and Research.* New York: Free Press.

———, ed. 1986. *A Sourcebook on Child Sexual Abuse.* Newbury Park: Calif.: Sage.

Forward, F. 1980. *The Best Kept Secret: Sexual Abuse of Children.* New York: McGraw Hill.

Groth, A. N. 1979. *Men Who Rape: The Psychology of the Offender.* New York: Plenum.

Herman, J. 1981. *Father-Daughter Incest.* Cambridge, Mass.: Harvard University Press.

Horton, A., B. Johnson, L. Roundy, and D. Williams, eds. 1990. *The Incest Perpetrator.* Newbury Park, Calif.: Sage.

Laws, D. R., ed. 1989. *Relapse Prevention with Sex Offenders.* New York: Guilford.

Levant, D. 1995. *Masculinity Reconstructed.* New York: Dutton.

Maletzky, B. M. 1991. *Treating the Sexual Offender.* Newberry Park, Calif.: Sage.

Marshall, W. L., D. R. Laws, and H. E. Barbaree, eds. 1990. *Handbook of Sexual Assault.* New York: Plenum.

Meiselman, K. D. (1978). *Incest.* San Francisco: Jossey-Boss.

Money, John. 1988. *Lovemaps.* Buffalo, N.Y.: Prometheus Books.

Money, John, and M. Lamacz. 1989. *Vandalized Lovemaps.* Buffalo, N.Y.: Prometheus Books

Nathanson, D. 1992. *Shame and Pride.* New York: Norton.

Prendergast, W. 1991. *Treating Sex Offenders.* New York: Haworth.

Van Der Kolk, B., A. McFarlane, and L. Weisaeth, eds. 1996. *Traumatic Stress.* New York: Guilford.

Donald Specter and Terry A. Kupers

Litigation, Advocacy, and Self-Respect

Lawsuits are now a fact of prison life, and they have changed the legal and psychological dynamics of prisons. Wardens who once operated with little concern about the law now must look over their shoulders and consult with their attorneys. Courts that once left prison management exclusively to correctional administrators are now obligated to scrutinize certain policies and procedures. Prisoners who suffered civil death as one result of their incarceration now have some rights. Wardens, whose responsibilities include every facet of a prisoner's life, have lost some of their control and power, and prisoners have gained some small measure of autonomy.

The right to file a lawsuit and to make the warden justify his or her actions also has important psychological ramifications. In one very important sense, it is a symbolic recognition of the prisoner's continuing citizenship and worth as a human being. It tells the guards and the warden and the whole world that prisoners have rights that must be respected, and it provides prisoners with the means to assert those rights and obtain that respect.

The purpose of this chapter is to begin a discussion of how the struggle for prisoners' rights has changed prisoners' sense of themselves as men as well as the conditions under which they live and their prospects for rehabilitation. This is certainly not to say that litigation should be initiated because of its psychological benefits. There first needs to be a just legal grievance, for instance a profound violation of prisoners' constitutional rights. But in addition to the legal issues, litigation has other personal and social ramifications.

The History of Prison Litigation

Since 1791, when the Eighth Amendment was added to the Constitution of the United States, it has been unconstitutional to impose "cruel and unusual" punishment on prisoners. For most of our history as a nation, this constitutional precept has been little more than an empty phrase when it comes to prisoners. Until recently, the courts turned a blind eye toward conditions in our prisons. The judicial system created a separate rule for prisoners, the "hands-off doctrine," to avoid any examination of prison conditions or practices. In *Stroud v. Swipe,* the court declared that "it is not the function of the courts to superintend the treatment and discipline of prisoners in penitentiaries" (187 F.2d 851 [9th Cir. 1951]).

Wardens, unfettered by public scrutiny or legal constraints, were absolute rulers of the prison kingdom. With just a bare-bones budget to provide for the feeding, care, treatment, employment, and housing of prisoners, the living conditions were generally poor at best. Often they were barbaric.

Much of the judiciary's long history of reluctance to intervene in prison affairs changed after the 1971 Attica rebellion exposed the widespread brutality behind prison walls. Putting aside the popular notion that the rule of law did not apply to prisoners and their wardens, a few courageous judges began to examine prison conditions and were horrified at what they found.

One court noted the "rampant violence and jungle atmosphere existing throughout Alabama's penal institutions," using as an example the case of a twenty-year-old inmate who, "after relating that he has been told by medical experts that he has the mind of a five year old, testified that he was raped by a group of inmates on the first night he spent in an Alabama prison. On the second night he was almost strangled by two other inmates who decided instead that they could use him to make a profit, selling his body to other inmates" (*Pugh v. Locke,* 406 F.Supp. 325 [M.D. Ala. 1976]). Another court characterized the Arkansas prison system as a "dark and evil world completely alien to the free world" (*Holt v. Sarver,* 309 F.Supp. 381 [E.D. Ark. 1970]). The Supreme Court summarized the conditions of punitive isolation in Arkansas:

> Confinement in punitive isolation was for an indeterminate period of time. An average of 4, and sometimes as many as 10 or 11, prisoners were crowded into windowless 8' × 10' cells containing no furniture other than a source of water and a toilet that could only be flushed from outside the cell. At night the prisoners were given mattresses to spread on the floor. Although some prisoners suffered from infectious diseases such as hepatitis and venereal disease, mattresses were removed and jumbled together each morning, then returned to the cells at random in the evening. (*Hutto v. Finney,* 437 U.S. 682 [1978] [footnotes and citations omitted])

After courts from Rhode Island (*Palmigiano v. Garrahy,* 443 F.Supp. 956 [D.R.I. 1977]) to California (*Jordan v. Fitzharris,* 257 F.Supp. 674 [N.D. Cal. 1966]; *Madrid v. Gomez,* 889 F. Supp. 1146 [N.D. Cal. 1995]) discovered similar, but not always as dramatic abuses, the legitimacy of prison litigation began to take hold. For instance, in *Jones v. Wittenberg,* the court noted, "Not all the toilets in the cells work. The soil pipes and waste pipes leak, and the leakage runs upon the floor, which causes problems for those prisoners who, for lack of bunks, are required to sleep on the floor" (323 F.Supp. 96 [N.D. Ohio 1971]). In rhetorical terms, this legitimacy culminated in 1974 in a remarkable statement by the U.S. Supreme Court: "There is no iron curtain drawn between the Constitution and the prisons of this country" (*Wolff v. McDonnell,* 418 U.S. 555 [1974]). This statement, made during the waning years of the Cold War, has some remarkable implications. Prisons were being compared, at least implicitly, to communist dictatorships. On the other hand, the Court recognized explicitly that prisoners—just like everyone else, even if not to the same extent—have basic rights protected by the Constitution.

The recognition that prisoners have legal rights has had some profound consequences for individual prisoners and prison officials. As Jacobs (1977) notes, a paradigm shift occurred when wardens were forced to sit side by side with prisoners in a courtroom, with each having the same due process rights. Even more shocking from the wardens' viewpoint was that prisoners could make them answer questions and justify their positions.

Over time the shock of due process wore off, and wardens who had begun their careers in the 1970s became familiar with litigation and the idea of due process. A February 27, 1997, *San Francisco Daily Journal* article entitled "Prison Law Firm Toils on Behalf of California's Inmates" reported the following response by one prison official who was asked to comment about the significance of a law firm devoted to prisoners' rights: "We put no value judgment on [the lawsuits they bring]. It's just the reality of the situation."

That reality has changed not only prisoners' perceptions of themselves but also the way prison guards behave. The power that wardens lost prisoners gained. Prisoners are no longer completely helpless and entirely dependent on their keepers. They now have some ability to hold guards accountable for their actions. Guards and prison administrators are trained about prisoners' rights and are presumably affected by the fact that they may be sued for their day-to-day activities and policy decisions.

What has not changed is the continuing need for lawsuits. Despite the prophylactic effect of the threat of suit, prison administrators are responding to the public's cry for retribution and punishment by designing modern dungeons, such as sypermaximum-security units, that stretch the limit of human tolerance. In *Madrid v. Gomez,* the court declared that the conditions in the Security Housing Unit at Pelican Bay State Prison "press the outer bounds of what most humans can psychologically tolerate" (p. 1267). Prison officials are coping with an ever-increasing prison population that is more and more overcrowded. Even if they are well meaning, prison officials are not often provided the resources necessary to properly care for and treat the people in their custody.

Thus, in recent years courts have been forced to issue injunctions against a pattern of brutality on the part of guards (*Madrid v. Gomez*) and order prison systems to provide adequate staff to treat the severely mentally ill (*Coleman v. Wilson,* 912 F.Supp. 1252 [N.D. Cal. 1996]) and reasonable accommodations for the disabled (*Armstrong v. Wilson,* 942 F.Supp. 1252 [N.D. Cal. 1996]). Without these kinds of lawsuits, there is little doubt that the absence of outside scrutiny would permit correctional officials to return to the barbaric practices that the courts discovered when they began to review conditions in the prisons in the 1970s.

The Personal Impact of Litigation on Prisoners

In order for a man to feel good about himself, he has to be able to affect his situation. The traditional ideal is the man whose fortunes—or good looks or brains or talent—provide him with significant power to control his situation as well as the situations of others. Of course, this need to feel powerful drives many men to commit terrible acts in terms of gender relationships. Men need to learn that feeling powerful does not require power, or domination, over others. But ever since the American Dream established the illusory standard that anyone can climb to the top of the heap, men who cannot achieve their aims and men who feel they have fallen or are about to fall to the bottom believe they have only themselves to blame. For example, many men believe that only their personal inadequacies prevent them from maintaining sufficient control of their situation to avoid unemployment, poverty, homelessness, and so forth. Getting locked up in prison is not exactly a reflection of a man's power to control his situation. On the contrary, according to traditional values, the prisoner is at the bottom of the barrel.

Prisoners insist on being respected as men, even though many admit they have behaved in ways that they regret and that have lost them a certain amount of respect from others. But most prisoners feel they have been disrespected by teachers, employers, the police, and the courts for many years. As if to compensate for past humiliations, they insist they must be respected on the prison yard. The areas reserved for weight lifting are the most thickly populated in the prison. The men's bodies are muscular, their mean stares penetrating. Fights are often about respect, one man feeling that another has disrespected him. Unfortunately, the stakes are very high. An all-out battle over respect can end a life—or many lives.

In spite of the posturing and gladiatorial battles on the yard, the sad reality is that prisoners have very few ways to earn lasting self-respect and respect from others. Prisons are designed to minimize a prisoner's individuality and force him to give up to his warders total control over his daily life. The more repressive the prison, the less control prisoners have over their circumstances and the more humiliated and disrespected they feel. Probably more than anything else, enhanced repression causes the prisoner to feel a sharp loss of control. The dismantling of rehabilitation programs and the shrinking of educational and recreational opportunities that has occurred in recent decades adds to the prisoner's sense that there are no positive outlets for him. Many prisoners say they feel there's nowhere to go, no means of earning self-respect by gaining competence at something, no way to learn to cope better with the outside world. And there is even a move to take away the weights and the other recreational outlets.

The efficacy of rehabilitation programs is under debate, but it is fair to say that in cases where rehabilitation has been effective—that is, when a released prisoner finds work in the area he was trained for and is able to avoid rearrest—the former prisoner typically reports that the training for postrelease employment, more than anything, helped him maintain his self-respect and stay out of trouble on the prison yard and back on the streets. It makes sense: A self-respecting man who has an opportunity to improve himself and find a satisfying niche in society after his release is not as likely to join a fight to the death as is an inmate who feels he has nothing to lose.

In a similar way, litigation, although certainly not an end in itself, provides prisoners with a sense that they have some stake, however meager, in the larger system. It can also provide a civilized and nonviolent means of resolving disputes within the prison community. In *Morrissey v. Brewer,* the Supreme Court noted that a perception that prison procedures are fair enhances the prospects for rehabilitation "by avoiding reactions to arbitrariness" (408 U.S. 485 [1972]). In the same sense, litigation promotes self-respect and rehabilitation. Prisoners who believe that their constitutional rights are being respected and that they have some legal recourse are less likely to resort to illegal or violent means to attain some control over their situation.

The Prisoner's Self-Esteem

Dannie Martin was a federal prisoner when he wrote a series of articles for the *San Francisco Chronicle*'s Sunday magazine. In the book he coauthored with *Chronicle* editor, Peter Sussman, Dannie tells of the enhanced self-esteem that came with the publication of his writing. He was not the only prisoner who felt pride. According to one prisoner, "Every time an article came out, it was kind of big news around the institution. Everybody waited for them. . . . We all felt that through Mr. Martin we had a voice going out to the public, telling our side of it" (Martin and Sussman, 1993:49).

Dannie was the plaintiff in a lawsuit that went to trial in the federal district court of San Francisco. Did a prisoner have the right to operate a business (that is, to be paid for his published writing) while in prison? At a sensitive moment in the litigation process, just before Dannie decided to appeal an unfavorable ruling, he received a letter from another prisoner, saying that the federal correctional authorities were "afraid of inmates such as Dannie Martin because he restores the individual inmate to a higher degree of self-worth than they would allow" (p. 242). Dannie's case eventually went to the Ninth Circuit Court of Appeals, where it was ruled moot because by that time Dannie was out of prison.

The case of *Cain v. Michigan Department of Corrections* (MDOC) (No. 88-61119-AZ, Mich. Court of Claims) provides another example of the pride prisoners feel about their litigation and the courage they express. At a time when corrections departments are rationalizing as security measures endless restrictions on prisoners' freedoms and federal courts are refusing to intervene, eight male prisoners acting "*in pro per*" in Michigan state court on behalf of forty-one thousand men, joined by two thousand women prisoners and their attorneys, have halted implementation of a new, cruelly restrictive policy for over ten years. *Cain v. MDOC* finally went to trial in April 1997, and the litigation continues at this writing.

The prisoners were successful in slowing the institution of a new policy that would take away personal clothing, force prisoners to wear flimsy uniforms that are inadequate in the cold season and uncomfortable in the summer, and take away all prisoners' possessions—including televisions and radios—except what fits into a duffel bag or a duffel bag and a small footlocker. Also, only new property ordered from an approved store catalogue would be permitted into the prisons. Thus, if a prisoner were sent to a higher-security institution on a disciplinary infraction, if he beat the rap on appeal, and if he were then returned to a lower level, he would have to send all possessions out or lose them, without ever being able to get them back. Obviously, this policy would create immense hardship for prisoners without means.

The courtroom is a gymnasium in a local jail near Jackson with tables for the judge, the lawyers, and the witness and rows of benches for the press and audience. Over a dozen men and women prisoners arrive in shackles to sit at the plaintiffs' table. These plaintiffs are proud to participate in the lawsuit. The fact that the prisoners were able to organize a lawsuit and have it heard in a court of law bolsters their feeling that they are still citizens with legal rights, and that permits them to retain the hope that they might have some control over their destiny.

Indeed, prisoners are proud of their participation in class action litigation that improves their plight, whether it is to end double-celling or improve the quality of mental health services behind bars. By taking action against their jailers, they express their capacity to act and demand redress for their grievances. And, in terms of the discussion of "toxic masculinity" and men's need to dominate, the pride men feel in standing up for themselves does not require power over others. Rather, it is a positive struggle to maintain a sense of dignity while demanding what, after all, is every citizen's constitutional due.

Conversely, when prisoners are denied the opportunity to express their side of the story and receive a fair hearing, their self-regard suffers, as does their ability to follow the rules and their programs. For instance, inside prison guards bring many disciplinary "cases" against convicts. A guard may charge a prisoner with fighting, possessing drugs, brandishing a handmade weapon or merely disobeying a command. These cases usually do not go back to the courts; rather, the prison's rules establish the punishment and provide procedures for prisoners to appeal the punishments that the guards mete out.

A prisoner who is given a fair hearing is more likely to serve his sentence peacefully. But a prisoner who believes he is being punished unfairly and denied a fair hearing will go to the punitive segregation unit begrudgingly, and he will feel disrespected. And this may cause him to fall into a depression, or it may make him that much more prone to violence the next time he believes someone is disrespecting him. As we noted earlier, the Supreme Court has recognized that the potential for rehabilitation decreases when prisoners believe they are being treated unfairly (*Morrisey v. Brewer*).

Correctional staff members often have difficulty accepting enhanced self-esteem on the part of prisoners. They subscribe to the intermale dominance hierarchy, even to the equivalent of the prisoners' code, and they view the prisoners as at the bottom of the heap. When prisoners appeal staff decisions, staff members feel that their authority is being undermined. Some say they feel disrespected themselves, with the injury compounded by any coworker who may believe the prisoner's side of the story. Usually the panel selected to hear the prisoners' appeals is composed almost entirely of security staff, so it does not often rule in favor of a prisoner. In many states, 90 to 95 percent of the disciplinary hearings go against the prisoners. When we consider a situation in which a guard strikes a prisoner and then writes him up for "assaulting an officer," this one-sided procedure does not bode well for the maintenance of inmates' sense of fairness in the prisons.

The prisoner who wins an appeal or a grievance against a staff member always runs the risk that the staff will retaliate. In fact, in the states that permit prisoners to call witnesses to support their side of the story at disciplinary hearings, fear of retaliation by guards prevents many prisoners from testifying in favor of fellow inmates. Here, in fact, is one of the many ways that prison policies serve to prop up the toxic male tendency to view life as a war of all against all, with nobody coming to the defense of his neighbor for fear of the consequences. Obviously, prisoners tend to suffer a loss of self-esteem when they are unable to present their cases and receive fair hearings. At the same time, correctional authorities are not happy about court interventions that weaken their hand and give prisoners a renewed sense of pride and agency.

The Move to Weaken Prisoners' Rights

The decline in prisoners' access to court remedies began, ironically, with the same 1974 Supreme Court decision that drew the parallel to the iron curtain. In *Wolff v. McDonnell* the Court decided that prisoners who faced disciplinary charges that could result in longer prison terms through a loss of credits were due less process and fewer protections (including the right to attorneys) than in the trial that resulted in the original conviction and loss of liberty. Several years later the Court handed down a pair of decisions (1) granting jail officials wide latitude to restrict the rights of pretrial detainees, even though they were still presumed innocent, and (2) making it very difficult to limit the population, by ruling that double-celling was not in itself cruel and unusual punishment (*Bell v. Wolfish*, 441 U.S. 520 [1979]; *Rhodes v. Chapman*, 452 U.S. 337 [1981]). By that point the Court's membership and ideology had changed, as had its metaphors. Instead of focusing on the totalitarian control exercised by prison officials as the Court had done for a decade and a half, prisoners' complaints about conditions were met with mocking phrases such as "Nobody promised them a rose garden" (*Atiyeh v. Capps*, 449 U.S. 1316 [1981]).

More recently, the Court has made it much easier for prison officials to defend against prisoners' lawsuits (*Turner v. Safley*, 482 U.S. 78 [1987]). And the Court has restricted access to the law library so that prisoners who file a case may be denied the right to research the law to prosecute it (*Lewis v. Casey*, 518 U.S. 343 [1996]). This one-two punch has taken much of the air out of lawsuits initiated by *pro per* prisoners and those challenging specific prison regulations.

Not to be outdone, the Republican-controlled Congress passed a "reform" bill in 1996 that imposes new and sometimes insurmountable barriers to both class action litigation and lawsuits by individual prisoners. Under this new bill, known as the Prison Litigation Reform Act (PLRA), many existing settlements can be terminated at will, funds available for attorneys' fees for the representation of prisoners are greatly reduced, and a combination of increased liability for filing fees and a "three strikes and you're out" provision has sharply curtailed prisoners' ability to challenge the actions of prison officials and the conditions under which they live.

Perhaps the most distressing part of this long trend backward is that it is not over. The states have now realized that through Congress they may be able to achieve what even the William Rehnquist Court will not grant—a return to the good old days when they had virtual impunity in running the prisons and immunity from suit.

The Future of Prison Litigation

Litigation, in addition to its legal merit and objective effects, serves to give prisoners a sense of their agency and helps control gross excesses on the part of insensitive guards and correctional administrations. In a large number of class action lawsuits and individual habeas corpus suits, the courts have ruled that prisoners suffer cruel and unusual punishment on account of harsh prison conditions, staff brutality and inattention, and inadequate medical and mental health services.

Advocates of the law-and-order approach, who want to "lock 'em up and throw away the key," do not accept the courts' rulings lightly. In some states, they campaign for the electoral defeat of judges who they accuse of "coddling" prisoners. These campaigns are so effective that, in ruling on prison litigation, sitting judges have to be very careful that they do not antagonize the law-and-order lobby.

Then, if pressuring the courts does not accomplish their purposes, and there are too many judgments against correctional systems for violating prisoners' constitutional rights, legislators get busy passing laws to deny prisoners some of those rights. An example is the recent Supreme Court decision about prisoners with disabilities. The Court held that the Americans with Disabilities Act (ADA) applies to state prisoners (*Pennsylvania Department of Corrections v. Yeskey,* 524 U.S. 206 [1998]). Immediately after the Supreme Court handed down that decision, Senators Strom Thurmond and Jesse Helms proposed legislation to change the ADA to exclude prisoners. Fortunately, that effort has not resulted in any amendments to the ADA to date.

When prison riots occur, the public is led to believe that the riot proves the wisdom in harsh criminal justice policies. In other words, the convicts are animals, there is no place for them in civilized society, and they deserve whatever harsh punishment they receive. But this cynical view overlooks the fact that most riots occur only after the prisoners have suffered overcrowding and brutalization and after they have become enraged by every aspect of their deprivation and feel there is no legitimate mechanism for them to air their grievances. Hans Toch reflects the thinking of most informed criminologists when he writes, "Riots are sparked by grievances rather than lax security" (1997:23).

In a time of conservative hegemony and wide support for the law-and-order approach to public policy, governmental agencies are unlikely to support or even explore the possibility of prison reform. In this context, class action lawsuits may still be the best available avenue for improving prison conditions and guaranteeing prisoners constitutional protections. Moreover, when prisoners are able to maintain some hope that they will be heard and there will be some redress of their grievances, their self-esteem rises and they have an opportunity to channel their energy into productive pursuits.

Conversely, if Congress and the courts permit the states to strip prisoners of their rights under the Constitution and federal law, prisoners' hopes for humane treatment under the cruel-and-unusual punishment clause will have been resting on a hollow stump. No longer will prison litigation bring some light into the dark recesses of this country's prisons. And desperate men will be left with none but destructive recourse.

References

Jacobs, J. B. 1977. *Stateville: The Penetentiary in Mass Society.* Chicago: University of Chicago Press.

Martin, D. M., and P. Y. Sussman. 1993. *Committing Journalism: The Prison Writings of Red Hog.* New York: Norton.

Toch, Hans. 1997. *Corrections: A Humanistic Approach.* Guilderland, N.Y.: Harrow and Heston.

Christian Parenti

Rehabilitating Prison Labor: The Uses of Imprisoned Masculinity

Prison labor is back. Inmates now work for states and private corporations doing data entry, manufacturing plasma, building stretch limousines, slaughtering ostriches for export, and booking holiday reservations. Accompanying this new "inside" labor market are occasional bursts of rhetoric about "rehabilitation" and "job training," as well as a cryptic appeal to traditional, positive notions of masculinity. But this appeal to rehabilitation and masculinity is (1) a way of extracting more effort from inmate laborers and (2) a means of justifying the return of prison labor in general.

As the essays in this book make clear, prison strips men of any positive form of "masculinity." The assumption in this essay is that masculinity, like all gender expressions, is historically constructed. Moreover, this essay does not privilege "traditional" notions of "breadwinner" masculinity as inherently good. There should be room for a multiplicity of masculinities and a cultural freedom to move between them. The concern with "traditional," positively defined masculinity arises from its political uses as a mobilizing cultural story. What is usually left is a hyperviolent masculinity necessitated by prison's increasingly Hobbesian total war of all against all.

In addition, rehabilitation has been jettisoned from the official goals of most prison systems. Thanks in part to the theoretical intervention of James Q. Wilson, John Diulio and other New Right criminologists, U.S. prisons are now places for "incapacitation" and retribution. Social engineering, the original and rather utopian goal of prisons, is all but dead. People see and endorse prisons for what they are: brutal warehouses.

The California Department of Corrections (CDC) officially abandoned the goal of rehabilitation in 1984; other states have also dropped it as an official goal or have all but abandoned it in practice. Yet as prison labor reemerges, we hear echoes of the "treatment model" and notions of the traditional "responsible male" bouncing back from the past.

For example, California's Joint Venture Program (JVP), which encourages private industry to use prison labor, boosts its program in a state brochure as follows: "Now ... business can gain a competitive edge and provide the opportunity for inmates of California correctional institutions to begin to rebuild their lives." Similarly, the largest employer of prison labor in the country—the federal government's UNICOR, which uses over twenty thousand inmates in a myriad of industries—justifies itself with extensive appeals to rehabilitation and inmate responsibility. "Properly organized prison industrial programs such as FPI [Federal Prison Industries] can be justified on several grounds. . . . The primary task of prison is to confine offenders, but the secondary task is to provide inmates with ways to improve themselves during confinement. Prisons cannot magically rehabilitate offenders, but they can provide opportunities for inmates to reform their behavior and rehabilitate themselves" (Roberts, 1996:11).

What is going on? Does prison labor rehabilitate inmates? Is prison labor part of reconstructing violent and "impulsive" (childlike) outlaws into "responsible" (adult) men? Or does the rhetoric of rehabilitation and the cryptic appeal to positive notions of masculinity merely legitimize the exploitation of prison labor? The facts on the ground indicate that it is the latter; the rhetoric of rehabilitation has returned as a means of camouflaging the morally dubious return of prison labor.

What Is Wrong with Chain Gangs?

Before we address the cryptic appeal to masculinity, it is worth clarifying the case against prison labor. Historically, convict workers in the United States have been horribly mistreated. For example, the southern convict leasing system used whipping, small metal cells called sweatboxes, and numerous other forms of abuse to manage inmate laborers. In most southern states, prisoners called "trusty shooters" served as guards, often the trusties were known psychopaths whose only qualifications were loyalty to their overseers. Punishment was brutal, death rates reached 10 percent per year, and in some of the worst cases—such as Arkansas, where only twenty-seven civilian employees kept three thousand prisoners until the 1970s—escape rates reached 25 percent (Oshinsky, 1996; Feely and Rubin, 1996).

The private corporations that leased convicts made huge profits as a direct result of this terror. Free workers also suffered; union power was undermined by widespread use of inmate scabs. For mine owners, "the cost advantages of forced labor in coal mining had indirect effects as well. The US Bureau of Labor estimated that the wages of free miners were reduced 10 to 20 per cent in areas where convicts were also used to mine coal" (Lichtenstein, 1996:82). Historically, prison labor in the United States has been a brutal affair guided by corporate avarice, racism, and concomitant layers of sadism.

Some would argue that forcing people to work against their will, regardless of the conditions, is inherently wrong. It is a question open to debate and one that is somewhat abstract. A more important, more specific question is What does forced labor mean in *this* system *today*?

If the United States had a "rational" prison system—one that incarcerated only the truly violent and dangerous (a tiny fraction of the current prison population) and attempted to rehabilitate and reintegrate most offenders—then requiring convicts to work might be justified. If this labor were mixed with job training, kept out of the hands of private capital, and administered humanely, requiring convicts to do some socially useful work could be good for both prisoners and society. But this hypothetical penal system bears little resemblance to current reality. Most new U.S. prisoners are, in fact, nonviolent offenders serving absurdly long sentences for either drug possession or property crimes. With 2 million people behind bars, the United States has the highest rate of incarceration in the world. Our prison system is a gluttonous beast, out of control; new corporate interests attach themselves to and insinuate themselves into it daily. Increasingly, these parasitic layers of interests are served by the state's official use of deadly force and outright torture to manage the bad world inside.

In other words, the main problem with prison labor today is the prison system within which it occurs. An unjust, bloated, violent, and corrupt gulag archipelago cannot be a place for useful, just, and humane prison labor. If one believes it unreasonable to lock up for ten years nonviolent crack addicts who are guilty of possession, then, by the same logic, it is unreasonable to force them to work against their will. When the initial terms of imprisonment are unjust, all else that follows is unjust.

Putting aside this more fundamental critique, there is also the question of just compensation and workplace rights. Most prison laborers today make between 23¢ and 40¢ an hour. The highest-paid prisoners in the country work for private firms that set up shop inside prison. In California such "joint venture" inmates earn $4.25 an hour (minimum wage). In Oregon a few inmates are reported to earn as much as $7.00 an hour. However, in both cases 80 percent of the prisoners' pay is taken by the state in the name of room and board, restitution, and fines. Although whipping is no longer allowed, prisoners nonetheless face dangerous conditions and on many occasions have expressed their discontent in lawsuits demanding improved pay and working conditions. In *Hale v. Arizona* (967 F2d 1356 [9th Cir. 1992]), a 1992 suit filed by Arizona prisoners working in the state's prison industry, at first the prisoners won a favorable ruling before a three-judge panel in the Ninth Circuit. But an en banc panel later vitiated the inmates' victory on appeal (*Hale v. Arizona* (993 F2d 1387 [9th Cir. 1993]). In Wisconsin there was even a brief prison strike in January 1996.

The Cryptic Appeal to Masculinity

Though masculinity is not an overt part of the new rhetoric of rehabilitation surrounding prison labor, traditional notions of man as "breadwinner" nonetheless form a significant subtext. Traditionally, "work" has defined the male world and psyche. And masculinity is ipso facto a central piece of the prison labor puzzle because of the simple fact that 92 to 93 percent of prisoners are men. Masculinity is one of the central discourses of incarceration, as well as one of the penal system's main psychosocial sites of intervention and destruction. Thus, a discussion of prison labor—even though many women work in U.S. prisons—always drags with it a subterranean set of assumptions about "manhood" and gender.

"Inmates receive 'real world' employment experience and develop a strong work ethic that enables them to become productive and responsible citizens," says an undated brochure from California's JVP. It also promises "a return to society of well trained, motivated adults with savings and skills to decrease recidivism and the level of violence in the community." One almost expects a line about JVP inmates becoming better fathers and husbands.

Invoking the "citizen" and "well-trained, motivated adult" is particularly interesting if we consider the historical treatment of women as nonadults and noncitizens. Raffter (1983) points out the infantilization of women in prison and the fact that the notion of "adult" was, at a certain level, only for men.

Masculinity and Labor Power

Work is not as simple as it may seem. The giving and taking of labor occurs differently depending on the historical and cultural context or for that matter when embedded in differently "gendered" experiences. Prison labor among men involves an intersection of all these questions; the male prisoner's labor is extracted or given not simply by force but also through an appeal to genderized norms and notions of identity. If we assume, as the evidence indicates, that prison constructs a primarily adversarial and predatory form of masculinity, then we can say that prison labor attempts to control men through a different, more traditional, mainstream gender norm—that of the responsible citizen. Before dealing specifically with the question of laboring inside, a discussion of how cultural notions of gender (in this case, masculinity) intersect with the labor process is necessary.

Despite the many years that have passed since its publication, one of the best books on masculinity and work is Paul Willis's (1977) *Learning to Labor*, an ethnography of rebellious working-class "lads" in northern England. Willis made the crucial observation that the social construction of masculinity in industrial Britain was, at least in part, a means of extracting "labor power." By "labor power," I mean physical and mental energy sold by the laborer. As Karl Marx put it, "That which comes directly face to face with the possessor of money on the market is in fact not labour, but the labourer. What the latter sells is his labour-power" (1906:588). "Labor power" here is distinct from the commodity "labor," that is the amount of labor time bought by an employer and sold by a worker. Labor time can be bought, sold, measured, standardized, and easily managed. But labor power—the real inalienable essence of the commodity labor, that is the physical and mental effort given by the laborer—is more elusive. One of the central dynamics in capitalist production is always how to extract more labor power per unit of labor time. The laborer sells his or her time; that part of the transaction is standardized. The amount of actual effort—physical and mental energy exerted by the laborer—varies. And the key to capitalist profit is to extract as much labor power for as little compensation as possible (Braverman, 1974).

Willis (1977) argued that many working-class young men were rendered macho and stoically anti-intellectual by their rebellion against state schools. According to Willis's ethnography, the lads experienced school as a hostile and emasculating institution run by middle-class missionary-like teachers. For Willis the youths were "experiencing" the cultural side of class conflict. And resistance to schooling was, for the lads, a resistance to authority in general, and because of the political economic context, that also meant a resistance to class hierarchy. The lads' resistance took the form of a hypermachismo, which valued physical power, brutality, and toughness (and was, incidentally, very racist). "Thus physical laboring comes to stand for and express, most importantly, a kind of masculinity, also an opposition to authority—at least as it is learned in school" (p. 104).

In the end, the lads, having protected their honor against the engineering of middle-class teachers, structured themselves out of any opportunities for class mobility that the larger society offered. The lads inevitably emerged from school with little more than a fatalistic, macho, anti-authoritarian ethos, which led them straight to the shop floor. In other words the lads' immediate short-term refusal to be obedient and physically docile, to sit at desks and learn boring subjects led them, in the long run, into a willingness to work hard on the shop floor. The lads' cultural resistance (a machismo that valued physical strength), in the end, made them docile, productive industrial workers.

Once in the factory, the macho ethos enabled the lads to bear, and in a sense willingly give their physical power to, the production process. To labor physically was to be a man. The hidden, unacknowledged mission of the school, concludes Willis, was to provoke a machismo that would ultimately render the lads compliant, even willing, laborers.

Thus, Willis illustrates the connection between traditional notions of masculinity and the extraction of labor power. The cultural story of the strong man, the stoic responsible and capable man, is intimately bound up with the nexus of the production process or the larger milieu of political economy.

So how then does masculinity meet work in the prison shop? And why are prison labor and its justifications enjoying a comeback?

The Return of Convict Labor

The fact of the matter is that all U.S. prisons are under increasing financial pressure. In California, for example—according to my December 1995 interview with criminologist Elliott Currie in Berkeley—the prison system is at 192 percent capacity, and despite tremendous state largess, CDC administrators are being forced to cut costs before they are permitted a renewed round of cage building. According to the CDC, the average California prison, already streamlined by a "cookie cutter design," costs at least $290 million to build and $150 million to $200 million per year to run. The Rand Corporation forecasts that the three-strikes policy alone will cost the state more than $5.5 billion annually—five times the original estimate.

In a telephone interview with the author on October 20, 1996, California Senate President Pro Tem Bill Lockyer stated, "We're cannibalizing higher education, and that can't continue." The CDC, like other state systems, is being forced to rein in costs. In 1996, state Republicans "didn't even get the $25 million they wanted for prison planning."

This momentary hurdle will no doubt be overcome, but it reveals the need for cost cutting, a pressure felt in prison systems throughout the country. As a result, prison labor takes on a new importance, and the mean future of prison as work camp begins to take shape. Senator Phil Gram summed up the idea when he told the 1995 National Rifle Association Convention, "I want to turn every federal prison in this country into a mini industrial park" (Gugliotta, 1997). Edwin Meese, U.S. attorney general under Reagan, editorialized in the May 1, 1996, *Wall Street Journal*, "The time is ripe to reduce the cost of incarceration by expanding inmate work programs." And, according to Meese, Pete Wilson—then California governor—"strongly support[s] the concept that prisoners should work rather than sit idly by at tax payer expense."

The Appeal to Imprisoned Masculinity

"Most inmates want to do a good job, they take pride in their work and they work hard to produce a quality product," according to an undated UNICOR brochure entitled "Federal Prison Industries: A Critical Correctional Program," published by the U.S. Department of Justice. Along with the hyperbole of the prison system itself, we have press accounts of prison labor, and there again we find the subterranean discourses of masculinity. An October 24, 1996, *San Francisco Chronicle* article by Sam S. Whitting, entitled "Prisoners at Work," tells about a for-profit silk-screen shop at San Quentin with the barely ironic name Inkarcerated. The article provides an excellent example of appeal to responsibility and cryptomasculine notions of redemption. "It helps me send money home to my daughter, and it helps me because when I hit the street I'll have a silk screen trade," said one Inkarcerated worker. "I won't go back out into society the way I came in here."

The entrepreneur in charge of this outfit said, "It gave the men pride and a sense of self worth. The work built their self-esteem." But "the work" served other purposes as well: making profits for the business owner and defraying the state's costs of incarceration. As Inkarcerated's owner, Darren Angus put it in my March 27, 1997, telephone interview with him, "They really worked hard, harder than guys on the outside."

So here you have it: the carrot of self-esteem, which in part is about some positive notion of what it is to be a man, dangled out as promise to a bunch of caged, overcrowded, and extremely vulnerable men. The result? Labor power is given willingly. In fact, all prison labor programs have huge waiting lists. Every prison employer lauds the productivity of its captive workforce. And despite declamations from the Left, most prisoners are extremely glad to have prison jobs.

Legitimation: The Appeal to Public Consciences

The story of prison labor's morally salubrious effects is not merely a means of extracting labor power; it is also a canard set afloat to camouflage the extreme violence of an out-of-control incarceration binge. The discourse of prison labor as training is a public relations fig leaf over the septic loins of a social monster: the Prison Industrial Complex. I do not mean that all claims of rehabilitation are fraudulent. As a principle I support the "rehabilitative model" of criminal justice. Despite its faults, massive failures, and implicitly coercive nature, the "treatment model" (or versions of it) is, practically speaking, a more humane corrections policy than the current vogue that sees prisoners as hopelessly damaged freight to be stored and slowly destroyed.

The specific point here is that, although rehabilitation is a worthy goal, the rehabilitative nature of prison labor becomes less convincing when we look more closely at the type of work that inmates do and at their real job prospects upon release.

For example, one of the most successful prison labor projects in the country is Oregon State's line of jeans called "Prison Blues." So far Uni-group, the state-owned company that makes the jeans, has an average yearly revenue of $2 million. Most of the inmates who make the denim pants and T-shirts for this internationally sold line are men. But on the outside, well over 90 percent of workers in the needle trades are women. Although the genderized parameters of apparel work are ultimately artificial and socially constructed, these parameters are nonetheless experienced as real. As a result, Uni-group prisoners are being "trained" for jobs that, given gender norms and employer preferences, do not exist. Indeed, upon release, very few of them go into sweatshops to make jeans.

The training aspect of prison labor is often quite dubious. In the 1960s, when the treatment model prevailed, inmate workers in the federal system often received "cluster training" in the form of work, classes, and job rotation. The idea was to give prisoners as many skills as possible. That is quite different from the minimal training of sewing, pressing, and folding jeans that the Uni-group's prisoners receive. So if the job training of prison labor is largely unreal, what is the hype all about? Political legitimation.

Exploiting prison labor is an extremely contentious issue. Some of the bloodiest battles fought by U.S. labor were over the use of inmate scabs. In 1891 and 1892 members of the United Mine Workers attacked five different Tennessee prison camps where inmates were forced to scab; in one case all the convicts were released, and the camp was burned to the ground (Lichtenstein, 1996:99). Labor is not so militant in its opposition to prison labor today, but there is a moral sanction against it nonetheless. Montgomery Ward, for example, has a policy prohibiting the use of child, slave, or prison labor by its subcontractors, according to an August 10, 1995, Reuters News Service article entitled "Montgomery Ward Sues Vendor, Pulls Clothes." In fact, our ironic, errant Inkarcerated eventually went out of business, because, as Angus put it in my March 27, 1997, telephone interview with him, "the retailers didn't want to be associated with prison made products. They weren't sure about the public reaction." Many people see prison labor for what it is, an exploitation of the most politically vulnerable part of the society. Given the prevailing moral climate, some other rationale is needed, and rehabilitation, plus an appeal to the reconstructed positive male, fits the bill.

Conclusion

Unfortunately, it is corporate avarice and state brutality, not a positively defined masculinity, that are being rehabilitated by the return of prison labor. In fact, well-paying jobs on the outside, one of the real bases of self-worth for both men and women, are being eroded by the expansion of the lockup labor market. According to my July 17, 1996, *San Francisco Bay Guardian* article, entitled "Captive Capitalism," thousands of jobs in furniture production have already been lost to UNICOR. Will the men left unemployed by these cuts now have to prove their "masculinity" by beating up wives, girlfriends, children, and each other? Will the pressure to be a "breadwinner" drive some of them into the sub-rosa economy of drugs? Chances are yes. But, hey, there is job training inside.

References

Braverman, H. 1974. *Labor and Monopoly Capital: The Degradation of Work in the Twentieth Century.* New York: Monthly Review Press.

Feeley, M. M., and E. R. Rubin. 1996. "Two Classic Cases of Judicial Prison Reform: Arkansas and Texas." In *Judicial Policy Making and Prison Reform*. Unpublished paper.

Gugliotta, Guy. 1997. "From Federal Prisons to an Agency Near You." *Washington Post,* July 15.

Lichtenstein, Alex. *Twice the Work of Free Labor: The Political Economy of Convict Labor in the New South*. New York: Verso, 1996.

Marx, Karl. 1906. *Capital: A Critique of Political Economy.* Vol. 1. New York: Modern Library.

Oshinsky, David. 1996. *Worse Than Slavery: Parchman Farm and the Ordeal of Jim Crow Justice*. New York: Free Press.

Raffter, N. H. 1983. "Chastizing the Unchaste: Social Control Functions of a Woman's Reformatory, 1894–1931." In *Social Control and the State,* ed. S. Cohen and A. Scull. Oxford: Blackwell.

Roberts, J. W. 1996. "Work, Education, and Public Safety: A Brief History of Federal Prison Industries." In *Factories with Fences: History of Federal Prison Industries*. Washington, D.C.: Federal Bureau of Prisons.

Willis, Paul. 1977. *Learning to Labor: How Working-Class Kids Get Working-Class Jobs.* New York: Columbia University Press.

Lige Dailey Jr.

Reentry: Prospects for Postrelease Success

I am convinced that the prospects for postrelease success depend critically on the personal resources and expectations of the parolee. If he believes that the criminal justice system will help him to reenter society successfully, he is predestined for failure. My postrelease story is told from an African American male point of view. I dedicate it with love and respect to my only son, Damu Dailey, and to other young, black males at risk of going to prison.

How Prison Prepared Me for Postrelease Success

After serving seven years for first-degree armed robbery, the parole board expected me to come out of prison, without job skills, and immediately get a job. The fact that I was a black ex-convict with a dishonorable discharge from the military did not appear to be a major concern to the board. But in my mind, it evoked a frightening image of being pushed into a boxing ring with both hands tied behind my back.

To say that I was "without job skills" is misleading. I should clarify that I had no "marketable" job skills. The skills that I had developed in the prison factories were worthless on the streets. When I was paroled, I quickly learned that outside businesses were not motivated to pay me minimum wage with benefits when they could pay a prison inmate twenty-five cents an hour to do the same job.

My prison counselors had lied to me. They had told me that working in the factories would develop my marketable skills and increase my chances for early parole. My choice was to work in the prison factory for twelve hours or be confined to my cell for twenty-four hours. Initially I refused to work, but after a few weeks of sitting alone in a dark, freezing cell, I changed my mind. I know for a fact that each prison where I served time had its own factory and corporate contract. At Soledad, I did piece work for a very famous underwear and blue jeans company. In Black Mountain Prison Camp, I fought forest fires; and at San Quentin, I made mattresses and quality office furniture.

I hated working for slave wages. I spent most of my time finding ways to get out of it. I even made numerous attempts to form a prison workers' union with other inmates. As a result, the prison staff continuously harassed and abused me and eventually threw me into the detention center as punishment. While in detention, we were able to smuggle out letters to the leaders of several radical California unions, asking for support and technical assistance, but we never received an answer. We had to accept this lack of response as an indication that outsiders did not really care about inmate employment rights.

I was never allowed to attend high school in prison because of my prior escape and political activities. However, I read as many books as I could find about human behavior. Fellow inmates began to come to me for advice and counsel, and I grew to enjoy and appreciate the confidence they placed in me. I felt that with my authenticity and with the problem-solving experience I was gaining with inmates, I could make an important contribution to the field of human services. One year before I was paroled, I put in a request to the education department to take the GED (high school equivalency) test, and it was approved. I took the test and passed it. My secret master plan was to go to college and major in counseling. The first time I shared my career goals with my fellow inmates, their hurtful reaction was to turn it into a joke. My prison counselor compounded the injury by telling me that my career goals were nothing more than "pipe dreams" and would never happen. He reminded me that I was a black convict doing time without skills and upon release I would be a black ex-convict on parole without skills. He advised me to find a gas station attendant job and try to stay out of trouble.

My first impulse was immediate anger. His professional advice was nothing less than a put-down. I started to return the insult but managed to suppress this strong urge. While in prison, I had learned the painful lesson that certain police types had enormous egos and were easily intimidated by the slightest demonstration of independent thought. It was not important that my prison counselor believe in me; I believed in myself.

Long ago I was forced to become a student of my keepers' moods and behaviors. Through observation and interaction, I learned their strengths and weaknesses and the self-serving stereotypes they had of themselves and of black inmates. This hard-learned knowledge sometimes allowed me to outwit prison staff. For example, there was a certain tobacco-chewing, white guard who routinely banged his club against the bars and pulled on his ear to indicate that the volume of our television was too load. This behavior occurred only when black inmates watched TV. One day I pretended to lower the volume and looked up to get his usual nod of approval. He gave it with a smile. I then realized that he had a need for his white presence to be acknowledged in this room full of black men. After I understood the true nature of his need, each time he asked us to turn the TV down, I played the game of "pretend." I would act as if I were turning the volume down and repeatedly ask him whether it was low enough. He would say, "No" the first two times, and usually by the third time, he would finally say, "Yeah. That's low enough. Now keep it like that, or I'll turn it off!" Actually, I never lowered the volume a single degree. It was all in his head. Satisfied, he would always walk away "struttin'" like a barn yard rooster, and I got to control the TV. At first I was tempted to expose the guard's racism in front of the entire inmate population. I wanted him to know that I, a black inmate, had psyched out his white superior ass! But my better judgment prevailed. I realized that I might have to cross that bridge again. With this lesson in mind, I allowed my prison counselor to believe that he had pursuaded me to pursue a more realistic career goal as a "gas station attendant." I was not going to allow my ego to get me into an argument with him. He had too much power over my release date.

Prison Release: Surprise, You're on Candid Camera!

When I was finally released from prison that following year, I was due for a real surprise. My counselors had not prepared me for the reality of parole. Despite my return to free society, the general disrespect and infringement upon my personal freedom remained unchanged. My "outside prison" was similar to my inside prison. The outside prison guards were called "parole officers," and they, like the inside prison guards, had the duties of controlling and monitoring my behavior. They initiated arbitrary "strip searches" and invaded my residence looking for contraband, renaming this intrusion "unscheduled home visits." Like prison guards, the parole officers carried guns and used clubs; they also had the discretionary power to return me to prison without the benefit of trial. The restrictions that parole placed on my ability to "fit into society" were counterproductive. My status as a parolee was public record. My parole officer was mandated by the state to talk to any potential employer before allowing me to take the job. And if by a miracle someone did hire me after talking to my parole officer, all my fellow workers somehow knew that the "new black guy" was on parole.

Public knowledge of my parole status made it very difficult for my fellow workers to accept and trust me. It also did absolutely nothing for my sense of belonging and self-esteem. I resented the treatment I received from my fellow workers. I felt like a leper in biblical times—forced to wear an "unclean" sign around my neck. In hindsight, I recognize that my presence created self-esteem problems for my fellow workers as well. I imagine that for them to work side by side with a newly released, unskilled, black parolee did absolutely nothing for their self-esteem. They were motivated to alienate me. In this way they were able to say to themselves, "I may be at the bottom of the educational and economic heap, but at least I'm better than a parolee!"

My first year outside the walls was much more lonely and restricting than my seven years inside prison. In prison, interaction with fellow inmates was expected, accepted, and normal. But in this outside prison, association with parolees or ex-convicts was an unforgivable violation of parole. This particular taboo was the most difficult for me to understand and obey. I felt that this restriction was cruel and mean-spirited. It demanded that I sever my ties with people I had known for nearly ten years. Among them were people whose behavior had demonstrated that they respected my values and wanted me to succeed. This abomination was made even worse by the fact that a third of these people had been friends of mine before I went to prison. I could not, would not, and did not deny or desert them. I clearly violated parole. Why wasn't I taken back to prison? I'm not sure. But I am absolutely certain that the friendships I formed while in prison prepared me for my future life on the outside.

Consider the following interdependent variables: In prison, my friend Johnnie Moore introduced me to Pawho, who introduced me to Albert. Albert and I formed a poetry team in prison called the Soledad Prison Poets (Soledad Prison Poets, 1987). This partnership helped to develop my powers of critical analysis, elevated my consciousness, and prepared me for an outside life of political activism. When I was released from prison, my outside support system further assisted in my development. Pawho's wife, Lora, introduced me to her friend Ardella, who became my wife, who in turn introduced Albert and me to her friend Oni, the West Coast representative for Bravo Black Productions. Under Oni's management, the Soledad Prison Poets became well-known artists and political activists in the California prison movement. If I had obeyed my parole officer and refused to associate with my ex-convict and parolee friends, my life would have been much more limited. I took a big risk and held fast to my friendship support group, and it paid off!

My inside and outside support system was not a one-sided arrangement for the inept, selfish, and lazy. Everyone in our group, including my immediate family, was expected to be able to give and receive support equally. My friends had the age, experience, and skills to be good advisors. They were especially honest risk takers, and they were mature enough to recognize dangerous decisions and situations.

For me, the word "support" is important, and it played a significant role in my life inside and outside the prisons of the United States. My history of support has assumed many forms. It has been experienced as affection; protection; knowledge; or access to a friend's wisdom, financial assistance, and influence. In my group, the word "support" did not mean that we were obligated to go along with any of our friends' self-destructive behaviors and schemes. We had the responsibility to confront each other when issues such as these emerged. Often it is only the people who love us who tell us the truth or disagree with us. My friends are my life's greatest treasure. I have found that searching for genuine friendships is similar to panning for gold. After painfully sifting through tons of worthless rocks and dirt, if we are truly blessed, we might discover one or two gold nuggets.

I have in my possession an old prison snapshot of me and several friends. If I look at it too long, it brings tears to my eyes. As a support group, we kept each other alive and sane. It still fills me with rage and sadness to know that, out of a group of eight black males in the photo, I am the only one still alive. Most of my friends were victims of violent crimes, shattered dreams, and other stress-related conditions. I helped carry their caskets to several different burial sites. Pieces of my soul were buried along with them in each of their graves. As a result of their deaths, I sometimes feel a little tinge of what psychologists call "survivor's guilt." I remember asking myself, "Why them and not me?" Some of these brothers were smarter, more creative, and more evolved than I was. Why did I survive when everyone in that prison snapshot died? Was it sheer circumstance, divine providence, or something more? Whatever it might have been, it has motivated me to live every second of my life with honesty, courage, and passion. My life is precious, and I do not take it for granted. You never really know when it just might be your time to say good-bye to this plane of existence. There is one truth I have learned about death: It comes and goes without warning!

Reentry Insights: The Revolving Door

I gained my first insight about reentry while in prison. I knew several inmates who had been released on parole and six months later returned to prison. These prisoners were arrested for the same crimes they had committed before. The stories these individuals told me about their outside experiences were typically about fast women, drugs, and expensive cars. They always focused on the "fast life" and how well they had been "getting over" just before they were arrested. No one ever accepted responsibility for being arrested for criminal incompetence. It was always a "snitch" or some outside "fluke" that caused their temporary setback. It is now clear to me that their self-esteem, sense of belonging, and identity were tied to living the fast life, despite the cost. Prison had failed not only to equip them with marketable skills but also to inspire them to change their behavior. Being accepted by their peers as gangsters, hustlers, and pimps was much more rewarding than the humiliating uncertainty of working a nine-to-five job for minimum wage. I know from personal experience that to rebel against society, to take what you want by your wits and courage, is truly an ego boost. Sure it is dangerous and stressful. But according to the news media, so is working at the post office.

As a former criminal, let me state that criminal activity is a powerful narcotic. For many of us, it was the only empowering experience we ever knew. We were addicted to a lifestyle that excited us and fueled our fantasies. However, it is interesting to note that, although many of us knew that we were poor excuses for criminals, our only regret about our past crimes was "being caught."

When I was paroled back into my community, I met parolees who failed to remain on the outside because of their lack of academic skills and confidence. Two good examples were my former jailhouse friends Charles and Hank. They had somehow managed to graduate from the prison high school system without adequately learning how to read or write. I tried to help them, but they were too sensitive about their problems to accept assistance. They returned to a life of crime, and eventually they returned to prison. When we think about functionally illiterate parolees like Charles and Hank, who can we honestly blame for their reentry failure? The prison school system? Their outside schools? Their parents? Charles and Hank? Society?

I believe that, in most cases, successful reentry has a great deal to do with what the general community thinks and feels about the person. I was generally liked and respected by my neighbors, and my crimes took place outside of my community. Many of my fellow parolees were not so fortunate. For example, my homeboy Bibi, who threw acid into the neighborhood bully's face, was never forgiven by people in our community. He and the parolees who went to prison for victimizing their families, friends, or communities did not receive the quality of support I received when I was released on parole. These people usually committed new crimes and were returned to prison.

My successful reentry was facilitated by the support, encouragement, and love I received from my family, friends, and community. They helped me to achieve my prison "pipe dream" of becoming a counselor—and much more. Thirteen years after I was released on parole from San Quentin Prison, I earned a doctorate in clinical psychology. I am now a certified hypnotherapist and organizational consultant, and I currently practice as a licensed marriage, family, and child counselor in the San Francisco Bay area. I teach at two community colleges and at a postgraduate institution. I am a published author and poet and have involved myself in the field of human services in a variety of ways (Dailey, 1996). I have served my community as mental health director for the AIDS Minority Health Initiative Program, as president of the Bay Area Association of Black

Psychologists, as manager of Parental Stress Services, and as oral commissioner for the California Board of Behavioral Science Examiners. I have also worked with inner-city schools, gangs, drug addicts, the homeless, and lead domestic violence prevention groups.

However, I ask the reader not to reduce my story to a Hollywood happy ending. I still experience residual effects from my incarceration. I have occasional nightmares and sometimes grind my teeth when I sleep. Inside buildings, I am most comfortable sitting with my back against the wall, facing the door. But I can safely say that I now know and appreciate who I am—that I have noteworthy goals and strong beliefs and passions about freedom, friendship, and love. But for the reader to believe that I have somehow made a so-called successful reentry into society would be an exaggeration. How can any black parolee or ex-convict reenter a society of which he has never truly been a part? Furthermore, white racism is immune to black success. To demonstrate this reality I use myself as an example.

Last week, on my way home from work, a police vehicle with flashing lights and a screeching siren pulled my car over. Two white, male cops cautiously approached my car with their guns drawn. They asked me to slowly get out of my car, and they searched me. Then they handcuffed me and placed me in their police car, where I sat for over an hour. After they checked my name for warrants and searched my car for contraband, they released me. When I asked them why they had stopped me, they responded that it had appeared that my rear license plate lights were out. I learned later that this was not true; my lights had not been out. They did not apologize. Indignities such as these are common experiences for many black men in the United States. Although I should know better than to expect anything different from these pigs, it still pisses me off to no end. After achieving my career goals, literary notoriety, and middle-class membership, the police are still harassing me. This was not the first such incident. As usual, these racist cops could not see my noteworthy contributions and positive societal value. All they could see was my black, male face. And once again, I was manipulated into another psychological "dick fight" with the law. So far, I have managed to survive these conflicts with the police without being assaulted or taken to jail. This outcome has more to do with my background and experience than with luck or police color blindness. Unfortunately, this quasi-neutral result is not the general rule for younger black males.

Young Black Males Are at Risk of Going to Prison or Worse!

I believe that, between the ages of fifteen and thirty, black males tend to be more vulnerable to the deadly games of white police officers. African American parents should worry especially about the safety of their male children. I am convinced that the criminal justice system targets black males for violence, and they require special knowledge and skills to survive and progress in this country. Although I did my best to prepare my twenty-two-year-old son, Damu, at a very young age, I yet worry about his safety. At the age of ten, he was trained to protect himself. He earned a black belt in martial arts and was taught self-discipline and how to think on his feet. I have given him the benefit of my experiences, my support, and a more accurate map of reality than I received from my father. My son is more of an exception to the rule. There are many other young black males who grow up without the love and tutelage of concerned fathers or mentors. As a young man, I was generally unaware that I had been clothed in the projected guilt and fears of white society. I had no idea that I had been maliciously typecast and scripted to play the ominous role of the Bogeyman: a character identified in the dictionary as a mythical hobgoblin who carries off naughty children. As a consequence of the black Bogeyman myth, black males are viewed as a part of America's ills and a menace to society.

The Bogeyman Is Gonna Get You!

When people believe in myths, these myths can often take on a life of their own and cause great harm. A black parolee reentering society must deal with the enormous burden of the Bogeyman stigma. This anti–black male stigma is in operation before he goes to prison and while he serves his prison sentence, and it greets him upon his return to outside society. The social conditions that put black males at risk of being harassed, abused, and sent to prison are an inherent part of white U.S. culture. Remember the 1989 case of Charles Stuart? He was a white man who killed his wife in her eighth month of pregnancy and blamed the black Bogeyman. What about the white woman in Philadelphia who killed her three children and blamed the black Bogeyman?

Finally, consider the infamous case of Susan Smith, a twenty-three-year-old white mother who blamed the black Bogeyman for abducting her two small children to cover up the fact that she had drowned them herself. She set off a nationwide manhunt for a black man who, she claimed, hijacked her car at gunpoint and then sped away with her boys in the back seat. Law enforcement agencies nationwide, equipped with fabricated facts and a detailed composite sketch, were prepared to find a black Bogeyman by any means necessary! Smith's racist lie caused the South Carolina police to trample upon the civil rights of hundreds of black men in a frenzied search for a make-believe suspect. These national news stories represent a small sample of the lies that failed. We must seriously wonder about the success rate of those lies that never came to light. These white killers concocted lies that they knew the white media and law enforcement would eagerly embrace. They knew instinctively that, without a black Bogeyman to blame, it would be very difficult for white racists to conceal the scope and the horror of their violence.

It has become very apparent to me that the legacy of African American slavery often expresses itself in the emasculating treatment of black males. I believe that white males are generally intimidated by black masculinity and the imagined threat that we pose to their authority and white women. I am sure that many white males have vivid images of black males rampaging through dark city streets, waiting for the opportunity to rob them and pounce on their women. Although this popular white notion is statistically groundless, it nonetheless fuels ritualistic acts of white male violence against black males. The vicious beating of Rodney King was neither the first nor the last of its kind. Just recently, two white Klansmen in Texas dragged a black man to death behind their truck. In New York City, two white "peace officers" beat and sodomized a black man with police clubs in the rest room of their own precinct. And in California, Bill Cosby's son was beaten and shot to death by a nineteen-year-old neo-Nazi skinhead!

Black males have historically paid a terrible price for crossing the paths of insecure and violent white males. This environmental threat has influenced black males to be unusually creative in the development of their masculinity. We risk intimidating white males if we are "too" masculine, and we give women the wrong impression if we are "too" effeminate. Caught between these two stereotypical demands, we are seriously challenged in developing a positive gender identity—one that is nurtured and shaped by the strengths and needs of our people and not simply the result of a fear reaction to white society. To prove our manhood, we often displace our violent frustrations onto one another or become compulsive womanizers in a feeble attempt to increase our self-esteem. These self-galvanizing behaviors have to stop. They discourage trust and respect among African American people and contribute to our own demise. In my opinion, we need black mentors who have successfully navigated the treacherous waters of racism. Older black males are the most qualified to teach young black males how to progress beyond simple survival, with dignity. Without their rescue, young black males are at risk of going to prison or, even worse, becoming homicide victims.

Prison: My Manhood Rite of Passage

Although I did not become a victim of homicide, I was sent to prison at age eighteen to serve a five-year-to-life sentence. It became my destiny to find my mentors and develop my goals in prison. I met black mentors who helped to stabilize my identity. They assisted me in identifying the responsibility I had to myself, my family, African American people, and the rest of humanity. Prison was a university where I was introduced to the inspiring ideas and contributions of African people. It was in prison that I was introduced to the Kwanzaa celebration and its seven principles of black liberation (Karenga, 1989).

My new self-respect empowered me to believe in myself and steered me away from the discouraging U.S. propaganda. This propaganda tried to convince me that, because of my race and crimes, I had nothing of value to contribute to society. Prison counselors made no attempt to endorse black people who had served prison time and had gone on to make significant contributions to society. But with the help of my prison mentors, I was introduced to such books as Alex Haley's *Autobiography of Malcolm X* (Malcolm X and Haley, 1964). Through this book, I learned that my biggest enemy was not the white man "per se" but my overdependence on white people and their definitional system. It was these types of revelations that inspired my vision and unlocked my mind (Cross, 1971).

In no way, however, am I attempting to endorse, glorify, or recommend prison. I would not ever want to repeat the horror, the violence, and the degradation of the prison experience. I was able to accomplished my major reentry goal "in spite of" and not "because of" any constructive assistance from the criminal justice system. I am certain that my "postrelease success" hinged on the *cultural relevance* of my support and education. I sincerely believe that prison rehabilitation will never become more than empty rhetoric in the United States. The U.S. penal system is clearly not designed to rehabilitate; it is designed to punish. Law-abiding citizens will never agree to give preferential treatment to people like me who have broken the law. They feel that providing worthwhile skills training to felons would be a slap in the face of most "decent folks" who have not committed crimes and cannot afford to pay for specialized education. This position is understandable, but it does not address the reality that the majority of prison inmates will commit new crimes and return to prison. I believe that society's thirst for revenge has blinded it to our escalating cycle of recidivism. It was Dr. Martin Luther King Jr. who said, "The eye for an eye philosophy will ultimately lead to a nation of blind people."

I propose that the successful completion of marketable skills become a major prerequisite for inmate parole. In support of this skill-based program, the state must legalize a prison workers' union and guarantee contracts to ensure its continued existence. Finally, ex-convicts who have demonstrated postrelease success should occupy at least 50 percent of the seats on the parole board. If this plan is properly implemented, it has the potential to reduce crime and recidivism dramatically. But it will also cut off an enormous amount of money and control currently enjoyed by the criminal justice system. The law enforcers who constitute the criminal justice system (politicians, judges, lawyers, police detectives, correctional officers, and the like) will never passively allow anyone to strip them of their power. They have a vested interest in maintaining their current power relationships with felons. They want more power, not less! For these reasons, any systematic change of the kind proposed here is unlikely to happen in the United States.

Closing Remarks

Putting my reentry memories into words has been a bittersweet experience. Self-editing this essay was an even greater challenge. I am thankful to my editors for offering me this opportunity to tell this portion of my story. There is a lot of work yet to be done in this country. I long ago committed myself to constructive involvement in social change. This work is often difficult, dangerous, and thankless. As a realist, I am aware that I will occasionally run into a racist wall. I will constantly face obstacles of ignorance, fear, and hatred of one kind or another. I have learned to manage this American dilemma without being in a perpetual state of paranoia and rage. I now know that I must always make conscious decisions and take responsibility for the quality of my interactions with others. I view my past mistakes as lessons and not letdowns. I am a living example that, given a chance, human life can have significant redeemable value. I am a survivior and a visionary who has just celebrated his fifty-second birthday this month! It is hard to believe that I have been out of prison for well over twenty-five years. I guess I have been lucky. But who really knows?

Peace.

References

Cross, William E. 1971. "The Negro to Black Conversion Experience: Toward a Psychology of Black Liberation." *Black World* 20 (9): 13–27

Dailey, Lige Jr. 1996. *Do We Really Know What Love Is? A Guide for Improving Love Relationships*. Emeryville, Calif.: SPP.

Karenga, Maulana. 1989. *The African American Holiday of Kwanzaa: A Celebration of Family, Community and Culture*. Los Angeles: University of Sankore Press.

Malcolm X and Alex Haley. 1964. *The Autobiography of Malcolm X*. New York: Ballantine.

Soledad Prison Poets. 1987. *Who Is the Real Criminal?* San Francisco: Julian Richardson Associates.

For Further Reading

Abbott, Jack Henry. *In the Belly of the Beast: Letters from Prison.* New York: Vintage, 1982.

Abu-Jamal, Mumia. *Live from Death Row.* New York: Addison-Wesley, 1995.

———. *Death Blossoms: Reflections from a Prisoner of Conscience.* Farmington, Pa.: Plough, 1997.

American Civil Liberties Union (ACLU). "Prisoners' Assistance Directory." National Prison Project, New York, 1997. Available from ACLU National Prison Project, 132 West Forty-third Street, New York, New York 10036.

Amnesty International. *United States of America: Rights for All.* London: Amnesty International, 1998.

Bandele, Asha. *The Prisoner's Wife: A Memoir.* New York: Scribner, 1999.

Braithwaite, R. L., T. M. Hammett, and R. M. Mayberry. *Prisons and AIDS: A Public Health Challenge.* San Francisco: Jossey-Bass, 1996.

Churchill, W., and J. J. Vander Wall, eds. *Cages of Steel: The Politics of Imprisonment in the United States.* Washington, D.C.: Maisonneuve Press, 1992.

Cohen, S., and L. Taylor. *Psychological Survival: The Experience of Long-Term Imprisonment.* New York: Vintage, 1972.

Currie, E. *Confronting Crime: An American Challenge.* New York: Pantheon Books, 1985.

———. *Reckoning: Drugs, the Cities and the American Future.* New York: Hill and Wang, 1994.

Daly, Kathleen. *Gender, Crime and Punishment.* New Haven, Conn.: Yale University Press, 1994.

Denborough, David, ed. *Beyond the Prison: Gathering Dreams of Freedom.* Adelaide, South Australia: Dulwich Centre Publications, 1996.

Donziger, Steven, ed. *The Real War on Crime: The Report of the National Criminal Justice Commission.* New York: HarperCollins, 1996.

Dyer, Joel. *The Perpetual Prisoner Machine: How America Profits from Crime.* Boulder, Col.: Westview, 2000.

Faith, K. *Unruly Women: The Politics of Confinement and Resistance.* Vancouver, Canada: Press Gang, 1993.

Foucault, Michel. *Discipline and Punish: The Birth of the Prison.* Trans. Alan Sheridan. New York: Pantheon Books, 1977.

Gilligan, James. *Violence: Our Deadly Epidemic and Its Causes.* New York: Grosset/Putnam, 1996.

Glaser, David. *Preparing Convicts for Law-Abiding Lives: The Pioneering Penology of Richard A. McGee.* Albany: State University of New York Press, 1995.

Herman, Judith. *Trauma and Recovery: The Aftermath of Violence–From Domestic Abuse to Political Terror.* New York: Basic Books, 1992.

Human Rights Watch. "Sexual Abuse of Women Prisoners in the U.S." In *The Human Rights Watch Global Report on Women's Human Rights.* New York: Human Rights Watch, 1995.

———. *Cold Storage: Super-Maximum Security Confinement in Indiana.* New York: Human Rights Watch, 1997.

Irwin, John. *The Felon.* Englewood Cliffs, N.J.: Prentice-Hall, 1970.

Irwin, John, and James Austin. *It's about Time: America's Imprisonment Binge.* Belmont, Calif.: Wadsworth, 1994.

Jacobs, J. B. *Stateville: The Penetentiary in Mass Society.* Chicago: University of Chicago Press, 1977.

James, Joy, ed. *States of Confinement: Policing, Detention, and Prisons.* New York: St. Martin's Press.

Kupers, Terry A. *Prison Madness: The Mental Health Crisis behind Bars and What We Must Do about It.* San Francisco: Jossey-Bass, 1999.

Martin, D. M., and P. Y. Sussman. *Committing Journalism: The Prison Writings of Red Hog.* New York: Norton, 1993.

Masters, Jarvis. *Finding Freedom: Writings from Death Row.* Junction City, Calif.: Padma, 1997.

Mauer, Marc, and T. Huling. *Young Black Americans and the Criminal Justice System: Five Years Later.* Washington, D.C.: Sentencing Project, 1995.

Mauer, Marc, and M. C. Young. *Truths, Half-Truths, and Lies: Myths and Realities about Crime and Punishment.* Washington, D.C.: Sentencing Project, 1996.

McCall, Nathan. *Makes Me Wanna Holler: A Young Black Man in America.* New York: Vintage, 1995.

Menninger, K. *The Crime of Punishment.* New York: Vintage, 1969.

Messerschmidt, James W. *Masculinities and Crime: Critique and Reconceptualization of Theory.* Lanham, Md.: Rowman and Littlefield, 1993.

———. *Nine Lives: Adolescent Masculinities, the Body, and Violence.* Boulder, Col.: Westview Press, 2000.

Miller, Jerome G. *Search and Destroy: African-American Males in the Criminal Justice System.* New York: Cambridge University Press, 1996.

Parenti, Christian. *Lockdown America: Police and Prisons in the Age of Crisis.* New York: Verso, 1999.

Prejean, H. *Dead Man Walking.* New York: Vintage, 1993.

Prison Focus. Quarterly publication of California Prison Focus, 2489 Mission Street, No. 28, San Francisco, California 94110.

Prison Legal News. Monthly publication of Prison Legal News, 2400 N.W. Eightieth Street, No. 148, Seattle, Washington 98117.

Rideau, Wilbert, and Ron Wikberg. *Life Sentences: Rage and Survival behind Bars.* New York: Times Books, 1992.

Rierden, A. *The Farm: Life Inside a Women's Prison.* Amherst: University of Massachusetts Press, 1997.

Rosenblatt, E., ed. *Criminal Injustice: Confronting the Prison Crisis.* Boston: South End Press, 1996.

Rothman, D. J. *Conscience and Convenience: The Asylum and Its Alternatives in Progressive America.* Boston: Little, Brown, 1980.

Sabo, Don, and David F. Gordon, eds. *Men's Health and Illness: Gender, Power and the Body.* Thousand Oaks, Calif.: Sage, 1995.

Scacco, A. *Rape in Prison.* Springfield, Ill.: Charles C. Thomas, 1975.

Selke, W. I. *Prisons in Crisis*. Bloomington: Indiana University Press, 1993.

Shapiro-Bertolini, E. *Through the Walls: Prison Correspondence*. Culver City, Calif.: Peace Press, 1976.

Toch, Hans. *Mosaic of Despair: Human Breakdowns in Prison*. Washington, D.C.: American Psychological Association, 1992.

———. *Corrections: A Humanistic Approach*. Guilderland, N.Y.: Harrow and Heston, 1997.

Tonry, M. *Malign Neglect: Race, Crime and Punishment in America*. New York: Oxford University Press, 1995.

Wimsatt, William Upski. *No More Prisons: Urban Life, Homeschooling, Hip-hop Leadership, the Cool Rich Kid's Movement, A Hitchhiker's Guide to Community Organizing, and Why Philanthropy Is the Greatest Art Form of the 21st Century*. New York: Soft Skull Press, 2000.

About the Contributors

MUMIA ABU-JAMAL is a prisoner at the state prison in Waynesburg, Pennsylvania. He writes widely on prison and social issues. His books include *All Things Censored, Death Blossoms: Reflections from a Prisoner of Conscience,* and *Live from Death Row.* He has written for the *Yale Law Journal,* the *Journal of Prisoners on Prisons* (Canada), and (among other newspapers) the *Philadelphia Tribune* and the *Philadelphia Inquirer.*

ALICE is an author and consultant who spent an extraordinary year loving an extraordinary man.

STEPHEN WAYNE ANDERSON is a prisoner at San Quentin Prison, California.

HORACE BELL is a freelance poet/writer currently incarcerated at California State Prison at Pelican Bay. His poems have appeared in *The Sentinel* (Los Angeles newspaper) and *Prison Focus,* a publication of California Prison Focus.

T. PETE BONNER is the pseudonym for a journalist formerly affiliated with the magazine *PrisonLife.*

HARRIS BREIMAN, PH.D., helped to start the Shawangunk Men's Council within the New York State prison system. He is the director of OASIS—the National Prison Council Project—and codirector of the Mustard Seed Center for Healing in Woodstock, New York. He also maintains a private practice as a therapist and is active in the men's movement.

DANIEL BURTON-ROSE is a freelance journalist and editor (with Dan Pens and Paul Wright) of *The Celling of America: An Inside Look at the U.S. Prison Industry.* He is currently working on a book about the George Jackson Brigade.

DERRICK CORLEY is a writer and prisoner at Clinton Corrections Facility, Dannemora, New York.

WILL H. COURTENAY, PH.D., received his doctorate from the University of California at Berkeley. He is an adjunct professor in the Women's and Gender Studies Program, Sonoma State University, California. Courtenay's research focuses on the influence of masculinity on the health of men and boys. He is a regular contributor to professional journals and is currently completing a book on men's health for Temple University Press. He provides consultation, program development assistance, continuing education, and training to colleges, public health departments, medical centers, and health professionals nationwide. He is also a practicing psychotherapist in Berkeley and San Francisco. (E-mail: *courtenay@menshealth.org*.)

LIGE DAILEY JR., PH.D., is in private practice as a licensed psychotherapist in the San Francisco Bay area. He currently holds faculty positions at Contra Costa Community College and the American School of Professional Psychology.

ANGELA Y. DAVIS, PH.D., teaches at the University of California at Santa Cruz in the History of Consciousness Program. Her books include *Angela Davis: An Autobiography; Women, Race and Class;* and *Blues Legacies and Black Feminism.*

DAVID DENBOROUGH was employed within the New South Wales prison system from 1963 to 1966. During this time he was also working in scools with young men on issues of violence and masulinity. He now works as staff writer at Dulwich Centre Publications in Adelaide, Australia. He is the author of *Beyond the Prison: Gathering Dreams of Freedom.*

STEPHEN "DONNY" DONALDSON was a former prisoner who was brutally raped while incarcerated. After his release, he became a strong voice for prison reform and directed the national organization Stop Prisoner Rape (see www.spr.org). He was 49 when he died in 1996.

STEVE FRALEY is a prisoner and active writer at Collins Correctional Facility, New York.

CARL BRYAN HOLMBERG, PH.D., is a professor in the Department of Popular Culture at Bowling Green State University, Ohio.

CARLOS HORNSBY is a former prisoner at Attica Correctional Facility, Attica, New York.

MARC E. KANN, PH.D., is a professor of political science who holds the University of Southern California Associates Chair in Social Science at the University of Southern California. He is the author of *A Republic of Men: The American Founders, Gendered Language, and Patriarchal Politics.*

JACKSON KATZ, ED.M., is the founder and director of MVP Strategies, an organization that provides gender violence prevention training to the U.S. Marine Corps, colleges, high schools, law enforcement agencies, and community groups and corporations. He lectures across the country on the connections between masculinities and the U.S. epidemic of men's violence against women. His educational video, *Tough Guise: Media Images and the Crisis of Masculinity,* is a production of the Media Education Foundation.

MICHAEL KECK is an actor, writer, and composer whose works have been featured at theaters across the United States and internationally. He facilitates workshops in various settings including schools, universities, community centers, and correctional facilities, primarily as a component to his performance of *Voices in the Rain.* Michael has served as a panelist for the National Endowment for the Arts, the New York State Arts

Council, Georgia Council for the Arts, and Meet the Composer. He is a member of AEA, AFTRA, ASCAP, and the Dramatists Guild.

TERRY A. KUPERS, M.D., a psychiatrist, serves as an expert witness in legal cases regarding conditions of confinement and the quality of psychiatric care in jails and prisons. He has served as consultant to the Civil Rights Division of the U.S. Department of Justice, Human Rights Watch, and Amnesty International. Kupers teaches at the Wright Institute in Berkeley. His recent books include *Prison Madness: The Mental Health Crisis behind Bars and What We Must Do about It* (1999) and *Revisioning Men's Lives: Gender, Intimacy and Power* (1993).

NANCY LEVIT, ESQUIRE, PH.D., is a professor of law at the University of Missouri in Kansas City, Missouri. She is also the author of *The Gender Line: Men, Women, and the Law.*

WILLIE LONDON, B.S., is a poet, essayist, and prisoner at Eastern Corrections, Napanoch, New York. He is general editor of the prison publication *Elite Expressions*. He also coedited, with Don Sabo, the 1992 special issue of *Men's Studies Review*, on men in prison. He is a prison educator who worked with the Consortium of the Niagara Frontier College program at Attica Correctional Facility, and he currently tutors young and aspiring prisoners at Eastern New York Corrections Facility. He also works with blind and deaf prisoners at Eastern.

JARVIS MASTERS is a prisoner at San Quentin Prison, California. He is the author of *Finding Freedom: Writings from Death Row.*

MARC MAUER is the assistant director of the Sentencing Project, a national organization located in Washington, D.C., that seeks to create alternatives to incarceration and promote criminal justice reform. He is also the author of *Race to Incarcerate.* Mauer has been a consultant to the Bureau of Justice Assistance, the National Institute of Corrections, and the American Bar Association.

JAMES W. MESSERSCHMIDT, PH.D., is a professor of sociology in the Criminology Department at the University of Southern Maine. He is the author of *Nine Lives: Adolescent Masculinities, the Body, and Violence; Masculinities and Crime: Critique and Reconceptualization of Theory; Crime as Structured Action: Gender, Race, Class, and Crime in the Making;* and, with Piers Beirne, the third edition of *Criminology.*

SUSANNE V. PACZENSKY, PH.D., is a German journalist living in California, who tries to explain the United States to her German readers.

CHRISTIAN PARENTI is the author of *Lockdown America: Police and Prisons in the Age of Crisis.* He lives in San Francisco and writes regularly for *The Nation, In These Times, Salon,* the *San Diego Union Tribune,* the *Christian Science Monitor,* and *The Baffler.*

RUDY CHATO PAUL SR. was a prisoner at Attica Correctional Facility, Attica, New York.

DAN PENS is editor, with Daniel Burton-Rose and Paul Wright, of *The Celling of America: An Inside Look at the U.S. Prison Industry* and a frequent contributor to *Prison Legal News,* a national publication written and edited by prisoners.

CAROL POLYCH, M.S.N., is a community activist and registered nurse. She is currently in the doctoral program at the Ontario Institute for Studies in Education of the University of Toronto, Canada. Her research focuses on help seeking/helping in relationship to illegal drug use.

CHARLES J. SABATINO, PH.D., is a professor of religious studies and philosophy at Daemen College, Amherst, New York. For more than twenty years, he has been a prison educator and an advocate for the mentally ill in western New York. Sabatino also facilitates therapy groups for men on parole who are making transitions into communities.

DON SABO, PH.D., is a professor of sociology at D'Youville College. He has worked to develop the study of men and masculinities in a variety of areas, including sports, gender, health, and prison. He has been a prison educator for sixteen years. He is coauthor, with Jim McKay and Michael Messner, of *Masculinities, Gender Relations and Sport;* with David Gordon, of *Men's Health and Illness: Gender, Power and the Body;* and with Michael Messner, of *Sex, Violence, and Power in Sports: Rethinking Masculinity.*

DONALD SPECTER is an attorney and the director of the Prison Law Office at San Quentin, California, a nonprofit and public-interest law firm that provides free legal services to California prisoners concerning their conditions of confinement.

O'NEIL STOUGH passed away in January 2000, following his release only two months before, after serving over twenty-five years in Hawaii and Arizona state prisons. He was a freelance writer with many published articles and essays, including those in *Prison Legal News* and in *The Celling of America: An Inside Look at the U.S. Prison Industry.* He dedicates his two essays in this volume to his daughter, Holly, and to his granddaughter, Brittany.

ANTHONY THOMAS is a former prisoner at Attica Correctional Facility, Attica, New York.

Index

Page numbers followed by *f* indicate figures.